Traditions and Renewals

MARIE BORROFF

Traditions and Renewals

CHAUCER, THE *GAWAIN*-POET,
AND BEYOND

Yale University Press
New Haven
& London

Printed in the United States of America.

Library of Congress Cataloging-in-Publication Data
Borroff, Marie.
    Traditions and renewals : Chaucer, the *Gawain*-poet, and beyond / Marie Borroff.
       p.   cm.
Includes bibliographical references and index.
    ISBN 0-300-09612-7
1. English poetry — Middle English, 1100–1500 — History and criticism. 2. Gawain (Legendary character) — Romances — History and criticism. 3. Chaucer, Geoffrey, d. 1400. Book of the Duchesse. 4. Chaucer, Geoffrey, d. 1400. Canterbury tales. 5. Gawain and the Grene Knight. 6. Pearl (Middle English poem) 7. Judgment in literature. 8. Clergy in literature. I. Title.
PR313 .B67 2003
821'.109 — dc21   2002151340

A catalogue record for this book is available from the British Library.

The paper in this book meets the guidelines for permanence and durability of the Committee on Production Guidelines for Book Longevity of the Council on Library Resources.

10 9 8 7 6 5 4 3 2 1

Contents

Acknowledgments

Some of the essays collected in this volume have appeared in books or periodicals. I am grateful to the publishers and editors for permission to reprint the following: " 'Loves Hete' in the *Prioress's Prologue and Tale*," in *The Olde Daunce: Love, Friendship, Sex and Marriage in the Medieval World*, ed. Robert R. Edwards and Stephen Spector (Albany, N.Y.: SUNY Press, 1991); "Chaucer's English Rhymes: The *Roman*, the *Romaunt*, and *The Book of the Duchess*," in *Words and Works: Studies in Medieval English in Honour of Fred C. Robinson*, ed. Peter S. Baker and Nicholas Howe (Toronto: U. of Toronto Press, 1998); "*Sir Gawain and the Green Knight*: The Passing of Judgment," in *The Passing of Arthur: New Essays in Arthurian Tradition*, ed. Christopher Baswell and William Sharpe (Garland, 1988); "*Pearl's* Maynful Mone," in *Acts of Interpretation: The Text in Its Contexts: Essays on Medieval and Renaissance Literature in Honor of E. Talbot Donaldson*, ed. Mary J. Carruthers and Elizabeth D. Kirk (Norman, Okla.: Pilgrim Books, 1982); "Systematic Sound Symbolism in the Long Alliterative Line in *Beowulf* and *Sir Gawain and the Green Knight*," in *English Historical Metrics*, ed. C. B. McCully and J. J. Anderson (Cambridge University Press, 1996); "Reading *Sir Gawain* Aloud," in *Approaches to Teaching "Sir Gawain and the Green Knight*," ed. Miriam Youngerman Miller and Jane Chance (New York:

viii   *Acknowledgments*

Modern Language Association of America, 1986); "A Cipher in *Hamlet,*" in *Philologia Anglica: Essays Presented to Professor Yoshio Terasawa on the Occasion of His Sixtieth Birthday,* ed. Kinshiro Oshitari et al. (Tokyo: Kenyushka, 1988).

Texts and Short Titles

I quote the poetry of Chaucer from *The Riverside Chaucer,* 3d ed., ed. Larry D. Benson et al. (Boston: Houghton Mifflin, 1987). Short title: Riverside. For passages quoted from the *Canterbury Tales,* I give the Roman numeral and letter identifying the fragment in question, plus line numbers, except for series of passages in a single tale, where I give line numbers only.

I quote *Sir Gawain and the Green Knight* from Tolkien and Gordon's 2d ed., rev. Norman Davis (Oxford: Oxford University Press, 1967).

I quote *Pearl* from the edition of E. V. Gordon (Oxford: Clarendon Press, 1953).

I quote *Cleanness* from *The Poems of the Pearl Manuscript,* ed. Malcolm Andrew and Ronald Waldron (Berkeley and Los Angeles: University of California Press, 1982). Short title: Andrew and Waldron.

All translations from the *Gawain*-poet are mine. See Borroff, *Sir Gawain and the Green Knight, Patience, Pearl, Verse Translations* (New York: W. W. Norton, 2001). For passages quoted from *Pearl,* I supply literal versions where the wording of my verse translation departs too far from that of the original to be helpful to readers not conversant with the language of the *Gawain* poet.

I quote the Bible in Latin from *Biblia Sacra Iuxta Vulgatam Versionem,* 4th ed. (Stuttgart: Bibelgesellschaft, 1994). Each quotation in Latin is followed by the Douay-Rheims translation, quoted from *The Holy Bible Translated from the Latin Vulgate* (Rockford, Ill.: Tan Books and Publishers, 1971; photographic reproduction of the edition published by John Murphy, Baltimore, 1899). Since the Latin version is unpunctuated, I supply punctuation in accordance with Douay-Rheims.

Transliteration

I have modernized the alphabet in all passages quoted from Middle English, substituting *th* for the letter thorn, *y, gh,* or *z* for the letter yogh, depending on its position in the word, and *v* for *u, u* for *v,* and *i* for *j,* in accordance with modern spelling. I have also modernized passages quoted from Old French by substituting *v* for *u* where the consonant *v* is so spelled.

Dictionaries

The *Middle English Dictionary,* ed. Hans Kurath, Sherman M. Kuhn, Robert E. Lewis, et al. (Ann Arbor: University of Michigan Press, 1954–2001). Short title: *MED.*

The Oxford English Dictionary, 2d ed. on Compact Disc (New York: Electronic Publishing, Oxford University Press, 1995). Short title: *OED.*

Introduction

Most of the essays in this book are concerned with two late medieval poets whose works have continued to command interest and attention over a span of six centuries: Geoffrey Chaucer and the anonymous author of *Sir Gawain and the Green Knight* and *Pearl*. I have inquired into the nature of the powers vested in the intelligible and audible words of these poems, as they interact with and reinforce one another in forms of smaller and greater compass. The essays reflect my training at the University of Chicago under the "Chicago critics" R. S. Crane, Norman Maclean, and Elder Olson, whose methods I have gratefully adapted to my own purposes as a critic of poetry. My desire to learn how the expressive values of modern English words were founded on the earlier history of the language led me to Yale, where I studied philology under Professors Helge Kökeritz, John C. Pope, and E. T. Donaldson. As a result of these studies, my long-standing interest in metrics widened to include the verse of Chaucer and of the alliterative tradition as represented in Old and Middle English. More recently, I have turned my attention to sound symbolism as an essential feature of poetic language, developing a set of theoretical distinctions, and a terminology for expressing them, that is put to use in the essay in this collection entitled "Systematic Sound Symbolism in the Long Alliterative Line: *Beowulf* and *Sir Gawain and the Green Knight*."

The previously published essays included here do not address themselves to social or political issues, or, with the minor exception of the essay on the *Prioress's Tale,* to issues of gender. Likewise, my two essays on *Pearl,* one written two decades ago, the other during the past few months, are concerned with the poet's use of the resources of language to give form to his experience as a private person, and not primarily as a member of late medieval society. I believe that the questions these essays raise are of continuing importance, and that the validity of the conclusions they draw is not threatened by other questions reflecting other interests. With Chaucer, it is a different story. A few years ago, in thinking about the *Summoner's Tale,* I stumbled on a link between that tale and the reformist views of the Lollards which eventually resulted in the writing of an essay entitled "Dimensions of Judgment in the *Canterbury Tales*" The enlarged understanding of Chaucer that I gained in writing that essay was the foundation for another, entitled "Silent Retribution in Chaucer." Both are included in this collection.

R. S. Crane thought that the proper object of humanistic study in literature was the achieved work, shaped by its time and tradition but not fully predictable in historical terms, and manifesting an excellence eliciting admiration and wonder. Literary criticism, too, is at its best when it arrives at insights which the reader could not have predicted but which, once encountered, compel assent. If this volume, in its treatment of familiar materials, contains a few such surprises, it will have fulfilled my highest hopes.

PART I

Chaucer

I

Dimensions of Judgment in the Canterbury Tales:
Friar, Summoner, Pardoner, Wife of Bath

The ongoing project of reading Chaucer's poems against their historical moment has given us good reasons for thinking that the poet was seriously concerned about political tyranny and ecclesiastical corruption in his day — indeed, that his opinions on these matters might well have endangered him had he expressed them directly.[1] David Wallace, for example, has shown that in presenting a "Boccaccian" version of the *Clerk's Tale* rather than the Petrarchan version the narrator says he will relate, Chaucer is implicitly repudiating Petrarch's affiliations with the despotic power of the Visconti in Lombardy, at a time when the "descent into tyranny" of Richard II was becoming more and more troublesome.[2] Furthermore, in restoring "the commons to the narrative" (p. 200), Chaucer implies that "an aristocracy might save itself from tyranny . . . by counting upon the sound instincts of 'the peple' at moments of social crisis," and may be remembering "the efforts of the House of Commons [especially in the mid-1380s] to curb the king's tyrannical tendencies" (p. 202).[3] As for religious controversy, Alan J. Fletcher has recently noted the presence in the *Summoner's Tale* of a number of "Wycliffite nuances" indicating that, as against the prevailing view of the relation of the *Tale* to its historical background, "some of the antimendicant elements [of the *Tale* and its *Prologue*] are not traditional and dehistoricized but in fact contemporary, answering to dominant tropes of a controversial and partisan [that is, Lollard] antimendicancy."[4]

In what follows, I argue for the presence in the *Summoner's Tale* of a hitherto unrecognized allusion, confirmed by the affiliations discussed in Fletcher's
essay, to the Wycliffite polemic against the friars. This allusion, in turn, implies
a judgment on Chaucer's part of Friar John (along with his *alter ego* Friar
Hubert) transcending the secular sphere of antifraternal satire and fabliau. My
conclusions follow from a reexamination, first of the most relevant aspects of
the antifraternal background, then of the *Tale* itself and its *Prologue* in the
context of Fragment D, a seamless whole in which the *Summoner's Prologue*
and *Tale* are retrospectively linked with the Wife of Bath's *Prologue* and *Tale*
and those of the Friar himself. In the line of descent connecting the earliest
stage of antifraternal discourse to Chaucer's writings, I find the confessional
disquisition of Fals-Semblant in *Le roman de la rose* to have an importance
that has not yet been fully recognized. I am thus led to bring the Pardoner into
the compass of my essay, since Chaucer's indebtedness to this part of the
Roman is double: what he dramatizes naturalistically in the portrait of Friar
John, he represents quasi-allegorically in the Pardoner. I begin by discussing
allusiveness specifically of language, as it bears on some of the well-known
problems of judgment presented by some of the portraits in the *General Prologue*, including that of the Friar.[5]

The views attributed to Chaucer by the new historicist studies I have cited are,
of course, buried beneath the surface of the poetry — hidden in their time, it
would seem, from all but a sympathetic few. The cautious self-protectiveness
that made him avoid antagonizing people in high places is generally recognized and seems to have taken many forms.[6] It is reflected in the *General
Prologue*, for example, in the difference between the narrator's forthright
accounts of the wrongdoings of those pilgrims who occupy the lower end of
the social scale, and his notoriously problematic hints at less than admirable
behavior on the part of those at the upper end. The Shipman drowned his
prisoners (see [I (A) 400] and the note in Riverside); the Miller stole corn and
charged three times for it (562); the Summoner was a lecher and an accomplished con man (625, 652); the Pardoner passed off a pillow-slip and pigs'
bones as relics (694, 700). But the worldliness, promiscuity, and greed of the
three representatives of the regular clergy who inhabit the upper stratum of the
social hierarchy and are described immediately after the Knight and his companions are imputed to them by implication only, if at all. In the portraits of
the Prioress, the Monk, and the Friar, Chaucer allows the bottom line to
remain a blank; it is by no means clear how he judged them or how we should
judge them in our turn.

The most satisfying analysis of Chaucer's evasiveness in describing these
and certain other pilgrims, his willingness to make disparaging innuendos

coupled with his reluctance to say anything that could be read as outright condemnation, is presented by Jill Mann in her indispensable study *Chaucer and Medieval Estates Satire*.[7] Mann reads the portraits in the *General Prologue* against their backgrounds in literary tradition, chiefly that of "estates satire," in which representatives of the various professions are portrayed as failing to make their proper contributions to the social body as a whole. Comparing and contrasting the descriptions in Chaucer's gallery with their precursor analogues, she explains the perplexing ambiguities of some of them as reflecting the perennial shiftiness of language itself in the realm of valuation, whereby the significance of an approving word can range from profound to trivial, depending on how it is used.[8] Human nature is the culprit: "the shifting semantic values we give to words reveals in us relative, not absolute, standards for judging people" (196). We tend, in everyday social intercourse, to like people who are attractive and congenial, without worrying about what sorts of people they are in a more profound sense. Chaucer exploits this tendency of ours in the portraits by praising such characteristics as good looks, fine clothing, and congeniality, while suggesting, without actually saying so, that the behavior of the pilgrim in question is immoral. We respond sympathetically to the praise and at the same time are disturbed by the suggestions, unsure of how they should figure in our bottom-line assessment of the person portrayed. The Chaucer of the *General Prologue* practices what Mann describes as the "consistent removal of the possibility of moral judgment" (197). This technique can readily be understood as a self-protective maneuver, particularly when persons of importance are being described: the implications may be planted by the poet, but it is we who must draw the damaging inferences.

The importance of verbal allusiveness in creating such effects is brought out in a number of Mann's discussions of individual portraits. She shows, for example, how in the portrait of the Friar Chaucer "reduces traditional satiric topics to a series of brief hints" expressed in language that "emphasises the façade" (p. 39). The opening lines contain several words that express an ostensibly innocent meaning while, especially to a reader aware of "the stereotyped notion of the friar as womaniser" (p. 40) which was part of antifraternal tradition, they unmistakably suggest a less innocent one:

> A frere ther was, a wantowne and a merye,
> A lymytour, a ful solempne man.
> In alle the ordres foure is noon that kan
> So muchel of daliaunce and fair langage. (208–11)

Mann remarks on the ambiguity of the words *daliaunce* (p. 39) and *wantowne* (p. 41),[9] as well as on that of *rage* in the statement (257) that the Friar could "rage . . . as it were right a whelp" (ibid.), and points out that the suggestions generated by these extend to what we hear of "the Friar's connections with 'yonge wommen,' 'worthy wommen of the toun', 'faire wyves', 'tappesteres' and 'wydwes'" (ibid.). But she sees the disapproval evoked by these suggestions as qualified by another aspect of the portrait: its emphasis on "the attractiveness of the Friar; his music, his pleasant speech, his twinkling eyes and white neck, his muscular physique" (45). (One might add that two of these details are placed at the very end of the portrait, so that our final impression is favorable.) "Yet," Mann continues, "sinister overtones may be felt throughout . . . ; the Friar's cunning manipulation of the world to his own advantage, the possibility that he is a 'fixer', and a blackmailer . . . , lurk just out of the range of our vision" (ibid.). She concludes that "what Chaucer brings to [the antifraternal] tradition is . . . the constant use of ambivalent words which make it hard to subject the Friar to moral analysis. . . . And finally, what is new in the portrait is the growing realisation that there is much in common between the approval of this 'worthy' and 'merye' Friar, and everyday social standards of judgment. . . . [The Friar's] estate reveals more clearly than any other the gulf between the standards of an ordered society and of Christianity" (p. 54).

Despite occasional references to Christianity such as the one above, the purview of Mann's study is almost wholly secular: she is chiefly concerned with relationships among individuals within society rather than with relationships between the individual and the supernatural realm whose existence is affirmed by the Christian faith. Contrasting Chaucer with William Langland, she concedes the validity of the accepted distinction between the former as a secular writer and the latter as a religious one: "It is true that Langland, and most of the army of estates writers before him, have a continual sense of the rewards of Heaven and the punishments of Hell, which of itself provides a 'reason' for moral behavior, and that this sense is lacking in Chaucer" (pp. 191–92). My concern here is to supplement Mann's account of the ambiguities of Chaucer's language by showing how the wording of certain descriptive details is such as to remind the reader of aspects of Christian faith and doctrine ostensibly irrelevant to the content of a given passage. The problems of judgment elucidated by Mann are further complicated by such allusions: we are made uncomfortably aware that beyond the social and moral judgments we ourselves bring to bear on our fellow creatures, there exists, for the Christian believer in Chaucer's time and our own, an austere tribunal that exonerates or condemns *sub specie aeternitatis*.

When, in presenting the portrait of the Prioress, the narrator announces that he is going to speak of her *conscience* (142) and remarks, in that connection, on how "charitable and . . . pitous" (143) she was, we naturally expect to hear something pertinent to her life as a nun. What we do learn about, of course, is her tenderness toward mice caught in traps. We are thus made the victims of a kind of verbal practical joke. The irony of this anticlimax is enhanced by the specifically Christian associations of the words *charitable* and *pitous*. The word *charitable* is particularly powerful in its direct relationship to *charite*. Both this and the *caritas* of the Latin Vulgate signify what was described by Saint Paul, in a key passage of the New Testament, as the greatest of all virtues — that which, in medieval Christianity, figured as the positive component of a fundamental opposition between love of God and love of the world, or *cupiditas*.[10] Such allusiveness, in language that primarily describes worldly preoccupations, serves to remind us of unworldly preoccupations that are not described. We are left to wonder whether or not to suspect that the Prioress's concerns about animals get in the way of the spirituality mandated by her station in life, and, if they do, how much importance Chaucer means us to attach to that fact.[11] This opposition was placed in the foreground of Chaucer scholarship forty years ago and more by D. W. Robertson, but the sweeping generalizations applied by Robertson to all forms of medieval literature, and the black-and-white reductiveness of his conceptual scheme, have recently been subjected to corrective reappraisal. Concurrently, Chaucer scholars have turned their attention from questions of Christian doctrine and salvation to social and political issues, with special attentiveness to class- and gender-based oppression. Yet these new concerns point us back, paradoxically, to those of Robertson. Chaucer's awareness of royal tyranny, of unrest in the lower echelons of society, and, perhaps, of the misfortunes suffered by some of the women he knew simply because they were women cannot well be separated from his awareness of the corruption conspicuous in the lives of certain representatives of the contemporary religious establishment. And it must be remembered that the possibility, if not the certainty, of eternal and unspeakable torment after death loomed far larger in the fourteenth century than it does for most of us in the twenty-first. Chaucer knew sinfulness and injustice when he saw them, and there is every reason to think that he believed, or at least hoped, their perpetrators would reap their just rewards. At times he freely expresses his distaste for morally reprehensible behavior, as in his treatment of the Summoner and the Pardoner. More often, we can sense his feelings in full only by reading between the lines, apprehending, whether in local verbal structures or in larger ones, what is never directly expressed.

Returning to the Prioress, we can sum up Chaucer's method in her portrait by saying that language alluding to Christian doctrine makes the attentive reader mindful of a discrepancy between the actual preoccupations of the head of a convent and the spiritual life she professes. But having said this, we are faced with further questions. Granted our awareness of the discrepancy, how seriously are we to take it? And how can we delineate the limits of allusiveness, particularly in considering the portraits of those pilgrims whose vocations are secular? What, for example, are we to make of the appearance of the word *charitee* in the portrait of that egregiously worldly personage, the Wife of Bath? According to the narrator's account, no woman in the parish dares go to the *offrynge*, that is, the offertory, ahead of her; if anyone does, she becomes so angry that she is "out of alle charitee" (449–52). Here I take it that the very presence of an allusion is a matter of dispute, let alone its implications if present. Should we condemn the ungraciousness of the Wife toward other female parishioners as a departure from the supreme Christian virtue? Should we view as ironic the fact that it is displayed at a time when members of the congregation make donations to the church? Or should we take it less seriously as a foible, referred to with playful suggestiveness, that might be displayed by an otherwise "good Christian"?

A similar problem is presented by the Wife's use of the word *grace* in the story of her fifth and final marriage. She "loved to be gay," she tells the other pilgrims, "And for to walk in March, Averill, and May Fro hous to hous" (III [D] 545–47). She tells of how one year, in Lent, she went out into the fields with her husband's handsome young apprentice Jankin and a close woman friend. Her fourth husband was away in London.

> I hadde the bettre leyser for to pleye,
> And for to se, and eek for to be seye
> Of lusty folk. What wiste I wher my grace
> Was shapen for to be, or in what place? (551–54)

In the course of this outing, the "dalliance" she enjoyed with Jankin impelled her to tell him that if she became a widow he would be her husband (564–68). She had presumably dressed for the occasion, as was her wont, in her "gaye scarlet gytes," of which she says that

> Thise wormes, ne thise motthes, ne thise mytes,
> Upon my peril, frete hem never a deel;
> And wostow why? For they were used weel. (III [D] 559–62)

The echo in this passage of Matthew 6:19–20, "Lay not up for yourselves treasures on earth: where the rust, and moth consume," which is noted without quotation or comment in Riverside, seems inescapable. Those who hear it must surely be struck also by the stunning irrelevance of the Christian concept of grace to the Wife's story.[12] But what conclusion are we to draw from these and other profane inversions of Christian doctrine in her Prologue?[13] I shall return to the problem of judgment presented by the Wife at the end of this chapter.

In the language of the Friar's portrait, Christian allusiveness is infrequent and inconspicuous. The narrator's description of him as one who consorted with franklins, worthy women, and innkeepers and avoided the company of poor folk reflects antifraternal tradition (see below) but could also have reminded late fourteenth-century readers directly of the charge Jesus says is brought against him, that he consorts with tax-gatherers and sinners, that is, people of low social station (Matthew 11:19; cf. *Parson's Tale* 760, "for humble folk been Cristes freendes"). In the statement that

> over al, ther as profit sholde arise,
> Curteis he was, and lowely of servyse, (249–50)

the word *profit* has the general meaning "benefit" or "advantage" (*MED* s.v. *profit(e* n.[l] sense 1[a]), but by virtue of another meaning, "wealth, riches" (sense 4[d]), it reinforces the suggestions of materialism in the portrait. A third meaning, "spiritual benefit; . . . spiritual well-being" (sense 1[b]), works ironically as a reminder of the Friar's own unsound spiritual state. The cognate verb has a corresponding range of meaning in Middle English (see especially the citations s.v. *profiten* sense 1[b] "to be spiritually beneficial or helpful"). It was used in Wycliffite translations of the Vulgate into English as an equivalent of Latin *prosum* in such important texts as Matthew 16:26, "For what doth it profit a man, if he gain the whole world, and suffer the loss of his own soul? (Quid enim prodest homini si mundum universum lucretur, animae vero suae detrimentum patiatur?)." And though *lowely* had not yet acquired its present-day biblical associations, the attribute it signifies, expressed in Latin by the word *humilis*, is of primary importance among those ascribed to Jesus (cf., for example, Matthew 11:29, "because I am meek, and humble [AV: lowly] of heart (quia mitis sum et humilis corde)."

I see in the portrait an additional allusion whose presence has not, so far as I am aware, been previously noted. It appears as a kind of supererogatory element in the narrator's language when he speaks of the Friar's familiarity with taverns, innkeepers, and barmaids:

> He knew the tavernes wel in every toun
> And every hostiler and tappestere
> Bet than a lazar and a beggestere. (240–42)

The narrator goes on to defend the Friar from the charge implicit in this statement. It is not fitting, he says, that a man of so high a social position should

> have with sike lazars aqueyntaunce.
> It is nat honest; it may nat avaunce,
> For to deelen with no swich poraille,
> But al with riche and selleres of vitaille. (246–48)

What I find salient, and important, in these passages is the word *lazar*, which appears twice, and which I have not found used in other references in anti-fraternal literature to the poor folk whom friars avoid. Its source in English is the Latin proper name Lazarus, designating not the Lazarus whom Jesus is said to have raised from the dead in John 11, but the beggar in the parable he tells in Luke 16:19–31. This Lazarus, covered with sores, lay at the gate of Dives ("rich"), who dressed splendidly and feasted every day, "desiring to be filled by the crumbs that fell from the rich man's table (cupiens saturari de micis quae cadebant de mensa divitis)" (21). The two men died; the beggar was transported by angels to Abraham's bosom, and Dives was consigned to hell. Looking up from his place of torment, he vainly pleaded with Abraham to send Lazarus down, that he might dip his finger in water and cool his tongue. Abraham replied that between the two places there lay a great chasm that could not be crossed in either direction (26; the *chasma* of the Vulgate is rendered "chaos" in Douay-Rheims). Once reminded of this parable by the narrator's choice of words, one cannot but see Friar Hubert's way of life, with its avoidance of *lazars* and *beggesteres* and preferred associations with taverners and sellers of food, as emulating that of Dives. Furthermore, it is surely significant that the allusion latent here becomes explicit in the *Summoner's Tale* put into the mouth of Friar John himself as he sanctimoniously dwells on the self-mortification practiced by himself and his brothers:

> We lyve in poverte and in abstinence,
> And burel folk in richesse and despense
> Of mete and drynke. . . .
> Lazar and Dives lyveden diversly
> And divers gerdon hadden they therby. (III [D] 1873–75, 76–77)

The action of the *Summoner's Tale* culminates in a sustained allusion to Christian history and iconography whose latent presence, though undetected until the 1960s, is now generally if not universally acknowledged. The case for it was first made in print in 1966 by Bernard S. Levy. Levy acknowledged his indebtedness to Alan Levitan, whose essay was to appear five years later. Both argued that Thomas's gift to Friar John of a fart louder than could have been produced by any carthorse (2149–51) must be understood as a parodic analogue of the descent of the Holy Ghost on the assembled apostles at Pentecost, accompanied by the "sound . . . as of a mighty wind (sonus . . . tamquam advenientis spiritus vehementis)," as described in Acts 2:2. Furthermore, the "cartwheel solution" devised by the Squire at the manor to the problem of dividing the fart into twelve equal parts corresponds to certain representations of the event in medieval iconography, in which twelve radii leading to the heads of the twelve apostles extend from a central image of the Holy Ghost in the form of a dove.[14]

The presence of the parody, as analyzed by Levy and Levitan, has not been accepted by all Chaucer scholars.[15] However, a learned and judicious essay by Glending Olson, "The End of *The Summoner's Tale* and the Uses of Pentecost,"[16] has now, I believe, established once and for all its centrality in the tale's culmination. Olson sees the iconography of the cartwheel itself as one element of a larger pattern: "[the squire's] solution depends on something from outside and above the wheel traveling through it to a set of recipients. The wheel is only part of the narrative scenario" (p. 216). (See, however, the references to wheel iconography in John V. Fleming, "Anticlerical Satire as Theological Essay: Chaucer's *Summoner's Tale*" [*Thalia* 6 (1983), 5–21], p. 21, n. 30.) Olson's essay contributes further to our understanding of the cultural background of the tale by showing that "among [Chaucer's] possible sources of inspiration . . . are earlier imitations and parodies of Pentecost, some of which [Chaucer] was in all likelihood acquainted with" (p. 217). Of special interest are medieval accounts of "phony Pentecost[s]" (p. 218) in which Antichrist appeared, brought down fire from heaven, and performed false miracles. Such lore, popularly disseminated, was exploited in Wycliffite antifraternal discourse, which "appeal[ed] often in a general way to the idea of Antichrist" and even accused friars of exemplifying Antichrist's miracles (p. 221). Fleming's essay refers to the "quasi-dramatic . . . representations of the descent of the Spirit, which . . . almost certainly would have been familiar to Chaucer and his audience." In these representations, doves or flowers were "made to descend . . . to the sound of a mechanically contrived rushing of wind" (ibid.). I would add only that the presence of the Pentecostal analogy need not rule out the presence of other, subsidiary analogies, such as that with the wheel of the winds, adduced by Robert Hasenfratz ("The Science of Flatulence: Possible Sources for the *Summoner's Tale*," *Chaucer Review* 30 [1995–96], 241–61), and the Wheel of Fortune, mentioned by Kolve in the article cited in note 15, above, as associated in Hugh's treatise with the Wheel of Religious Hypocrisy (pp. 283–85).

It is one thing to be aware of such a parodic relationship, but quite another to incorporate that awareness into our response to the tale as a whole. After all, it lay buried there, unsuspected, for more than five and a half centuries. Does it give the tale a deeper meaning? and if so, in what does that additional depth consist? Derek Pearsall, in his study of the *Canterbury Tales*, concedes that the Pentecostal allusion is surely present but maintains that "such an allusion defies exegesis, or interpretation in relation to any moral or satirical theme in the tales," belonging rather to the "realm of what may be called 'pure' comedy."[17] He goes on to quote a negative assessment made by John Burrow in an article predating the discovery of the parody: "[The Tale] is 'poetry of the surface'. . . . In the end the poem does not add up to much. It remains an extended anecdote." "In a sense," Pearsall continues, "this is [still] true"; the virtue of the tale consists, not in its moral or religious profundity, but in its display of one of the "many kinds of literary and intellectual virtuosity from which we do not expect such calculable rewards but which nevertheless give delight."[18] I find it possible to agree as to the virtuosity and the delight, while maintaining that our recognition of the presence of the tale's parodic dimension cannot but enlarge our response to its central figure and the indignity that befalls him.

The antifraternal tradition that underlies the portraits of Friar Hubert and Friar John in the *Canterbury Tales* was handed down over a wide cultural range or spectrum, from learned to popular. The learned end is represented by a series of polemical treatises, written for the most part in Latin, of which the earliest dates back almost to the lifetime of Saint Francis. On the popular side, we find a body of material which must have been transmitted orally as well as in writing in English and the continental vernaculars. This includes stories, many or most of them now lost, of the sort that presumably supplied Chaucer with the joke in the *Summoner's Prologue* as well as the incident of the fart, if not its parodic elaboration, in the tale. Literary works of greater or lesser sophistication — for example, the *Roman de la rose* by Guillaume de Lorris and Jean de Meun, *Piers Plowman* by Langland, and the anonymous early fourteenth-century fabliau "Li dis de le vescie à prestre (The Tale of the Priest's Bladder)," which is "the only extended analogue [of the *Summoner's Tale*] known to scholars"[19] — fall at various points between learned and popular extremes. At the learned level of antifraternal polemic, three figures have been identified by scholars of the subject as being of major importance: William of St. Amour, a secular master of theology in the faculty of the University of Paris in the mid–thirteenth century; Richard FitzRalph, archbishop of Armagh in Ireland in the mid–fourteenth century; and Chaucer's near-contemporary John Wyclif.[20] In the following discussion of the literary background as it was or may have been known to Chaucer, Jean de Meun's continuation of *Le roman de la rose*, in which William's thought is recapitulated and dramatized at considerable length, will take pride of place, though its importance in the line of transmission has not hitherto been fully acknowledged.[21] FitzRalph will prove significant as a witness to the problematic relationship between the secular clergy and the friars in Chaucer's century, rather than as a contributor to the intellectual content of antifraternal discourse. And the thought of

Wyclif, as I have said, will be found to provide a hitherto unrecognized subtext for the *Summoner's Tale*—occluded by Chaucer almost successfully, yet, once recognized, profoundly enlarging the meaning of the tale and our responses to it.[22]

In the first major work to be directed against the friars, the *De periculis novissimorum temporum (Concerning the Perils of the Last Days)* by William of St. Amour, we find both the themes of later attacks and the scriptural allusions that would be used to support them. The treatise was published in 1256, only thirty years after the death of Saint Francis.[23] William took the part of the "secular masters" at the University of Paris in its antagonism toward the "mendicant masters," a group of friars who had recently joined the faculty and whom the secular faction had finally succeeded in expelling from the university's *consortium magistrorum* or magisterial governing body. The immediate occasion of the treatise was the appearance in 1254 of the "Liber Introductorius ad Evangelium Aeternum (Treatise Introductory to the Eternal Gospel)" by one Gerard of Borgo San Donnino, a Franciscan friar. The "Introductorius" (as it is usually called) is no longer extant. It was published by Gerard in an edition of certain of the prophetic writings of the famed twelfth-century abbot Joachim of Fiore and was based, with some simplification and distortion, on Joachim's ideas. According to Gerard's version, the first two ages of world history, associated with the Gospels of the Father and the Son, that is, the Old and New Testaments, respectively, were almost at an end. A third age, that of the Holy Spirit, was imminent; with its coming, a third testament, the "Eternal Gospel" or "Gospel of the Holy Ghost," would supersede the earlier two. What most aroused the indignation of William and his party was Gerard's assertion that the harbingers of the third age were none other than the newly founded orders of friars, who were to have a role in the transition analogous to that of John the Baptist in the coming of the second age. In his counterattack, William adapted, and took his title from, a passage of eschatological prophesy in 2 Timothy. Chapter 3 of that epistle begins with a warning: "Know also this, that, in the last days [of the world], shall come dangerous times (Hoc autem scito, quod in novissimis diebus instabunt tempora periculosa)." The church will find itself beset by enemies, "lovers of themselves (se ipsos amantes) [2]," "lovers of pleasures more than of God, having an appearance . . . of godliness but denying the power thereof (voluptatum amatores magis quam Dei, habentes speciem . . . pietatis, virtutis autem eius abnegantes) [4–5]," and "corrupted in mind, reprobate concerning the faith (corrupti mente, reprobi circa fidem) [8]." William agreed that the "last days" were at hand, as Gerard maintained, but he saw them rather as the last days described in 2 Timothy 3. The signs of the times portended, not a glorious third age, but the end of the world prophetically described in the Book of Revelation, and the members of the fraternal orders, far from being the messengers of an Eternal Gospel of the Holy Ghost, were the very lovers of themselves, hypocrites, and infidels whom Paul had warned of. Though in the *De periculis*, as in other writings, William prudently avoided explicit topical references, he described the "seducers (seductores)" posing an imminent threat to the church in terms that clearly pointed to the friars.[24]

The details of William's polemic, which are rather repetitively deployed, can be seen as substantiating three main allegations: (1) that the friars, despite their pretensions to holiness, were morally corrupt, (2) that they lacked a legitimate position within the church, and (3) that they falsely claimed to be following the apostolic way of life as inculcated in the New Testament, particularly in their reliance exclusively on mendicancy for support. The argument is conducted in scholastic fashion, each assertion being accompanied by supporting evidence in the form of excerpts from the Bible and the patristic authorities, chiefly the *Glossa Ordinaria*.[25] Little or nothing that is pertinent in scripture is overlooked; as a result, this earliest of the antifraternal treatises cited virtually all the texts that were to reappear in the works of later writers. The opening statement of the passage from 2 Timothy 3 provides a framework for the work as a whole, its fourteen chapters being devoted to answering a series of questions bearing on the predicted dangers, those who will cause them, and how they can be averted.[26]

In charging the friars with moral corruption, William drew first of all on the long list of vices attributed by Paul in 2 Timothy 3 to the men of the last days.[27] He also made use, briefly in the *De periculis* and more extensively elsewhere, of a rhetorically similar passage in the Gospels that had been used in earlier denunciations of religious hypocrisy and would now become a locus classicus of antifraternal polemic: the denunciation of the scribes and pharisees by Jesus in chapter 23 of the Gospel of Matthew.[28] Though the two passages differ in context, they resemble each other in purport and overlap in detail. In both, sinful actions, cloaked by a pretense of righteousness, are implicitly linked with denial of or alienation from the Christian faith; such actions manifest outwardly an inward repudiation of charity, or love of one's neighbor and of God, in favor of cupidity, or love of oneself and the world.[29] Once either passage was interpreted as having referred prophetically to the friars, details from it could, by a circular argument, be cited as evidence of fraternal corruption. Thus the statement in Matthew 23:6 that "they [the scribes and pharisees] love the first places at feasts (amant autem primos recubitus in cenis)" (6), and the description of the men of the last days in 2 Timothy 3 as "lovers of pleasures more than of God" (4), were cited in support of a persistent charge of gluttony. The desire of the scribes and pharisees to be called Rabbi or Master (7) corresponded nicely to the aspirations of the friars, not only at the University of Paris in the mid–thirteenth century, but also in later times and other places. The erudition for which the friars became famous early on[30] was thought to be rebuked by Paul's description of the men of the last days as "ever learning, and never attaining to the knowledge of the truth (semper discentes et numquam ad scientiam veritatis pervenientes)" (7). Each passage charged the wrongdoers in question with preying on women: the scribes and pharisees were accused by Jesus of devouring the houses of widows ("Vae vobis . . . quia comeditis domos uiduarum") (23:14), and the men of the last days were said to "creep into houses, and lead captive silly women laden with sins, who are led away with divers desires (penetrant domos, et captivas ducunt mulierculas oneratas peccatis quae ducuntur variis desideriis)" (3:6). William gave this latter verse a figurative interpretation: the friars, taking it upon themselves to act as confessors, pried into the secrets of the "houses," that is, the consciences, of those who confessed to them (*De periculis*, pp. 20, 24). Variations on the Latin phrase "penetrant domos" were to become perhaps the most familiar of all the clichés of antifraternal polemic.[31]

Arguing that the fraternal orders had no place in the historically established structure of the church, William applied to their activities the question Paul had asked in his Epistle to the Romans, referring to the need for preachers to spread the gospel to the Jews: "How shall they preach unless they be sent? (Quomodo vero praedicabunt nisi mittantur?)" (10:15; *De periculis*, p. 21).[32] The friars had not been "sent" in the traditional way and thus lacked the priestly calling or vocation in Paul's literal sense: "Neither doth any man take the honour [of the role of high priest] to himself, but he that is *called* by God, as Aaron was (Nec quisquam assumit sibi honorem, sed qui *vocatur* a Deo, tanquam Aaron)" (Hebrews 5:4; *De periculis*, ibid.) (emphasis added). They were outside the administrative structure of the church in being exempt from the authority of the bishops, answering only to their own superiors and to the pope. From the latter they had obtained such privileges as preaching and hearing confessions. The monies they had acquired by performing these services would otherwise have gone to the parish priests, to whom the care of souls had been properly committed and who were therefore entitled to "live from the gospel."[33] The friars could not claim to be the legitimate successors of the twelve apostles, like the bishops, or of the seventy-two disciples, like the priests; nor had a third order ever been established to which they might belong (ibid.).[34] Clearly, then, they were the usurpers prophesied by Paul, threatening the church in the last days of the world with dangers which must be inquired into and expelled without further delay ("videlicet quod non longe remota sunt illa pericula novissimorum temporum, & quod eorum inquisitio & repulsio non sit magis differenda" [p. 27]).

As usurpers, the friars were to be identified with the "false prophets (pseudoprophetae)" spoken of by Jesus, who came as wolves dressed in sheep's clothing (Matthew 7:15; cf. Matthew 24:11 and *De periculis*, pp. 21, 23), the "false apostles (pseudoapostoli)" referred to by Paul in Second Corinthians (11:13; *De periculis*, p. 35), and the "many Antichrists (antichristi multi)" who in the First Epistle of John were said to be present in the last hour (2:18; *De periculis*, p.19). They behaved after the fashion of the wolf in the parable told in John 10:1–13, who entered the sheepfold not "by the door . . . but . . . another way (non . . . per ostium sed . . . aliunde)" (1) and came only "to kill, and to destroy (non venit nisi ut . . . mactet et perdat)" (10; *De periculis*, p. 26). Linking this parable with Paul's warning in 2 Timothy 3, William identified entry otherwise than by the door with the penetration of houses, since those who enter "by the door do not penetrate (intrando per ostium, non penetrant)" (ibid.).

What seemed to William the self-evident viciousness of the friars, spelled out in prophetic detail in Matthew 23 and 2 Timothy 3, was in itself proof that their way of life differed diametrically from that preached by Jesus and supremely exemplified by "the apostle," that is, Paul. Moreover, he charged them with disregarding in a number of specific respects the explicit instructions given in the New Testament concerning the apostolic mission. Most conspicuous among these was the practice of mendicancy itself, concerning which William asserted categorically, "That the Lord begged, or his apostles, is nowhere found [in the New Testament] (Quod autem Dominus vel mendicaverit, vel ejus Apostoli, nusquam reperitur)" (*De periculis*, p. 33). Paul told his followers, "Work with your own hands, as we commanded you (operemini manibus vestris sicut praecepimus vobis)" (Thessalonians 4:11; *De periculis*, p. 32; cf. Sermon I, p. 44), and assured them that he himself had acted in accordance with his own precept.[35] And there were numerous other disparities. Jesus had instructed the disciples and apostles to find, in each town they visited, one person who was worthy and to stay in his house, eating and drinking what was set before them, whereas the friars sought out the homes of the wealthy, where they were served sumptuous meals.[36] Paul had not coveted gold and silver or the possessions of those to whom he preached, whereas the friars performed their services out of love of money.[37] Paul had endured reproaches and persecution in patience, whereas the friars could not bear correction.[38] A pun on the word *frater*, which by William's time had come to mean "friar" as well as "fellow-congregant," lent itself to his purposes: Paul had told his followers to withdraw themselves "from every *brother* walking disorderly, and not according to the tradition which they have received from us (ab omni *fratre* ambulante inordinate, et non secundum traditionem quam acceperunt a nobis)" (emphasis added).[39] He cited the interpretation of "ambulante inordinate" in the *Glossa Ordinaria* as referring to "those who concern themselves with other people's business, wandering here and there (illi qui aliena negotia curant, vagantes hac & illac)."[40] The friars habitually "wandered here and there" and often served as brokers and legal advisors. The warning against stirrers up of dissension given by Paul at the end of his epistle to the Romans was found equally apt. Such men "serve not Christ our Lord, but their own belly; and by pleasing speeches and good words, seduce the hearts of the innocent (Christo Domino nostro non serviunt, sed suo ventri, et per dulces sermones et benedictiones seducunt corda innocentium)."[41] Paul acknowledged that he was "rude in speech (inperitus sermone)," whereas the friars devoted themselves to learning and loved to show off their eloquence.[42] Finally, nothing in the way of life of Jesus or the apostles anticipated the magnificent churches and convents that were erected by the friars once they had gained wealth and power; such edifices, in fact, had been specifically condemned by Saint Francis. William said that in constructing them the friars had not turned stones into bread, as Satan had told Jesus to do, but had turned the bread rightfully due to the poor, of which the friars had deprived them by their begging, into stones.[43] Later antifraternal writings repeated these charges of William's and the biblical texts cited to support them.

Though in practical terms, the *De periculis* accomplished little, its influence and that of William's later writings was lasting.[44] Penn Szittya cites ample evidence to the effect that they were read by English clerics and scholars in Chaucer's time. Moreover, they were used in the latter half of the fourteenth century by opponents of the friars in the monastic orders in England as well as by FitzRalph and Wyclif, whose writings I discuss below.[45] We cannot be sure which of these materials, if any, Chaucer saw, but of his knowledge of William's life and work there can be no doubt, for he was a devoted reader of *Le roman de la rose*, including the part of it most relevant to this essay, the continuation by Jean de Meun of the narrative begun by Guillaume de Lorris.[46]

Jean was probably a colleague of William's on the faculty of the University of Paris. He apparently completed his work on the *Roman* in 1275 or a few years later, that is, about twenty years after the publication of the *De periculis*, and he may well have been working on it while William was still alive.[47] He incorporated an account of the controversy at the university in which William took part, along with much material from the *De periculis*, in his own brilliant contribution to antifraternal tradition, the long confessional monologue of Fals-Semblant.[48] This part of the *Roman*, we know, made an especially profound impression on Chaucer. Not only did it convey to him, or supplement, or both, the knowledge of fraternal abuses that he dramatized for his own purposes in the *Summoner's Tale*; it also played a part in the genesis of one of his most memorable fictional creations: the Pardoner.

In Jean's narrative, Fals-Semblant is accepted as an ally in a campaign on the lover's behalf mounted by Amors, who is called Love in the *Romaunt* (*Roman* 10409 ff.).[49] Ordered by Love to reveal to the assembly where he may be found and how he may be recognized (*Romaunt* 6073–81; *Roman* 10943–51),[50] he at first demurs, then, at the god's insistence, launches into a self-revealing discourse of more than a thousand lines (6138 ff.; 11006 ff.). He begins by saying that whoever wishes to find him must seek him out "in worldly folk. . . . And, certes, in the cloistres (Si le quiere au siecle ou en cloistre)" (6141–42; 11008), but not equally in both, for he likes to stay where he can best be concealed (that is, in the cloister). Later, he claims to play a protean variety of roles in society, assuming both female and male guise.[51] At such moments, his allegorical significance enlarges to encompass hypocrisy and fraud in general. But there is general agreement that his primary *persona* is that of a friar. In this episode, as in the *De periculis*, this aspect of his identity remains implicit, though in a later episode, when he sets off with Dame Abstynence-Streyned to see Wicked-Tonge, he dons "the cope of a frer" (7408; 12084). The accusations made by William in discursive form — of moral corruption and hypocrisy, usurpation of the functions of the secular clergy, and fraudulent pretense to the apostolic way of life — take on dramatic life in the *Roman* as, in a startling contradiction, hypocrisy frankly acknowledges itself, while charity clashes with cupidity in diametrically opposite formulations. When Amors, amazed by Fals-Semblant's candor, protests that he seems to be "an hooly heremyte," he replies, "Soth is, but I am an ypocrite" ("Tu me sembles .i. sainz hermites." "Cest voirs, mes ie sui ypocrites.") (6481–82; 11231–32).

> "Thou gost and prechest poverte."
> "Ye, sir, but richesse hath pouste ('power')."
> "Thou prechest abstinence also."
> "Sir, I wole fillen, so mote I go,
> My paunche of good mete and wyn,
> As shulde a maister of dyvyn;
> For how that I me pover feyne,
> Yit alle pore folk I disdeyne." (6483–90; 11233–40)

More shocking still is an interchange in which Fals-Semblant remains unmoved even by Love's invocation of the name of God:

Quod Love, "What devel is this that I heere? . . .
Thanne dredist thou not God?"
"No, certis" (6797, 6800; 11525, 28)

That this unabashed display of viciousness made a deep impression upon
Chaucer is clear in the *Pardoner's Prologue*, where Fals-Semblant's across-the-
board declaration, "To wynnen is alwey myn entente" (683; 11565) is echoed
by the Pardoner's "For myn entente is nat but for to wynne" (404). Elsewhere,
the Pardoner shows his indifference to divine judgment, at least as it bears on
the souls of his auditors (405–06), describes himself as a serpent spitting out
his venom in the guise of holiness (421–22), and boasts that his viciousness
does not detract from his skill as a teller of moral tales (459–61).[52]

The antifraternal attack that Jean puts into the mouth of Fals-Semblant in
confessional form is heavily indebted to the *De periculis* in content and echoes
a number of the scriptural texts William had marshaled in support of his case,
though in the *Roman* the specific biblical sources are seldom given. Thus,
although Fals-Semblant warns his auditors that he and his compeers represent
an imminent danger to the church,[53] 2 Timothy 3 is not mentioned. However,
to help his audience recognize "hem . . . that usen ["are accustomed"] folk
thus to disceyven (les felons . . . Qui ne cessent des gens decoivre)" (6883–
84; 11599–600), Fals-Semblant repeats several of the accusations made in
"Seynt Matthew (saint Maci)" (that is, Matthew 23), including the desire to
be called master (6885–922; 11601–36). William's moral abstractions are
brought down to earth by catalogues of specifics, as when Fals-Semblant lists
the bribes he and his fellows demand from those whose vices they threaten
to reveal:[54]

> "But ['unless'] they defende them with lamprey,
> With luce ['pike'], with elys, with samons,
> With tendre gees and with capons,
> With tartes, or with cheses fat,
> With deynte flawnes ['custard puddings'] brode and flat,
> With caleweis ['fine pears'], or with pullayne ['poultry'],
> With conynges ['rabbits'], or with fyn vitaille,
> That we, under our clothes wide,
> Maken thourgh oure golet glide;
> Or but he wole do come in haste
> Roo-venysoun, bake in paste;
> Whether so that he loure or groyne ['grumble'],
> He shal have of a corde a loigne ['leash'],
> With whiche men shal hym bynde and lede
> To brenne hym for his synful deede."[55] (7038–52; 11740–53)

William's firm belief that the fraternal orders have no legitimate place in the church is implied by Jean in Fals-Semblant's monologue. His account of his activities as a confessor recalls William's charge in the *De periculis* that the friars penetrate the houses of the faithful, both literally and figuratively, find out their secrets, and alienate them from their parish priests. Two passages bearing on this topic, found in a small group of manuscripts of the *Roman* but rejected as spurious by modern editors, are included in the *Romaunt*. Both are noteworthy in the boldness of the claims they impute to the friars, and because they appear in the *Romaunt* and thus, we may assume, in a version of the *Roman* that circulated in England, it seems probable that Chaucer knew them. The first runs to more than one hundred lines (6361–472); it is numbered parenthetically from line 1 to line 98 in Sutherland, pp. 127–29 and includes a sequence of lines numbered 8 plus a number in superscript. It begins with Fals-Semblant's assertion that he makes all Christians fall into his "traps (piges)" through his "privileges" (6361–63), and continues,

> "I may assoile and I may shryve,
> That no prelate may lette me,
> All folk, where evere thei founde be.
> I not no prelat may don so ['know no prelate who may do so']
> But it the pope be, and no mo,
> That made thilk establisshing." (6364–69; p. 127, (3)–(8))

In lines that would be echoed by Chaucer in the *Pardoner's Prologue*, Fals-Semblant boasts that he has become wealthy by preaching and hearing confessions, leading "right a joly lyf, Thurgh symplesse of the prelacye — They knowe not al my tregettrie ['trickery']" (6380–82). (The line corresponding to 6382 in the *Roman* is "Qui trop fort redoutent mes las [who greatly fear my snares])" [p. 127, (16)]. There follows a long imaginary speech by a parishioner, who tells his parish priest that he need not confess to him because he has already been confessed by "Friar Wolf (frere Lovel)" (6424; p. 128, [50]). If for this reason the priest threatens to bar him from taking communion, the friar will readily administer it to him. What is more, the friar is "full redy hym [the priest] to accuse, And hym punysshe and hampre so That he his chirche shal forgo (Je sui prest que je l'en escuse, E de lui punir en tel guise Que perdre li ferai l'eglise)" (6444–46; p. 128, [70]–[72]). A little later in the passage, Fals-Semblant repeats the admonition in Proverbs 27:23 which was applied in the *De periculis*, as it had been in Christian tradition generally, to the priest's responsibility for his "cattle," that is, the souls of those in his care: "Know the countenance of thy cattle (agnosce vultum pecoris tui)" (*De periculis*, pp. 20, 25). When the role of confessor is taken over illegitimately by the friars, the priest

"may never have myght
To knowe the conscience aright
Of hym that is undir his cure.
And this ageyns holy scripture,
That biddith every heerde honest
Have verry knowing of his beest." (6449–6454; p. 128, (75)–(80))

(Here the French, in which the last line reads, "Congnoistre le voult [face] de sa beste," follows the scriptural text more closely than the English.) The second of the two interpolated passages is short (6841–48; p. 136, [B¹]–[B⁸]). In it, Fals-Semblant claims flatly that he has "cure," or priestly responsibility, throughout the world; he can preach and give counsel everywhere because he has the pope's bull.

Later in the monologue, when Fals-Semblant describes his method of prying into the secrets of the lives of those he confesses, the word *proprete* (*proprietés* in the French text) echoes the *proprietates* into which William accuses the friars of prying (*De periculis*, p. 20; cf. note 31):

"And, for her soules savete ['salvation'],
At lord and lady, and her meyne,
I axe, whanne thei hem to me shryve,
The proprete ['nature, character'] of al her lyve,
And make hem trowe, bothe meest and leest,
Hir paroch-prest nys but a beest
Ayens ['compared with'] me and my companye,
That shrewis ['villains'] ben as gret as I." (6869–76; 11587–94)

As we saw, the analogy, alluded to in the appellation Friar Wolf, of the wolf that breaks into the fold bent on destroying the sheep, was an important weapon in William's rhetorical armory. It appears also in Fals-Semblant's description of his own predatory activities, though Jean melds with the parabolic style of the New Testament the anthropomorphic humor of the beast fables, calling the sheep "dam Belin" and the wolf "sire Ysengrin" (11123, 25). To these characters he adds the cat, Tibers, who is intent only on killing mice (11068–69).[56]

Jean follows William in arguing, in the person of Fals-Semblant, that the friars' reliance on mendicancy contravenes apostolic practice. Fals-Semblant's monologue cites the prayer of "Salamon . . . in his Parablis," that is, the Book of Proverbs, to be spared from riches and beggary alike, and Paul's instructions to the faithful to work with their hands, as William's treatise had done.[57] It repeats William's assertion that nothing in the New Testament shows that Jesus or his apostles engaged in begging,[58] as well as his warning that one who takes the alms rightfully due to those weak in body or otherwise incapable of labor, "etith his owne dampnyng (il mangue son dampnement)" (6643; 11373; cf. *De periculis*, p. 33). Other departures from the apostolic model on the part of the friars that William had noted include Fals-Semblant's admission that he is fond of rebuking others but averse to being rebuked himself (6987–94; 11693–700) and his professed penchant for meddling in secular affairs. He boasts that he serves as a broker, negotiates reconciliations and marriages, acts as an executor of wills and as a *procuratour* (agent or attorney), and makes legal inquiries (6971–80; 11679–86). His statement that the apostles "neither bilden tour ne halle, But lay in houses smale withalle (Ne fondoient palais ne sales, Ains gisoient en mesons sales ["filthy"])" (6571–72; 11315–16) implicitly condemns the magnificent edifices in which the friars live and worship.

Having named "William Seynt Amour" as a source of his statements on the subject of mendicancy (6763; 11488), Fals-Semblant admits that it was his own mother, Ypocrysie, who was responsible for William's exile (6779–80; 11507–08). He refers to an argument in "a book" written by William, evidently the *De periculis*, to the effect that he, and presumably others like him, should work for a living but dismisses it contemptuously; he would rather recite the paternoster and pray before the people, wrapping himself in a cope of "papelardie," or religious hypocrisy, to disguise his "foxerie (renardie)" (6781–96; 11509–24; see *foxery* in *OED*). Later (7089–154; 11791–844), he tells of how the University of Paris rose against a book styling itself "the gospel perdurable, That fro the Holy Goost is sent (l'Evangile pardurable, Que li sains Esperis menistre)" (7102–03; 11802–03), which falsely claimed to surpass the four Gospels as much as the sun surpasses the moon, and the nut the shell (7111–26; 11811–24). This "fals horrible bok (cele orrible monstre)" (7132; 11830) has now been hidden away, to be brought out again when it can be successfully defended. It sets forth many commandments that are "ayens the lawe of Rome expres (contre la loy de Romme)," and its proponents are allies of Antichrist (7190–91; 11878–79).[59] The gospel it preaches has not prevailed; nevertheless, and "maugre the Holy Gost (Malgré qu'en ait Sainz Esperis)" (7216; 11900), the lineage of Fals-Semblant and his mother and father now reigns over all the world. Their falseness is not perceived by "the folk (les gens);" in any case, no one who did perceive it would dare betray it, even though such cowardice on their part warrants the anger of Christ (7213–26; 11897–910). In fact, Fals-Semblant and his fellows are generally loved and respected; it is the "beggers with these hoodes wyde (beguins aus grans chaperons)" and "graye clothes nat ful cleane (larges robes et grises)" (7254, 56; 11938, 40)[60] to whose wisdom princes and lords should commit the governance of their affairs in war and peace (7261–64; 11944–46). He concludes by singling out for special condemnation those who dress humbly and pretend to have forsaken the world but in actuality covet worldly glory:

> "Who may that begger wel excuse,
> That papelard ['hypocrite'], that him yeldith so,
> And wole to worldly ese go,
> And seith that he the world hath left,
> And gredily it grypeth eft?
> He is the hound, shame is to seyn,
> That to his castyng goth ageyn."[61] (7280–86; 11962–98)

I have recapitulated Fals-Semblant's confession at considerable length with a view to showing its importance — indeed, what I consider its primary importance — as a literary source of the antifraternalism dramatized by Chaucer in his portraits of Friar Hubert in the *Prologue* and Friar John in the *Summoner's Tale*. Whether or not he had direct access to the writings of William of St. Amour and whether or not he read them if he did, Chaucer would have gained ample knowledge from the *Roman* of the charges mounted by William against the friars. He would have learned about the *Eternal Gospel* and the fraternal orders' association with it, the supposed authorship of this treatise by the Holy Ghost, its claim to supersede and surpass the four Gospels of the New Testament, and the hostility toward it on the part of the University of Paris that, according to Jean, caused it to go into hiding.[62] This section of the *Roman* not only served Chaucer as background for the *Summoner's Tale*, but was an essential source for the character of the Pardoner, to whom Chaucer assigned the brazen indifference to the threat of divine judgment he had seen in the disquisition of Fals-Semblant. Though the Pardoner is not a friar, he is akin to the friars in that he too is a kind of wandering mendicant who obtains monies for his support from the congregations he visits and thus deprives the local parish priests of some of their legitimate revenues. I shall have more to say later about the relation between the two figures.

The life and antifraternal writings of Richard FitzRalph can be discussed more briefly in that he contributed little or nothing to the rhetoric William had developed a century earlier. His career had begun at the University of Oxford, but he spoke as an opponent of the friars not so much for the academic community, which William of St. Amour had represented, as for the secular clergy, addressing those of highest rank in the ecclesiastical establishment from his own high position within it.[63] FitzRalph did not identify the friars categorically as the "lovers of themselves" against whose dangerous presence Paul had warned in 2 Timothy 3, as William had done; neither did he attribute to them the promulgation of a diabolically inspired gospel of the Holy Ghost. He saw them rather as inheritors of an ideal model of the religious life from which, since the death of their founder, they had diverged more and more sharply in practice. In taking this view, he allied himself, paradoxically, with a radical branch of the fraternal orders themselves, known as the "Spiritual Franciscans," who objected to the laxity with which, in their view, the original rule had come to be interpreted.[64] FitzRalph's activities as a reformer began with a series of sermons, some preached in English, attacking the corruption of the clergy generally.[65] His relations with the friars, cordial at first, became increasingly antagonistic, evidently as a result of his experiences as archbishop.[66]

FitzRalph's antagonism received its first important public expression in the treatise usually called *Unusquisque*, preached by FitzRalph before the pope in 1350.[67] This treatise was concerned with one of the major problems originally identified by William of St. Amour, namely, the position of the fraternal orders with relation to the historically established church. FitzRalph turned his attention to one aspect of that problem: who should control church income and property? As a way of answering it, he interpreted figuratively the injunction of Paul in 1 Corinthians 7:18, that the circumcised and the uncircumcised among the faithful should remain as they were ("Is any man called, being circumcised? let him not procure uncircumcision. Is any man called in uncircumcision? let him not be circumcised [Circumcisus aliquis vocatus est? non adducat praeputium. In praeputio aliquis vocatus est? non circumcidatur]"). Metaphorically equating the friars' professed renunciation of worldly goods in the state of "highest poverty" with "circumcision," he argued that the prelates of the church were uncircumcised; accordingly, it was their responsibility to administer the regulations of the church and dispense its temporal goods.[68] Since the ecclesiastical hierarchy made up of the "uncircumcised" included those lowest in rank, that is, the parish priests, it followed that, as William had maintained in the *De periculis*, the friars were acting illegitimately in accepting payment for pastoral services like preaching and hearing confessions, which had traditionally been performed by priests. In refusing to remain in their "circumcised" state, they were depriving the secular clergy of monies rightfully due them and breaking the rule of "highest poverty" originally established by their founder (pp. 56–57, 70–71). This legalistic or, to use Szittya's term, ecclesiological line of thought was supplemented at the end of the treatise by a logically superfluous argument: that the privileges acquired by the friars ought in any case to be abolished because the friars notoriously abused them.[69] In that he approved of the ideals originally espoused by Saint Francis, FitzRalph's views, as noted above, diverged from William's, resembling rather those of the friars who wished to reform the fraternal orders from within.

In 1356, FitzRalph published his major opus, a seven-volume treatise entitled *Concerning the Poverty of the Savior (De pauperie Salvatoris)*,[70] dealing with the complementary concepts of property and poverty as preached and practiced in the Gospels. Its historical importance consists in the fact that FitzRalph's view of divine grace as a necessary condition of earthly lordship was adopted, and its social implications further explored, by Wyclif.[71] Immediately after its publication, he resumed his antifraternal activities, attacking the friars with increasing intensity in a series of sermons preached in the vernacular in London. The resultant controversy culminated in the treatise entitled *Defensio Curatorum* (1357), delivered by FitzRalph before the pope and cardinals meeting in consistory. In the *Defensio*, as in a formal petition submitted separately, he asked that the fraternal orders be stripped of their privileges. He died three years later, his struggle against the friars, like William's, having been of no avail. In Szittya's words, "The case . . . simply vanished. No decision was ever recorded for either party."[72]

FitzRalph's main concern in the *Defensio*, as its title implies, is to defend the priests under his jurisdiction against the threat posed by the illicit pastoral activities of the friars.[73] Much of what he has to say as well as many of the biblical texts he cites in support of his charges can be found in the earlier writings of William of St. Amour, especially the *De periculis*. To these he adds quotations from the rule of Saint Francis, and the rhetorical force of his attack is often heightened by passages in which a personal note is sounded. So far as I have observed, 2 Timothy 3 is nowhere cited in the treatise, yet there is an unmistakable suggestion of it in FitzRalph's charge that the friars disregard the instructions of Saint Francis to beg meekly at the gate or the door; on the contrary, they come uninvited ("domos . . . penetrantes" in the Latin) into houses and courts. When they leave, they bear away "corn, other mele, brede, flesche other chese — though there be but tweyne ['two'] in the hous thei bere with hem that oon ['they take one of them away'] (aut grana aut similia, aut panes aut carnes seu caseos [loaves of bread or meats or cheeses] etiam si in domo non fuerint nisi duo, secum extorquendo [by wresting away or extortion] reportant)" (pp. 60, 1399). (The Latin version implies that the friars take away not one but both items of food.) The reader is reminded of Friar John's pitch at the beginning of the *Summoner's Tale*:

> "Yif us a busshel whete, malt, or reye,
> A Goddes kechyl ['small cake'], or a trype of chese,
> Or elles what yow lyst, we may nat chese." (1746–48)

FitzRalph takes literally, perhaps with reason, the accusation interpreted figuratively by William (see p. 15 and n. 31) that friars, in serving as confessors, gain influence over women (the *mulierculas* of 2 Timothy 3). They hear "the privyeste counseile of wymmen, of queenes, & of alle othere, & leggeth [lay] hed to hed. . . . Therfore in al the worlde wide sclaunder springeth of freres, the wiche sclaundre y wole nought reherse at this tyme (consilia secretissima mulierum reginarum & aliarum omnium indistincte [indiscriminately], etiam capite inclinato ad caput. . . . Unde per orbem scandala, quæ nolo exprimere)" (pp. 73, 1403). Other excerpts could be added, but these suffice to illustrate the content and tone of FitzRalph's complaint.

The *Defensio* has been described in dismissive terms as a specimen of "not very original anti-mendicant preaching,"[74] but its influence was both far-reaching and long-lasting. It survives in no fewer than eighty-four manuscripts, one or two more than exist of the *Canterbury Tales* in whole or in part (see Riverside, p. 1118). And FitzRalph himself was not forgotten either. Although an attempt to canonize him was unsuccessful, the tomb in his native town of Dundalk to which his body was translated after his death in Avignon became a local center of devotion, and many miracles were said to have been wrought there. Later writers piously invoked his name. Wyclif refers to him as "Seynt Richard," the pro-Wycliffite author of a late fourteenth-century Latin poem calls him "the Armachan, whom the Lord hath crowned in heaven (Armacan, quem cœlo Dominus coronavit)," and a quatrain inscribed early in the seventeenth century on an Irish manuscript reads as follows:

> Manny a mile have I gone,
> and manny did I walk,
> but neuer sawe a hollier man
> than Richard of Dundalk.[75]

Of the three figures who stand out in the intellectual history of medieval antifraternalism, John Wyclif (1328?–1384) is the best known and the most worthy of consideration in his own right.[76] Like FitzRalph, Wyclif was affiliated with the University of Oxford; he was elected master of Balliol perhaps as early as 1358 ("Chronology"; cf. Workman 1, 77–78). Around 1372, shortly before receiving his doctorate in theology, Wyclif entered the service of the crown. As a result, he came to be closely associated with John of Gaunt, who had become duke of Lancaster in 1361 and who in the years before the death of Edward III in 1377 was gradually obtaining for himself a "semi-regal jurisdiction" in England (ibid., 284). In 1374, Wyclif was rewarded by being made rector of Lutterworth in his native Yorkshire (ibid., 209). Later that year, he was appointed to a deputation sent to Bruges to carry out negotiations between the English king and the pope. On his return that same year, he retired to Oxford, devoting himself to preaching and writing; a collection of forty sermons preached "in or around Oxford or London," apparently to an audience of laymen as well as clerics, dates from this time.[77] His treatises on divine and secular lordship, entitled *De dominio divino* and *De civili dominio* (1375–76), were heavily indebted to FitzRalph's *De pauperie salvatoris* (see above, p. 25 and note 71). In them he argued in favor of disendowment, taking the position, which lent itself to Gaunt's purposes, that members of the clergy, if not in a state of grace, could be deprived of their property by the state.[78] His unorthodox views on the nature of transubstantiation having been condemned by a group of theologians at Oxford in 1380, he retired to Lutterworth. There, for the few remaining years of his life, he worked tirelessly, proclaiming, in a vast body of writings in Latin and English, his ever more intense and radical antagonism toward the established church and its hierarchy from the pope down. In 1382, at a synod convened at Blackfriars in London by William Courtenay, the archbishop of Canterbury, a number of his doctrines were branded as heretical, and his two most prominent followers were condemned; one fled overseas, the other recanted. But Wyclif himself was left alone, evidently as a result of the intervention of John of Gaunt. Thereafter, "all official records are silent concerning his further life."[79] He died at Lutterworth in 1384.

His early alliance with Gaunt would have brought Wyclif into contact with the friars: the duke chose his "special henchmen" from among them, the Carmelites being his favorites (1, 282). For a short time, his relations with them seem to have been amicable, but by the time of his departure for Lutterworth, he had developed the antipathy that took on an almost fanatical intensity in his last years.[80] In his antifraternal writings,[81] Wyclif acknowledged his indebtedness to William of St. Amour and especially to Richard FitzRalph.[82] It is thus anything but surprising that we should find him repeating the charges made by these two predecessors and citing again the by-now classic biblical texts that William had originally assembled: the denunciations of the scribes and pharisees by Jesus and of the dangerous men of the "last days" by Paul, the warnings against "false prophets" and "false apostles," the parable of the wolf bent on destroying the sheep, entering not by the door but another way, and the words of Jesus and Paul concerning the nature of the apostolic life.[83] But these materials are incorporated into Wyclif's intensely personal version of Christianity and presented in terms of his characteristic preoccupations and way of thinking.

For Wyclif, the Bible was for all practicing Christians a clear, reasonable, and sufficient source of doctrine. To prove that the friars were interlopers, encroaching upon the rightful domain of the secular clergy, nothing more was needed than to point to the simple fact that there was no reference to them in the New Testament. All four of the "newe ordris" or "newe sectes" that came in after the time of Jesus, namely, the friars, the monks, the Augustinian canons, and the prelacy, were, in Wyclif's view, superfluous and should be done away with. But the friars were the most recently founded and the most pernicious; the privileges to which they laid claim had been granted them by authorities as suspect as they.[84] Recognizing that the word *sect* was derived from the past participle *secutus* of Latin *sequor* "to follow," Wyclif maintained that the sole authentically Christian "sect" was that founded by Jesus, who said, "Follow me (Tu me sequere)" (John 21:22; cf. Matthew 8:22, Mark 2:14, Luke 5:27).[85] To ascertain the spiritual status of any professed member of the church, it was necessary only to observe his actions and see whether they accorded with the teachings of Jesus. Though the company of the saved on earth can be fully known only to God, human faith and works being insufficient without the operation of divine grace, it is reasonable to suppose that it is made up of those who live in accordance with Christian charity, keeping the ten commandments and loving God and their neighbors as Jesus told his followers to do. Those whose lives are visibly founded on cupidity, even if they conceal their true motives, can be safely supposed to be apostates or antichrists destined for the eternal sufferings of hell.[86] Adversary Christianity, in the Wycliffite as in other versions, admitted no middle ground.

Again and again, in the writings of Wyclif and his adherents, the way of life of the friars is condemned with a white-hot indignation such as we rarely find in William of St. Amour or FitzRalph. A particularly sore point is the friars' claim that they, more than other men, are followers of Christ. The English treatise *Concerning Blasphemy, Against the Friars* (*De blasphemia contra fratres*) — unattributed but thought by its editor to be the work of Wyclif himself — invites us to "se . . . whether thes newe sectis seyn soth upon Crist, that thei suen ['follow'] hym in lif bifore all other men; bot hit semes nay. . . . If freris, in more spense ['expense'] of housyng and mete, in clothyng, in juwels, chargen more tho puple then Crist with his apostils, how suen thei Crist in this maner of lyvynge? And so hit were al one ['the same thing'] to grounde ['establish'] soche ordiris of beggers, and grounde Anticristis clerkis and blasphemes ['blasphemers'] of Crist" (pp. 415–16). A similarly worded item in the Wycliffite tract entitled *Fifty Heresies and Errors of Friars* vibrates with detestation: "in covetise thei con nevere make an ende, bot by beggynge, byqueethyng ['(handling of) legacies'], by birying, by salaries and trentals, and by schryvyngis, by absoluciouns, and other fals meenes, cryen evere after worldly godis ['goods'] . . . And thus for this stynkynge covetise thei worschippen tho fend as hor God" (p. 373).

Of the sins imputed to the friars by Wyclif and his followers, that of blasphemy — speech or action constituting an insult to the divinity — is most basic and all-inclusive. It is the central concern of the Latin *Tractatus de blasphemia* (*Treatise Concerning Blasphemy*), which attacks the officials of the institutional church, rank by rank, from pope down to pardoner, as well as of the aforementioned *De blasphemia contra fratres*.[87] But references to blasphemy turn up in Wyclif's polemical writings with a frequency that the reader comes to recognize as distinctive. Most profoundly, Wyclif considered the friars to be blasphemers in that they insisted, while displaying the fruits of their covetousness for all to see, that they were perpetuating the way of life of the apostles.[88] In the *Tractatus de blasphemia*, he asserts that the "aforesaid sects" (of monks and friars) have, under the devil's guidance, so lapsed in the direction of worldliness that Jesus, if he came again and saw their magnificent dwelling places replete with sumptuous furnishings and treasures, would not recognize them as his sons.[89] Similarly, in the Latin treatise *Concerning the Foundation of the Sects* (*De fundatione sectarum*), he argues that "since [the friars] so magnify their sects over Christ, it is obvious that they are blasphemers. For Christ did not wish to have more than twelve apostles, but these dare to gather together many convents under a patron or governor who is a notable sinner. Who, I ask, would be a blasphemer if not he who goes beyond Christ and does not justify his excess?"[90] A comprehensive account of the blasphemies of the friars appears in *De Quattuor sectis novellis*:

> This sect, brought in by the devil, seduces many through its crafty wiles, and especially through the hypocrisy in which it abounds and which descends from the shifty lies of their father. Its very foundation is the blasphemous lie that Christ begged as the friars do. They blaspheme also in maintaining the lie that their religion and life are more perfect than those of the apostles, that their habit, their letters of fraternity, and their other meritorious works are more perfect and more needful than those that earlier marked other orders. And they lie blasphemously in a fourth way, that their special form of prayer is of more benefit to the people than the Lord's Prayer, as the form of their preaching, even when it consists of trivialities, is singularly to be praised.[91]

The writings Wyclif directed against the friars were part of an across-the-board attack on the institutions of the church which, like the antifraternalism of William and FitzRalph, came to little or nothing. Yet his influence persisted as an important aspect of what Anne Hudson has called "the continuity from native dissent of the medieval period into the new reformation of the sixteenth century" (*The Premature Reformation*, p. 446). And at the very least, his indignation against those who profaned the religious vocation they professed was something of which Chaucer could hardly have been ignorant, even if he had not lived his life at the political and cultural center of things.

That Chaucer was in fact vividly aware of Wyclif from the early 1370s on cannot be doubted.[92] He would have known him, at least by sight, at court; he would have had some degree of familiarity with his radicalism and reformist views, and he would have heard of such major events of his life as the condemnation of his views by the Council at Oxford in 1380 and the Synod at Blackfriars in 1382.[93] Connections with John of Gaunt were important for both men. Wyclif, who was perhaps twenty years older than Chaucer, began his association with Gaunt in 1372; from 1372 to 1380 he lived first in London, then at Oxford, removing permanently to Yorkshire only in 1380. Chaucer wrote *The Book of the Duchess*, an elegy for John of Gaunt's first wife, shortly after her death in 1368.[94] He first traveled to Italy in 1372, during his time of service as esquire of the king's chamber; two years later, Wyclif served on a deputation sent to Bruges on behalf of the crown. During the 1370s, Chaucer could have heard some of the sermons Wyclif preached in London (see Hudson, *The Premature Reformation*, p. 393). In addition to the coincident life-trajectories of the two during these years, a more specific link exists in the form of Chaucer's friendships with certain of the so-called "Lollard knights" at the court of Richard II, the most important of these friendships being with Sir Richard Stury, Sir Lewis Clifford, and Sir John Clanvowe.[95] Clanvowe is the author of two extant literary works. *The Boke of Cupide*, a love-vision in five-line stanzas in the Chaucerian manner, begins by quoting two lines from the *Knight's Tale*. *The Two Ways*, a religious treatise in prose, takes its title from the distinction drawn by Jesus in Matthew 7:13–14 between the narrow way that leads to salvation and the broad way that leads to destruction. (The verse that immediately follows, a favorite antifraternal text, denounces the false prophets who are wolves in sheep's clothing.) Clanvowe warns his readers that, because we do not know how soon we shall depart from this world, it is important to keep at all times to the narrow way that leads to eternal bliss, lest we be found at the moment of death in the broad way that leads to eternal suffering (p. 57). There follows a lengthy exhortation to the individual Christian to renounce all that worldly men most value, including bodily lusts, riches, and fame. These ideas are certainly in accord with the views of Wyclif, but Clanvowe does not carry them further; he shows no interest in attacking ecclesiastical corruption or engaging in doctrinal controversy. In the words of Anthony Tuck, "If Clanvowe's treatise is in any way representative of the spiritual beliefs of [the Lollard knights], they were attracted to the pietistic and moralistic attitudes of the early Lollards rather than to their more specifically antisacramental, antihierarchical and pacifist teachings" (pp. 152–53).[96] Such men would no doubt have responded with warm admiration to Chaucer's portrait of an ideal parson. They would have been equally appreciative of his portrayals of the worldly excesses of the Monk and the Friar.[97]

The traditional charges against the friars with which Chaucer shows his familiarity in the *Summoner's Tale* can readily be documented from the writings of William of St. Amour, Jean de Meun, Richard FitzRalph, and John Wyclif discussed above. But the antifraternal background of the tale includes popular traditions as well — traditions which, because the works representing them were not usually recorded, remain elusive.[98] There are no prior written versions of the anecdote told in the *Summoner's Prologue* or of the trick played in the *Tale*. The closest extant analogue of the trick is a fabliau entitled "Li dis de le vescie à prestre (The Tale of the Priest's Bladder)," which tells of a priest's bequest of the aforementioned organ to a group of friars who have been asking him for money.[99] There must have been many unpretentious rhymes on the order of the two stanzas of macaronic verse, extant in a single manuscript of the fifteenth century, that begin, "Flen, flyys, and freris populum domini male cædunt" and "Fratres Carmeli navigant in a bothe apud Eli," respectively.[100] A proverb in use in late Middle English which translates into modern English as "Three foxes and three friars make three villains" provides additional evidence of the pervasiveness of antifraternal sentiments at the popular level (see *MED* s.v. *frere* sense 2[c]). In three anonymous collections of "terms of association," *skulk* (a noun of agency derived from *skulken* v. "to go . . . furtively, slink") designates groups of friars and foxes; in two of them, of thieves as well.[101] The Summoner's indignant exclamation, "Lo, goode men, a flye and eek a frere Wol falle in every dyssh and eek matere" (III [D] 835–36) has a proverbial ring.[102] These and other, similar sayings would have been disseminated by nonliterate as well as literate speakers of the language. All such materials imply a concept of the corrupt friar that was in general circulation[103] — one that must, moreover, have had at least some basis in reality, as do the perennial jokes, jingles, and sayings about domineering mothers-in-law. I once heard a variant of the joke in the *Summoner's Prologue* in which was described an infernal scatological indignity inflicted on priests. In the *Summoner's Tale*, as, spectacularly, in the *Wife of Bath's Prologue*, Chaucer joins learned and popular materials in a fiction that compels acceptance as a representation of reality in all its fullness.[104]

The sizeable body of criticism, commentary, and annotation that has grown up around the *Summoner's Tale* during the past forty-five years has revealed, in steadily increasing measure, its depth and richness of meaning. The discovery of the Pentecostal parody figures in this history as an important milestone.[105]

Friar John has been assiduously exposed as a walking, talking exhibition of the faults complained of in antifraternal literature. We first see him as a preacher, using all his eloquence to elicit donations that would otherwise go to the parish priest whose place in the pulpit he occupies. Speaking on the subject of "trentals" (sets of thirty requiem masses sung on behalf of souls in purgatory), he assures the congregation that a group of friars in a convent can accomplish the deliverance of the tormented souls "hastily," whereas a priest, who will use the monies received for his services to make himself "joly and gay" (1727), "syngeth nat but o ['one'] masse in a day" (1728). He also asks for money to build "hooly houses" in which religious services will be reverently performed by himself and his brothers, taking a swipe in passing at the "possessioners," that is, the monastic clergy, who don't need more money and will waste whatever is given them. After the service, Friar John goes forth to beg from house to house, playing to perfection the part of *Penetrans Domos*. In the house he elects to visit at the end of the day there lives, not unexpectedly, a "silly woman, laden with sins" such as Paul predicted would be preyed on by the dangerous men of the last days.

A survey of the published criticism of the *Tale* results, among other things, in an enhanced sense of its intellectuality, a feature shared to a lesser degree by its more schematic companion piece, the *Friar's Tale*.[106] Ample tribute has been paid to the exactitude with which, in the course of the story, the crime is shaped to fit the punishment, as one noxious emission of hot air brings forth another.[107] The story itself arouses, toward the end, a more cerebral kind of interest. It does not conclude with the tricking of the trickster at the bedside of the intended victim, as does the *Tale*'s closest analogue, "The Tale of the Priest's Bladder (Li dis de le vescie à prestre)," but moves on to a phase of the action in which the central question becomes, not How will Thomas put this intolerably insistent visitor in his place? but How will the problem of equal division imposed by Thomas upon Friar John be solved?[108] Once "Jankin hath ywonne a newe gowne" (2293), the friar vanishes along with the rest of the *dramatis personae*, and the curtain is rung down with startling abruptness. The *Tale* makes intellectual demands on us, too, in its symbolic aspects. The relationship between the cartwheel and the wheel of Pentecostal iconography, which for the reader disposed or alerted to recognize it is there for the finding, participates in a larger, more profoundly significant relationship between the original gift of the fart and the Pentecostal gift of the Holy Spirit to the apostles.[109] And Roy Peter Clark has made the plausible and intriguing suggestion that there is an additional element of parody in the tale: the "groping" of Thomas's cleft by the friar alludes, with a reversal of roles, to the "groping" of the wounds of the risen Jesus by the Doubting Thomas of the New Testament.

This Thomas later became the Thomas of Inde whom the friar holds up to Thomas of Yorkshire, early in his appeal for a money gift, as an example of zeal in the building of churches.[110]

Furthermore, language as such, over and above narrative and descriptive content, requires our attention as we read. Much of what "happens" prior to Thomas's act of defiance consists in the making of speeches by Friar John which exhibit the showy rhetoric attributed by Saint Paul to the false apostles of his day, and, by their opponents, in later times, to the friars. Before the narrative is set in motion, excerpts from Friar John's sermon show how a preaching friar could play on the personal feelings of his auditors to elicit their "voluntary contributions." Later, hearing from Thomas's wife that their son has died, the friar launches without missing a beat into an account, suffused with false sentiment, of the "revelacioun" of the event (1854) that was vouchsafed him personally by Christ (1867–68). This segues effortlessly into a disquisition on the abstinence that brings friars especially close to God, impressively garnished with Old Testament materials and adorned at the end by a pun (on *chaced* "chased" and *chaast* "chaste" [1915–17]). The discourse that follows, addressed to Thomas specifically, begins with a further encomium on friars, including the claim that their prayers on behalf of their clients have special efficacy (1918–80). Its showpiece is a lengthy denunciation of the sin of wrath (1981–2089) which in itself takes up a total of more than one hundred lines in a tale of fewer than 600 lines. This last passage, with its "fables" redolent of secular learning, typifies the spiritually barren displays of erudition of which the preaching friars were thought guilty.[111] Insofar as exasperation at its inordinate length more and more detracts from enjoyment of its aptness as parody, we identify with Thomas, who like us is a captive audience.[112] Finally, the language of the tale is distinguished by a conspicuous series of plays on words. At least two of these are especially noteworthy in that they are woven into the action itself, portending its later stages, as in the friar's rhetorical question to Thomas, "What is a ferthyng worth parted in twelve?" (1967), and his assurance that Thomas will find him "as just as is a squyre" (2090).[113]

These aspects of the *Summoner's Tale* give rise to a problem of generic definition. Is it a fabliau? Most of those who have deposed on the matter have taken for granted the legitimacy of linking it with other examples of the genre in Chaucer; some have differentiated it from them.[114] Certainly Derek Brewer's succinct but comprehensive definition of the fabliau as "a versified short story designed to make you laugh," whose subject matter "is most often indecent, concerned either with sexual or excretory functions" and whose "plot is usually in the form of a practical joke carried out for love or revenge,"[115] fits to perfection the story told in the tale — until Friar John sets out to make his complaint to the lord of the village. It is true that Chaucer fleshes out the bones of the plot with a wealth of detail, dwelling lovingly (so to speak) on the petty manifestations of human hypocrisy at its most egregious. But he elaborates in similar fashion the plots of other tales whose classification as fabliaux has not been thought problematic. In the end, we should think of the tale as containing a fabliau rather than being one: its generic affiliations make one contribution, among others, to a "gret effect," a meaning that is elusive and many-layered in distinctively Chaucerian fashion.

Much has been written on Chaucer's portrayal of the thoroughgoing moral corruption and hypocritical dissembling of his friar: the gluttony shown by his fastidious choice of dinner menu and belied by the professions of abstinence that follow, the covetousness that leads him to be tenacious in beggary beyond the point of diminishing returns, the outburst of anger proving, if proof were needed, that his sermon against anger was an empty show. Lechery, too, is part of the picture, though those who have alluded to this aspect of the satire have shown an odd reluctance to put one and one together and state flatly that they make a couple.[116] Odd, because there can be no doubt of what we are meant to infer: that Friar John's visits as confessor to the husband have regularly included sexual relations with the wife. When he is described as embracing her closely and smacking his lips as he kisses her, the sparrow simile merely confirms what we can and should understand by the narrator's initial reference to Thomas's house as one in which the Friar was accustomed to being "refresshed" more than in a hundred other places (1766–67): "refreshment" is one of the Wife of Bath's euphemisms for sexual pleasure.[117] On consideration, in fact, we can recognize Thomas's wife as one of several *alter egos* of the Wife who appear in the secular tales.[118] Her complaint about her husband's irascible disposition, made in the sick man's presence, consists of a series of double-entendres signaling her discontent with his inadequacy as a sexual partner. Though, as she tells her visitor, Thomas has everything he can desire — though she makes him warm at night by covering him or by putting her leg or her arm over him — he only lies in bed groaning, affording her no other form of "desport" (1826–31). Her exhortation to the friar to chide him well (1824) tells us that she is in the habit of chiding him herself. What we might have guessed in the opening episode is later made explicit: the husband is an "olde cherl with lokkes hoore" (2182), possessing enough property to make him an attractive target for the friar's solicitations. All in all, the marital scenario sketched in the *Tale* is reminiscent of the Wife's description in her *Prologue* of her first three marriages to old, wealthy, and sexually unsatisfactory husbands. They could not please her in bed, she says — "in bacon ['preserved old meat'] hadde I never delit" (III [D] 418) — and she admits, or rather boasts, that she treated them severely:

> I governed hem so wel, after my lawe,
> That ech of hem ful blisful was and fawe ['eager']
> To brynge me gaye thynges fro the fayre.
> They were ful glad when I spak to hem faire,
> For, God it woot, I chidde hem spitously ['cruelly']. (219–23)

Later in the tale, in the course of the friar's bedside sermonizing, we are further reminded of Alison of Bath: the language used by the friar in rebuking Thomas for chiding his wife, "the sely innocent . . . that is so meke and pacient" (1983–84), is disingenuous and, from our point of view, blatantly ironic. His rhetorical question,

> Now sith ye han so hooly meke a wyf,
> What nedeth yow, Thomas, to maken stryf? (1999–2000)

implies a piece of advice fully in accord with Alison's views on marriage: let the husband cede the *maistrie* to his wife, in the hope of a fairy-tale happy ending.

I believe that the evidence I have adduced justifies the conclusion that Friar John's behavior in Thomas's house goes beyond mere flirting. But in fact there is a simpler basis for the same conclusion: the action of the *Tale* unfolds in the imagined world of the fabliau, which is characterized, among other things, by "the perennial sexual activity of priests, monks, and friars."[119] In this world, the miller's wife is the daughter of the local priest, a visiting monk dispassionately makes a sexual and financial arrangement with his host's wife (who has complained to him that her husband does not satisfy her sexually), and itinerant friars have replaced the incubi of former times in threatening women who walk abroad with rape (III [D] 878–81).

A pattern in the characterization of Friar John that can bear more emphasis than it has received so far is the systematic contradiction of speeches in which he professes a given virtue by an exhibition on his part of the corresponding vice, the two being either juxtaposed or in close proximity to each other. Closeness amounts to simultaneity when he takes care to make it clear that he does indeed deserve to be called Master in the course of his protest against being so addressed. A frequently noted example of this pattern is Friar John's outburst of anger immediately following his lengthy sermon against anger.[120] Other such contradictions are equally blatant. In the opening account of Friar John's performance in the local pulpit, paraphrase and quotation show us that his eloquence is aimed at the purses of his listeners. But soon afterward, at

Thomas's house, we hear him assuring his host and hostess that the sole purpose of his preaching is to save souls by spreading the words of Christ:

> in prechyng is my diligence, . . .
> I walke and fisshe Cristen mennes soules
> To yelden Jhesu Crist his propre rente;
> To sprede his word is set al myn entente. (1818–22)

His request for an elegant and ample meal (including a reference to that meal as mere "hoomly suffisaunce" [1843]) concludes with his claim to be "a man of litel sustenaunce" (1844), one who is abstinent in body but sustained spiritually by reading the Bible. The ensuing eulogy of the fraternal orders is replete with statements so worded as to contradict the evidence of gluttony we have just been given, not to mention the more indirect, but no less clear, evidence of adultery:

> We lyve in poverte and in *abstinence*, (1873)

and

> The *clennesse* ['sexual purity'] and the *fastynge* of us freres
> Maketh that Crist accepteth oure preyeres, (1883–84)

and

> Therfore we mendynantz, we sely freres,
> Been wedded to poverte and *continence*,
> To charite, humblesse, and *abstinence*,
> To persecucioun for rightwisnesse,
> To wepynge, misericorde, and *clennesse*. (emphasis added) (1906–10)

Friar John supplements these protestations by attributing to others the vices he claims to be innocent of himself. He accuses the monastic orders of wasting and devouring the wealth with which they have been endowed by indulging in gluttony and lewdness (1719–20, 1722–23, 1926–28), and he deplores the "negligence" of the secular clergy, the parish priests, in caring for the souls of their parishioners, as compared with his own "diligence" and superior ability "to grope tendrely a conscience" (1816–19). As for lay folk, they live, as he tells Thomas,

> in richesse and despence
> Of mete and drynke, and in hir foul delit ["sexual pleasure"], (1874–75)

so that the prayers of friars

> Been to the hye God moore acceptable
> Than youres, with youre feestes at the table. (1913–14)

The most important of the ways in which Friar John himself blatantly embodies the sins of which he accuses others has heretofore gone almost unnoticed. Although its placement in the narrative does indeed make it easy to overlook, its implications for the meaning of the *Tale* are profound and, once recognized, profoundly affect our response as readers. I mean the charge of blasphemy directed by Friar John, after the incident of the fart, against Thomas. Telling the lord of the village that no one, not even the poorest page, would fail to find abominable a "despit" (2176) such as he has received, he goes on to say,

> yet ne greveth me nothyng so soore,
> As that this olde cherl with lokkes hoore
> Blasphemed hath oure hooly covent eke. (2181–83)

A little later, when the lady of the manor dismisses Thomas's action as that of a "churl" or a madman, hence not worth taking seriously, the friar pays no attention to her words. On the contrary, he assures her that he is determined to be revenged on

> This false blasphemour that charged me
> To parte that wol nat departed be
> To every man yliche, with meschaunce! (2213–15)

Though we have not been prepared for this particular charge, it is apt enough. A deliberately aimed fart is certainly an insult, whether its target is one person or, by extension, a group, and an insult is blasphemous if its intended recipient is "hooly." *Blasphemy* originally had to do with language (Greek *phēmē* "speech"), and a fart, with a little ingenuity, can be (and has been) construed as linguistic, an "utterance" which, like the friar's hypocritical declamations, is at once empty of significance and disgusting. In the second passage I have quoted, the meaning of *blasphemer* is a little strained in relation to the content of the clause that modifies it, the charge of blasphemy now being based not on the giving of an insult, but on the imposition of an unreasonable task. There would thus seem to be, in the repetition of the word, a touch of insistence on Chaucer's part. In any case, it does appear, and it is repeated, and once we have noticed it, it takes on a saliency that is impossible to ignore. If, mindful that the sins of which the friar accuses others have so far been his own as well, we ask ourselves if he is guilty of this one too, I believe the answer is inevitable: he is. And if we go on to ask ourselves wherein his blasphemy consists, I believe we cannot avoid giving that question a Wycliffite answer: his claim that he supremely personifies apostolic sanctity is grossly insulting to the divinity whose emissaries on earth he claims to resemble and whose special favor he claims to enjoy.[121]

I have already cited some instances of Friar John's repeated identification of himself and his brothers with the original apostles.[122] He speaks of his calling — "I walke and fisshe Cristen mennes soules" (1820) — in the language Jesus used when he invited Andreas and Peter to follow him (Matthew 4:19). This follows his assertion that in his diligent preaching he "studie[s] in Petres words and in Poules" (1819). Antifraternal polemic, as we know, was founded on one of the epistles of Saint Paul; it continued to draw more heavily on his writings than on any other biblical source. The two epistles of Peter contain passages attacking the enemies of the early church in similar terms and were cited, along with those of Paul, from William of St. Amour on.[123] Later in the *Tale*, the friar boasts that, "as seith th'apostle [that is, Paul]," he and his brothers find simple clothing and food sufficient (1881–82; Riverside cites 1 Timothy 8). In describing himself and his fellow friars as wedded "to per-secucioun for rightwisnesse" (1909), he alludes to Paul's statement that "all that will live godly in Christ Jesus, shall suffer persecution (omnes, qui pie volunt vivere in Christo Iesu, persecutionem patientur)" as he himself has suffered it (2 Timothy 3:12); this in turn harks back to the eighth Beatitude, "Blessed are they which are persecuted for righteousness' sake (beati qui persecutionem patiuntur pro iustitiam)" (Matthew 5:10). (Friar John also "glosses" the first Beatitude in favor of himself and his brothers, claiming that Jesus, in saying that the poor in spirit are blessed [Matthew 5:3], had the friars especially in mind [1919–23].) Perhaps most outrageous of all is his appropri-ation for his own purposes of one of the texts most often cited against the friars' claim that, in supporting themselves by begging, they are emulating Jesus and the disciples:

> "The hye God, that al this world hath wroght,
> Seith that the werkman worthy is his hyre." (1972–73)

It is important for us to realize that the blasphemy committed by the friar is more than a matter of making claims we know to be false. That is, we must understand that he is not an egotist who has deceived himself into believing that his holinesss is pleasing to God, but an inveterate sinner who lives consciously and willfully in defiance of Christian (and fraternal) teaching. It is to ensure this realization on our part that the description of his greeting of Thomas's wife is so phrased as to indicate unmistakably the nature of the relationship between them, and that his tale of the "revelacioun" (1854) through which he sup-posedly learned of the death of the woman's son is made to include the evidence of its own falsity.[124] In putting himself and his brothers forward as incomparable exemplars of holiness, the friar is not simply stating untruths, he is lying, and he knows he is lying.

The sign that points most clearly to blasphemy as a theme that ultimately demands inclusion in our thinking about the *Tale* remains implicit — indeed, remained unrecognized until thirty years ago. I mean, of course, the iconographic parody of the cartwheel, which confirms in retrospect what the narrative has made obvious: this friar and, by implication, others like him are enacting a debased version of the enterprise initiated by the gift of tongues at Pentecost. Central to both the Pentecostal miracle and the apostolic mission, in turn, is an entity whose tacit presence in the narrative, like that of the iconographic pattern parodied by the cartwheel, we must sense as part of a sacred narrative conjured up by inverted analogy with a profane one. This entity is the Holy Spirit, in its all-important role in the founding of the Christian church and the ongoing dissemination of the Christian faith.[125] Chaucer, who knew his Bible intimately,[126] would have known that blasphemy against the Holy Spirit was said by Jesus to be the one unforgivable sin (Matthew 3:31–32; Mark 3:28–29; Luke 12:10). The charge of blasphemy against the friar, thus understood, must remind those familiar with it of Wyclif's antifraternal polemic; it also harks back to the very beginnings of antifraternalism: to the indignation aroused in William of St. Amour by a treatise proclaiming that the age of the Holy Spirit, heralded by the friars, would shortly supersede the ages of the Father and the Son.

I spoke earlier of the evident effect on Chaucer of the graphic and shocking display of sinfulness, including indifference to divine judgment, displayed in Fals-Semblant's monologue. Its influence on the *Pardoner's Prologue* is unmistakable. The Pardoner is not a friar, as Fals-Semblant is understood to be, but his professed way of life is such as to evoke familiar antifraternal themes. He assures the company that because he can acquire gold and silver by preaching, he has no intention of remaining poor; rather, he asserts, he intends to maintain himself in prosperity by what he calls his begging, and he differentiates himself vehemently from the apostles:

> For I wol preche and begge in sondry landes;
> I wol nat do no labour with myne handes . . .
> I wol non of the apostles countrefete;
> I wol have moneie, wolle, chese, and whete,
> Al were it yeven of the povereste page,
> Or of the povereste wydwe in a village. (443–44, 447–50)

(Compare the widow of Friar Hubert's portrait, from whom, though she "hadde noght a sho" [253], he would manage to extract a farthing ere he departed.) In creating the character compounded of Friars Hubert and John and building a narrative around the latter, Chaucer imagined Fals-Semblant's modus operandi, discursively analyzed in his own monologue in the *Roman*, as shown in action in a certain place at a certain time, disguised by hypocrisy yet revealing to a percipient reader the same unabashed and willful attachment to sin. In Jean de Meun's allegory, of course, Fals Semblant is a conventional "vice figure," playing his part in a cast of animated abstractions. Chaucer, drawing us into his more naturalistic fiction, induces us to respond to Friar and Pardoner alike as if they were our fellow human beings.[127] Insofar as we believe, or willingly suspend our disbelief in, the Christian doctrine governing the world of that fiction, we must assume that damnation is in store for both.[128]

If Friar John's most profound sin is blasphemy, and blasphemy in turn implies damnation, then what one might call the metaphysical significance of Thomas's gift takes on special prominence. In Christian symbolism, farting exemplifies the association of scatology and the stench which is its corollary with the infernal realm; this in turn has its complement in the association of fragrance with sanctity.[129] The stench of the literal fart suffered by the friar at Thomas's bedside, of the theoretical fart suffered at and around the cartwheel by him and his brothers, and, last but not least, of the "fartes thre" which in the view of the perceptive young Squire would be the appropriate reward for his preaching corresponds figuratively to the perceived quality of his behavior in life and looks forward in turn to the stink of hell. This correspondence is emphasized by a pun which, so far as I am aware, has not previously been identified. It occurs in the polite remonstrance of the lord of the manor to the furious friar: "Distempre yow noght; ye be my confessour; Ye ben the salt of the erthe and the savour" (2194–95). D. Thomas Hanks, Jr., has pointed out that the text of Matthew 5:13 in the Vulgate Bible, to which the lord is alluding and which is cited by Riverside's note, does not contain *sapor*, the Latin equivalent of *savour*. It reads, not "if the salt has lost its savor, wherewith shall it be salted," as the familar text of the Authorized Version does, but "if the salt shall vanish (si sal evanuerit)." This, Hanks finds, is also the reading of the Wycliffite Bible and other English texts of the Gospels available to Chaucer; the *Geneva Bible* (1560) was the earliest English translation to use the wording familiar to us today. *Sapor* does, however, appear in a couplet paraphrasing the same verse in John Gower's *Vox Clamantis*: "They are the salt of the earth. . . . And without their savour mankind could scarcely be salted (Hii sunt sal terre, . . . Absque sapore suo vix salietur homo)," and Hanks believes that Gower's formulation is Chaucer's source.[130] Whether or not this is so, Chaucer seems to have availed himself, in expanding the standard biblical text, of the fact that the word *savour* meant not only "taste" in Middle English but "odor," offensive as well as agreeable. (Compare the reference in line 2226 of the *Tale* to "the soun or savour of a fart.") Wittingly or unwittingly, the lord is telling the friar that he is the salt of the earth — and the smell. In addition, the *Summoner's Prologue* contains a premonitory vision of the disgusting stink of hell whose graphic vulgarity is matched nowhere else in Chaucer.[131]

Though the threat of damnation as it bears on Friar John (and, by logical extension, on Friar Hubert) remains tacit, it cannot but be significant that we are reminded more than once, in the tales of both Summoner and Friar, of the fearful punishments visited upon sinners in the afterlife. We hear in Friar John's own preaching a Dantesque description of the torments of purgatory:

> "Ful hard it is with flesshhook ['meat-hook'] or with oules ['awls']
> To been yclawed ['lacerated'], or to brenne ['burn'] or bake." (1730–31)

Such references occupy more space in the *Friar's Tale* than the story requires. The denouement, recounted with relish by the tale's vindictive narrator, is, of course, the snatching away of the summoner, body and soul, to hell, where, as the yeoman-devil assures him, he will come to know more about its secrets than any master of divinity (1637–38). After the benediction with which we might have expected the Friar to conclude, he returns to his infernal theme, assuring his audience that the wages of sin after death are

> Swiche peynes that youre hertes myghte agryse,
> Al be it so no tonge may it devyse,
> Thogh that I myghte a thousand wynter telle
> The peynes of thilke cursed hous of helle. (1649–52)

The idea of damnation is also evoked by an allusion to the New Testament early in the *Summoner's Tale*, first noted by Fleming (p. 694), which takes on saliency when considered together with other references to the topic. Describing himself to Thomas's wife as "a man of litel sustenaunce," Friar John says that

> "The body is ay so redy and penyble
> To wake, that my stomak is destroyed." (1846–47)

This formulation ominously echoes 1 Corinthians 6:13, "Meat for the belly, and the belly for the meats, but God shall destroy both it and them (Esca ventri, et venter escis, Deus autem et hunc et has destruet)."[132] That the Pardoner quotes this same verse in his *Tale* is a further sign of the connection between the two characters in Chaucer's mind:

Of this matiere, O Paul, wel kanstow trete:
"Mete unto wombe, and wombe eek unto mete,
Shal God destroyen bothe," as Paulus seith. (VI [C] 521–23)

Considered retrospectively, the allusions to the parable of Lazarus and Dives in the portrait of Friar Hubert and in the words of Friar John (see above, pp. 9–10) also take on a deeper meaning: if these allusions are indeed in point, the similarity between the friars and Dives must not only pertain to their behavior in life, but must silently presage the suffering after death described in the parable.

As the portrait of the friar in the *General Prologue* is linked with the portrait of the friar in the *Summoner's Tale* by an allusion which, fully understood, implies damnation, so too references to damnation link the portrait of the Summoner in the *Prologue* and his fictional counterpart in the *Tales*. The narrator of the *Prologue* reports the Summoner's radical scepticism as to the danger posed by the "ercedekenes ('archdeacon's') curs" (655), that is, excommunication. "'Purs is the ercedekenes helle,' seyde he" (658)—that is, the torments after death to which the ecclesiastical curse consigns a sinner can safely be discounted; it is the temporal penalty that really hurts. The narrator is shocked by this opinion and roundly condemns it:

wel I woot he lyed right in dede;
Of cursing oghte ech gilty man him drede,
For curs wol slee right as assoillyng savith. (659–61)

This ostensible rebuke, on consideration, proves ambiguous. As J. S. P. Tatlock put it, "The curse and the absolution stand or fall together, but do they stand or do they fall?" (p. 261). He adds that Chaucer's "implied doubt of the value of assoiling is fully paralleled in Wyclif" (p. 71). Wyclif did indeed deny the efficacy of excommunication and absolution as formal actions of the church, for he believed that membership in the congregation of the saved, and the forgiveness of sins, depended alike on the state of the soul in question, something concerning which only God could have knowledge. What the church does either accords with God's judgment, in which case it simply has the value of signifying what is true, or diverges from God's judgment, in which case it has no value at all. The qualification of the statement in the Summoner's portrait—"each *guilty* man should fear excommunication"—clearly implies this line of thought.[133] An example of a formulation in Wyclif to the same effect is, "And as the assoiling serveth of nought, but as it acordith with Cristis keies ['keys'], so the cursyng noieth not, but as Crist above cursith" (*The Church and Her Members*, p. 361). The fictional summoner in the *Friar's Tale* is similarly scornful of the threat of punishment after death posed by the church, defying it forcefully in a manner reminiscent of Fals-Semblant and the Pardoner:

Nere myn extorcioun, I myghte nat lyven,
Ne of swiche japes wol I nat be shryven.
Stomak ne conscience ne knowe I noon;
I shrewe ['curse'] thise shrifte-fadres ['confessors'] everychoon. (1439–42)

The *Summoner's Tale*, understood in accordance with the interpretation set forth here, elicits two divergent but not mutually exclusive responses. On the one hand, we apprehend it in terms of its perceived literary genre or genres. It fits Brewer's definition of the fabliau in that it is a story designed to make us laugh involving an indecent practical joke carried out for the sake of revenge, and it is satiric in that it exposes manners and motives obnoxious to society. It shows us a trickster in action; we hope and expect that he will be tricked; he is, with an indecency that appropriately undercuts his self-importance; we are duly amused, and we need think no more about it. Such a reaction is in fact hinted at late in the tale, in the words spoken by the lady of the manor after the friar has made his complaint to her and her husband. When he asks her what she thinks, she replies,

"How that me thynketh? . . . So God me speede,
I seye a cherl hath doon a cherles dede." (2205–6)

But the tale is more, does more, than that. It is laden with meanings above and beyond those proper to it as fabliau and satire, meanings that transcend the framework of secular society and must be "taken seriously." Reading the *Summoner's Tale*, especially after the *Friar's Tale*, we are continually reminded that its protagonist is not only obnoxious but evil, that he is offensive not only to society but to the God in whom that society believes, and that he may ultimately suffer pains in comparison with which the most outrageous humiliations inflicted by other human beings are negligible. The tale, then, does in its way what certain portraits in the *General Prologue* do: it evokes the supernatural realm beside the secular one but leaves it to us to see whether the former bears on the latter, and if so, how.

The second response need not interfere with the first. There is no reason our awareness of meanings *sub specie aeternitatis* should interfere with our enjoyment of the tale's brilliance as satiric comedy: we can smile when the friar commits the trivial sin of driving the cat from its chosen bench, even though we understand fully the ominous implications of his statement that his stomach is destroyed. The conviction—or, given a momentary suspension of nonbelief, the suggestion—that in the fullness of time such persons as Friar John will be condemned by a judgment not of this world generates a kind of penumbra of grim satisfaction surrounding our amusement, supplementing our *prima facie* response rather than diminishing it.[134]

To return to the Wife of Bath, who has laid up her treasures on earth and for whom "grace" is a stroke of good luck in her ongoing search for her next husband: Should her comic monologue also give rise to intimations of a more serious sort, in terms of which our primary response to it should finally be enlarged? I shall answer this perennial question indirectly, by contrasting two kinds of morality — or rather, of immorality — one underlying the Wife's self-revelations, the other, the behavior of Friar John. Each takes as its point of departure the self-interest that in medieval times was called cupidity; each is displayed in a way of life contrasting radically with the saintly way shown in the religious tales. Yet Chaucer clearly differentiates the two, and the contrast between them accords with a principle stated by the hero of *Troilus and Criseide*: "Ther is diversite requered Bytwixen thynges like" (3.405–06).

Certainly the characterizations of the friar and the Wife of Bath seem designed from the outset to elicit two quite different kinds of emotional response. We first see the friar in the ascendant, enjoying deferential treatment as a house guest, his sanctimonious facade intact.[135] We first see the Wife, an illiterate who has been told all she thinks she knows by men, on the defensive, asserting her heartfelt preference for the marital state and the sexual pleasure it legitimizes against the barrage of belittlement and reproof to which she has long been subjected. When, shortly after the beginning of her monologue, she confesses her perplexity over what Jesus said to the Samaritan woman at Jacob's Well (John 4), she reveals that she has been made the butt of an intellectual practical joke. In the gospel story, Jesus amazes the woman and convinces her, by knowing all about her life even though he has never seen or heard of her before, that he is the Messiah. She has been married five times, he tells her, and what is more, she is now living with a man she is not married to. Someone has misrepresented this statement to the Wife as a case of *post hoc, ergo propter hoc*: the woman's current partner, whom she takes to be "the fifthe man," is not her husband because four husbands are the legal limit. The Wife naturally cannot see why the difference between four and five should be so important and is baffled by the statement ascribed to Jesus:

> "What that he mente therby, I kan nat seyn;
> But that I axe, why that the fifthe man
> Was noon housbonde to the Samaritan?
> How manye myghte she have in mariage?" (III [D] 20–23)

If the perpetrator of the joke had been Jankin the clerk, as there is every reason to suspect, the fact that he was her fifth husband would have made the story wickedly apropos and deeply disconcerting to his wife.[136]

A more important contrast between Friar John and the Wife of Bath consists in the fact that, whereas she admittedly lives by "winning" whatever she can in the sexual and marital marketplace (cf. III [D] 413–14), the friar lives by wholesale extortion. Furthermore, such disapproval as we may feel on hearing of the Wife's callous treatment of her first three husbands (all "goode men, and riche, and olde" [197]) is mitigated by a tenet of popular morality: old men who marry attractive young women in the hope of prolonging their sexual activity bring their misfortunes on themselves. The friar, on the other hand, preys on innocent and culpable alike; his victims have only one fault in common: they are susceptible to his plausive rhetoric. Then again, the Wife's main commodity, the pleasure she dispenses out of her sexual plenitude, has genuine value in the world of human interaction: "And trewely, as myne housbondes tolde me, I hadde the beste *quoniam* ['sexual organ'] myghte be" (607–08). What the friar "sells" — including his promises of prayer on behalf of his clients and the trentals and letters of fraternity that were favorite targets of Wycliffite attack — is worthless because he himself is worthless; its recipients are endangered by relying on him for spiritual help which they might otherwise have sought from priests like the Parson. Most important of all, the Wife is devoid of hypocrisy; she presents what seems to us to be the whole truth about herself and her life history, her triumphs and her defeats. In the course of doing so, she shows herself momentarily in a sympathetic light, revealing that passion made her unwontedly generous in leading her to give up "al the lond and fee" she had previously acquired to the young fifth husband, whose well-shaped legs and feet had won her heart (630–31; cf. 596–99). That she contrasts with Friar John in these respects is blindingly obvious. Indeed, in one of her admissions she seems to invite comparison between herself and the friars, since the fault in question was frequently mentioned in antifraternal criticism:

> I hate him that my vices telleth me,
> And so doo mo, God woot, of us than I. (662–63)

The friar uses scriptural allusions to elaborate the false image of his holiness. It is true that the Wife also cites the Bible to serve her own purposes and that she conveniently forgets texts she finds uncongenial. But at times she makes scriptural authority work in her favor, as, for example, in her metaphorical interpretation of "barley bread." And she is correct in saying that the instructions given by Jesus in Matthew 19:21 were conditional on the desire of his questioner to be perfect: "If thou wilt be perfect, go sell what thou hast, and give to

the poor (Si vis perfectus esse, vade, vende quae habes, et da pauperibus)."
From the standpoint of the church, her choice to eschew the "counsel of
perfection" is, if not admirable, at least acceptable. Indeed, her professed
commitment to sexual generosity in marriage, "In wyfhod I wol use myn
instrument As frely as my Makere hath it sent" (149–50), is not wholly discor-
dant with the spirit of the injunction it would seem to echo, "Freely have you
received, freely give (gratis accepistis, gratis date)" (Matthew 10:8).

Everything the Wife says about herself and her life implies a complete and
consistent system of human activity, motivation, and values. She herself delin-
eates it with striking exactitude in what is probably the *Prologue*'s best-known
passage:

> But — Lord Crist! — whan that it remembreth me
> Upon my yowthe, and on my jolitee,
> It tikleth me aboute myn herte roote.
> Unto this day it dooth myn herte boote
> That I have had my world as in my time. (469–73)

The word *boote*, like *grace*, has important associations with Christianity in
that it signifes, among other things, the salvation brought about by the life and
death of Jesus. As used here, it means the satisfaction that comes from remembering earthly possessions and pleasures passed. The *herte* in which the Wife's
satisfaction resides is complemented by the *soule* of the *Prioress's Prologue*:
"For [the Virgin Mary] hirself is honour and the roote Of bountee, next hir
Sone, and soules boote" (465–66). The heart is physical; it is "rooted" in the
temporal "world" that the Wife is happy to have possessed in her "time." And
the complementarity of world and time harks back to the ancient form of the
word *world* in Germanic: it originated as a compound of *wer-* "man" and *ald*
"old" (*OED*).

Friar John is a Satanic adversary of God. The values exhibited by his way of
life differ conspicuously from those celebrated in the *Wife of Bath's Prologue;*
they are anti-Christian, whereas the Wife's ought rather to be called non-
Christian, inhering in a world of temporal process (and, concomitantly, of
decay) separated off from the eternity posited by religious doctrine. There is
no denying that, in taking possession of her world in her time, the Wife has on
many occasions behaved very badly indeed. Chaucer has so structured her
monologue as to make her condemn herself in her own words: it is clear that
she has been grasping, promiscuous, and dishonest. Indeed, as she defends
herself, and her sex generally, against antifeminist attacks, she inadvertently
reveals that she herself has been guilty of the faults of which women, particularly wives, have traditionally been accused. The language assigned her in

the recital of her autobiography conveys all this; it also reminds us from time to time, with a tacit force that seems peculiarly Chaucerian, of the relationship between supernatural and natural realms affirmed by the Christian faith — a relationship the Wife herself ignores. Chaucer keeps silent as to the consequences of bringing the one to bear upon the other. Those who attempt to do so should remember that the intimations of eternal punishment so conspicuously present in the *Friar's* and *Summoner's Tales* are absent here.[137]

Chaucer's silence in the *Summoner's Tale* is far more portentous. The grim satisfaction I described earlier as a penumbra surrounding our primary response to the tale derives from our understanding, once Friar John has been identified as a blasphemer, that he is obnoxious not just to Thomas and the Squire at the manor, but to a being who is not mocked and whose timeless justice will ultimately destroy him. It also answers to an intensity in the antipathy aroused in us as we read the tale that cannot be satisfied within the confines of literary structure or by the clichés of antifraternal satire. The antifraternalism of Chaucer's time could not have been merely self-perpetuating; it must have been sustained in part by the existence of certain men who were conspicuously vulnerable to its critique. Nor can the interest in antifraternalism that led Chaucer to lavish some of his finest artistry on the *Summoner's Tale* have been purely intellectual.[138] Within the tale, the life story of Friar John comes to an end when the narrative of his humiliations by Thomas and the Squire comes to an end. In reality, the friar or friars in Chaucer's time who resembled him, and who may indeed have served as models for this or that feature of his portrait, would have remained on intimate terms with the wealthy and the powerful and would have continued to enjoy the wealth and power they had accrued. The Friar Hubert of Chaucer's fiction may have been prone to sexual and other forms of self-indulgence, but he is also a man of dignity, as the Host's language shows even as he reproves him for insulting the summoner:

> "A, sire, ye sholde be hende
> And curteys, as a man of youre estaat." (III [D] 1286–87)

If Chaucer had wished to vent his antipathy toward such a person in a fiction, while protecting himself from the consequences of giving offense to high-ranking personages or their patrons, what better stratagem could he have have devised than to use as his mouthpiece a man at the bottom of the social ladder, the disreputable and repulsive Summoner who by virtue of his profession was predictably an enemy of all friars? And if he had wished to mount an attack whose seriousness and devastating force went beyond the boundaries of satire, what better stratagem could he have devised than to bury beneath the surface of a comic tale a parodic relationship whose implications could not be proven, whose presence remains implicit, and which he was evidently content to allow to go unrecognized — save, we may suppose, by a chosen few?

The *Summoner's Tale* is, I think, the product of exactly these strategies. I began this essay by referring to two recent studies, of the *Clerk's* and *Summoners Tale*, respectively, which have revealed similar strategies on Chaucer's part, and there have been others.[139] Chaucer was a master of camouflage, among other things, and it is not in the least surprising that the latent meanings of some of the *Canterbury Tales*, including whatever is meant by the Pentecostal parody underlying the *Summoner's Tale*, were apprehended only late in the day. He was not a Laodicean, lukewarm in matters of good and evil, as Tatlock in passing once implied that he was. But though he knew iniquity when he saw it and found it abhorrent, he stopped short of taking the risks consequent on a direct confrontation, maintaining rather the discretion that characterized his professional life throughout and that enabled him finally to survive, pension intact, the violent replacement of one English king by another at the end of the century. Ten years ago, S. Sanderlin, at the conclusion of a thoroughly researched, judicious account of the last fifteen years of Chaucer's life, had this to say: "If the *Canterbury Tales* leave an impression of an urbanite author, the dry financial and legal records I have been considering leave an impression of the political Chaucer as a cautious nonpartisan. He was not necessarily a fence sitter, but he was prepared to be quiet when it was better to be so. . . . How much of this prudence was ever reflected in the *Canterbury Tales* remains to be shown."[140]

Addendum
Some Further Intimations of Wycliffite Resonance in
the Canterbury Tales

In 1916, J. S. P. Tatlock, in an essay entitled "Chaucer and Wyclif," identified two passages in the *General Prologue* as "[agreeing] strikingly with certain of Wyclif's most emphatic opinions not often found elsewhere" (p. 259). The first was Chaucer's admiring reference to the Parson's reluctance to threaten his parishioners with excommunication as a means of compelling them to pay their tithes (486). The second was the narrator's statement, in the portrait of the Summoner, that "curs wol slee, right as assoillyng saveth" (661). I discuss this statement on pp. 42–43, above. Roger Loomis, in "Was Chaucer a Laodicean?" (*Essays and Studies in Honor of Carleton Brown* [New York: New York University Press, 1940], pp. 129–48), reaffirmed Tatlock's view that the portrait of the Parson has a Wycliffite slant and presented additional evidence for thinking so. In three details in the portrait, "Chaucer hammers home the point that the Parson took his doctrine from the gospel" (p. 141): he "Cristes gospel trewely wolde preche" (481), "first he wroghte, and afterward he taughte. Out of the gospel he tho wordes caughte" (497–98; cf. Matthew 5:19); and "Cristes loore and his apostles twelve He taughte; but first he folwed it hymselve" (527–28). The Parson thus is presented as exemplifying the "fundamental thought characteristic of Wyclif, . . . the authority of the Bible and especially the gospels as opposed to the Fathers, philosophers, councils, and all commentators and canonists whatsoever" (p. 141). Furthermore, line 527 echoes the "one phrase [namely, 'Christ and his apostles'] which occurs inevitably and often monotonously in the English writings of Wyclif and his followers" and "is . . . notably absent from the contemporary writings of the orthodox" (p. 142). A discussion of the Parson's portrait in Hudson's *The Premature Reformation* begins by pointing out certain aspects of the Parson, including the tale he tells, that emphasize his orthodoxy and differentiate him from the followers of Wyclif: "The Parson is without doubt no paid-up member of the Lollard party" (p. 391). However, she then asks, "Is this the end of the story?" and answers her own question by saying that "such a conclusion seems reductive and misleading. . . . Within his description of the Parson Chaucer included many of Wyclif's ideals for the clergy. . . . Had Wyclif set out to versify his own ideals, he could not have wished to alter [Chaucer's lines]. What is omitted is, for the date, as significant as what is included: there is no mention of the Parson's administration of the mass, no allusion to his role as confessor. Taking this together with the biting condemnation of religious figures such as the Monk, Friar, Summoner, Pardoner and the mockery of the Prioress, the early critics' assertion of Chaucer's Wycliffite sympathies looks rather more credible" (ibid.).

2

Silent Retribution in Chaucer:
The Merchant's Tale, *the* Reeve's Tale,
and the Pardoner's Tale

And with a mighty meaning of a kind
That tells the more the more it is not told.
—Edwin Arlington Robinson, "The Sheaves"

In "Apologies to Women," her inaugural lecture as Professor of Medieval and Renaissance English in the University of Cambridge, Jill Mann drew attention to an interesting discrepancy between two passages of Chaucer's *Merchant's Tale*.[1] Describing what happens immediately after May climbs into the pear tree in January's garden, the narrator addresses the "ladies" in his audience:

> Ladyes, I prey yow that ye be nat wrooth;
> I kan nat glose, I am a rude man —
> And sodeynly anon this Damyan
> Gan pullen up the smok, and in he throng. (IV [E] 2350–53)

Which is to say—I too, for the purposes of this essay, must speak rudely—

> this Damyan
> Pulled up her smock, and into her he thrust.

Yet a mere eight lines later, after the restoration of January's eyesight through the kindness of Pluto, the narrator tells us that January looked up into the pear tree

And saugh that Damyan his wyf had dressed
In swich manere it may nat been expressed,
But if I wolde speke uncurteisly. (2361–63)

Mann discusses this odd switch — from directness of speech, covered by a prefatory apology, to an across-the-board denial of any wish to speak "uncurteisly" — in terms of the psychology of the narrator, his successive states of mind as he tells the story. When the literally climactic event finally takes place, "the narrator's ability to describe what is going on in polite language momentarily gives way" (p. 11), as a result, it would seem, of vicarious excitement. But "given a little time . . . [he] recovers himself, and does better when he has to describe January . . . taking in what is going on over his head" (ibid.). I shall argue that the first, graphic statement has been put by Chaucer into the mouth of the narrator because only such a statement can convey to the reader a fact essential to the tale's implied denouement: copulation between May and Damian has been fully accomplished and has made her pregnant. The fate that January thought to avert by marrying a young wife in old age — the passing on of his wealth to another man's child — is visited upon him at the end of the tale in richly deserved retribution.[2] But the meaning of the pear tree episode remains implicit; there are clues that point us in its direction, but we must reach it ourselves. This same obliquity, this same holding back from overt statement, can be found in at least three other tales: the *Summoner's Tale*, which I discuss in detail in chapter 1 of this book, and the *Reeve's* and *Pardoner's Tales*, which I discuss below. It seems to be associated particularly with politically sensitive materials.

The *Merchant's Tale* appears in Mann's lecture as a late example in a series of works exemplifying medieval attitudes toward women, beginning with Benoît de Sainte-Maure's *Roman de Troie* in the mid–twelfth century and concluding with the poetry of John Lydgate and Thomas Hoccleve in the fifteenth. These texts are set in one array and examined *seriatim* as discourses, in terms of a set of variables consisting of author-narrator, audience, subject matter, and language. The fictional works of Benoît and Chaucer, the didactic allegory of Jean de Meun, and the prose polemic of Christine de Pisan are drawn upon in turn as generically undifferentiated source materials enlarging our understanding of the stated subject.

For the purposes of this chapter, however, I need to look at the *Merchant's Tale* not as a discourse but as a mimetic narrative, in the sense in which the term *mimetic* was defined by R. S. Crane and his followers in the Chicago school of criticism.[3] That is, I shall consider it as a representation of the actions and thoughts of a set of characters portrayed in moral as well as in physical and social terms, in which its central character suffers a change of fortune.

Such a work elicits emotional responses bound up inescapably with the moral judgments it enables its readers to make. And it arouses expectations based in part on its readers' familiarity with the genre to which it belongs. Premises presented early on imply conclusions; causes portend effects; from certain actions and events other actions and events may be expected to spring. Reading a fabliau, we encounter comically unsympathetic characters and expect them to be subjected to appropriate punishments, often of an indecent nature. All this is conveyed to us by a narrating voice that is itself part of the representation. The narrating voice, in turn, is governed by an authorial agency that, in the words of Wayne Booth, "chooses, consciously or unconsciously, what we read" and appears to us in the completed work as nothing more or less than "the sum of [its] own choices."[4]

The choices made by the author — the poet, insofar as we can know him from his work — are of many kinds. Most obviously, he chooses the words of which the work consists and which appear to the reader as a seamless whole, a continuous utterance whose source is the narrator of the tale. This is its form at the most immediately perceptible level, the verbal form susceptible of description in terms of features of language. What Mann singles out in the *Merchant's Tale* for comment and resolves in terms of the narrator's psychology is a pair of references to the same subject, the first couched in graphic, the second in euphemistic terms — that is, two successive components of its verbal form. While I accept Mann's resolution, I believe I can resolve the disparity on a deeper level by attributing it to what I call the conceptual form of the tale — the idea (not necessarily formulated as a conscious intention) that governed Chaucer's shaping of it. The idea on which the *Merchant's Tale* is based demands, as I said earlier, that we be given to understand beyond all doubt that copulation between Damian and May in the tree has been fully accomplished. We learn this from the words of the narrator in the lines I first quoted; when he refers again to the same act, there is no need for "discourteous" language, and he can use a formulation that will not offend the ladies present.

Lest I be accused of "intentionalism," I hasten to disclaim any suggestion that the idea underlying a narrative fiction need be expressed in words in the mind of the author as the literary critic seeks to express it. It may be present subliminally, guiding him to the inclusion, at this or that point, of materials extraneous to the story, or to elaboration or succinctness in realizing this or that episode verbally, or to the preference (as in the passages discussed by Mann) for one kind of language rather than another at a given point. All these kinds of choices cooperate to determine the form of the work in the full sense of that word, and from form, fully realized, derives the peculiar effect of the work, which is inseparable from its power.[5] Chaucer chose to devote six lines to the wedding of May and January (1703–08), and forty-one, almost seven

times that many, to their wedding night (1817–57). Choices of this sort determine the magnitude (to ring in an old-fashioned but valuable concept) of the
successive parts of the story and thus of the whole. Chaucer also chose to
describe the priest's actions at the ceremony briefly and in words that have a
dismissive, if not derisive, ring:

> [He] croucheth hem, and bad God sholde hem blesse,
> And made al siker ynogh with hoolynesse — (1707–08)

Choices among alternatives of formulation and verbalization both render into
words the successive parts of the narrative content and give the language of the
narrator its expressive qualities — qualities such as straightforwardness or in-
direction, politeness or rudeness, formality or informality. In the lines quoted,
they sound one of the "sour notes" that E. T. Donaldson thought characteristic
of the tale.[6]

The *Merchant's Tale* is perhaps the most notable of Chaucer's generic hy-
brids. To the basic fabliau armature of the trick in the pear tree, he has added a
good deal of discursive material alien to the genre. At the beginning of the tale,
he inserts two disquisitions on marriage, the first spoken by the narrator, the
second by January to his friends, drawing on Eustache Deschamps and other
learned writers (see the prefatory note to the tale in Riverside, p. 884). Together these take up almost one-fifth of the tale's length. I believe he makes use,
in his account of the wedding night, of Boccaccio's allegorical pastoral, the
Ameto (noted only as a possible source in Riverside, ibid.; but see below,
p. 54). Later, he brings in Pluto and Proserpine as witnesses to May's deception
and stages a domestic altercation between them. Even though these divinities
are desolemnized into "faerye" beings, such as might appear in a Breton lay,
their presence reminds fit audiences though few of the somber and portentous
rhetoric of Claudian's *De raptu Proserpinae* (alluded to explicitly in 2232). At
the most immediately perceptible level of form, he couches the narrator's
speech in high-flown rhetoric — for example, in his reference to the coming of
night after January has married May:

> Parfourned hath the sonne his ark diurne;
> No lenger may the body of hym sojurne
> On th'orisonte, as in that latitude. (1795–97)

No undercutting here, as in the *Franklin's Tale*, with "This is as muche to seye
as it was nyght" (V [F] 1018)!

The contents of these expansions, from the opening disquisition and debate
on marriage through the account of the wedding night, have an important
effect on our reactions to the unfolding narrative. In the analogous fabliaux,
the jealous, blind husband and his sexually frustrated wife are stock figures in

whom we have a minimal emotional investment. We expect and hope, without being deeply concerned about it, that the wife will escape the unnatural constraints of her situation and that she will deceive her husband, after the fact, in word, as she has earlier in deed. We react to the events more with amusement than with sympathy or indignation: amusement first at the mechanism of the deceit, then at the plausibility of the excuse. In the *Merchant's Tale*, however, these events are framed and recounted in such a way as to elicit reactions of quite a different order. As the action begins, we are subjected, via the materials brought in from the *Miroir* and elsewhere, to a prolonged and distasteful encounter with January. We are made part of the entourage that is his captive audience, hearing him out perforce as he expatiates gloatingly on his sexual gourmandise and boasts of his virility. We watch him basking in the hypocritical flattery of Placebo and testily repudiating the therapeutic home truths proffered by Justinus. Particularly trying to our patience is his confession of a single misgiving: the insufferably fatuous notion that he may not be allowed to enjoy the eternal bliss of heaven in addition to the earthly bliss in which he plans to spend the remainder of his life.

After the wedding, we are vicariously subjected to an even more intimate encounter with him in the marriage bed, where the point of view of the narrative is that of his bride. Chaucer incorporates into this scene a number of details taken from an episode in the *Ameto* in which a beautiful young nymph who is a votary of Venus describes the old husband who was forced on her early in life and the unwelcome amorous attentions he lavished upon her night after night in the course of their marriage. Because of the way these details are dramatized by Chaucer, they have a shocking immediacy lacking in Boccaccio. In the *Ameto*, the nymph is far from the marital scene in time and place as she describes her husband's repellent physical features and distasteful behavior (she is now happy, possessed of a young lover who fully satisfies her). In the *Merchant's Tale*, similarly repellent features are withheld from us until we vicariously experience May's wedding night. In the *Ameto*, for example, the husband's beard is a visual characteristic, one of several that indicated to the nymph when she first saw him that he was an old man:

> His head, which had little hair (and that white), gave a clear indication of this; and his cheeks, rough with wrinkles, and his furrowed forehead, and his thick and heavy beard — no more and no less stinging than the needles of a porcupine — made me still more certain of his advanced age.[7]

The tactile effect of the beard is something that at this point in her narrative she has yet to experience. Compare the way we learn about January's beard in the *Merchant's Tale*:

> He lulleth hire, he kisseth hire ful ofte;
> With thikke brustles of his berd unsofte,
> Lyk to the skyn of houndfyssh, sharp as brere ...
> He rubbeth hire about hir tendre face. (1823–27)

These additions to the basic story line, from January's discourse on marriage through the details of the wedding night, have a cumulative effect, serving to make us desire ever more fervently the retribution that the old husband deserves and that the tale as fabliau leads us to expect.

Chaucer's additions to the first phase of the tale also make clear a reason for January's decision to marry that figures importantly in its unfolding plot: his desire to beget a legitimate heir. This motive is prefigured within thirty lines of the opening, in the course of the narrator's ironic disquisition in praise of marriage — especially the marriage of an old man:

> And certeinly, as sooth as God is kyng,
> To take a wyf it is a glorious thyng,
> And namely when a man is oold and hoor;
> Thanne is a wyf the fruyt of his tresor.
> Thanne sholde he take a yong wyf and a feir,
> On which he myghte engendren hym an heir. (1267–72)

Here, for the first time, we hear the fateful word *fruit*. Though the phrase "the fruit of his treasure" means primarily "the best part of it" (*MED* s.v. *fruit* n. sense 2[c]) — "the flower of it," we might say, varying the metaphor — the word *fruit* carries, especially in view of the lines that immediately follow, an inescapable suggestion of its most common cluster of metaphorical meanings in Middle English, which include not only "offspring, progeny" but "unborn child, fetus" (sense 4[a]). The importance for January of a fruitful marriage is again brought out when he is rationalizing his preference for a young wife. An old wife would not be able to bear children, he says, and adds,

> Yet were me levere houndes had me eten
> Than that myn heritage sholde falle
> In straunge hand. (1437–40)

Our understanding that this very fate is in prospect for January at the end of the tale depends on certain prerequisites, and each of these is duly established as the story unfolds. First, May must not have been impregnated by January before she climbs the tree. Second, January must have reason to believe, as May falsely implies when she pleads with him to let her climb it, that he has in fact impregnated her. At some point or points in their married life, then, he must have been sexually potent — capable of penetration and ejaculation.

Third, we must, as I said earlier, understand the copulation of Damian with May to have been fully accomplished.

As to the first prerequisite — that May has not been, and indeed cannot be, impregnated by January — it was a widely held tenet of medieval gynecology, which it would seem Chaucer accepted, that women as well as men produced seminal fluid and expelled it during orgasm. For conception to take place, "female seed" had to be combined with male; hence the possibility of conception depended on the woman's experiencing orgasmic pleasure during the sexual act.[8] That May had no such experience in her marital relations with January — a fact implied also by her unwifely eagerness to copulate with Damian — is made clear by the narrator, during his account of her wedding night, in contemptuous words: "She preyseth nat his pleyyng worth a bene" (1854).

In the *Ameto*, the nymph states flatly that her old husband was incapable of sustaining an erection. "He worked uselessly," she tells her listeners, "for that plough, eroded by age, moving its pointed part in a circle like the [limp] willow, refused to carry out its due office in the firm fallow" (p. 90).[9] The narrator of the *Merchant's Tale* says that January, when first in bed with May, mounts her and "labors" at length, but within the frame of the wedding night episode he does not make it clear what the outcome of those labors may be. Later, however, he unambiguously describes what January was able to accomplish in his pleasure garden:

> And whan he wolde paye his wyf hir dette
> In somer seson, thider wolde he go,
> And May his wyf, and no wight but they two;
> And thynges whiche that were nat doon abedde,
> He in the gardyn parfourned hem and spedde ["succeeded"]. (2048–52)

That is to say, sexual acts not completed in bed were successfully performed in the garden.

Given the symbolic implications of that venue, January's success there is not in the least surprising. Chaucer does not need to bring in Priapus to let us know that January has built himself a pleasure garden in a highly specific sense. It has been argued, I believe with justice, that Chaucer's use of the word *wyket* to refer to its small locked entry gate and of *clyket* to refer to the latchkey involves indecent plays on the meanings of English and cognate Old French words.[10] But the locked entrance to an enclosed place and the key that penetrates the lock have natural symbolic meanings in the sexual realm, entirely aside from the words used to refer to them. The meaning of the former was familiar to the medieval Christian in the metaphorical description of the sister-spouse, in the Song of Songs or Canticle of Canticles, as *hortus con-*

clusus, fons signatus, "a garden enclosed, a fountain sealed up" (4:12), that is, a virgin in her prenuptial state (Douay-Rheims translation). And these images are the basis, as we know and Chaucer knew, of the typological interpretation of the passage: the image of the enclosed garden was thought to prefigure the unviolated virginity of Mary. The garden of the *Merchant's Tale*, among other things, effects a profane reversal of this condition: the repeated unlocking and entering of the garden by January symbolizes the repeated penetration of the wife (in that same garden) by her insatiably priapic husband.

The gate and the pleasure garden, then, are natural symbols of May's external and internal sexual anatomy, respectively. January, as householder and husband, has access to both. The *wyket* stands for the entry point of penetration, and the key for the penetrative organ. If these specific symbolic meanings are valid, it seems likely that the pear tree within the garden's enclosed and penetrated space has a meaning as well. It is first referred to, in the words of the narrator, as "a tree / That charged was with fruyt" (2210–11). The fact, referred to above, that *fruit* could in Middle English mean "fetus" and the fact that the Middle English phrase "charged with child" meant "pregnant" are both relevant here (for the latter, see *chargen* v.sense 2b [a]). In order to gain his permission to climb the tree, May tells the now-blind January that she longs to eat some of the small unripe pears on its branches and falsely implies (again using the word *fruyt*) that she is with child:

> I telle yow wel, a womman in my plit
> May han to fruyt so greet an appetit
> That she may dyen but she of it have. (2335–37)

(In *Le debat sur le Roman de la rose*, Christine de Pisan, objecting to Reason's use of graphically sexual language in the poem, says that Reason is acting as she herself would act if she spoke to a pregnant woman and mentioned "pommes aigres ou *poires nouvelles* ou autre fruit," thus arousing her appetite for them [emphasis added].)[11] The fruit-bearing tree enclosed within the garden corresponds, then, to the womb, the place where "fruit" grows within the body, so that intercourse in that location, if anywhere, symbolically portends conception.

The narrator's rude description of what Damian does to May in the tree presents us with the final "necessary cause" of May's pregnancy: what January could not and did not do, Damian has done. But the wording of January's anguished response to May's explanation that she had to "struggle" with a man in a tree to restore his sight seems designed to make doubly sure that we understand what has happened: " 'Strugle?' quod he, 'Ye, algate in [all the way in] it wente' " (2376). (This last line, I must confess, has always struck me as resembling a report to a farmer of a successful encounter between a cow in his herd and a stud bull hired to impregnate her.)

When May climbs down from the tree (Damian seems to disappear, once he has served her turn), she is indeed pregnant, as, and yet not as, the deceived January thinks. Once she has explained away the sight he thought he saw,

> This Januarie, who is glad but he?
> He kisseth hire and clippeth hire ful ofte,
> And on hire wombe he stroketh hire ful softe,
> And to his palays hoom he hath hire lad. (2412–15)

I am as certain that the impregnation of May by Damian is part of the idea underlying the verbalized form of the *Merchant's Tale* as I am that I am writing these words. How else to explain the presence of allusions to the engendering of heirs and to pregnancy, such as appear nowhere even in the most elaborate of the tale's analogues? But I must admit that in the fullness of the tale as we read it, this culmination is not so much thrust upon our attention as half-concealed, embedded in materials that attract, and may also distract, our attention. One reason May's pregnancy is not generally recognized is that it is never made explicit. The delighted January leads May back into his "palays," and the story is brought to an end with three lines of prayer and benison. The reference in the opening section of the tale to the begetting of an heir, as an important reason why an old man should marry, appears in a long, brilliantly mordant disquisition, ostensibly in praise of marriage, whose relation to the views of its speaker, not to mention those of Chaucer himself, has roused critics of the poem to continuing debate. And January's own expression of his desire to leave his wealth to his legitimate offspring comes as an afterthought to his repudiation of the physically unappetizing idea of an old wife. We are more apt to remember the lines

> "Oold fissh and yong flessh wolde I have fayn.
> Bet is," quod he, "a pyk than a pykerel,
> And bet than old boef is the tendre veel" (1419–21)

or, in retrospect,

> "a yong thyng may men gye,
> Right as men may warm wex with handes plye" (1429–30)

than the significant but less intrinsically striking lines about child begetting that follow. And so too with the graphic language revealing to us that Damian has achieved full physical possession of May: we may be so struck by its boldness that we disregard the further implications of the fact it states.

We can respond adequately, if not fully, to the tale without taking this final interpretive step, taking satisfaction in seeing May's husband first cuckolded, then deceived. In addition, we can grasp what the tale, through Chaucer's realization of the basic story line, has to say about the relationship between men and women. Regardless of what has or has not happened at the end, the addition of materials from Deschamps, the bringing in of Pluto and Proserpine from Claudian and faeryland, and the dressing up of an indecent and amusing little fabliau in the trappings of high-style rhetoric contribute to the tale's meaning in two mutually supplementary ways. They universalize January and May (already made quasi-allegorical by their names) as representatives of their respective genders and of the marital relationship and thus give them a dignity denied the protagonists of the analogous fabliaux. And the extension of Proserpine's promise that May will be able to excuse herself to "alle wommen after, for hir sake" (2267) confers on the story the importance of origination myth: "How white roses came to be red," "How crows came to be black," "How women came to be able to excuse themselves in compromising situations."

The particular relationship between the sexes presented in the *Merchant's Tale* is governed by January's atrocious, unbridled egotism and the indignities he inflicts on May as a result of it — granted that, in paying him back, she operates on as low a plane as he. The elevation of the narrator's language throws into relief the sordid character of the events that inevitably follow. Especially notable, in connection with this aspect of the tale, is the attitude of men toward women embodied in the language of *amour courtois*. And here I cannot do better than to paraphrase Mann's analysis in "Apologies to Women." The traditional rhetoric expressing the romantic idealization of women by men purports to exalt them above the crudities of the physical act which is love's natural goal. Yet women, like men, are physical beings and to deny them this aspect of common humanity is to relegate them, via a form of "patronising protectiveness," to "a linguistic ghetto" (p. 12). The shocking contrast between the fictional May January sees in the mirror of his mind and the real woman who comes to life in response to Damian's appeal — initiating what J. D. Burnley calls "the contest of rapacity with duplicity"[12] — implies a skeptical critique of the conventions of *amour courtois* that seems to point beyond the tale's narrator (who, as I argue below, may have originally been the Monk) to Chaucer himself.

Whatever May's behavior may tell us about women's sexual appetites or their aptitude at infidelity and deceit, her story also shows what is done to young women by much older men. January, who controls the course of events, including the events of May's life, at the outset and is controlled by them in turn, stands at the center of the drama; the retribution we anticipate as the tale moves toward its denouement will be visited on him. And as it has been interpreted by most readers, that retribution has seemed satisfactory: the victimized wife has found a means of pleasuring herself, in the course of which she has successfully deceived her old husband. Fully understood, as the fate to which he says he would have preferred being eaten by dogs, the retribution visited on January satisfies more completely than the lesser punishment of unwitting cuckoldry the intense indignation his behavior has aroused in us; it fits the crime to perfection. Yet Chaucer does not force this fullness of meaning on us; he allows us to arrive at it by ourselves.

My sense that this pattern of silent retribution is present in the *Merchant's Tale* is confirmed by what I take to be manifestations of the same pattern elsewhere in the *Canterbury Tales*. I have argued at length elsewhere for the presence in the *Summoner's Tale* of occluded but undeniable signs, the most notable of these being an iconographic parody that went undetected for centuries, that Friar John is more than an avaricious hypocrite fully deserving the comeuppance that befalls him at the end of a comic story. Rather, in Chaucer's conception of the tale as I understand it, he is what Wyclif believed all friars were: a confirmed and unrepentant blasphemer against the Holy Spirit, who deserves and will ultimately be consigned to the pains of hell. The satisfaction we derive from recognizing that this form of retribution is intended for him, whether we are believers in damnation or willing suspenders of disbelief, supplements the satisfaction afforded us by the social humiliation that is his punishment within the fabliau frame.[13]

The *Reeve's Tale* does not, like the *Merchant's Tale*, contain discursive materials alien to the fabliau genre, or flights of high-style description — though Chaucer does complicate and enrich the response of the tale's original audience (and ours) to the students Aleyn and John by having them speak in accents that would have sounded ridiculously uncouth in the literal sense of that word, that is, unfamiliar, to London ears. Chief among the victims of its comic mayhem is Simkin the miller, in whose person the Reeve of the *General Prologue* takes revenge on the teller of the *Miller's Tale*. In the concluding six lines, the "unimpersonated artistry" (to use Donald Howard's helpful phrase)[14] of the rest of the tale gives way to the maliciously triumphant accents of the Reeve's own voice:

> Thus is the proude millere wel ybete,
> And hath ylost the gryndynge of the whete,
> And payed for the soper everideel
> Of Aleyn and of John, that bette him weel.
> His wyf is swyved, and his doghter als.
> Lo, swich it is a millere to be fals! (I [A] 4313–18)

But retribution at the end of the tale has another aspect, understood in the last analysis as transcending the designs of the pilgrim who tells the story. Its premises are spelled out in the opening expository section. There we learn that Simkin's wife is the daughter of "the person of the toun" (3943). This information functions, in its immediate context, to explain the social pretensions of the couple: the readiness of the miller to do violence to anyone who speaks familiarly to his wife, and the haughty manner of the wife herself. Knowing that we are "in" a fabliau, we look forward to seeing them punished for their disagreeable behavior. We are then told about their children: their baby son and their twenty-year-old daughter, whose name, we later learn, is Malyne. The son's cradle will become a prop in the bedroom farce in which the action culminates. The daughter too will serve a purpose in the plot: having been "swyved" along with her mother, she will complete the triumph of the two visiting students over her father by returning to them the wheat he had stolen. So far so relevant, but the content of the verse-paragraph following the description of Malyne has no bearing on the sequence of events that is to unfold. Here, in lines 3977–86, we learn, from the narrator's account of the parson's intended bequest to his daughter, that he has accumulated a not inconsiderable amount of property—*catel*, or material possessions, above and beyond his *mesuage*, or place of residence. (See *catel* n. sense 1[a], and *mesuage* n., in *MED*.) Not only does the Reeve's parson look forward to passing these worldly goods along to his granddaughter; he also intends to arrange a marriage for her to a man whose lineage he considers worthy of hers.[15] All this information is conveyed to us in matter-of-fact language, devoid of any suggestion of shock or disapproval—as is not unexpected, given the fact that "sexual misbehavior on the part of priests is . . . a pervasive fabliau theme."[16] But now the narrator's matter-of-fact tone changes, first to scathing sarcasm, then to a direct accusation unparalleled, to my knowledge, elsewhere in Chaucer's comic tales:

> For hooly chirches good moot ben despended
> On hooly chirches blood, that is descended.
> Therfore he wolde his hooly blood honoure,
> Though that he hooly chirche sholde devoure.[17] (3983–86)

Given the Wycliffite notes that a number of his readers, including myself, have detected in recent years in Chaucer's writings, it is natural to associate this passage with the reformist views current in his time. The Parson of the *General Prologue* has been recognized as a man of whom Wycliffite sympathizers would have thoroughly approved; any mention of *catel* or *mesuage* in the portrait of such a man would be irrelevant, indeed downright shocking. The Reeve's parson is his antitype: a "shiten shepherd" to whom material gains and the social status of the child of his concubinage mean more than the spiritual welfare of his flock.[18] And the events that occur later in the tale are disastrous not only for Simkin and his wife but, tacitly, for him. His castle in the air will have crashed to the ground; his granddaughter is no longer a suitable candidate for the sort of marriage by means of which he had hoped to pass "hooly chirches good" on to "hooly chirches blood." In the words bellowed by the outraged miller when he realizes what has happened to his daughter, Chaucer adroitly reminds us of this strand of the story which, once introduced, had dropped out of sight.

> "Who dorste be so boold to disparage
> My doghter, that is come of swich lynage?" (4271–72)[19]

The word *disparage* here is stunningly relevant: it meant primarily "to degrade . . . socially . . . [by] marrying below rank or without proper ceremony" (*MED* s.v. *disparagen* v. sense 1; cf. *parage* n. sense 1 "descent, lineage"). As for poor innocent Malyne, once she has had her tearful moment at center stage she is forgotten, a pawn in a drama moved forward by men.

As a final exemplar of the pattern of silent retribution whose recurrent presence in the *Canterbury Tales* I am arguing for, I offer the *Pardoner's Tale*. My view of the Pardoner is, I take it, the standard one: he is a quasi-allegorical being, at once wholly vicious and wholly impenitent. In transforming the figure of Fals-Semblant in *Le roman de la rose* into a pilgrim in late fourteenth-century England, Chaucer chose to make him an unabashedly fraudulent representative of a profession legitimate in origin though corrupted in practice. He also visited upon him a physical abnormality that would have been understood to reflect conspicuously the inner perversion of his soul. However we may want to describe his condition in medieval or modern medical terms, the Pardoner clearly lacks normal male sexual equipment as well as what in Chaucer's time would have been considered normal male sexual desires. Yet he passes himself off — or so he believes — as a fine young fellow, thinking himself dressed in the latest style (I [A] 682), desirous of having "a joly wenche in every toun" (VI [C] 453), even "aboute to wedde a wyf" (III [D] 166). His physical deficiency is counterbalanced by what comes to seem a dreadful potency in the realm of language: his ability to mesmerize the congregations to which he preaches into believing in his false relics and offering up money and valuables in return for supposed supernatural benefits. Once he has finished the tale that serves as the *exemplum* of his sermon, he embarks on yet another sales pitch. When he makes a dangerous gamble, asking the Host for an offering and insulting him gratuitously in the process, he brings upon himself a brutal, obscene, and public humiliation.

As we read the specimen sermon and the tale that follows, the world as the Pardoner imagines it slowly but surely closes around us. Everything in it locks together in dark inevitability: a malign rhetoric triumphantly demonstrates its own power to lead ignorant and gullible human beings into sin;[20] a trio of sinners, impelled onward with ever-increasing momentum by their own flagrantly sinful actions, move toward the denouement in which they will murder one another for money.[21] The tale alludes along the way to elements of Christian doctrine but blasphemously inverts them: the rioters' oath that "death shall be dead" if they can seize on him parodies the triumph of Christ over death thought to be prophesied in Hosea 13:14 (710), the planned sharing of the bread and wine (797) is a communion service of the damned, and so on.[22] One aspect of this imaginative encapsulation that can bear more emphasis than it has hitherto received is the certainty with which the Pardoner describes his benighted spiritual state, like a doctor diagnosing the disease from which he himself suffers. According to his own confident self-exegesis, he is a man possessed by a single sin, namely, the covetousness or desire for wealth described by Saint Paul in 1 Timothy 6:10 as "the root of all evils." And he explicates his way of life in terms of a single paradox: that by using his great rhetorical powers to preach against his own chosen form of sin, he acquires the wealth that enables him to practice it. But this analysis, while correct as far as it goes, does not tell the whole story. For one thing, it leaves out the place of covetousness in the whole panoply of sins as it was understood in Chaucer's time. Though evils in their numbers were indeed thought to spring from it, it was predicated on something more profound: the turning away of the soul from God brought about by pride, which, in the typical formulation of Chaucer's Parson, was considered "the general roote of alle harmes" (X [I] 389). The relationship is spelled out in a passage in the Old Testament book of *Ecclesiasticus:* "But nothing is more wicked than the covetous man. Why is earth and ashes proud? . . . The beginning of the pride of man, is to fall off from God: Because his heart is departed from him that made him: for pride is the beginning of all sin" (10:9, 14–15).[23]

The Parson, opening his discussion of covetousness, says that "whan the herte of a man is confounded in itself and troubled, and that the soule hath lost the comfort of God, thanne seketh he an ydel solas of worldly thynges" (X [I] 740). It is inevitable that the world as imagined by the Pardoner should be crammed with "things" in what amounts to a reification of sin, from his opening description of the various "relics" he carries about, through the "moneie, wolle, chese, and whete" (448) he intends to have, to the eight bushels of gold florins in which the rioters' fatal greed is embodied, the daggers, the poison, and the "botelles thre" (671) that are the instruments of death, and the "nobles or sterlynges, . . . silver broches, spoones, rynges" (907–08) and "wolle" (910) sought for in the invitation to receive pardon that closes the sample sermon.[24] The omnipresence of objects weighs the tale down to the point where even its moral locates itself within the physical world. Covetousness is a source of evil: burglars caught in the act may be shot and killed.

But although covetousness dominates the imagination of the Pardoner, and though the murders at the end of the tale are indeed motivated by desire for gold, its protagonists are not shown from the outset as exhibiting that sin in particular. Rather, their behavior seems intended to manifest all seven deadly sins at once, including even the one in which the Pardoner himself has no share. The "yonge folk" (464) described at the beginning of the tale, in addition to being covetous, are slothful, gluttonous, irascible,[25] and lecherous (463–82). To these five sins, the three rioters of the tale proper soon add the remaining two. They exhibit pride in boasting that they can easily dispose of "this false traytour Deeth" (699) and especially in their disrespectful behavior toward the old man.[26] And envy is as important a cause of their death as covetousness: each of them desires to have more gold than the others. There is, in fact, a well-known biblical text that fits this story of sinners hastening toward their inevitable destruction better than the Pardoner's 1 Timothy 6, a text that fairly cries out from between the lines of the tale, namely, Romans 6:23: "For the wages of sin is death." But this text lies beyond the Pardoner's ken. The second half of the verse, "But the grace of God, life everlasting, in Christ Jesus our Lord (gratia autem Dei vita aeterna in Christo Iesu Domino nostro)," retroactively defines "death" as damnation, the "second death" of the soul (Revelation 2:11, 20.6). Such is the spiritual meaning that we should be led to assign to death by the Pardoner's fable. But the all-too-vivid materiality of his narrative gets in the way, though the Pardoner does seem to gesture in its direction when he says that the glutton, seeking ever more delicate dishes to stimulate his appetite, "is deed, whil that he lyveth in tho vices" (548). Here I find useful the distinction between "notional awareness" and "substantial knowledge" made, and applied to the tale, by Malcolm Pittock.[27] Pittock notes the identification of death in medieval Christian culture with both a physical condition and a spiritual state: "For the sinner, . . . physical extinction . . . is itself a prelude to an immortality that is merely a more intense experience of physical death" (pp. 108–09). The Pardoner realizes that he is "a ful vicious man" (459) and impenitent and thus knows that this death is in store for him, but his tale epitomizes his "alienation from the substantial knowledge of [it]," an alienation likewise symbolized within his tale by the rioters' mistaken "identification of death with a real person" (pp. 112–13).

Once he has finished his sermon, breaking off with "And lo, sires, thus I preche" (915), the Pardoner makes a statement that has struck many of the tale's readers as oddly out of key with the cynicism of his performance up to that point:[28]

> And Jhesu Crist, that is oure soules leche,
> So graunte yow his pardoun to receyve,
> For that is best; I wol yow nat deceyve. (916–18)

He then does something even more puzzling: he turns to his fellow pilgrims and exhorts them to obtain from him, through "offerings" of money, the pardons whose fraudulence he has confessed — indeed, flaunted — in his confessional monologue. We hear in this new solicitation what we have heard before, but with a difference that is literally dramatic. In the *Prologue* and *Tale*, the Pardoner is reciting a monologue, speaking words such as he has used repeatedly in the course of his professional activities, like an actor reading aloud a part he has memorized. Once the performance is over, having rung down the curtain with "And lo, sires, thus I preche" (915), he leaves his imaginary pulpit for the "real" world of the *Canterbury Tales* framework, in which he is one of a company of pilgrims traveling to Canterbury. But like a computer governed by one program, he continues, in these changed circumstances, to act in accordance with his sole aim in life, which is to acquire money. Readily improvising a sales pitch adapted to the circumstances, he carries himself away by the power of his own rhetoric to the point of making the outrageous suggestion that his fellow pilgrims should avail themselves of "pardoun . . . Al newe and fressh at every miles ende" by repeatedly offering him "nobles or pens, whiche that be goode and trewe" (927–30). But then his elation brings about his downfall: he turns toward the Host, singling him out as the member of the group most urgently in need of pardon because he is "most envoluped in synne" (942), and invites him to kiss all his relics "ye, for a grote" (945).[29]

With the Host's obscene retort, the large-scale drama starring the Pardoner, which begins in the *Prologue*, is picked up again briefly in the Wife of Bath's *Prologue*, and resumes in earnest after the Host asks the Pardoner for a story, moves into its final scene. Targeted by the Host's brutally graphic language, the Pardoner undergoes what would have been for him the most devastating of all humiliations: the exposure, in the presence of the whole assembly of pilgrims, of the abnormality he thought he had successfully disguised. This punishment, like the one undergone by the Friar in the presence of the lord and his household in the *Summoner's Tale*, is social and public in nature. So too is the brief sequel that closes the Fragment: the Knight now intervenes, from his position of authority as the most noble member of the pilgrimage, to restore peace.

The speech that follows the Knight's peremptory "Namoore of this" (962) well deserves our attention. It is phrased with impeccable courtesy, as a polite request rather than a command. And this courtesy is directed equally toward the Host, who is a good fellow and a prosperous bourgeois, and the Pardoner, who is, both morally and socially, at the low end of the scale represented by the pilgrims (the Knight addresses the Host as *yow*, the Pardoner, less respectfully, as *thee*). The kiss that follows is a secular version of the *Pax*, or Kiss of Peace, that forms part of the church service: in this setting, it affirms, not love and unity among the faithful, but civility among members of a social group. The Knight's final speech also includes, in passing, an expression of affection toward the Host — "And ye, sire Hoost, that been to me so deere" (964) — which I have always found both unexpected and oddly moving.

This extended sequel surely makes a more satisfactory ending for the *Pardoner's Tale* than an abrupt breaking off, such as takes place at the end of most of the other tales, would have done. It satisfies us partly, I think, because it liberates us at last from the claustrophobic spell cast on us by the Pardoner's command of language, in both the hypocritical moralizing of his sermon and the doom-ridden world of his tale. The Host's retort comes as a punishment whose savage indecency fits the Pardoner's own lack of decency; in it, our expectations are grimly fulfilled. But the Knight's unexpected intervention, which follows, is of a different order. It shows us that the cynical vision of the world that has been held up before us so long is incomplete — that something more, and better, is possible. I venture to suggest that as the kiss is a secular version of the Pax, so the Knight's gratuitous and beneficent intervention is a secular version of divine grace. I quote again the startling reference to Christian redemption with which the Pardoner concludes his tale:

> And Jhesu Crist, that is oure soules leche,
> So graunte yow his pardoun to receyve,
> For that is best, I wol yow nat deceyve. (916–18)

No realistic explanation for his reason for saying this, among the many that have been offered, has been accepted as fully convincing. I believe that in fact there can be no such explanation, that there is no motive, such as we look for in realistic fiction, for the Pardoner's action. Rather, the statement is there because Chaucer himself wanted it there: it is he, through the Pardoner, who is telling us that the pardon of Christ is the best pardon of all, that it alone bestows on us the grace which saves us from the death of the soul. The promise in Romans 6:23, of "life everlasting, in Christ Jesus our Lord," is conspicuous in the *Pardoner's Tale* by its omission.[30]

For those who have been convinced by me and others of the reformist sympathies covertly signaled here and there in Chaucer's writings, a further, and final, interpretive step suggests itself. The statement that Christ's pardon is best, considered as part of what the Pardoner says after telling his tale, means that divine pardon exceeds in value those offered by dishonest Pardoners such as himself. Considered, however, as a statement put into the Pardoner's mouth, without clear dramatic motivation, by Chaucer the poet, it takes on a wider and more dangerous meaning: Christ's pardon excels not only those of fraudulent pardoners, but those of pardoners who serve as licensed and honest officials of the institutional church. This idea is, of course, thoroughly in accord with the views of Wyclif, who in one of his polemical treatises condemned *quaestores* as blasphemers, along with the members of all other ranks of the ecclesiastical hierarchy.[31]

In the *Merchant's Tale*, the *Reeve's Tale*, the *Pardoner's Tale*, as also in the *Summoner's Tale* (discussed elsewhere in this volume), Chaucer points the way to a final step in interpretation but leaves us to take it for ourselves. The meaning of each of these tales involves some sort of retribution visited upon a character who richly deserves it. But the full punitive force of each is, so to say, "occluded": not only is the punishment in question allowed to remain implicit, but the tale is presented in such a way as to distract us from, or cause us to stop short of, full understanding. Reading the *Merchant's Tale*, we may not realize that January's wealth is going to go to another man's child; reading the last episode of the *Reeve's Tale*, we may not think with satisfaction of the materialistic parson, suddenly deprived of the heir on whom he had intended to bestow his ill-gotten gains. Reading the *Summoner's Tale* and the *Pardoner's Tale*, we may not think of the eternal pains of hell.

In signaling interpretations that we are left to spell out for ourselves, in putting us in mind, beyond the language of the poem, of things not expressed there, the *Reeve's*, *Pardoner's*, and *Summoner's Tales* resemble each other in form. They also resemble each other in purport: in each case the tacit or occluded meaning implies an author (and perhaps a group of readers as well) critical of the workings of the institutional church. And each of these interpretations corroborates the others. Once we see how deeply the Wycliffite conception of friars as blasphemers permeates the *Summoner's Tale*, we can more fully sense the indignation of the narrator of the *Reeve's Tale* as he speaks of those who devour the goods of holy church and can more readily read into the Pardoner's strange assurance that Christ's pardon is best a Wyc-liffite scepticism concerning all pardoners, crooked and straight alike. One part of the *Canterbury Tales* casts light upon another. We can readily resolve the much-discussed verbal ambiguities of the portraits, in the *General Prologue*, of those two imposing personages the Monk and the Friar, by reading them in conjunction with the *Shipman's* and *Summoner's Tales*, respectively: there we learn that "venerie" (I [A] 166) for the Monk, at least in his younger days, was an indoor as much as an outdoor sport[32] and that "dalliance and fair language" (I [A] 211), for the alter ego of Friar Hubert in the *Summoner's Tale*, were rewarded by more than culinary refreshment. The final comment on these portraits is made by the Prioress, to whom the Host turns with a request for a tale, after deducing from the *Shipman's Tale* the moral that husbands should not entertain monks in their homes. Toward the end of her story, she blandly refers to the abbot who appears in it as

> an hooly man,
> As monkes been — or elles oghte be. (VII.642–43)

On consideration, we can see these three cases as linked by a common feature. All involve a personage of some consequence: members of two branches of the regular clergy and a well-off secular priest. In incorporating these figures into the design of the *Canterbury Tales*, Chaucer carefully refrains from saying anything in his own voice that might imply a critical or condemnatory attitude. Rather, he retreats behind a variety of fictional surrogates, including the nonjudgmental pilgrim Chaucer in whose person he speaks in the *General Prologue*. The appearance of the Monk, or an alter ego of the Monk, in the role of a *pricasour* in the indecent sense is the responsibility of the Wife of Bath, for whom the *Shipman's Tale* was originally written. The humiliations of the friar are recounted by the vulgar and vicious Summoner, and the collapse of the ambitions of the unpriestly parson can be thought of as a by-product of the vindictiveness of the Reeve.

At this point, I find it impossible to keep Chaucer the poet separate from the "real" Chaucer, whose ambiguous though comparatively high social status is made clear to us by the account presented in Paul Strohm's *Social Chaucer*. This Chaucer was, it is true, a member of the "gentil" class, but one who belonged to the lower rather than the upper level of that large and miscellaneous body, lacking the secure aristocratic status confirmed by the possession of hereditary lands and income. Such a man may well choose to refrain from impugning ecclesiastics as imposing as the Monk and Friar of the General Prologue, or even an ordained priest of some worldly pretensions. We note, in this connection, that Chaucer the Pilgrim does not hesitate to attribute outright knavery to the group at the low end of the social scale whose portraits follow those of the Parson and the Plowman: the Miller has the proverbial golden thumb, the Manciple diddles all his employers, the Reeve lends his lord what he has stolen from him; the Summoner knows how to pluck a finch, and the Pardoner passes pigs' bones off as relics.

The occluding of January's punishment in the *Merchant's Tale* can be viewed in this same light. January is referred to from the outset as a knight, but as the tale presents him, he is also a lord of consequence, possessed of wealth, a magnificent *palays* complete with pleasure garden, and a large entourage — the sort of person whose story would normally be suited to the high style. A subsidiary theme of the tale is the flattery to which such persons are subjected and the egotistic delusions they may entertain as a result, though any suggestion of similarity to English lords is deflected by January's removal to an Italian locale.

I believe, in fact, that the *Merchant's Tale* was originally written, not for the Merchant, but for the Monk.[33] The narrator's references to "this fooles that been seculeer" (1251) and "folk in seculer estaat" indicate this, as do what has been called his "supercilious intellectualism" and the withering contempt for the institution of marriage implied by his ironic praise of it in the opening section of the tale. By virtue of his higher social status, moreover, the Monk is better qualified than the Merchant to tell a tale in which the private vices of a member of the aristocracy are exposed, just as the Knight is better qualified than the Host to ask the Monk to break off the tale now labeled as his. Yet Chaucer does not permit even the Monk to make clear the full extent of January's punishment.

The *Canterbury Tales* can never be definitively interpreted, and this is probably just as well, if it means that much valuable criticism, representing a multiplicity of approaches, will continue to be written about them. One reason for this elusiveness is the fact that the tales as we have them represent several stages of an authorial conception that evolved over a long period of time. I believe we can detect in them an earlier stage, at which the Wife of Bath was to tell what is now the *Shipman's Tale*, the Man of Law was to tell what is now the *Tale of Melibee*, and the Monk was to tell what is now the *Merchant's Tale*. In a later stage, Chaucer's enlarged conceptions of the Wife of Bath and of his fictional self and his deepening interest in the question of the relations between the two sexes, most notably the marital relationship, led to such breakthroughs as the *Wife of Bath's Prologue* and the supremely parodic *Sir Thopas* and to the retrospective alignment of the *Merchant's Tale* with that of the Clerk. In a third stage, we see the wide horizon of the tales closing in. The giving up on this world of the *Second Nun's Tale*, the association of the human quest for knowledge with damnable human cupidity in the *Canon's Yeoman's Prologue* and *Tale*, and the repudiation of tale telling itself in the *Manciple's Tale* lead abruptly to the *contemptus mundi* of the *Parson's Tale* and Chaucer's own *Retractation*.

This shifting ground is rendered more unsteady still by what I cannot help thinking of as Chaucer's willful evasiveness, his staging of the public exposures and punishments of the vicious and corrupt in an overarching fiction — a "meta-fabliau," in Traugott Lawler's ingenious conception of it[34] — made up of fictions recounted by fictional beings. To this must be added his habit of occluding his most profound meanings, of scattering clues to them in contexts in which they tend to be overlooked. It is at the end of the *Nun's Priest's Tale* that he comes the closest to responding to our desire to understand him, first telling us to single out the "morality," then blandly assuring us that everything that is written is written to our doctrine — that nothing is ultimately irrelevant — and finally advising us to "take the fruit, and let the chaff be still" (VII [B2] 3443). I am inclined to think that the second instruction overrides the other two, that we must pay attention to everything in the *Canterbury Tales*, from the page of discourse to the whole complex of the tales at a given stage of Chaucer's conception of it, in the light of everything we can find out about the poet and his times. With Chaucer, more than with any other writer in English I know of, our quest for understanding will prosper to the degree that we cast our nets wide.

3

"Loves Hete" in the Prioress's Prologue and Tale

When, in book 1 of *Troilus and Criseide*, Pandarus encourages the despondent Troilus to try to win Criseide's love, he cites, as is his wont, a number of general truths. Among them is something he has heard wise men say, to the effect that

> Was nevere man or womman yet bigete
> That was unapt to suffren loves hete,
> Celestial, or elles love of kynde. (1.977–99)

In view of Criseide's beauty and youth, he continues, it is not appropriate that love in her case should be celestial "as yet," even if she were inclined toward that kind of love or capable of it. Criseide herself, however, seems at a later stage of the action to have a rather different opinion. After Pandarus, making his opening move in the conversation in which he plans to reveal to her that Troilus loves her, tells her to take off her wimple, dance, and observe the rites of May, she professes to be aghast. It would be more becoming for her, she says, to sit in a cave, praying and reading "holy seyntes lyves"; let maidens and young wives go to dances (2.110–19).

If we take our lead from the anachronistic "saints' lives" and translate Criseide's cave into a fourteenth-century convent, we can think of the opposition between cave and dance as paralleling that between Pandarus's love

71

celestial and "love of kynde," and of both pairs as representing two opposite modes of life available to women of gentle birth in Chaucer's time. A life based on natural love would manifest itself in social relationships with members of the opposite sex, leading to marital ties and in turn to the begetting and rearing of children; a life based on celestial love would be spent for the most part in cloistered isolation, in prayer and the contemplation of holy deeds.

Was the Prioress inclined to, or capable of, love celestial? To this question, the details making up her portrait in the *General Prologue* to the *Canterbury Tales* are, as everyone knows, wholly irrelevant — or, as regards the brooch inscribed "Amor vincit omnia," hopelessly ambiguous. We are probably right in inferring from them that, so far as outward appearances are concerned, she is a sentimental, snobbish, self-indulgent lady of some worldly pretensions. (Though it is true that she sings the divine service well, it is also true that the Pardoner, the most morally reprehensible of the pilgrims, is "a noble ecclesiaste.") Yet nothing in her portrait rules out the possibility that she had an inner spiritual life suffused with devotional ardor, and it is this latent aspect of her that we see displayed when she reappears at the end of the *Shipman's Tale*.[1]

To the Host's elaborately deferential, indeed almost reverent, request that she be the next teller, she makes a gracious but brief and businesslike response which should perhaps remind us of the much-praised brevity of Mary's answers in scripture: " 'Gladly,' quod she, and seyde as ye shal heere" (452). The *Prologue* that follows is in part an apologia or self-justification. Alluding to the "infants and sucklings" of Psalm 8, out of whose mouths God has perfected his praise, the Prioress implicitly distinguishes this miraculous activity (an infant [Latin *infans*] being literally "one incapable of speech") from that of the adult "men of dignitee" who are most fully qualified, by authority and learning, to "perform" God's praise in the natural order of things. She herself, a woman and therefore presumably lacking the qualifications of these male divines, resembles rather the inarticulate infants, and she invokes their praise of God as a precedent justifying her in her own attempt. Her story, she says, will be told in praise not only of God but of the Virgin Mary, who, though she is the mother of God and the "blisful queene" of heaven, was once a mortal woman like herself. After the Virgin has been invoked, she remains, though envisaged in meticulously correct subordination to the members of the Holy Trinity,[2] the center of the Prioress's rapt attention, contemplated with ardent veneration in all her transcendent power, glory, and goodness.

Given Mary's importance in the tale, it is appropriate that the Prioress should appeal to her in particular for help in telling it (473). In the sixth and last stanza of her Prologue, as she figuratively expresses her sense of her inadequacy to the task, this appeal takes a turn of some psychological interest:

My konnyng is so wayk, O blisful Queene,
For to declare thy grete worthynesse
That I ne may the weighte nat sustene. (481–83)

The image of bearing a weight recalls one of the sources of the *Second Nun's Prologue*, a hymn by Venantius Fortunatus:

Quem terra, pontus, aethera,
Colunt, adorant, praedicant,
Trinam regentem machinam,
Claustrum Mariae bajulat.[3]

The verb *bajulat* in the last line is emphatic in meaning; *bajulare* is defined in Lewis and Short's *A Latin Dictionary* as "to carry a burden, to bear something heavy." In her miraculous parturition, Mary bore within her body and brought forth into the world nothing less than the divine ruler of the earth, the sea, and the heavens. The Prioress, too, is by analogy pregnant at this moment, but what she carries within her is not a child; it is the theme of her tale, the "great worthiness" of the Virgin, which she feels herself too weak to "declare" or bring into the light.[4] The idea of weakness serves as a pivot, harking back to the image of the "children . . . on the brest soukynge" of the opening stanza. From the figurative pregnancy that overwhelms her, the Prioress imaginatively retreats or regresses to the condition of "a child of twelf month oold, or lesse, That kan unnethes any word expresse" (485). She thus becomes one of the infants of the Psalm, and the Virgin, by implication, becomes the mother suckling the infant upon her breast. Insofar as her "declaring" of her story, despite this virtually inarticulate state, is made possible by the help and guidance of the divine mother, it is itself a miracle of the Virgin, spreading her praise through her own intercession, as does the miraculous singing of *O Alma redemptoris mater* by the martyred little boy in the story itself.[5]

Positioning herself thus in her Prologue in relation to the telling of her tale, the Prioress moves from the "real" world of the pilgrimage, and specifically that of the *Shipman's Tale*, to an imagined world existing far away in an unspecified past ("Ther was in Asye, in a greet citee, Amonges Cristene folk a Jewerye" [488–89]). As is true in medieval hagiographical literature generally, this world and the things that happen in it reflect the simplest and most reductive oppositions of adversary Christianity. Those who inhabit it are either faithful or infidel, labeled a priori and viewed as such beyond a shadow of a doubt; they are thus imbued either with a love of God, Jesus, and Mary which makes everything about them them loveable and good or with a hatred which makes everything about them hateful and evil. These identifications are confirmed, if confirmation were needed, by a series of direct interactions between natural and supernatural realms: in addition to the part the Virgin plays in the story, we see Satan inciting the Jews to do away with the boy and his singing (558–66), Jesus guiding the boy's mother to the pit in which the Jews have thrown him (603–06), and the Holy Trinity, invoked by the abbot, causing the boy to answer his question (645 ff.). This is a world, one might add, in which the Prioress herself, as Chaucer portrays her in the *General Prologue*, does not and indeed could not exist.

The events of the tale move, on the model of New Testament salvation history, from suffering through martyrdom to triumph; in the Prioress's narration of them, an emotional fervor associated with pathos and "affective piety" predominates over intellectuality, ruling out the possibility of qualified moral judgment.[6] As, in her Prologue, she identifies herself both with the infant on the breast and the human mother of the infant Jesus, so in her tale she identifies herself both with the little boy and the Virgin, sharing equally in his devotion to her and her tender care for him. The love felt by infant and boy for the mother or mother-figure, and thus, implicitly, by the Prioress herself for the Virgin, is inarticulate, prerational, all-absorbing, wholly dependent on the unfailing reciprocal love and nurturance of the beloved, distanced from the adult world of "dignitee" and learning. Explaining to the abbot at the end of the story how it is that he can continue to sing even though his throat has been cut, the boy begins by telling of the emotion which is the first cause of the sequence of events in its entirety:

> This welle of mercy, Cristes mooder sweete,
> I loved alwey, as after my connyng. (656–67)

(The phrase "as after my connyng" significantly resembles the Prioress's "as I best kan or may" in the Prologue.) His immediate attraction toward the anthem praising Mary was caused by this love that had "always" possessed him and was itself miraculous, in that he knew no Latin and therefore had no rational understanding of its content. He learned the anthem later not as a text set to music, but "by rote" (545), that is, as a sequence of discursively meaningless verbal sounds linked to the notes of a melody.

The pathetic simplicity of the tale, with its binary oppositions between goodness and evil, love and hate, is enhanced by complementary sets of images evoking the two emotions. The Virgin and the little boy are associated with the whiteness, respectively, of the emblematic lily and of the Lamb followed by the Holy Innocents in Revelation. The Lamb itself represents Christ in a sentimentally appealing aspect. Both Virgin and child are "sweet"; it was the "sweetness" of Christ's mother that had pierced the boy's heart from the beginning of his life on, and the Prioress refers to the martyred corpse as "his litel body sweete" (682). The boy is symbolized by two precious stones, the emerald of chastity and the ruby of martyrdom (609–10), and he is entombed at last in a sepulchre whose "marbul stones cleere" (671) would seem to derive from the liturgy of the Feast of Holy Innocents.[7] The attractiveness of these images is heightened by contrast with the repulsiveness of the "foule usure" practiced by the Jews, the Satanic serpent swollen with outraged pride, the wasp's nest, and the filth of the "ordure" in the Jews' privy (which last cannot do away with the sweetness of the body of the dead saint).[8]

The contrast between the inarticulate helplessness associated in the Prologue first with the infants sucking at the breast, then with the Prioress herself, and the articulate or discursive powers associated with worldly "men of dignitee," is symbolized by a pervasive opposition, in Prologue and tale alike, between song and speech. At the end of the Prologue, in the Prioress's final prayer to the Virgin, she refers to the tale that is to follow as a song: "Gydeth my song that I shal of yow seye" (487), that is, "Guide my song that I shall utter concerning you." A song, specifically, the anthem heard by the boy in school, is, of course, crucial to the tale's plot, and in learning it "by rote," the boy learns it, as I have said, primarily as music, including the sounds of words. This thematic distinction is made explicit at the end of the account of the anthem's meaning given the boy by his "felawe": "I kan namoore expounde in this mateere. I lerne song; I kan but smal grammeere" (535–36). Song takes on an anagogical or otherworldly significance when, at the moment of the boy's murder, the Prioress suspends the telling of her story to address him directly, joyfully visualizing him in the company of 144,000 virgins whom John, in Revelation, saw following the Lamb:

> O martir, sowded to virginitee,
> Now maystow syngen, folwynge evere in oon
> The white Lamb celestial — quod she —
> Of which the grete evaungelist, Seint John,
> In Pathmos wroot, which seith that they that goon
> Biforn this Lamb and synge a song al newe,
> That nevere, flesshly, wommen they ne knew. (579–85)

We infer that, for the Prioress, an eternity of singing in the company of the Holy Innocents represents the greatest imaginable bliss.[9]

The *Prioress's Tale* is also songlike in that it is composed, not in the iambic pentameter couplets in which Chaucer wrote most of the tales, but in the seven-line stanza called *rime royal* which he seems to have thought appropriate to devotional stories. Since, by metrical convention, the end of each stanza of rime royal must also be the end of a sentence, the language of the tale is measured out in units of even length. It is in this sense as well as by virtue of the elaborate rhyme pattern of the stanza itself more artificial, distanced from speech by one further remove, than the language of the *Shipman's Tale*, which precedes it. The language of the tale is also marked, as has often been noted, by the incantatory or songlike feature of reiteration. Phrases such as "Cristene folk" (489, 495, 614), "Cristes mooder" (506, 510, 538, 550, 597, 656, 678), and "litel child" (516, 552, 587, 596, 667), which occur again and again, become particularly conspicuous, and the words *singen* and *song* resound, appropriately, from beginning to end.

We see the unworldly innocence of a child taking precedence over the worldly experience of a "man of dignity" at the end of the poem in the effect of the boy's martyrdom on the abbot. It is he, as the person of highest authority in the scene, who takes upon himself the responsibility of finding out what has caused this supernatural event. Confidently invoking the Trinity in high for-mulaic language, he "conjures" the boy to explain how it is that he can con-tinue to sing, though he should have died long since "by wey of kynde" (650). After he has been told about the grain placed by the Virgin on the boy's tongue and has, by removing it, delivered him into her hands, he is overcome. He weeps copiously and falls prostrate, lying "stille . . . as he had ben ybounde" (676), reduced to helplessness and silence.

Once the body has been entombed, the *Prioress's Tale* is at an end, and she closes as the Shipman had done, but to opposite effect, with a prayer on behalf of her fellow pilgrims: "Ther he is now, God leve us for to meete!" She prays, that is, that God may allow all of those present to meet in the company of the Holy Innocents in which she had earlier visualized the martyred boy. But seven more lines follow, and in the space between the penultimate and final stanzas we are brought back from the faraway place and unspecified time of the tale to Lincoln, a city in England, and an event that occurred "but a litel while ago," in a historical past not far distant from the present. ("History is now and in England.") This is the "real world" of the *Canterbury Tales*, inhabited by the Prioress herself and her beloved little dogs, by the Monk of the pilgrimage, and by the Monk of the *Shipman's Tale*. Here, professed Christians, even members of the regular clergy, can also be "sinful folk unstable," desperately in need of the mercy of a merciful God, multiplied unstintingly in honor of the Virgin queen of heaven. From it, the Prioress has imaginatively retreated to a realm in which the truths of salvation history are self-evident and unquestioned. The relation of the mortal Christian to divine beneficence in this realm is modeled not on adult eroticism, the soul's recognition of and passionate response to its divine wooer, but on the thoughtless and instinctual bliss of the child encircled by the loving care of its mother, exempt for the time being from all danger and doubt. This is celestial love as the Prioress knows it, and in reading her Prologue and tale we can, if we allow ourselves to be beguiled by Chaucer's consummate verbal and metrical artistry, experience it temporarily for ourselves.

4

Chaucer's English Rhymes: The Roman, *the* Romaunt, *and* The Book of the Duchess

Rhyme — the repetition of the sounds of words at regular intervals — has been a distinctive feature of verse in English from the earliest times to the present. The displacement of alliteration, or initial rhyme, by rhyme in the more familiar sense, or end-rhyme, was part of the process whereby French literary culture came to dominate English culture after the Norman Conquest. But the total vocabulary of rhymes and the range from the most obvious to the most ingenious combinations offered by the shapes and meanings of particular words are unique to each language, and poetry in English naturally developed a tradition of its own. Chaucer, the first major English poet to use end-rhyme, was thoroughly conversant with French poetry. In his early writings especially, we can see the French influence interacting with the native inheritance. In this chapter, I shall explore this interaction in two of Chaucer's earliest poems: his translation of *Le roman de la rose*, known as the *Romaunt*, and his first important narrative poem, *The Book of the Duchess*.

End-rhyme was evidently invented more than once.[1] It appears infrequently in classical Greek and Latin poetry but becomes common in Medieval Church Latin, whence it makes its way into the European vernaculars.[2] We find it also as a constituent feature of poetry in two unrelated non-European languages, namely, Arabic and Chinese. In modern English, rhyme appears everywhere and at all cultural levels: in the poems of the classical canon, in light verse, in the early babblings and traditional games of children, in proverbs, in nursery rhymes, in Cockney slang, in the nicknames of popular celebrities, on greeting cards, in the fugitive verses written for informal occasions. As one branch of what I call "systematic sound symbolism,"[3] rhyme derives its power from our counterrational, deeply rooted sense that identities of sound imply connections among meanings and even among things. Such connections are implicit in the traditional rhymes familiar to English speakers in literary and popular poetry alike: "kiss" and "bliss," "spring" and "sing," "moon" and "June." The reinforcing implications of identities of sound can also work ironically to underline oppositions or discrepancies between meanings, as in "death" and "breath" or "night" and "bright."

The responses of individual readers to rhyme in literature will vary in depth and breadth. There is a primary pleasure associated with the "incantatory" repetitions of the rhyming sounds themselves. We are also affected, consciously or unconsciously, by the symbolic power of rhyme in the realm of meaning. And we may find pleasures of a more sophisticated kind in the transcendence of technical difficulties or the creative handling of a tradition.

In an important article entitled "One Relation of Rhyme to Reason,"[4] W. K. Wimsatt compared Chaucer's rhymes with those of "the English poet whose rhyming shows perhaps the clearest contrast to [his]," namely, Alexander Pope (p. 157). Wimsatt began with some general observations about rhyme such as I have made above, noting that the repetitions of rhyme "impose upon the logical pattern of expressed argument a kind of fixative counterpattern of alogical implication" (p. 153). It was his view that rhyming words that also exhibit "parallels of meaning" are characteristic primarily of "balladry and other primitive types of poetry," though he conceded that "even in sophisticated poetry such as Tennyson's *In Memoriam* one may find some stanzas where a high degree of parallel is successful" (p. 154). Going on to compare Chaucer's rhymes with Pope's in detail, he clearly showed his preference for combinations in which identities of sound in pairs of rhyming words are played off against various kinds of differences between them. A rhyme like Chaucer's *resoun / condicioun*, for example, is dubbed "dullish," in comparison with the "quaint minor contrast in length and quality of words" in Pope's *maids / masquerades* (p. 158). Syntactic differences, such as those among the parts of speech, can also add piquancy to rhymes. Pairings like *thriftily / yemanly*, *bracer / bokeler*, and *sheene / grene* in Chaucer's portrait of the Yeoman are "tame" because the rhyming words belong to the same part of speech; furthermore, the words linked in the first two pairs are formed with the same suffixes (p. 160). Rhymes between nouns and verbs in Pope, such as *eyes / rise* and *(with civil) leer / (to) sneer*, have more "piquancy." When Pope does rhyme words that are grammatically alike, the pairs not infrequently present interesting formal differences, for example, that between singular and plural in the nouns *laws* and *applause* (p. 161).

Though, so far as I am aware, Wimsatt never included *Le roman de la rose* in his purview, he would surely have taken the same sort of pleasure in the rhymes of the *Roman* that he took in the rhymes of Pope. I have in mind, in particular, the rich rhymes which appear in the verse with such frequency as to constitute a conspicuous feature of its style. Before I go on to discuss some of these within the framework of Wimsatt's comparative analysis of Pope and Chaucer, I need to present and define my terms. Rhymes in French verse have been classified according to many schemes, some involving distinctions of word origin and meaning as well as of sound.[5] Mine is based entirely on degrees of phonic identity. I distinguish the following categories, in order of increasing degrees of "richness" and decreasing frequency of occurrence, in the octosyllabic couplets of the *Roman*. I add the terms applied to them in French prosody:[6]

  1. "Simple rhymes" (*rime suffisante*) between the eighth syllables of successive lines, in which phonic identity is restricted, as is usual in English rhyming, to the vowels and the consonants that follow them.
     Examples: *plot* "pleased" / *n'ot* "(there) was not" (27–28), *feirë* "to make" / *peirë* "pairs, sets" (61–62)[7]
  2. "Rich rhymes" (*rime riche*) between the eighth syllables of successive lines, in which phonic identity includes the consonants immediately preceding the rhyming vowels.
     Example: *argent* "silver" / *gent* "pretty" (91–92)
  3. "Double rhymes" (*rime léonine*),[8] in which a simple rhyme between the seventh syllables of successive lines is followed by a rich rhyme between the eighth syllables.
     Example: *romanz* "romance" / *comanz* "(I) commence" (35–36)
  4. "Double rich rhymes," in which both the seventh and eighth syllables of successive lines rhyme richly.
     Example: *songier* "dream [infin.]" / *mençongier* "false" (3–4)
  5. "Triple rhymes," in which a simple rhyme between the sixth syllables of successive lines is followed by rich rhymes between the seventh and eighth syllables.
     Example: *covertement* "secretly" / *apertement* "openly" (19–20)[9]

In the two passages of the *Roman* I have tabulated, 40 out of 64 rhymes, or 63 percent, and 20 out of 25, or 80 percent, respectively, are rich, belonging to the second, third, fourth, and fifth of the above categories. Thirteen out of 64, or 20 percent, and 6 out of 25, or 24 percent, belong to the last three.[10] The ear of the reader familiar with the conventions of the verse is thus constantly made aware of variations among lesser and greater degrees of phonic identity in rhyming pairs. As regards meaning, form, and grammatical function, these same pairs exhibit a range between similarities of the sort Wimsatt found "dullish" in Chaucer and differences of the sort he found "interesting" or "piquant" in Pope. My concern for the moment is with the differences.[11]

Linkages between words of different parts of speech are found in rich rhymes (category 2 above) such as *mais* "May" / *mais* "more" (45–46), *chantant* "singing" / *tant* "so much" (71–72), *atempree* "mild" / *pree* "meadow" (125–26), *portast* "carried, possessed" / *tast* "touch" (543–44), and *mignot* "pretty" / *n'ot* "did not have" (551–52), as well as in double rhymes (category 3), such as *aparant* "apparent" / *garant* "guarantee" (5–6), *forment* "strongly, deeply" / *dormant* "sleeping [ger.]" (25–26), and *atornee* "adorned" / *jornee* "day, day's work" (569–70). A notably ingenious double rich rhyme, involving a lexical contradiction, links *verdure* "greenery" with *yver dure* "winter lasts" (53–54). In the rhyme *die* "should say" / *musardie* "foolishness" (11–12), the basic grammatical disparity between verb and noun is doubly enhanced: the two words differ in length and as diction, the former being a more ordinary word, the latter more unusual and colorful. The effect is rather like that of the *maids* / *masquerades* rhyme cited from Pope by Wimsatt. Grammatical similarities between pairs of richly rhyming words belonging to the same part of speech are sometimes qualified, as in Pope, by minor contrasts in form or length. Thus *ganz* "gloves" and *Ganz* "Ghent" (563–64) differ in that the first is a common noun, the second a proper noun; in addition, the first is plural, the second singular. The triple rhyme *ai ge fiance* "have I trust" / *senefiance* "significance" (15–16) links the three-syllable noun *fiance* (counting the final *e*) with a noun of five syllables.

As I indicated above, the passages I have examined in detail also contain numerous rhymes of the sort viewed by Wimsatt as "tame." A large proportion of these involve simple homeoteleuton, that is, the repetition of an inflectional ending or suffix: *aloie* "(I) went" / *souloie* "(I) was accustomed" (23–24), *amee* "(to be) loved" / *clamee* "(to be) called" (43–44), *levé* "(I) rose" / *lavé* "(I) washed" (89–90), *esbanoiant* "taking my pleasure" / *costoiant* "passing alongside" (126–27), *savoree* "made savory" / *coloree* "colored" (535–36), *enbesoignie* "(was) busied" / *pignie* "(was) painted" (567–68). Given the technical virtuosity of the poet, and thus his presumable ability to have avoided these simplest forms of rhyme had he so wished, it seems wrongheaded to compare them invidiously with rhymes of greater elaboration, viewing them as occasional dull patches in an otherwise brilliant fabric. They ought rather to be seen as part of an array in which each element throws into relief the qualities of the others. In the art of rhyme as practiced in the *Roman*, variety is of the essence in more ways than one, as we will see. And in fact, simple linkages of form as well as sound may, when the meanings of the rhyming words are akin or antithetical, felicitously emphasize either of these relationships, as happens with *amoreus* "amorous" / *savoureus* "pleasing" (79–80), *frarin* "miserable" / *serin* "serene, enjoyable" (69–70), and the triple rhyme *covertement* "covertly" / *apertement* "openly" (19–20).

I cannot conclude this discussion of the *Roman* without singling out, as of particular interest, the two rhymes that occur in the first four lines of the poem. The first is a double rhyme, the second, double rich.

> Maintes genz dient que en songes
> N'a se fables non et mençonges;
> Mès l'en puet tex songes songier
> Qui ne sont mie mençongier.

[Many men say that there is nothing in dreams but fables and lies, but one may have dreams which are not deceitful.][12]

The phonic identity of *songes* "dreams" with the second syllable of *mençonges* "lies" in the first couplet "confirms," on the level of sound, the opinion the poet is referring to: that dreams are lies, just as virtual phonetic identity in the Italian proverb "Traduttore, traditore" "confirms" the idea that translators are traitors to their texts. In the second couplet, the identity of *songier* "(to) dream" with the last two syllables of *mençongier* "deceitful, lying" "contradicts" the poet's affirmation that "one may have dreams which are not deceitful." But these phonic identities in Old French have resulted from the fortuitous convergence of pairs of words that were once entirely distinct in sound as well as in meaning. Old French *songe* is derived from Latin *somnium* "dream," which in turn is based on *somnus* "sleep," whereas *mençonge* is thought to derive from an unattested popular Latin word **mentionica*, based on *mentio* "a lie." The rhymes thus symbolize a disparity between outward appearance (the shapes of words) and truth (the origins of words), just as a dream may seem when one experiences it to be a deceptive illusion, yet signify a truth that will emerge later: "Qui li plusor songent de nuiz / Maintes choses covertement / Que l'en voit puis apertement" (18–20) (For most men at night dream many things in a hidden way which may afterward be seen openly). In that this same distinction between surface appearance and latent meaning is basic to allegorical narrative generally, the difference between the seeming and actual relationships between the words of the two opening rhyme-pairs is profoundly relevant to the poem as a whole.

I turn now to Chaucer's use of French-style rhymes in the *Romaunt* and in

his first major independent poem, *The Book of the Duchess*.[13] Anyone familiar with Chaucer's verse will know that to examine it in search of witty and
ingenious linkages of meaning and form, such as enhance the verses of the
Roman, is to place him at a disadvantage. Especially is this true for the *Romaunt* because Chaucer's choices among words here are constrained by his
line-for-line adherence to the meaning of the French original.[14] I shall make
this more invidious part of my discussion as brief as possible.

Whereas rich rhymes of various kinds occur 63 percent and 80 percent
of the time, respectively, in the two passages of the *Roman* I tabulated, the
proportions of such rhymes in the corresponding passages of the *Romaunt* are
a comparatively low 15 percent and 17 percent.[15] A number of the rich rhymes
that do occur involve linkages, based directly on the French original, of words
of French derivation by homeoteleuton; thus *apparaunt / warraunt* (5–6) corresponds to *aparant / garant, amorous / saverous* (83–84), to *amoreus / savoureus, pitous / delytous* (89–90), to *piteus / deliteus*, and *fasoun* "fashion" /
resoun (551–52), in part to *moison* "dimension" / *reison*. Of the remaining
rich rhymes, a large proportion are formed by repetition of native suffixes—
most frequently of *-ly*, which sometimes, but not invariably, echoes the corresponding suffix *-ment* in the French: *covertly / openly* (19–20), *redily / erly*
(93–94), *queyntely / fetisly* (569–70), *fetisly / richely* (577–78), *oonly / un-
couthly* (583–84). The rich rhyme *here / here* (37–38) is a simple reiteration
of word and meaning; the rhyme *also / so* (33–34) is likewise reiterative in
slightly disguised form, since *also* was originally a phrase with *so* as its second
element. The second syllable of the double rhyme *pleiyng / costeiyng* (133–
34), corresponding to *esbanoiant / costoiant*, is a homeoteleuton in which the
native ending of the participle is substituted for the French ending; there is also
a simple rhyme between the stems of the two verbs, as in the original. Only in
seyne "say" / *Seyne* "Seine" (117–18) has the translator contrived an original
linkage in which phonic identity is set off by a grammatical difference (the
corresponding rhyme in the *Roman* is not a rich rhyme but a simple one:
fontaine / Saine [111–12]).

In *The Book of the Duchess* (*BD*), Chaucer is adapting materials from
French poetry rather than translating line by line and is thus presumably freer
to rhyme according to his own bent. But this freedom does not result in an
increase in the number of rich rhymes. The percentage for the poem as a whole
is slightly over 7 percent, about half as great as the percentages cited above
from my two sample passages of the *Romaunt*. A number of the rich rhymes
that appear in *BD*, like those taken directly from the original in the *Romaunt*,
involve homeoteleuton, linking words of French derivation having the same
suffixes, for example, *creature / portrayture* (625–26) and *suffisance / plesance*

(703–04). As in the *Romaunt,* native suffixes also appear in such linkages. There are four rhymes on -*ly*, including a notable five-line sequence in which *why / comlily* (847–48) is immediately followed by *swetely, womanly, debonairly* , and *frendly* (849–52). -*Nesse*, which I did not find in the rhymes of my sample passages of the *Romaunt,* appears in four rhymes in *BD* (601–02, 607–08, 827–28, and 1155–56). Grammatical differences or differences in meaning sometimes add interest to rhymes between words of identical shape, for example, in *here* "here" / *here* "hear" (93–94), *countour* "mathematician" / *countour* "counting-house" (435–36), and *noumbre* "to enumerate" / *noumbre* "number" (sb.) (439–40).

To sum up: in the *Roman,* we find a heavy proportion of rich rhymes of various degrees of intricacy and ingenuity to simple rhymes. Though such rhymes are by no means absent from Chaucer's early verse, it does not exhibit what might be called the systematic formal variation with respect to rhyme that we find in the French poem. This comparative lack of variety manifests itself in two additional ways: there is more repetition of rhyming syllables, that is, of rhyming sounds, in Chaucer's verse than in the verse of the *Roman,* and there is more repetition of rhyming words and of particular rhyming pairs. Repetition of rhyming syllables results in part from linkages between pairs of words ending in native suffixes of frequent occurrence such as -*ly* and -*nesse*; a number of these were cited above from the *Romaunt* and *BD* as examples of Chaucerian rich rhyme. To these should be added simple rhymes in *BD*, such as *trewely / why* (33–34) and *gesse / sicknesse* (35–36), in which only one rhyming word contains the suffix in question (for additional examples with -*ly*, see lines 669–70, 721–22, 745–46, 777–78, 1047–48, 1111–12, 1151–52, 1197–98, and 1269–70; for -*nesse*, see lines 797–98 and 1059–60). The native suffix -*ing(e)* is likewise conspicuous in its frequency; it appears in the *Romaunt* in simple rhymes in lines 25–26, 75–76, 91–92, 105–06, and 133–34, as well as in the rich rhyme *pleiyng / costeying* which was cited earlier, and in *BD*, mostly in simple rhymes, in lines 229–30, 349–50, 599–600, 605–06, 611–12, 633–34, 639–40, 761–62, 795–96, 801–02, 869–70, 959–60, 995–96, 1313–14, and 1327–28 — fifteen times in all. But repetition of rhyming syllables in English is also a function of something we do not find in French: the repeated use of sets of rhymes made up entirely or chiefly of lexical words. One such set rhymes on the *e* of *be*; its members rhyme among themselves and with a variety of words ending in a stressed *e* (spelled -*y* in modern English) corresponding to the *e* in certain French suffixes. Thus *be* rhymes with *nycete* in *Romaunt* 11–12, with *me* in 15–16, and with *she* in 45–46; *me* rhymes with *she* in 35–36, with *jolite* in 51–52, and with *se* in 121–22; *me* rhymes with *entre* "entry" in 537–38, *see* with *she* in 549–50, and *she* with *cuntre* and *journe* in 559–60 and 579–80, respectively. The second rhyme of the *Romaunt* links *sen* and *ben*, alternative fuller forms of the infinitives of *see* and *be*; *ben* rhymes with *wren* "cover (v.)" in 55–56, and *grenë* rhymes with the inflected infinitive *senë* in 57–58. Words rhyming in *-ight* make up another such group: *aright* rhymes with *lyght* in *Romaunt* 31–32, *ryght* with *wight* in 47–48, and *light* with *myght* in 77–78; *sightë* rhymes with *brightë* in 73–74, and *wightës* with *nyghtës* in 17–18. Among repeated pairs of words, *wel* rhymes with *del* in *Romaunt* 27–28 and with *everydell* in 125–26; *is* rhymes with *ywis* in 43–44 , 69–70, and 555–56, *faire* rhymes with *payre* in 65–66 and 107–08, and *here* rhymes with *clere* in 87–88 and 101–02. Sets of words rhyming with *se* and *bright* are similarly conspicuous in *BD*, leading off with *lyght* / *nyght* in 1–2 and *me* / *be* in 9–10. Of the three rhyming pairs that repeat in the passages of the *Romaunt*, *fair* / *pair* and *here* / *clere* do not occur in *BD*, but *wel* rhymes with *(every)del* a total of eleven times (221–22, 231–32, 543–44, 697–98, 845–46, 863–64, 1001–02, 1013–14, 1041–42, 1147–48, 1159–60), and *ys* rhymes with *iwis* in 657–68. Two other groups of rhyming words, ending with *-oon* (as in *oon* "one") and with *-ought*, should also be mentioned as especially conspicuous,[16] and four pairs of rhyming words, in addition to *wel* / *(every)del*, occur with notable frequency: *slep* / *kep* in 5–6, 127–28, 137–38, and 223–24, along with *slepë* / *kepë* in 43–44; *wif* / *lif* in 63–64, 75–76, 85–86, 201–02, and 1037–38; *sorwe* / *morwe* in 213–14, 595–96, and 1255–56, along with *a-morwe* / *sorwe* in 1103–04 and *morwes* / *sorwes* in 411–12; and, last but not least, *rowthe* / *trowthe* in 96–97, 465–66, 591–92, 999–1000, and 1309–10.[17]

The patterns presented by the *Roman* are quite different. The rhyming syllables that recur are almost invariably suffixes linked in both rich and simple rhymes by homeoteleuton (a group that appears in two adjacent rhymes, consisting of the words *ueille* "wishes," *fuelle* "foliage" [51–52], *s'orgueille* "prides itself," and *mueille* "moistens" [55–56], is a notable exception). Among rhyming suffixes, *-ment* appears in *covertement* / *apertement* (19–20), *cointement* / *apertement* (559–60), and *seulement* / *noblement* (573–74); *-er*, the ending of the infinitive, appears in *rimeer* / *agaeer* (31–32), *enfiler* / *aler* (93–94), and *miroer* / *treçoer* (557–58); the variant infinitive ending *-ier* appears in *songier*, rhyming with *mençongier* "false" (3–4). The rhyming syllable of most frequent occurrence in the passages I examined was the suffix *-ant*, found in the present participle, the gerund, and adjectives of participial origin. It appears in *esbatant* / *escoutant* (99–100), *pleisant* / *reluisant* (117–18), and *esbanoiant* / *costoiant* (127–28) and is linked with words of other parts of speech in *aparant* / *a garant* (5–6) and *chantant* / *tant* (71–72). It also rhymes with *-ment* in *forment* / *dormant* (ger.) (25–26) and *dormant* (pple.) /

durement (87–88). The proportion of repeated rhyming syllables to the total number of rhyming syllables in lines 1–128 and 524–74 of the *Roman*, however, falls short of the proportion in the *Romaunt*: about 35 percent of the couplets I tabulated in the former are repetitive in sound versus about 62 percent of those in the latter. More significantly, the verse of the *Roman*, in the passages I tabulated, exhibits almost no repetition among rhyme-words themselves, and no repetition at all of rhyming pairs. The sole exception I found was *apertement*, which appears twice, rhyming with *covertement* in lines 19–20, and with *cointement* in 559–60 (but see note 21, below).

The above data suggest some across-the-board generalizations concerning English and French rhyming practices. First, though rhymes on suffixes are found in English, the proportion of these to rhymes between the stems of independent words is considerably smaller in English than it is in French.[18] Second, rhyme in English is much more repetitive than it is in French with respect both to rhyming syllables and to rhyming words. Furthermore, the groups of words that rhyme repeatedly among themselves in English are linked by similarities other than sound. They are in general "common" as diction, in that they are neither colloquial nor literary, and "common" in their familiarity, in that they occur frequently in the language at large. With a few exceptions, such as the interjection *ywis*, they are lexical words, having referential meanings. And they are of native, rather than of French, origin. In French verse, we do not find groups of repeated rhyming words such as are ubiquitous in English.[19] We do find repeated rhyming syllables, but these are almost all suffixes attached to a variety of bases.

Thus far I have described Chaucer's rhymes in disparaging language, speaking of their lack of variety in form and of their repetitiousness in syllables and wording as compared with the rhymes of the *Roman*. A positive description will prove equally valid and more illuminating. Considered in their own right, the repeated words in Chaucer's rhymes can be thought of as systems, formulaic in nature and, like all sets of formulas, serving the poet as a technical resource. Readers familiar with rhymed verse in Middle English will be aware that the systems to which combinations like *be* and *me* or *sight* and *bright* belong are part of an inherited tradition. The groups of common words that rhyme with each other in the *Romaunt* and *The Book of the Duchess* appear also, along with other such groups, in the poems of Chaucer's predecessors and contemporaries, not least the metrical romances whose "rime doggerel" he deliciously satirized in *Sir Thopas*.

The rhymes of *Le roman de la rose* are equally traditional and, paradoxically, equally repetitive in their very variety of form and wording. The high proportions of rhymes of various degrees of richness, the heavy reliance on rhyming suffixes, and the ingenious ways of devising syllabic sequences of identical shape which are characteristic of the verse of Guillaume de Lorris appear also in the verse of Chrétien de Troyes, who wrote a century earlier than Guillaume, and in the verse of Guillaume de Machaut and Jean Froissart, who wrote a century later.[20]

The two ways of rhyming represented by the English and French traditions might be called simple and elaborate, respectively — or, to use more qualitative language, naive and sophisticated. They require different skills of the poets who practice them, and they produce different effects. In the French tradition, rhyme is literally recherché. The lack of readily available sets of simple rhyming words, the comparative intolerance of repetition,[21] the necessity of adorning passage after passage with rhymes of various degrees of richness: these aspects of the French tradition continually challenge the resourcefulness of the poet and press him toward linguistic diversity. Rhyme itself, and the techniques of rhyme, are highlighted; as a result, the reader's attention is divided, as also in the verse of Pope and his contemporaries, between the content and the surface of language. Robert Frost's observation, in "In a Poem," that "The sentencing goes blithely on its way, / And takes the playfully objected rhyme" seems designed to fit this kind of verse. The Middle English poet, for his part, may avail himself of the established groups of rhyming words and, if he wishes, supplement them with similar groups of his own devising. Within the groups, he is free to repeat pairs of rhyming words that are particularly relevant to his subject matter. The skillful poet is able to do this unobtrusively, in part by working the repeated words and rhymes into the stream of narrative or descriptive detail in such a way that their presence at each point seems natural, in part by using them for a variety of purposes and in a variety of ways: in different meanings or collocations, or in different idioms or grammatical constructions. Effectively used, they become transparent; the reader sees through the verbal surface to the meanings that help the narrative or descriptive content unfold.[22]

Each of these traditional styles has its characteristic vices. Elaborate formal linkages of the sort that enhance the elegance and wit of the verse of a Guillaume de Lorris may, when contrived by a lesser poet, seem artificial and pretentious, and the hindrances to direct statement presented by the constant need for a variety of form and wording in rhyme may retard the pace of exposition, description, or narration to the point of prolixity. In Middle English verse, the traditional words, when used again and again in the same way and for the same purpose, seem dragged in "for the sake of the rhyme";

repetition becomes tiresome, and simplicity seems merely flatfooted. There is an additional danger for the Middle English poet in the form of an inherited body of expressions, suitable for use in rhyme, which are general and adaptable in meaning and thus can suggest themselves all too readily for use in filling out the line when inspiration flags. In the metrical romance *Sir Degravant*, for example, the expressions "both hardy and wight," "both squire and knight," "to see with sight," and "By day or / and / ne by night" recur, with a frequency that soon becomes noticeable, among an unconscionably large number of rhymes on *-ight*.[23] The more accomplished poet may draw on such phrases but, if he does so, will succeed in incorporating them inconspicuously, along with the traditional rhyming words, into the flow of language.

Although the rhymes of *The Book of the Duchess* for the most part represent the native tradition, an admixture of French-style rhymes enhances at various points the dramatic expressiveness of the poem's language. A natural starting place for discussion is the opening passage, in which Chaucer imitates the opening of Froissart's *Le paradis d'amour*. I quote the French and English passages, with a modern translation of the French.

1	Je sui de moi en grant mervelle
	Coument tant vifs, car moult je velle,
	Et on ne poroit en vellant
	Trouver de moi plus travellant,
5	Car bien sachiés que par vellier
	Me viennent souvent travellier
	Pensees et merancolies
	Qui me sont ens ou coer liies.
	Et pas ne les puis desliier,
10	Car ne voel la belle oubliier
	Pour quelle amour en ce travel
	Je sui entrés et tant je vel.

[I wonder greatly about myself, how I live so long, for I stay awake a great deal, and no one would be able to find anyone who suffers more than I do in staying awake. For know well that as a result of staying awake, thoughts and fits of melancholy often come to torment me, which are attached within me to my heart. Nor can I detach them, for I do not wish to forget the beauteous one for whose love I have entered into this torment and stay awake so much.][24]

1	I have gret wonder, be this lyght,
	How that I lyve, for day ne nyght
	I may nat slepe wel nygh noght;
	I have so many an ydel thoght

5   Purely for defaute of slep
      That, by my trouthe, I take no kep
      Of nothing, how hyt cometh or gooth,
      Ne me nys nothyng leef nor looth.
      Al is ylyche good to me —
10   Joye or sorowe, wherso hyt be —
      For I have felynge in nothyng,
      But as yt were a mased thyng,
      Alway in poynt to falle a-doun;
      For sorwful ymagynacioun
15   Ys alway hooly in my mynde.

The passages well exemplify their respective traditions as regards patterns and techniques of rhyme.[25] All the rhymes in the French passage are rich; three (*vellant / travellant, vellier / travellier,* and *desliier / oubliier*) are double rich. Three couplets out of the six rhyme on suffixes, and three couplets exploit identities of sound between pairs of words related to the verbs *travellier* "suffer" and *vellier* "stay awake." The English passage contains one rich rhyme: *nothyng / thyng.* All the rhyming syllables are lexical words, and the words themselves are simple and familiar. Three of the seven pairs of rhyming words (*lyght / nyght, noght / thoght,* and *me / be*) belong to groups that I cited earlier as frequently represented in the *Romaunt* and *BD,* while *slep / kep* was cited from *BD* as a repeatedly used rhyming pair. The word *thing* reappears as a rhyme-word in *BD* 62, paired with *king*; this pair appears also in 83–84, 141–42, 219–20, and, in the plural, in 57–58. The words *adoun* and *doun* appear in rhyme five more times in the course of the poem (161, 348, 635, 749, and 1165), and *loothe,* in its plural inflected form, reappears as a rhyme-word in line 581. *Day ne night* is a traditional phrase which lends itself to use as a filler (see my earlier reference to *Sir Degravant*), but here the complementarity of day and night is in point.

The passage in Froissart is grave in tone, formal in style, and dignified in manner. Admittedly, it suffers in translation into English prose, but one might venture the judgment that even in the original it is a little prolix, ringing the changes on elected identities of sound to, if not beyond, the point of diminishing returns. The English passage, by contrast, sounds informal and unpremeditated, and the manner of speaking adopted by the Chaucerian persona is characteristically vehement and hyperbolic. (It is hard to imagine Froissart's speaker describing himself as "a confused creature . . . always on the verge of falling down.") The mild oath that provides Chaucer's first line with its rhyme-word is apparently drawn from the colloquial idiom.[26] Overall, the passage has in full measure the "naive intensity" described by J. A. Burrow as characteristic of the style taken over by Chaucer from earlier English poetry, and of the style of Ricardian poetry generally.[27] The ingenuousness, spontaneity, and strong feelings of the narrator of *The Book of the Duchess*, of course, are appropriate for one destined to respond sympathetically to and receive instruction from a member of the nobility in the person of the Black Knight. Interestingly, although the speakers of both the French and the English poems have been cured of their sleeplessness and their resultant states of disorientation and distress, by the time they begin to tell their retrospective tales, each describes his malady in the present tense, as if he were experiencing it now. This being the case, Chaucer's language must be judged the more dramatically appropriate of the two.

I said earlier that the proportion of rich rhymes to the total number of rhymes in *BD* is a little over 7 percent, considerably lower than that in my sample passages of the *Romaunt*. But this is only an average; the proportions vary significantly from part to part. In the language of the narrator, from the opening of the poem until he hears the complaint of the Black Knight (lines 1–474), 15 out of 237 couplets (not counting the anomalous linkage of *Morpheus* with *moo fees thus* in 265–66) rhyme richly, or about 6.7 percent. Shortly afterward, in the Knight's first long speech, the distribution of rich rhymes varies in an interesting way. The speech divides naturally into several sections. A lengthy description of the intensity and all-pervasiveness of his sorrow, taking up almost forty lines (560–97), concludes with a promise to explain what has caused it ("Allas! and I wol tel the why" [598]). The passage that immediately follows consists of a series of variations, couched in language marked by conspicuous repetitive schemes, on the antithesis between former joy and present grief first expressed as "My song ys turned to pleynynge" (599–619). Then comes a lengthy portrayal of the allegorical figure of "fals Fortune" (620–51), which leads to a narrative couched in metaphorical terms drawn from the game of chess (652–86). The speech ends, as it began, with a generalized lament (687–709). Lines 560–97 contain no rich rhymes at all, but in the remainder of the speech (lines 598–709), 12 couplets out of 55 rhyme richly, or a proportion of almost 22 percent. Literal truth is veiled, in the language of this same passage, by a maximum of rhetorical elaboration, and it seems fitting that the rhymes too should be unusually elaborate. (The proportions of rich rhymes in the Knight's three remaining long speeches are lower: about 3 percent in lines 759–1041 [but 5 out of 13 couplets in lines 827–52], 2 percent in 1052–1111, and 3 percent in 1144–1297.) The rhymes of the Black Knight's two "songs," on the other hand, exemplify the native tradition at its simplest; plain rhyme-words and familiar rhyme combinations seem designed to enhance their artful "sincerity" of language.

Tracking the pairs of rhyming words that occur most frequently in *The*

Book of the Duchess, we see that even at this early stage of his career, Chaucer has mastered the art of repeating without repetitiousness. One and the same word is made to serve a variety of purposes and is incorporated in a variety of constructions and phrasal combinations. *Del,* which rhymes only with *wel,* appears in the phrases "never a del" (543, 936) and "a gret del" (1158) as well as in the compound formation "everydel," which sometimes means "entirely," as in "I had be dolven everydel" (222) and sometimes, more literally, "every part," as in "Whan I had . . . overloked [the story] everydel" (231–32). In "[of trouthe] she had so moche hyr del" (1000), *del* has its full independent meaning, "share." *Morwe,* which rhymes only with *sorwe,* means "morning" in "I fond hyt redy every morwe" (1256), as does *a-morwe* in "That whan I saugh hir first a-morwe" (1103), whereas in "And deyede within the thridde morwe" (214), it means "day." *Morwe* also appears in the expression "ne nyght ne morwe" (22), which harks back to the earlier phrase "day ne nyght" (2) and is similarly meaningful in the context of the narrative. The expression "to meet with [that is, to experience] sorrow" (see *meten* v. [4], sense l[b] in *MED*) is wittily invoked in a rhyme between *morwe* and *sorwe* in lines 595–97, when the Black Knight says of himself that

> whoso seeth me first on morwe
> May sayn that he hath met with sorwe,
> For y am sorwe, and sorwe ys y.

Kep, which rhymes only with *slep,* appears several times, with a variety of meanings, in the expression "take kep." In "I take no kep / Of nothyng" (6–7), it means "I have no interest in anything"; in "or she tooke kep" (128), it means "Before she became aware [that she was falling asleep]"; in "Yif I ne had . . . take kep / Of this tale" (224–25) it means "If I had not remembered this story." The verb *kepë,* in "Our first mater is good to kepe" (43) means "continue with, stick to." The lexical and idiomatic potentialities of other repeated rhyme-words are exploited with similar resourcefulness.

Equally important for the avoidance of repetitious or monotonous effects is Chaucer's ability to incorporate frequently occurring rhyming words in passages of natural sounding dialogue, as when Juno gives her "messager" his instructions:

> "Go bet," quod Juno, "to Morpheus —
> Thou knowest hym wel, the god of slep.
> Now understond wel and tak kep!" (136–38),

or when the dreamer informs the Black Knight that the hunt for the hart has been unsuccessful:

"Sir," quod I, "this game is doon.
I holde that this hert be goon;
These huntes konne hym nowher see."
"Y do no fors therof," quod he;
"My thought ys theron never a del."
"By oure Lord," quod I, "y trow yow wel;
Ryght so me thinketh by youre chere." (539–45)

This last passage exemplifies, in the rhyme *del / wel*, another way of creating variety in the repetition of rhyming pairs: by separating the two members syntactically, here with a shift between speakers.

When the meanings signified by two rhyming words are of importance in the narrative, repetition may serve to bring them into prominence and, through the suggestive power of sound symbolism, to reinforce the connections between them. The rhyme thus acquires thematic significance. This happens, in the first part of the poem, with *slep* and *kep*. The activity of sleeping signified by the former and the faculty of attention or memory signified by the latter are related in several ways that bear on the action: lack of sleep results in an indifference on the part of the narrator which the stories of Ceyx and Alcyone and of the Black Knight effectively dispel; sleeplessness leads to reading a book; recollection of the book results in the restoration of sleep; out of sleep comes a dream worthy of being remembered. So, too, the ideas signified in the first part of the poem by the repeated rhyme-words *wif* and *lif* have connections with each other and with the story; these relationships remain relevant, though the rhyming pair itself disappears, in the part of the poem concerned with the successive self-revelations of the Black Knight.[28]

The repeated rhyme-words of most profound thematic import in *The Book of the Duchess* are surely *rowthe* and *trowthe*. The compassion signified by *rowthe* is felt by the narrator in the first part of the poem for Queen Alcyone: her sorrow causes him to experience "such pitee and such rowthe" that he continues to be afflicted by it all the following day (95–100). In the second part of the poem, the Black Knight's complaint strikes the dreamer as "the moste pitee, the moste rowthe" that he ever heard (465–66). *Rowthe* thus means both the feeling of compassion itself and that which elicits it. In these passages, *trowthe* rhymes with *rowthe* in the colloquial expression "by my trowthe," which adds emphasis rather than meaning to the statement in which it appears. The word's potential as a designator of the important concept of fidelity remains latent, here and in two additional occurrences of the expression (552, 591). When, however, the Black Knight, exhorting the dreamer to attend fully to the account he is about to give, says "Swere thy trouthe therto" (752), the meaning of *trouthe* comes to the fore. The oath is proposed in all seriousness, and the dreamer's assent to it allows him to show his own "fidelity" as a sympathetic auditor prepared to hear the story out. Fidelity is, of course, preeminent among the virtues attributed to Lady White in the story itself:

> And trewly for to speke of trouthe,
> But she had had, hyt hadde be routhe.
> Thereof she had so moche hyr del —
> And I dar seyn and swere hyt wel —
> That trouthe hymself over al and al
> Had chose hys maner principal
> In hir that was his resting place. (999–loo5)[29]

When the Black Knight completes the final phase of his account, telling of the years of happiness that he and his lady enjoyed together, the poem moves to its conclusion in several ways. The question Where is she now? asked immediately by the dreamer, brings on the literal revelation that he is at last prepared to understand; the hunting of the h(e)art comes to an end as the hunter-king rides home to his "long castle"; the surrounding dream dissolves as the clock in the castle strikes twelve; and once the narrator has told of his determination, on awakening, to "put this sweven in ryme," the "ryme" itself comes to its self-proclaimed conclusion: "This was my sweven; now hit ys doon." A single couplet, extraordinary in its rhetorical and metrical emphasis, its concentration of meaning, and its emotional charge, is pivotal:

> "She ys ded!" "Nay!" "Yis, be my trouthe!"
> "Is that youre los? Be God, hyt ys routhe!" (1309–10)

Needless to say, the familiarity of the rhyme does nothing to detract from these lines. On the contrary, this final linking of the words *trowthe* and *rowthe* underscores yet again the relationship between faithfulness and compassion that is essential to the meaning of the poem. It is also a sign of something new: the simplest of English rhymes playing their part in a complex drama resonant with human reality.[30]

P A R T II

The Gawain-*Poet*

5

Sir Gawain and the Green Knight:
The Passing of Judgment

It is a commonplace of the criticism of *Sir Gawain and the Green Knight* that the drama acted out at the Green Chapel both ought and ought not to be read as a confessional scene. John Burrow, tracing out the analogy between what he calls the "pretend, secular confession" made by the hero and "a real, sacramental one," finds that the mock-confession "ends, as it should," with a mock-absolution:[1]

> I halde the polysed of that plyght [Bertilak says], and pured as clene
> As thou hadez never forfeted sythen thou watz fyrst borne.
> [I hold you polished as a pearl, as pure and as bright
> As you had lived free of fault since first you were born.] (2393–94)

Elsewhere in late fourteenth-century English poetry, some of the same words are spoken by another confessor the validity of whose role is subject to question:

> I yow assoile by myn heigh power,
> Yow that wol offre, as clene and eek as cleer
> As ye were born.
> (*The Pardoner's Tale*, VI (C) 913–15)

Here, as always, similarity can instruct us about difference. The Green Knight's words, unlike those of Chaucer's Pardoner, are not, to use a modern term, to be taken as "performative." They do not purport to *bring about* the state of grace to which they refer.² Rather, they take the form of a lay judgment, a personal assessment based on observation and analysis of the facts. In the statement "I halde the polysed of that plyght," *halde* means not "pronounce" but "consider."

The judgment passed by the Green Knight on Sir Gawain in these lines comes as a reassurance following upon the hero's first angry outburst. It is preceded by another judgment of a more comparative and conditional nature, based specifically on the fact that Gawain had not yielded to the sexual temptations of the lovely chatelaine:

> I send hir to asay the, and sothly me thynkkez
> On the fautlest freke that ever on fote yede —
>
> . . . .
>
> Bot here yow lakked a lyttel, sir, and lewté yow wonted;
> Bot that watz for no wylyde werke, ne wowyng nauther,
> Bot for ye lufed your lyf; the lasse I yow blame.
> [She made trial of a man most faultless by far
> Of all that ever walked over the wide earth;
>
> . . . .
>
> Yet you lacked, sir, a little in loyalty there,
> But the cause was not cunning, nor courtship either,
> But that you loved your own life; the less, then, to blame.] (2362–68)

Here the element of subjectivity is again explicit: "sothly me thynkkez," "the lasse I yow blame."

Nonsacramental and hence nonauthorized though they may be, many if not most readers of the poem have nonetheless found the Green Knight's judgments satisfying. They are, indeed, the *only* considered judgments the poem provides. Sir Gawain's own anger and agonizings are exaggerated and, to the degree that they are so, slightly comic. As for King Arthur, Queen Guenevere, and the lords and ladies of the court, they do not make any explicit judgments at all. They kiss and embrace their returned comrade, they laugh at his story, they comfort him, and they end by arbitrarily transforming a mark of blame into a badge of honor. It is to the words of the Green Knight that we must look if we seek a rationale for such leniency.

It is all very well to accept the Green Knight's judgments at the end of the poem, but for those of us who do so, a further, formidable question must be faced. Why should we accept his views? If he does not, like a real confessor, speak with institutional and hence putatively divine authority, what kind of authority does he represent? These questions are inseparable from the question of his identity, and by this we must understand his identity not only as the Green Knight, but as the exuberant host and huntsman of Fitt III, Lord Bertilak. Of the various and contradictory interpretations of the figure of the Green Knight that have been put forward in the criticism of the poem, I have found none fully satisfying, and my own answer must itself be couched in paradoxical terms. The Green Knight/Bertilak figure is not, I take it, a spirit emanating from the cyclically renewed world of vegetative nature,[3] nor does he embody the word of God in its severe but ultimately benevolent aspect, descending upon a profane feast,[4] nor is he a latter-day Hades, a lord of the land of the dead,[5] nor is he "a fiendish tempter," if not the Prince of Darkness himself,[6] nor, finally, is he a bluff but genial country gentleman masquerading, mummer fashion, as a kind of green-uniformed *miles gloriosus* who is beheaded, then made to walk, talk, and ride horseback by means of stage magic.[7] I suggest, more generally, that his affiliations are twofold. On the one hand, he belongs to the real world, as medieval human beings experienced it and as we experience it today. On the other hand, he represents an illusory perception, likewise universal, of that reality.[8] Let me begin with the former.

It will be obvious that by "reality" as human beings experience it, I mean, not a changeless realm of absolute values apprehended from the mortal perspective, but the mortal perspective itself: the mutable, transient condition of the embodied psyche.[9] "Life," so defined, is what Sir Gawain had loved and had not wished to lose. In passing judgment on him, the Green Knight accepts this high valuation. He also sees Gawain's fault as temporary, a departure from his true character limited to a particular time (*here*, in line 2366, must be taken to mean "at this point"), and as relative, a "lack" or failure to live up to an ideal, rather than a lecherous or vulgarly covetous deed. He would, we presume, agree with Sir Gawain's own excuse for not accepting the lady's glove: "Iche tolke mon do as he is tan [A man must keep within his compass]" (1811).

Throughout the poems of MS. Cotton Nero A. x., the poet sympathetically conceives of human experience, and hence of human action, as defined by circumstantial limitations. He also conceives of it as part of a natural continuum, as linked by kinship to the experience of other creatures who inhabit sentient bodies, whose behavior is constantly affected by the circumstances in which they find themselves, and who instinctively avoid pain and cling to life. Here is a poet who can take time out to imagine the queasiness of a whale after swallowing an indigestible human morsel — "heartburn," one of my students called it — and who can render the desperation of the wild animals about to be drowned in the Deluge with at least as memorable a poignancy as that of the human friends and lovers who share their fate:

The most mountaynez on more thenne watz no more dryghe,
And theron flokked the folke, for ferde of the wrake.
Sythen the wylde of the wode on the water flette;
Summe swymmed theron that save hemself trawed,
Summe styghe to a stud and stared to the heven,
Rwly wyth a loud rurd rored for dred.
[The tallest of the mountaintops were taking on water;
Folk fled there in flocks, who feared the great doom.
The wild things took to water when woods went under;
Some set out to swim and thought themselves safe;
Some, stranded on the steeps, stared up to heaven
With heart-rending roars that reechoed afar.] (*Purity,* 385–90)[10]

When the narrator concludes his account by saying that "alle cryed for care to
the Kyng of heven" (393), he makes no distinction, among the antecedents of
alle, between "the wylde" and "the folke."

In *Sir Gawain and the Green Knight,* the affinities between human beings
and other living creatures take on particular importance. They are emphasized
by certain descriptive and verbal repetitions which I want now to discuss in
detail.

To begin with, an embodied mortal creature is, by definition, made of vulnerable flesh and blood. The poem contains a series of references to bleeding
which associate the Green Knight with Sir Gawain and, less conspicuously, associate both of them with the hunted deer. Phantasmal and faerielike though he
may seem in the first Fitt, the Green Knight does, it turns out, share with other
living beings the ability to bleed when cut. After Gawain has beheaded him, the
poet tells us, "the blod brayd fro the body, that blykked on the grene [The
blood gushed from the body, bright on the green]" (429), and he later refers to
the headless trunk as "that ugly bodi that bledde" (441). In the first hunting
scene, the deer, thrown into panic by the surrounding beaters, hounds, and
bowmen, are said to bray and bleed (1163), and the hounds are fed afterward
with bread bathed in their blood (1361). Most significantly, there is a clear
echo in the scene at the Green Chapel, after the *barbe* at the end of the Green
Knight's ax-blade has sliced into the flesh of Sir Gawain's neck, of the wording
of the earlier beheading scene. There, the blood of the Green Knight had
blykked, or gleamed, on his green garments. Now, Sir Gawain sees his own
blood *blenk,* or gleam, on the snow (2315). The two verbs are cognate. The
poet, as is his wont, makes us experience the action from the point of view of its
central figure, and we share his brief moment of relief and exultation:

Never syn that he watz burne borne of his moder
Watz he never in this worlde wyghe half so blythe

[Not since he was a babe born of his mother
Was he once in this world one-half so blithe.] (2320–21)

To have been born of a mother is to be a mortal creature, and to see yourself bleed is to know you are still alive.

The poet further links the Green Knight, the hunted deer, and Sir Gawain as fleshly beings by means of a phrase evidently original with him, or at least found nowhere except in his works: *schire grece*, literally, "shining fat." The noun *grece* itself denotes the fatty flesh of human beings only in *Sir Gawain and the Green Knight*.[11] When Sir Gawain beheads the Green Knight in the court, the poet says that the ax "schrank thurghe the schyire grece [of the Green Knight's neck], and schade hit in twynne [cut the flesh cleanly and clove it in twain]" (425). At the end of his first day's hunting, Lord Bertilak, presenting Sir Gawain with his day's winnings, shows him the flesh of the deer, "the schyree grece schorne upon rybbes [the hewn ribs, heavy with fat]" (1378). At the Green Chapel, the wounding of Gawain's neck is described in a line which, like that about the blood gleaming on the snow, unmistakably echoes the earlier passage. The barb at the end of the blade, the poet says, "schrank to the fleshe thurgh the schyre grece" (2313).[12]

A less conspicuous but significant echo links Sir Gawain and the fox as creatures compelled by instinct to avoid a life-threatening blow. At the end of the foxhunt, when the exhausted quarry emerges into view with the pack of hounds at his heels, Bertilak *castez*, or strikes, at him with his sword and, says the narrator, the fox "schunt for the scharp, and schulde haf arered" (1902), that is, he flinched before the blade and intended to have retreated. After Sir Gawain has flinched from the first stroke of the Green Knight's ax and been duly ridiculed, the words he speaks in his own defense include the same verb: "I schunt onez, And so wyl I no more" (2280–81).

As for the boar, a retrospective link between that animal and the Green Knight, which is also a proleptic link with Sir Gawain, is implied by the hewing off of his head at the end of the second hunt and its presentation to Sir Gawain by Lord Bertilak — "a seasonable though somewhat tactless gift," as Burrow wittily calls it.[13]

Warm-blooded creatures, human and nonhuman alike, are also vulnerable to cold, and this aspect of their kinship, too, is signified by the poem's descriptive content. When he sets forth in search of the Green Chapel at the beginning of November, Sir Gawain literally goes out into a cold world. The account of his travels from All Souls' Day to Christmas Eve, in lines 713 ff., falls into two parts. First, we are told of his many battles: not only against loathly and fierce, though otherwise unspecified, "foes," presumably human, but also against dragons, wolves, *wodwos*, bulls, bears, boars, and giants, all ticked off in a mere seven lines (715–17, 720–23). But these fade into the background of quest-romance convention as we learn that the winter weather was a worse hardship still (726), for the hero had to sleep in his iron mail on bare rocks, in falling sleet, with icicles hanging overhead. In the stanza that immediately follows, one of the poem's best-known details describes a company of Gawain's fellow-creatures, the wretched little birds on the bare twigs overhead "that pitosly ther piped for pyne of the colde" (747). At the beginning of Fitt IV, during the night preceding Gawain's fateful departure for the Green Chapel, the poet tells us how the wildest of winter storms kept him from sleeping, but, preoccupied though he is with the fate of his hero, his imagining of the scene outside the castle includes the pain inflicted by the driving snow on the creatures of the forest: "the snawe snitered ful snart, that snayped the wylde [Sleet showered aslant upon shivering beasts]" (2003).[14]

What is signified by descriptive details and verbal repetitions scattered throughout the poem is also signified, on a larger scale, by the hunting scenes considered in their entirety. So much critical acumen has been devoted to exploring the relations between these scenes, taken singly, and the bedroom scenes with which they are paired, that comparatively little has been said about their collective meaning and effect. In them, we see in vividly described action the overwhelming compulsion of vulnerable flesh and blood to save itself from death, as each of a series of three species of animal uses to the utmost the particular means of defense with which nature has endowed it. The deer summon up all their speed; the boar charges out with all his strength; the fox uses all his tricks. Reading or hearing these scenes, we are made to share the point of view of the hunted creatures as much as that of the hunters, hearing with the deer the arrows whizzing under branches at every turn (1161), feeling with the boar the stinging showers of arrows that drive him out into the open (1454–61, 1564–66), seeing with the fox the three hounds, "all gray," who rush toward him out of the hunting station at which he has unwittingly arrived (1712–14). As we follow the action in Sir Gawain's bedroom, seeing it build, on successive mornings, to his fateful acceptance of the green girdle, our attention is shifted periodically to the hunts in progress, where we witness, and much of the time experience vicariously, these desperate maneuvers on the part of living creatures who do not want to die. The proportionate extent of the shifts can easily be measured. Given a silent or oral reading rate of twenty lines per minute on the average, about forty minutes of "narrative time" elapse between Gawain's gleeful acceptance of Bertilak's invitation to stay and his promise to do whatever else he decrees (1079–82), and the moment of his acquiescence (1861). Of those forty minutes, the hunting scenes take up fourteen, or more than a third.

Insofar as the poet has made us sympathetic witnesses of the behavior of the animals in the hunting scenes, he has of course predisposed us to judge Gawain leniently when, bent on saving his own skin, he fails the Exchange of Winnings test. We ourselves thus become implicated in the action. But the sympathy we feel for our fellow-creatures in the poem does not, needless to say, include the Green Knight/Lord Bertilak figure. His flesh may have an outer layer of *schire grece*, he may bleed when his head is cut off, but for him the state of headlessness is strictly temporary—indeed, scarcely an inconvenience. And except for the beheading stroke, he is never, until the spared Sir Gawain joyously confronts him at the Green Chapel, threatened with physical violence. On the contrary. In both his aspects, he is himself the hunter, the threatener, the inflicter of wounds, the dealer out of death and dismemberment. We can imagine him saying, to adapt the words Ted Hughes gives to his "Hawk Roosting," "My manners are cutting off heads."

Yet in the person of Lord Bertilak, he belongs as clearly to the real world as the Green Knight had belonged to the world of phantom and faerie. Though the castle in which he lives materializes suddenly, shimmering and shining like a mirage beyond the hoar oaks of the winter forest, nothing about it is incommensurate with Sir Gawain's previous experience except its superlative splendor: it is "a castel the comlokest that ever knyght aghte [A castle as comely as a knight could own]" (767). (We have no reason to think that this judgment excludes Camelot; compare the similar judgment that Bertilak's wife is lovelier than Guenevere [945].) Sir Gawain is impressed but not shocked or daunted by the lord's great size and fierce demeanor, and he immediately does what all of us do, consciously or unconsciously, when we encounter anyone for the first time in real life: he estimates his age, judging him to be "of hyghe eldee," that is, of fully mature years (844–45).[15] All in all, he thinks him well suited to be the head of an important estate, "to lede a lortschyp in lee of leudez ful gode [to be a master of men in a mighty keep]" (849). All this smacks as much of late fourteenth-century reality as of quest-romance

What is more surprising is the fact that Lord Bertilak's alter ego, the Green Knight, becomes assimilated, by the end of the poem, to the mortal realm. In the course of the fourth Fitt, he changes, and the change he undergoes is also a diminishment. It would perhaps be more accurate to say that a change comes about in the way Sir Gawain and we perceive him, but I see no need to choose between the two alternatives now, if ever. In any case, by becoming, or seeming to become, less than he was, he defines himself as part of a world in which we must expect the end to be heavier than as well as different from the beginning. The lines I allude to are well known:

> Gawain watz glad to begynne those gomnez in halle,
> Bot thagh the ende be hevy haf ye no wonder;
>
> .   .   .   .
>
> A yere yernes ful yerne, and yeldez never lyke,
> The forme to the fynisment foldez ful selden.
> [Gawain was glad to begin those games in hall,
> But if the end be harsher, hold it no wonder,
>
> .   .   .   .
>
> A year passes apace, and proves ever new:
> First things and final conform but seldom.] (495–99)

As seen by King Arthur and the court, and at the same time by the readers or auditors of the first section of the poem, the Green Knight is overwhelmingly splendid and strange, a domineering, enigmatic, uncanny figure, invulnerable to word and blow alike. In the course of the action at the Chapel, these qualities, without our being consciously aware of it, fade away. One might say that between his entrance in the first episode of the poem and his departure in the last, the Green Knight suffers a sea change in reverse, becoming less rich and strange rather than more so. A close look at the descriptive style of the two passages will, I hope, confirm and clarify a shared perception of this difference.

I am aware that the entrance upon the scene of so in every way unprecedented a personage calls for a descriptive set piece — at least from this poet. All his readers know how brilliantly he rises to the occasion. Immediately after the Green Knight has been said to enter the court — "Ther hales in at the halle dor an aghlich mayster [There hurtles in at the hall-door an unknown rider]" (136) — the passage of time is suspended for eighty-five lines, whereupon the action resumes exactly where it had left off, with the line "This hathel heldez hym in and the halle entres [This horseman hurtles in, and the hall enters]" (221). The result, measured again in terms of "narrative time," is that both audiences — the smaller audience within the poem and the larger audience outside it — are made to stare fixedly at the Green Knight in admiration and amazement for over four minutes. This trick obviously cannot be played a second time with equal effect; the second entry of the Green Knight is not attended by another such description. But descriptive material in narrative need not be confined to set pieces; it can be incorporated in varying amounts in the treatment of unfolding events. As he tells us of the confrontation at court, the poet dwells on the Green Knight's least mannerism and action in such loving detail and in such a diversity of concrete and specific terms that he continues throughout the scene to loom larger than life. Nowhere is this more apparent or the effect of the technique more striking than in the account of his behavior after his head has fallen to the floor and gone rolling around to be kicked by the spectators:

> He brayde his bulk aboute,
> That ugly bodi that bledde;
> Moni on of hym had doute,
> Bi that his resounz were redde.
> For the hede in his honde he haldez up even,
> Toward the derrest on the dece he dressez the face
> And hit lyfte up the yghe-lyddez and loked ful brode,
> And meled thus much with his muthe, as ye may now here:
> [His bulk about he haled,
> That fearsome body that bled;
> There were many in the court that quailed
> Before all his say was said.
> For the head in his hand he holds right up;
> Toward the first on the dais directs he the face,
> And it lifted up its lids, and looked with wide eyes,
> And said as much with its mouth as now you may hear:] (440–47)

It is true that in the Green Chapel episode, the poet compensates for the lack of a pictorial set piece by a brilliant display of auditory imagery. Before the Green Knight finally emerges into view, he makes a prolonged and unconscionable racket with his ax and whetstone, and this noise is described in terms of three onomatopoetic similes occupying a total of four long lines, as a result of which we hear it almost as clearly as Sir Gawain himself does:

> Quat! hit clatered in the clyff, as hit cleve schulde,
> As one upon a gryndelston hade grounden a sythe.
> What! hit wharred and whette, as water at a mulne;
> What! hit rusched and ronge, rawthe to here.
> [Lord! it clattered in the cliff fit to cleave it in two,
> As one upon a grindstone ground a great scythe!
> Lord! it whirred like a mill-wheel whirling about!
> Lord! it echoed loud and long, lamentable to hear!] (2201–04)

Nor are details of gesture and action, couched in concrete terms, entirely lacking in the narrative that follows. Once he appears, the Green Knight is said to be "gered as fyrst, Bothe the lyre and the leggez, lokkez and berde [in form as at first, . . . His lordly face and his legs, his locks and his beard]" (2227–28). He sets the handle of his ax to the ground as he stalks along (2230) and uses it to vault over the stream (2231–32); he heaves it up for the first stroke "with alle the bur in his body [With all the force in his frame]" (2261); before striking the second stroke, he glares as angrily as if he were mad (2289); before striking the third stroke he "frounsez bothe lyppe and browe [scowls with both lip and brow]" (2306). But this is all, and all this, I submit, seems pretty thin beer when we compare its collective effect with that of the first episode. This becomes clear when we compare the last detail I quoted, "[he] frounsez bothe lyppe and browe," with a corresponding detail in the scene at court:

> The renk on his rouncé hym ruched in his sadel
> And runischly his rede yghen he reled aboute,
> Bende his bresed broghez, blycande grene,
> Wayved his berde for to wayte quo-so wolde ryse.
> [The stranger on his green steed stirred in the saddle,
> And roisterously his red eyes he rolled all about,
> Bent his bristling brows, that were bright green,
> Wagged his beard as he watched who would arise.] (303–06)

Once the third and last blow has been struck, we are told that the Green Knight desisted, set the haft of his ax on the ground, and rested his arms on the head — a relaxed, placatory, and in every sense down-to-earth series of actions. Immediately afterward, there occurs what A. C. Spearing calls an "almost vertiginous shift of perspective" (p. 189). The shift is spatial, as Spearing says — we suddenly find ourselves looking at Sir Gawain through the eyes of the Green Knight rather than the reverse. And it is accompanied by a more radical shift in our perspective in the psychological sense. For the first time, we are allowed to know *how* the Green Knight is seeing and what he is feeling, and this knowledge strips him once and for all of his aura of strangeness and menace. Come to find out, he likes Sir Gawain very much, just as we do, and has evidently liked him very much all along.

As the Green Knight becomes both more like Sir Gawain and more like ourselves, he becomes less green. A simple corollary of this change is the virtual disappearance, from the descriptive and narrative passages of the final phase of the Chapel episode, of the word itself. It appears immediately after the Knight has struck the second blow, in line 2295, "Then muryly eft con he mele, the mon in the grene [Then merrily does he mock him, the man all in green]" (I shall have something to say later about the wording of this line), and in the succinct account of the departure of the two from the Chapel in lines 2475–78:

> Gawayn on blonk ful bene
> To the kyngez burgh buskez bolde,
> And the knyght in the enker-grene
> Whiderwarde-so-ever he wolde,

[Gawain sets out anew;
Toward the court his course is bent;
And the knight all green in hue,
Wheresoever he wished, he went,]

But it does not appear between the two.[16] In a passage of roughly equal length in Fitt I (containing 405 words versus the 385 of the other), from the moment when Sir Gawain approaches the Green Knight, gisarme in hand (line 375), until he and King Arthur laugh together after the Knight's departure (line 464), the word *green* occurs six times, that is, in about one line out of eight.[17]

The difference in effect between the two episodes is of course more than a matter of frequencies of words and details. As seen at court, the Green Knight is not only dressed in green, he *is* green, as are his ax and his horse:

For uch mon had mervayle quat hit mene myght
That a hathel and a horse myght such a hwe lach,
As growe grene as the gres and grener hit semed,
Then grene aumayl on golde glowande bryghter.
[For much did they marvel what it might mean
That a horseman and a horse should have such a hue,
Grow green as the grass, and greener, it seemed,
Than green fused on gold more glorious by far.] (233–36)

(Note the three occurrences of the word *green* in the last two lines.) Once his knightly credentials have been established, he is called "the Green Knight" (390, 417); in the final reference to him in the episode, the poet uses the adjective as a substantive, saying of King Arthur and Sir Gawain that "at that grene thay laghe and grenne [laugh and grin]" (464). He is also called "the knyght [or gome] in the grene" (377, 405), but these appellations, taken together with the others, give us little or no sense of disjunction between the apparel and the figure itself. Such a disjunction is, however, suggested in a number of ways, and ever more insistently, by the poet's treatment of the Green Knight in the Chapel episode. At the moment when he first greets Sir Gawain, after he has vaulted over the stream on his ax,[18] he is, to be sure, referred to as "that grene gome" (2239). But thereafter he is called "the gome *in* the grene" twice (2227, 2259; emphasis added), and, immediately before the striking of the third blow, "the mon in the grene" (2295). (The presence of the everyday and realistic word *mon* in the line as originally composed is guaranteed by the alliteration on *m*.) The Green Knight himself, in this latter episode, seems to limit his own greenness to his attire. He tells Sir Gawain that he is giving him the fateful girdle as a memento because "hit is grene as my goune" (2396), not "as green as I am."

After he identifies himself as Sir Gawain's host and the husband of the temptress of Fitt III, the Green Knight's physical presence seems to change into that of Bertilak. The poet calls him "the lord" (2403) after he has invited Sir Gawain to return to Hautdesert, and the words in which Gawain finally addresses him indicate that he too now sees him in this embodiment, rather than his earlier one: "But on I wolde yow pray, displeses yow never: Syn ye be lorde of the yonder londe ther I haf lent inne, Wyth yow wyth worschyp . . . How norne ye yowre ryght nome? [But one thing I would learn, if you were not loath, Since you are lord of yonder land where I have long sojourned . . . How runs your right name?]" (2439–43).

When Bertilak explains what has set the sequence of events in motion, he tells Sir Gawain that Morgan le Fay had wanted to bereave the knights of the Round Table of their wits "with glopnyng of that ilke gome that gostlych speked With his hede in his honde bifore the hygh table [With awe of that elvish man that eerily spoke With his head in his hand before the high table]" (2461–62), as though the Green Knight had been someone else entirely: a *gome*, that is, a human being, who spoke "uncannily" as he performed a magical feat, rather like a stage magician who has just succeeded in sawing the lady in half.[19]

The process of demystification which runs its course in the final Fitt of the poem includes, of course, the domestication of the resident witch, Morgan the Goddess. A few words from Lord Bertilak (2463 ff.) turn her into Sir Gawain's aunt, the "old ancient lady" back home who knows him and all his compeers at Arthur's court and would presumably now welcome a second visit from her wandering nephew. The "grieve-Guenevere-and-cause-her-to-die" project, whatever we may or may not wish to make of it, has evidently been abandoned.

It is not enough to say that by the end of the Chapel episode the Green Knight has turned into Lord Bertilak, for the Bertilak of that episode differs from the Bertilak of Fitts II and III in the same way that the Green Knight at the Chapel differs from the Green Knight at court. In the interior scenes at Hautdesert, we see the host continually laughing, leaping around, thinking up ideas for fun and games, talking and joking extravagantly, and generally behaving in wild and crazy fashion, to the point where either those around him or he himself, depending on how we want to interpret line 1087, cannot imagine what he may do next. In the exterior scenes, as the leader of the hunts, he personifies to the fullest imaginable extent the joy of vigorous and masterful bodily activity, exultantly galloping from place to place, mounting and dismounting again throughout the day of the deer hunt; confidently striding into the running stream to confront the greatest of all wild boars; snatching the dead fox from the jaws of the hounds and waving it exuberantly in the air as he shouts to summon the rest of the huntsmen. Indeed, he might have been designed to personify the pronouncement of Gaston Phoebus in his late fourteenth-century treatise on hunting, that "hunters lyven in this world most joyfully of eny other men."[20] At the Chapel, once the Green Knight has set his ax down, leaned on it, and begun to assume his Lord Bertilak aspect, he remains immobile. In television parlance, he turns into a "talking head," saying his sensible say jovially, to be sure, but without the extravagance and irony that had characterized his language at Hautdesert.

At the beginning of this chapter, I suggested that the *Gawain*-poet presents the Green Knight as, on the one hand, emanating from the real world, that is, the mutable and transitory world in which we live out our lives as human beings, and on the other hand, as representing an illusory view of that world. More specifically, our view of him as he first appears in the poem involves an admixture of illusion, as does that of the court. As the action plays itself out, our view of him becomes more realistic, via a process of what I have called diminishment or demystification. The two views correspond to an earlier and a later phase of human experience generally. John Ganim has said that the action of the poem is "a journey into age,"[21] and this observation seems to me true in more ways than one. To make clear what I mean, let me derive from the story of Sir Gawain as I have analyzed it a more general, paradigmatic story, a story whose central figure is someone much like ourselves as we would like to see ourselves and to have others see us. In the first part of this story, someone older than we, having dominant or authoritative status, seems to us awesome, charged with a magical aura, invulnerable, larger than life.[22] Later, this same being comes to be seen as less awesome, less magical, less amazingly large — in short, as more like us. This change in mode of perception is linked with a change in ourselves: we learn that we are not quite all we had hoped we would be and had believed we could be. In the *Gawain*-poet's version of the story, we are led via a series of unpredictable, bewildering, and variously discomfiting situations to what seems the very brink of death,[23] at which point we betray an ideal to which we had confidently dedicated ourselves. After all is over, we are judged benevolently by a person or persons older than we, told that our trials are at an end, and assured that, even though our behavior did not measure up to an absolute standard of perfection, we have been found, not wanting, but acceptable, quite all right, in fact. The name I give this paradigm is maturation. I believe it corresponds to the experience of individuals of either gender, and it is what I see as the theme of *Sir Gawain and the Green Knight*.[24] Thinking about it, I am reminded of a line from Wordsworth: the Green Knight and Lord Bertilak, as they merge into a single presence, simultaneously "fade into the light of common day." We have come through intact — indeed, we have done well — but neither we nor the world is as wonderful as we had thought.[25]

Having been so bold as to write these words, I must immediately qualify them. The poem we call *Sir Gawain and the Green Knight* is neither a myth nor a fairy tale, nor is the story presented in spare, paradigmatic terms. It is a richly detailed narrative, coming to us from the hand of a poet who was fascinated by the circumstantial and contingent, the exigencies of time and place. The human identity of the central figure is specific in terms of gender and profession: he is a knight, the liege man of the king in the olden days of "Arthurez wonderez" (27). He thus belongs to a fictional past distant from the present time in which the poem was written. Yet his knightly status, which is kept in the foreground throughout, is relevant to that present. Toward the end of the fourteenth century, professionalism — money paid for services rendered — had encroached upon the older chivalric ideals of feudal fidelity and Christian selflessness,[26] and Sir Gawain is portrayed as an embodiment and upholder of those ideals. The meaning of his emblem, the pentangle, is expounded in terms of an interlocking set of *knightly* virtues, put into practice in activities proper to a knight, both afield, "in melly" (644), and at court among his compeers, "in mote" (635). In his angry burst of self-denunciation after all has been revealed to him, Sir Gawain accuses himself of having forsaken his *kynde*, his nature, "that is larges and lewté that longez to knyghtez" (2380–81). *Larges* "largesse" is the *fraunchise* or generosity enumerated among the five virtues signified by one of the five points of the pentangle; *lewté* "loyalty" is the *trawthe* that is "betokened" by the design generally (626). A moment earlier, the Green Knight had said that "as perle bi the quite pese is of prys more, So is Gawayn, in god fayth, bi other gay knyghtez [As pearls to white peas, more precious and prized So is Gawain, in good faith, to other gay knights]" (2364–65). The Green Knight/Bertilak figure is also a knight, but he is more: he is also a lord, the head of a knightly company, and this is one reason his judgment at the end of the poem carries weight. I have already quoted Gawain's estimate of him on first acquaintance, that he was well suited "to lede a lortschyp in lee of leudez ful gode" (849). That is exactly what the members of Arthur's court, complaining of the king's foolishness in involving himself in a *cavelacion* (683), had said Sir Gawain might have become if he had not committed himself to being beheaded:

> A lowande leder of ledez in londe hym wel semez,
> And so had better haf been then britned to noght,
> Hadet wyth an alvish mon, for angardez pryde.
> [A great leader of lords he was likely to become,
> And better so to have been than battered to bits
> Beheaded by an elf-man, for empty pride!] (679–81)

In terms of the legendary world of romance, Sir Gawain is the nephew of the most glorious king in Christendom, and Bertilak is nobody we have ever heard of. In terms of the poem's late medieval present, Sir Gawain is a member of a household and Lord Bertilak is the head of one. His judgment of the hero carries the weight of time-honored institutional as well as generational authority. In praising him as a knight, he holds up in pristine brightness an ideal that the passage of time had tarnished.

Kent Hieatt has pointed out that the echo of the opening line of *Sir Gawain* toward the end of the poem — "After the segge and the asaute watz sesed at Troye" — occurs at line 2525. This number seems clearly to allude, as he maintains, to the five fives of the pentangle; moreover, it corresponds in its symmetry to the 1212 lines of *Pearl*.[27] The reiterative long line is followed by an additional five lines, the single bob-and-wheel sequence that closes the poem (2526–30). In the first two lines of the wheel, the poet says that many such adventures have befallen in the past. In the third and fourth lines, which are the last lines of all, he invokes the divine judgment that follows life on earth, referring to Christ in terms of his human suffering at the time of the Crucifixion:

> Now that bere the croun of thorne,
> He bryng uus to his blysse!
> [May He that was crowned with thorn
> Bring all men to His bliss!]

This concluding invocation stands outside the circle, implied by reiteration, that encloses the dramatized narrative. That narrative, as we know, is set in a Christian world, much of it at two Christian courts. Even when the Green Knight first speaks to Sir Gawain in what had seemed a chapel fit for a fiend's devotions, he exclaims, reassuringly, "God the mot loke [May God keep you]!" (2239). I am certain that if we could ask the poet about the state of Gawain's soul after his return, he would tell us, perhaps somewhat bewildered by our inquiry, that of course he went to confession, told the whole story to a priest (as he had already told it to the entire court), and was absolved.[28] But the fact remains that he did not choose to say so. The poem as he wrote it ends with the nonsacramental, nonauthorized judgment of a human being by other human beings. In this respect, it anticipates, fleetingly yet clearly, the passing of judgment from the divine to the earthly realm which will so change the meaning of the Arthurian legends as they are handed down, from poet to poet, to our own day.

Addendum

In note 9 of this chapter, I make a distinction between readers of the poem who see the world of Arthur's court as innocent in terms of Christian doctrine and those who see it as condemned. Since the chapter was written, the former view has been presented, with a telling difference, by David Aers in " 'In Arthurus Day': Community, Virtue, and Individual Identity in *Sir Gawain and the Green Knight*," in *Community, Gender, and Individual Identity*, pp. 153–78 (see note 26, above), and, more recently, in "Christianity for Courtly Subjects: Reflections on the *Gawain*-Poet," in *A Companion to the Gawain-Poet*, ed. Derek Brewer and Jonathan Gibson (Cambridge, England: D.S. Brewer, 1997), pp. 91–101. For Aers, the poem presents "as unironic a celebration of 'the courtly culture of fourteenth century England' as ones provided by the ideal models in courtesy books or writings such as those by the Chandos Herald" (pp. 157–58). He sees Christianity, or rather a socially adapted form of it, as "unproblematically assimilated" into this culture, where "the King, knight, and ladies move easily from mass to games and feasting in hall, from public sacred space to public secular space with both areas legitimized by 'clerkez who, like the poet himself, join in the lay peoples' celebrations" (p. 157). But Aers opens his discussion by observing that the poem "set[s] aside the economic, political, and military practices of the landowning class in the late fourteenth century, as it looks back to 'Arthurus day' " (p. 153). It omits all concern with the economic and political forces operative in the poet's time; "also blocked out are the conflicts within the ruling class, including armed struggle between magnates and king, culminating in the deposition and murder of the king whose connections with the region in whose language the poem is written were so extraordinarily close" (p. 154). In the end, "even in his sharpest rhetorical self-flagellation, Gawain sees himself still very much part of the heroic, competitive community" (p. 172) which encapsulates him in the poem. His response to Sir Bertilak displays his continuing " 'intense and sensitive concern for reputation'," while ignoring basic theological concepts like grace, charity, and sacramental purification (pp. 172–73).

In addition to being limited in these ways, Aers argues, the poem ends by abandoning certain "troublesome issues" (p. 176) it has introduced, issues raised by "the privatization . . . of space" at Hautdesert (unlike Camelot) and the resultant "privatization or interiorization of consciousness" (exhibited in such passages as 1658–63, in which we are shown a contrast between the hero's troubled thoughts and his smoothly courteous outward manner). After the episode at the Green Chapel is over, and Gawain has returned to Arthur's court, there occurs an "exuberant and fraternal honouring" which is "simultaneously an affirmation of the solidarity in the upper-class community, . . . confidently projected into a future ('evermore after') which includes the poet's present" (175). Gawain may see himself as reincorporated into this community, but the poet provides no such evidence of his inner state as he has given us earlier. "Apparently [Gawain's] public identity will coexist with a shadowy private self bearing judgments and language which contradict it" (177). The poet refuses to imagine a new identity which might take shape from these shadows. Rather, he "just leaves us with this disjunction," unable to "escape [his] own historical horizons" (pp. 177–78).

While I respect these arguments, I cannot agree that exclusivity of social setting in fiction is an *esthetic* fault (one thinks, for example, of James's *The Golden Bowl*). To reprove the author of *Sir Gawain and the Green Knight* for ignoring actual and imminent threats to "the common knightly culture in the changed circumstances of the fourteenth century," in retreating to the time of King Arthur, is not only to judge him as a member of society rather than as a poet, but to project into his world political views held by the illuminati of a later millennium. When the *Gawain*-poet does talk, in *Patience*, of poverty and social subservience, he sees them, taking his cue from the Beatitudes, as indignities to be suffered meekly, rather than as causes for rebellion. Here, too, I assume that he falls short in Aers's terms.

As for the ending of the poem, I share the response of many, if not most readers in seeing nothing problematic about the fact that the poet, winding things up after the suspense is over, does not take time to describe Gawain's inner response to the court's insistence on celebrating his acquisition of the green girdle. Presumably he still feels as he felt when he and the Green Knight were alone together: furious at himself and the lady and burning with humiliation. I suggest that in the final episode, the members of the court too seem to have grown older. The king and queen "comfort" the returned hero as parents might (2513), and the laughter of all present echoes that of Bertilak-cum-Green Knight, just before he pronounces his authoritative judgment (2389). It implies that Gawain's agonizings have something about them of the melodramatic self-centeredness of youth and may justifiably evoke our amusement along with our sympathy as the story ends.

6

Pearl's *"Maynful Mone"*

It is true of the memorable poetic image that many lines of meaning converge toward it, and many lines of expressive force correspondingly radiate from it. In this chapter I shall trace a number of lines or radii whose center is the rising of the "maynful mone" in *Pearl*, line 1093.

The simile appears at the beginning of the nineteenth, or next-to-last, section of the poem. The two preceding sections have given an account of the celestial Jerusalem, as seen and described by Saint John in the Book of Revelation. Section 17 tells of the architectural plan of the city and the precious substances of which it is made; section 18 tells how God and the Lamb illuminate it, so that there is no need of sun or moon, and how the River of Life flows from the throne of God, with the twelve Trees of Life, bearing their fruit twelve times a year, ranged alongside it. The link word of this latter section is *mone*, and the word makes its farewell appearance in the lines I am concerned with here. The simile of the rising moon introduces the account of the processional within the city, where the dreamer ultimately sees his beloved Pearl. It is thus a transitional image, standing between a phase of the dream that corresponds with scriptural authority and a phase of personal experience, vouchsafed to the dreamer individually as a result of the maiden's intercession. (The poet's account of the processional does contain many details drawn from Revelation, but these materials are freely adapted and rearranged. Briefly, the poet converts the tableaux of the original into a scene of ongoing activity.)[1]

I quote eight lines, of which the vehicle and tenor proper of the simile ("as . . . so") take up the first four (lines 1093–1100):

> Ryght as the maynful mone con rys
> Er thenne the day-glem dryve al doun,
> So sodaynly on a wonder wyse
> I was war of a prosessyoun
> This noble cite of ryche enpryse
> Watz sodanly ful wythouten sommoun
> Of such vergynez in the same gyse
> That watz my blysful an-under croun.
> [As the great moon begins to shine
> While lingers still the light of day,
> So in those ramparts crystalline
> I saw a procession wend its way.
> Without a summons, without a sign,
> The city was full in vast array
> Of maidens in such raiment fine
> As my blissful one had worn that day.]

With regard to the compound *day-glem* (literally, "day-gleam") in line 1094, it should be observed that, whereas the modern reader thinks of a gleam as something fitful or fugitive, like the vanished "visionary gleam" of Wordsworth's *Intimations* ode, *glem* in Middle English could mean "beam or radiance of emitted light," as in *sonne glem* ("sunbeam"). *Day-glem* thus means "light of day."[2] The figurative use of the verb *dryve* with reference to the waning of the light at evening has parallels in other passages of Middle English poetry, where it is linked by alliteration with *day* (as here) or *dark*, or both.[3] Line 1094 cannot be translated literally; a reasonably close modern approximation would be "before daylight has wholly died away."

The mighty moon that rises while the last of the light of day lingers on earth is the moon at or near the full, appearing low in the east opposite the sun, which has just set in the west.[4] I feel certain that the poet has the full moon specifically in mind. If so, it is possible that *maynful* in line 1093 was originally two words, in which case "the mayn ful mone" would be the "the great full moon" itself.[5] In any case, the moon seen as a circle in the eastern sky is a fit symbol of the celestial realm within which the processional is about to appear. The place of its rising — *oriens* in Latin, "rising" and, by transference, "east" — is traditionally associated with the advent of Christ.[6] And its circular shape links it with several other exemplars of circularity in the poem, all associated with the kingdom of heaven.

The first and most important of these is, of course, the pearl. Invoked as a terrestrial gem in the opening stanza, in terms that gradually come to suggest a lovely young woman, the pearl is invested with a series of attributes, of which roundness is the third. First, it is pleasing to princes (or to a prince; the Middle English text does not have the apostrophe that would force the phrase to commit itself to one or the other reading in modern English). Second, it is peerless among gems that come "out of oryent" (in view of the symbolic significance of the east in the Christian tradition, *oryent* must be counted, along with *prynce* and others, among the bivalent terms in the passage having sacred as well as secular meanings). Third, the pearl is "round"; the attribute is here passed over lightly, merging immediately into the more general one of "rekennes," "rightness" in "uche aray," every setting.

When the pearl reappears in its symbolic aspect in the parable of the merchant, told by the Pearl maiden in section 13, it is again said to be round. It resembles the kingdom of heaven, "the reme of hevenesse clere" (line 735), "For hit is wemlez, clene and clere, / And endelez rounde, and blythe of mode" (lines 737–38). Roundness is an attribute of the heavenly kingdom because it is "endless." Here again the reader's sense of the modern value of a Middle English word may blur the meaning of the original. We tend to think of something "endless" as existing "without cessation." A circle can be traced around and around without stopping, as the planets rotate perpetually and move perpetually in their curved orbits. But *endelez* here means not so much "without an *end*" as "without *ends*" — that is, without termination rightward or leftward in space.[7] Being "end-less" in this sense, the circle contrasts with another figure, the line.

The two figures appear in *Pearl* with complementary symbolic significance. The line takes visible form as the *rawe*, or "row," of laborers in the parable of the vineyard, a detail added by the poet to the account in Matthew. When the time of payment comes, the lord of the vineyard tells his steward to set the workers in a row, in such a way (we infer) that those who began working earliest in the day stand "first," at the head of the line, and those who began latest stand "last," at the foot. The sequence is thus a spatial analogue to the temporal sequence made up of the successive hours of the day; each has a beginning and an end. The lord's decree concerning the order of payment reverses the expected order of both time and space. The line of laborers is to be read "back" in time, from later to earlier, and "backward" in space, as if, in terms of Western culture, a line of print were to be read from right to left instead of from left to right. Both reversals fulfill the prophecy that precedes the parable in the Gospel (it is the last verse of chapter 19; the parable follows in 20.1–16): "But many that are first shall be last, and the last shall be first." The prophecy is reiterated at the end of the parable in the final words of the lord to one of the those who have "murmured" against his decree: "And many that are first, shall be last: and the last shall be first."

Now the prophecy itself admits of two different and complementary interpretations, both of which are found in the patristic commentaries.[8] According to one interpretation it signifies reversal: the first and the last will change places. According to the other it signifies equation: the first and the last will be identical. The former interpretation applies to the literal subject matter of the parable, to the line of laborers with its series of positions in space corresponding to a series of points in time. The latter applies to what is signified by the parable, to the reward of eternal life in God's presence symbolized by the perfect roundness of the pearl. All the saved participate equally in this reward, and its value is infinite, literally "beyond compare," unlike earthly rewards, which are measured in terms of a quasi-linear scale of values or degrees ranging from high to low. In the parable the reward is symbolized by the daily penny, given to all who labored in the vineyard regardless of when they came to work. In earthly terms not all can be paid simultaneously; the line is a means of making the process of payment simpler and more orderly. In heaven the blessed have no places relative to one another; all are paid as one. Their relationship is like that of the 360 degrees of a circle, which can be counted off from any arbitrarily chosen point on the circumference.

Roundness, then, is an important symbol in *Pearl*; what it symbolizes is abstraction from the linear or dimensional, two-ended mode of earthly space, time, and value. In addition to the pearl, the poem contains three other emblems of roundness, though the attribute is not predicated of any of them explicitly. The first of these is the crown, which metaphorically signifies the kingly or queenly rank of all who enter the heavenly kingdom. The Pearl maiden is wearing a crown when the dreamer sees her on the other side of the stream; she doffs it to greet him but puts it on again to instruct and correct him. Mary, too, has a crown, as the dreamer knows. Puzzled by the maiden's assertion that she is now a queen in heaven, he wonders if she has displaced the Virgin, and asks (lines 427–28):

> The croune fro hyr quo moght remwe
> Bot ho hir passed in sum favour?
> [Now who could assume her crown, by right,
> But she in some feature fairer were?]

As the form of his question shows, he is thinking of crowns in terms of earthly scales of merit and rank. The order in terms of which Mary is "empress," as the maiden says, over all those who are kings and queens in heaven is not comparative but organic, mutually corroborative and fulfilling. The relationships among its members are like those among the parts of a living body, as is explained in lines 457 ff. in accordance with Saint Paul's simile in 1 Cor. 12. Finally, all the members of the procession within the celestial Jerusalem are crowned "of the same fasoun" as the maiden who has appeared to the dreamer, just as all wear "the blysful perle" even though in the parable there is but a single pearl of great price.

A second emblem of circularity, akin in significance to the crown, is the garland. After awakening from his dream, the narrator bemoans his expulsion from the heavenly kingdom but consoles himself by reflecting that his pearl is safely established there (lines 1185–88):

> If hit be veray and soth sermoun
> That thou so stykez in garlande gay,
> So wel is me in thys doel-doungoun
> That thou art to that Prynsez paye.
> [If you in a garland never sere
> Are set by that Prince all-provident,
> Then happy am I in dungeon drear
> That he with you is well content.]

The fact that the word *garland* in Middle English could mean "coronet" or "crown" (though the modern meaning, "wreath of flowers," seems primary in line 1186)[9] is additional evidence for the symbolic affiliations I am concerned with here.

Third, there is the penny in the parable. Since it is a daily wage, it was identified by the patristic writers with the "daily bread" asked for in the Lord's Prayer. And this in turn was identified with the communion wafer, likewise round in shape, "shown us every day," as the poet says (line 1210), by the priest at mass.[10]

Circularity of an abstract sort is exemplified by the plot and design of the poem itself. In its beginning is its end. In the first section the narrator lies down on the flower bed where his pearl is buried; his soul leaves that "spot" during the dream, but his body remains there (lines 61-62). In the last section he returns to the point of departure (lines 1171–72):

> Then wakned I in that erber wlonk;
> My hede upon that hylle watz layde.
> [I waked in that same garden-plot,
> My head on that same mound was laid.]

The *hylle* is the *huyle* or "mound" of line 41, "where perle hit trendeled doun [where Pearl went tumbling wide]," and the *hyul* of line 1205, over which, as the dreamer says, he received his fateful vision.[11] His gesture, after he awakens, of reaching out in longing — "Ther as my perle to grounde strayd I raxled [I stretched my hand where Pearl had strayed]"[12] — repeats that described in line 49 — "Bifore that spot my honde I spenned [Before that spot . . . I stretched my hand]." This circularity in the plot of the poem is found also in its verbal patterning. Each section is linked to the preceding one by the reiteration of rhyme words, and the rhyme word of the last section, which is also that of the first line of the poem, links the end back to the beginning to complete the design.[13]

The simile of the "maynful" (or "mayn ful") "mone" is significant in that it participates in a symbolic opposition between roundness and linearity that is thematically important in *Pearl*. But it also conveys a visual image, and in so doing it bears on the description that follows in an interesting way. Since we "see" the full moon just before we "see" the procession within the city, it is as if the moon's circular outline were superimposed on the city's perimeter — as if the celestial Jerusalem, for the purposes of this part of the vision, were round rather than square. The kingdom of heaven *is* round — the maiden has said so in expounding the attributes of the pearl of great price in section 13. If we object that the same city cannot be both round and square, we are thinking, like the dreamer, in terms of spatial dimensions as we experience them on earth. But the rules of geometrical or positional space (as one might term it) do not apply to the heavenly kingdom as it is imagined by the *Pearl* poet. For one thing, the river that separates the dreamer from the maiden is not "real"; it is a spatial symbol of the division between mortality and immortality. In order to "cross" it, we must change not our position in space but our mode of existence, through the death of the body. As soon as the dreamer takes the apparent dimensions of the dream scene literally and rushes down the bank toward the river, his dream dissolves. Again the maiden appears to him (and us) to be standing on the opposite bank, within hailing distance. But she is also discovered in the procession within the city, and we realize, on consideration, that in a sense she is always there. Her seeming position in space during the conversation within the dream symbolizes her divinely vouchsafed role as instructor-intercessor.[14]

This lack of conformity to the rules of positional space — space as we know it — is even more striking in the treatment of the procession. From the moment the dreamer first sees it, it fills the city (lines 1097–1100):

> This noble cite of ryche enpryse
> Watz sodanly ful wythouten sommoun
> Of such vergynez in the same gyse
> That watz my blysful an-under croun.
> [Without a summons, without a sign,
> The city was full in vast array
> Of maidens in such raiment fine
> As my blissful one had worn that day.]

This being the case, it must be moving not through any particular street but through all the streets, approaching the throne from every direction as if by way of the convergent radii of a circle "on golden *gatez* that glent as glasse" (line 1106). This centripetal movement complements the centrifugal movement of the River of Life as the poet describes it in section 18: there it is said to course powerfully "thurgh uche a strete" (line 1059). Again, if the river fills every street, there is no room, in earthly terms, for the procession. And what is true of space must be true also of time: if the procession occupies every part of the city, it is also simultaneously setting out, arriving, and moving at every point between departure and arrival.

I said earlier that the simile of the risen full moon is transitional, linked retrospectively to authoritative revelation and ushering in a personal, though equally valid, phase of the dream vision. It is transitional also in another way. The orbit of the moon, in the Ptolemaic system of astronomy, is the boundary between earthly and heavenly realms.[15] Although the word *sublunary* had not yet entered the language in the *Pearl* poet's time, expressions such as "under (the) moon" and "under the circle of the moon" were conventional designations in Middle English for the realm of earthly existence.[16] Since the moon as seen from earth is variable, perpetually waxing and waning, it was and is a natural emblem of the vicissitudes of mortal fate.[17]

In three of its appearances as link word in section 18 of *Pearl, mone* is used in the phrase "an-under mone," meaning "on earth." The dreamer says, of the sight of the celestial Jerusalem, that (lines 1081–83)

> An-under mone so great merwayle
> No fleschly hert ne myght endeure,
> As quen I blusched upon that bayle,
> [Beneath the moon so much amazed
> No fleshly heart could bear to be
> As by that city on which I gazed,]

and that (lines 1090–92)

> Hade bodyly burne abiden that bone,
> Thagh alle clerkez hym hade in cure,
> His lyf were loste an-under mone.
> [Had a man in the body borne that boon,
> No doctor's art, for fame or fee,
> Had saved his life beneath the moon.]

It is his spirit, not his "fleshly heart," that has experienced the vision, as he has told us at the beginning of section 2 (lines 61–62):

> Fro spot my spyryt ther sprang in space:
> My body on balke ther bod in sweven.
> [My soul forsook that spot in space
> And left my body on earth to bide.]

The spirit returns at the end of the dream to rejoin the body unharmed. (In view of the fact that the poet distinguishes so carefully between sublunary and translunary realms, it would seem that the dreamer's use of the phrase "under mone" when he inquires of the maiden where she and her companions dwell is to be taken as yet another sign of his characteristic mode of misapprehension. "As ye ar maskeles under mone [As you under moon are flawless found]," he says, "your wonez schulde be wythouten mote [Your lodgings should be wholly bright]" [lines 923–24]. They are not, of course, "under mone," any more than the city of Jerusalem the maiden is talking about is in the land of Judea.)

The moon in *Pearl* faces in two directions, literally and symbolically; it has both positive and negative aspects, a *sensus bonus* and a *sensus malus*. Seen as a circle of radiant white, the full moon can join the pearl it resembles in symbolizing the heavenly kingdom.[18] But the moon is also, by virtue of its astronomical position, associated with the limitations and flaws of mortality. Unlike the pearl, it is not only variable but maculate. The poet has singled out this latter characteristic for disapproval in explaining why it is excluded from the celestial Jerusalem (lines 1069–70):

> The mone may therof acroche no myghte;
> To spotty ho is, of body to grym.
> [The moon has in that reign no right;
> Too spotty she is, of body austere.]

But the negative aspects of the moon are canceled out in its final appearance, as the risen full moon of the simile that opens in section 19. Here the moon becomes a wonderfully apt symbol not only of the content of the dreamer's experience but of the manner of its befalling. For wherever his spirit may be during the dream, he himself is an inhabitant of the sublunary realm, and the rising of the full moon is a "sublunary" event in the most exact sense possible: it can be seen only from an earthly vantage point, by one looking up at the heavens.

Strictly speaking, the tenor of the simile is not the city within which the procession is about to materialize but the dreamer's sudden awareness that a procession is in progress: "So sodanly on a wonder wyse / I watz war of a prosessyoun." The risen full moon is a sight of which we may indeed "suddenly" become aware. Gaining in brightness as darkness falls, it draws attention to itself in the sky where it has actually been present for some time. So too the procession, though from the dreamer's point of view it suddenly fills the city, has in a profounder sense been there all along. Everything in the poem thus far has been preparing him to see it.

Considered as a natural event, the rising of the full moon has an additional and more important dimension of significance. It takes place at the end of the day, at the time in the parable of the vineyard when the laborers have finished their work and are about to be paid. A retrospective glance at the parable as told in *Pearl* reveals that the later passage in fact echoes the earlier one, though the repetition involved is more likely to attract the attention of the exegete than that of the common reader.

In lines 529–40 the Pearl maiden tells of the sending into the vineyard of the last group of laborers at the eleventh hour, called "evensonge" by the poet. This occurs "on oure byfore the sonne go doun." Then "the worlde bycom wel broun":

> The sunne watz doun and hit wex late.
> To take her hyre he made sumoun;
> The day watz al apassed date.
> [The sun long since had sunk from view;
> He summoned them to take their pay;
> The day had passed its limit due.]

(The statement that "the worlde bycom wel broun," I take it, refers to the thickening of dusk before darkness falls rather than to full darkness.[19] In terms of the later passage, the laborers are summoned before daylight has wholly died away.) The stanza describing the events of the eleventh hour and later and the stanza containing the simile of the rising full moon have the same B-rhyme, and the two stanzas share three rhyming words: *doun, sumoun,* and *boun* ["arranged, fixed"]. Of these, *sumoun* especially is an echo with a difference. The members of the procession within the celestial city need not be "summoned," for they have already been both called and chosen.

What the dreamer sees in section 19 is in fact the participation of the blessed in the reward symbolized by the penny in the parable. Unlike the row of laborers, the "lines" formed by those who move through the streets have neither beginning nor end. Nor can anyone in them be thought of as first or last because the entire group is constantly starting out, arriving, and moving at every intermediate point. The only specified position is that of the Lamb, who leads the way. He is the "head" of which the members of the procession are the body, since his voluntary self-sacrifice (of which his visible, freshly bleeding wound is the emblem) has made salvation possible and has established the church through whose sacraments the individual soul attains it. Salvation itself, the heavenly reward, is experienced as an eternity of bliss — eternity in the sense not of perpetual duration but of release from linear time.

Remembering that the daily penny was identified not only with salvation but with the daily bread of the Lord's Prayer, which in turn was identified with the communion wafer, we see that the blessed souls are in fact in a state of eternal communion with the divine presence. The penny in the parable is an element in a symbolic representation, but the consecrated communion wafer is real and symbolic at once. It is a part of the earthly experience of the faithful and a foretaste of the life to come. The comparison in line 1115 of the members of the procession to maidens at mass is profoundly in point: the celebration of communion on earth and the celebration within the celestial city are related to each other much as the vehicle and tenor of a metaphor are related. The latter is what the former means.

Following out the lines of meaning that converge on the simile of the "maynful mone" in *Pearl*, we are led into a number of interrelated areas of medieval learning: geometry (more exactly, the branch of geometry now called topology), theology, astronomy, patristic exegesis. The image is to that extent recondite, drawn from books rather than from life. But it is also based on a universal experience, an event that human beings have witnessed in all ages, and one to which many of them, not least the *Pearl* poet, have responded as a sign of the splendor of the created world. It thus typifies the combination of artifice and simplicity, of intellectuality and human emotion, that has perennially attracted and rewarded the attention of the critics of *Pearl*.

The Many and the One: Contrasts and Complementarities in the Design of Pearl

My starting point is a contrast between two aspects of sound patterning in *Pearl* that created difficulties for me in my attempt to replicate in modern English the phonic design, as well as the sense, of this most intricately wrought of medieval poems.[1] The first and more apparent of these difficulties is posed by the multiple rhymes the stanza form requires. In accordance with the scheme ABABABABBCBC, each of the poem's 101 stanzas must contain four instances of the A-rhyme and six instances of the B-rhyme. In addition, the final link-word of each section of the poem must appear as a C-rhyme at the end of five stanzas, rhyming with five other words. The second difficulty has its source, not in the repetitive demands of the poem's design, but in the perceptible diversity of its rhyme-sounds and rhyme-words. These two features pull the language of the poem in opposite directions. Once aware of their interaction, a translator is bound to try to recreate it.

Diversity of sound is part of a many-ness or multiplicity that I find pervasive in *Pearl*, exemplified also in the shifts of mode or genre of discourse, of emotional tone, of style, and of figuration that take place from section to section of the poem. As diversity of sound plays against a single prosodic design, so these other diversities play against the single line of the poem's dramatic action, which brings its central figure from an initial state of bafflement and despair to a final state of understanding and reconciliation.[2]

An opportunity to restate general impressions about repetition and diversity of sound in factual terms is provided by another poem in Middle English which shares its prosodic form with *Pearl*. *Pety Job*, that is, *Little Job*, consists of expanded paraphrases of passages taken from nine of the speeches made by Job in the biblical story, amounting in all to fifty-seven stanzas, or 684 lines, somewhat more than half the length of *Pearl*.[3] *Pety Job* has never been classed among the high watermarks of religious poetry in English, and few, I think, would quarrel with the judgment that its author, though competent, was not a notably gifted versifier. Reading it with an attentive ear, one becomes aware, as one does not in reading *Pearl*, that certain rhyme-sounds and rhyme-words are being used again and again without rhetorical or other expressive justification. Tabulations of passages of equal length bear out this comparative impression, and I have presented, in an appendix, complete figures for the first ten stanzas (lines 1–120) of each poem.

As a prelude to my discussion of the more deep-seated aspects of the interplay between diversity and repetition in *Pearl*, I offer a summary of the poem as a whole. The narrator describes himself at the outset as inconsolably mourning a lost pearl; we soon see that he is speaking metaphorically of a lost maiden. He goes to the herb garden where she is buried, falls asleep on her burial mound, and has a dream. The maiden appears to him, and they engage in a long conversation, in the course of which she dispels a number of misunderstandings on his part: that he can cross the dream-space separating them as if it were space on earth; that in becoming a queen in heaven, she must have usurped the title of Mary; that she did not live long enough or accomplish enough to merit her high reward in the afterlife; that in becoming the bride of the Lamb she must have displaced all other women; that the Jerusalem in which she dwells is in the kingdom of Judea. Her explanations reveal some of the differences between supernatural and earthly realms that the human mind finds difficult, if not impossible, to comprehend: all are of highest rank in the heavenly kingdom; the reward of eternal bliss, being absolute, has no relation to degrees of merit; thousands upon thousands of those who died in infancy are brides of the Lamb and share the single pearl of great price. Her discourse includes exegesis, argument, narration, and eulogy, supported by parables and other biblical passages, drawn from the Gospels and Revelation.[4] When the dreamer has heard it all, he makes a request reflecting another misunderstanding of the same kind as his earlier ones: he would like to be taken to the great walled city where she lives and to see her "blissful bower," that is, her chamber, within it. At this point, he learns that the dream has been a divine dispensation: he has already been granted permission by Christ, through the maiden's intercession, to see the celestial city, though not to enter it. At the end of the vision that follows, he sees within it a company of maidens, headed by the Lamb who is their bridegroom, moving toward the central throne. His gaze singles out the maiden who had appeared to him in the dream. Overcome by the desire to join her, he rushes toward the river that separates them—and awakens. In retrospect, he judges the dream to have been a "veray avysyoun," an authentic vision. If it is indeed true that she who was taken from him on earth lives in bliss in a kingdom that lasts forever, he is content to remain in the dungeon of this world and to submit himself, as a good Christian, to the will of Christ.

The story, as I have retold it above, exhibits on a large scale the interplay between singleness and multiplicity that pervades the poem: between the one line, or direction, of the narrative as a whole and its many episodes or stages. As I said earlier, the narrative traces a change in the central figure, brought about under divine auspices, from bafflement and despair to understanding and resignation. His change of inner state is accomplished by means of the dream, which reaches its own culmination within the frame of the first and last sections. So far, my description would, I think, be found acceptable by most readers of the poem. But it fails to address the problems of interpretation that arise when we compare the ending of the dream and the ending of the poem in the narrator's retrospective thoughts. He believes that his dream ended untimely, that there was more he could have learned from it had he only been less impetuous. Yet we are offered no clue as to what these additional "mysteries" (1194), as he calls them, might have been. Did he have a chance to enter into a mystical union with the divine that his mortal limitations caused him to forego? The answer to this question is not immediately clear. Neither is it clear whether he has indeed achieved a degree of enlightenment that we can find satisfactory. In the last three stanzas of the poem, both the intensity of the dream's culmination and the sound of the narrator's weeping (1181) have died away. But by that same token, he is no longer the impassioned visionary who pitied the bleeding Lamb and desired his "little queen." In his postvisionary state, he rather resembles the cured mental patient who has exchanged his brilliantly dramatic hallucinations for the prosaic world of everyday reality. At least one critic has found his bland statement that "to pay the Prince other sete saghte, Hit is ful ethe to the god Krystyin (to content that prince and well agree, Good Christians can with ease incline)" (1201–02) both "theologically superficial and psychologically superficial."[5] As the end of this essay, I shall offer a new interpretation of the ending, based on a section-by-section reading of the poem.

The dreamer himself, of course, is not aware he is being subjected to a spiritual reeducation. For him, the dream simply takes the form of a succession of many experiences of seeing and hearing, to each of which he responds in turn. The variety of the dream's successive stages reflects the complexity and profundity of the inward change it dramatizes. The poet wastes no time in making explicit the Christianity of the dreamer-to-be. The lines in section 1 that tell us this,

> Thagh kynde of Kryst me comfort kenned,
> My wreched wylle in wo ay wraghte,
> [Comfort of Christ might come to mind
> But wretched will would not forbear] (55–56)

are so phrased as to imply a distinction of central importance for our understanding of what follows: between knowledge that remains theoretical or abstract and knowledge attended by emotional and imaginative realization. Knowledge of the latter sort seems to be referred to late in the poem by the maiden, when she says of herself and her companions in heaven, "We thurghoutly haven cnawyng [we have comprehensive knowledge]" (859).[6] Only by acquiring it can the dreamer direct his "wretched will" away from earthly, transient objects of desire toward those that are heavenly and permanent. The dream makes him see what, as a Christian, he knows: that the being he had loved and lost on earth continues to exist. It also makes him see that although she retains the identity that linked her with him before she died, she has taken on a new and transcendent identity, and that the realm to which she now belongs is wholly separate from and incommensurate with the human world. He must not only understand but gladly accept all this if the design of the dream, and its designs on him, are to be fulfilled.

Our understanding of the direction of the story line is most conspicuously at odds with the dreamer's experience in the first stage of the dream, set in a gorgeously surreal landscape. Though he believes that he is present there by "Godez grace," he speaks for all the world like the hero of a quest romance, a disembodied knight-errant out for adventure, under the governance of fortune, in a "foreste" where he can expect to encounter "mervaylez" (63–64, 67, 98).[7] (One thinks of King Arthur, in *Sir Gawain and the Green Knight*, awaiting the "mayn mervayle" [94] that will allow him to take his seat.)[8] He moves effortlessly through a seemingly endless succession of pleasurable sights and sounds:

> I welke ay forth in wely wyse;
> No bonk so byg that did me derez.
> The fyrre in the fryth, the feier con ryse
> The playn, the plonttez, the spyse, the perez;
> And rawez and randez and rych reverez,
> As fyldor fyn her bonkes brent.

[I walked along with bliss at hand;
No slope so steep to make me stay;
The further, the fairer the pear-trees stand,
The spice-plants spread, the blossoms sway,
And hedgerows run by banks as gay
As glittering golden filament.] (101–06)

He can foresee no end to this series of delights, but he is soon brought up short (though at first he is unaware of the fact) when he comes "to a water by schore that scherez [I came to a waterway that marks a boundary along a shore]" (107).[9] This stream has the same splendor as the rest of the landscape, and he describes it in much the same language, but its presence brings his onward progress to an end. He has not, it turns out, been wandering freely; rather, he has been steadily approaching a barrier that will remain before him until he tries to cross it at the end of the dream. Looking with longing toward the farther shore, he moves into the next stage of his spiritual journey: his confrontation with the maiden whose loss in death had preoccupied him in his waking life.

Although the description of this landscape is, strictly speaking, a prelude to the dreamer's spiritual education and not a part of it, no reader would wish it absent from the poem. It not only gives imaginative pleasure in itself but, as a descriptive tour-de-force, contributes to the verbal elaboration the poet evidently thought appropriate to his theme, as a jeweler crafting a reliquary might lavish on it rich ornamentation befitting the preciousness of its contents.[10] But the leisurely, seemingly open-ended unfolding of this first stage of the narrative also plays a part in the developmental psychology of the dreamer. Awed and delighted, first by the glory of the crystal cliffs and the trees with their indigo boles and glittering silver leaves, and later by the gleaming beryl banks of the stream and the gems shining from its depths like stars on a clear winter night, he temporarily forgets the grief that had possessed him. The exemption of these substances from decay, their preciousness in worldly terms, and their beauty are signs (though he does not interpret them as such) that his dream is of divine origin, therefore beneficent in purpose. Moving along in his exalted state, nourished by sweet odors of fruits that refresh him like food, he is as ready as a mortal soul can be for the shock that awaits him.

When the maiden suddenly appears, seated before a crystal cliff, he identifies her at once and without hesitation as his "pearl" (241–42). Later, we can and should infer that in life she had been his daughter, and that she had died before reaching the age of two.[11] The importance of this immediate and confident recognition is emphasized by the repetitive language the poet assigns him. The moment he saw her, the dreamer says, he knew her well, he had seen her before. And he tells us that as he continued to gaze on her, his response gained in intensity and certainty:

> On lenghe I looked to hyr there;
> The lenger, I knew hyr more and more.
> [I gazed on her there at length;
> The longer, I knew her more and more.] (167–68)

This visionary confrontation with the person of his lost beloved is an essential step in the movement of his soul away from despair: it is an emotionally charged experience, confirming and deepening his belief in the personal immortality promised by Christian doctrine. He sees that his beloved pearl is still fully herself and is deeply moved by the sight. She, for her part, acknowledges the bond between them. Her first words implicitly answer in the affirmative his question, "Art thou *my* perle?" (242; emphasis added)

> Sir, ye haf your tale mysetente
> To say *your* pearl is al awaye,
> That is in cofer so comly clente
> As in this gardyn gracios gaye.
> [Sir, your tale is told for nought,
> To say your pearl has gone away
> That is closed in a coffer so cunningly wrought
> As this same garden green and gay.] (257–60; emphasis added)

But the question, of course, must also be answered in the negative. She is not "his" pearl in the sense in which the adored infant over whom he had the authority of a father was his in life. Most obviously, as he can plainly see, she is no longer an infant. Indeed, she wears a crown, and her demeanor is as solemn as that of a worldly nobleman, a duke or an earl. Instead of being subject to his authority, she has assumed the authority over him that a person of high rank in earthly society has over a commoner. She is now transformed in ways he could not have imagined, and his conception of her must change accordingly.

It does in fact change, as we can see if we observe the successive terms of address he directs toward her as the poem continues. During the first part of their conversation, he speaks to her, as he had in his waking state, in the conventional terms of *amour courtois*, "courteous love," which at once idealize the beloved and contain her within the limits of the lover's imagination:[12] she is his *iuel* (jewel) (249), his *swete* (325). She is responsible for all his earthly sorrows; he has "playned" her loss, concealing from others his "longeyng" for her, suffering "del [grief] and gret daunger" (242, 244, 250).[13] After she has lectured him at some length on his misapprehension of the state of things between them, including his misguided wish to join her then and there, he begs her to stop scolding him and make her "comfort" known to him instead (361–72). (The echo, in line 369 "kythez me kyndely your coumforde," of *kynde*, *comfort*, and *kenned* in the narrator's earlier reference to Christ in line 55 is surely significant.)[14] His petition contains a term belonging to the vocabulary of religious devotion that had not yet been coopted into the secular language of love. *Endorde* (368) is evidently the past participle, with an altered prefix, of the verb which has descended into modern English as *adore*. It meant in Middle English "to worship as a deity" and first appears in secular contexts at the end of the sixteenth century. Its source in English was Old French *aourer*, from Latin *adorare*, refashioned in the fourteenth century as *adourer*. See *OED* s.v. *adore* v., senses 1 and 5.[15] He also acknowledges the fact that her newly acquired faculty of courteous speech makes her his social superior:

> Thagh cortaysly ye carp con,
> I am bot mol and manerez mysse.
> [Though you speak courteously,
> I am of earth, and lack manners.] (381–82)

Here we have the first reference in *Pearl* to the "courtesy" that, as the poet somewhat idiosyncratically conceives it, will prove central to the maiden's description of the community of the blessed. These words and the immediately ensuing request to be told about the life she leads imply, as critics of the poem have observed, a new humility on his part, with a corresponding shift of attention from the attributes he had projected on her as a love-object to attributes she possesses in her own right—specifically, the dignity and high station, the "worschyp and wele" (394) that are now apparent.[16]

This more adequate awareness resonates eloquently in the two apostrophes he addresses to her after she has expounded the parable of the pearl. In the first of these (745–56), he invokes her as a being whose "properties" could not have been created by human art and cannot be apprehended by the human intellect. His reference to her "angel-havyng so clene cortez [her angelic behavior, so wholly courteous]" (754) reflects his newly acquired understanding that she is a member of "the *court* of the kyndom of God alyve" (445; emphasis added).[17] The second apostrophe (769–80) shows him vividly conscious of her royal status as bride of the Lamb, of the "reiatez . . . so ryche and ryf [royalties so rich and abundant]" (770) that make her so dazzling to behold. The denouement of the dream-drama is foreshadowed by the fact that, despite this deepened understanding, he continues to see her membership in the heavenly company in the comparative terms of his human experience. Because in earthly society a man has only one wife, she must have "driven" all other women out of the running, including many who had led long lives dedicated to Christ (773–80).

As their conversation proceeds, his language continues to express his realization that her mortal individuality, though in a sense perpetuated in death, has been enhanced by divine attributes and exists on a higher than mortal plane. Unsurprisingly, it also assimilates her more and more to the Virgin Mary. He prefaces his request that she teach him about the city in which she and her companions dwell by addressing her as a "reken rose" (906), seeing her now as transformed from the rose she had said she was in life, that "flowred and fayled as kynde hyt gef [that flowered and failed as nature granted to it]" (270), into an exemplar of eternal beauty. The Virgin is the primary instance of such a rose, one of her scriptural designations being "Rose of Jericho" (Ecclesiasticus 24:18; cf. *MED* s.v. *rose* n. (1), senses1[d], and 3[b]). And the appellation "gloryous withouten galle [blemish]" (915) in this same passage fits the Virgin above all other women. The last of his apostrophes, "Moteles may [spotless maiden] so meke and mylde" (961) could well be the first line of a Marian lyric.

The dreamer's recognition of the maiden's new identity is part of the "design" of the dream as I described it earlier, in that it involves emotional and imaginative as well as intellectual enlightenment. This change in him is abetted by a change of tone in the maiden's discourse which deserves extended consideration. It comes at the end of her lengthy response to the dreamer's insistence that her rank in heaven is too high. (The passage in question runs from line 493, in section 9, to line 745, in section 13, with one interruption by the dreamer.) First, she tells and explains the parable of the vineyard, following one line of interpretive tradition in equating arrival at the vine at the end of the day with death in infancy: the same "penny" of eternal life is paid to the faithful Christian who lived a long life and the infant who died shortly after baptism. When the dreamer says that this is "unreasonable" in that it means "more" pay for "less" work (589–600), she counters his objection by speaking of the gift of salvation poured forth by the infinite sufficiency of God's grace, to which the terms "more" and "less" do not apply. The infant who lives too short a life to act sinfully is in fact more certain of salvation than the righteous man, who must obtain absolution for the sins he inevitably commits. As she makes this point, the term *innocent* (625) appears for the first time in the poem, as an appellation for those whose lives on earth have been cut short, including herself. This anticipates her later account of St. John's vision of the 144,000 virgins following the Lamb (Revelation 14:1–5; *Pearl*, section 15), and her appearance in that procession in the last phase of the dreamer's vision of the celestial Jerusalem. The virgins in Revelation 14 were identified by the church with the infants under the age of two who were killed by the order of King Herod after the birth of Jesus, and whose martyrdom was celebrated on what in the *Pearl*-poet's time was called Childermas, later known as the Feast of the Holy Innocents.[18] Salvation for both the innocent and the Christian who has lived virtuously comes from God's grace, through the incarnation and crucifixion of Christ (646–48). Blood and water flowed from the wound made in the side of Christ when he hung on the cross; the blood redeemed mankind from original sin; the water established the sacrament of baptism, through which the original sin of Adam, inherited by all human beings, is washed away. Grace is available to the "righteous" Christian

> That synnez thenne new, yif him repente,
> Bot wyth sorgh and syt he mot hit crave,
> And byde the payne therto is bent.
> [Who is penitent, having sinned anew,
> If with sorrow at heart he cry and crave
> And perform the penance that must ensue.] (662–64)

Even so, his best hope of salvation is in him "on rode that blody dyed [on the cross that died bleeding]" (705).

This long and, at least to modern ears, sometimes dry discourse serves to prove to the dreamer, once and for all, that the maiden's translation to royal rank in the afterlife is justified. It rises to eloquence in justifying the salvation of "innocents" such as herself, whose lives on earth amounted to little. But it has an adversarial thrust and takes on, at times, an ominous tone. It includes the poem's only reference to damnation (641–44), and it cites and applies to the dreamer personally that most threatening of biblical dicta, that "no man living shall be justified" in the sight of God (Psalm 142.2; A.V. 143). Then, as if aware that her auditor needs consolation as much as correction, she speaks less sternly. She turns to a story drawn from the life of Jesus on earth, in which innocence is shown as deserving not only salvation but love, and thence to a parable representing the kingdom of heaven as precious and desirable beyond all else. In the latter, the symbolic meaning of the single great pearl upon the maiden's breast becomes explicit for the first time.

A comparison between the penny, in the parable of the vineyard, and the pearl of great price, in the parable of the merchant, makes clear this change of tone. Both, by virtue of their circular form, symbolize the eternity or exemption from time of the heavenly kingdom: a line depicting the circumference of a disk, such as the penny, or a sphere, such as the pearl, is "endless round" (738) — self-contained and without terminal points. But the responses elicited by the two symbols differ radically. We understand the significance of the penny as one item in an elaborate allegorical structure which also includes the workers, the vineyard, the lord of the vine, and the hours of the day. The pearl, too, has allegorical significance in a somewhat simpler story. But unlike the penny, it is itself an emotionally charged object of contemplation and is described, in language enhancing this aura, as

> wemlez, clene, and clere,
> And endelez rounde, and blythe of mode.
> [flawless, clean, and clear,
> And endlessly round and blithe of spirit.] (737–38)

After telling the parable of the merchant, the maiden identifies the pearl that appears in it with the "wonder perle" (221) upon her breast, telling the dreamer that it was placed there by her "Lorde the Lombe, that schede hys blode" (741). He then asks a question that, like his earlier inquiry about the nature of her life, betokens a shift away from his earthly preoccupations. Early in their conversation, the maiden had spoken of her lord the Lamb, who had taken her as his bride, crowned her queen, and made her his heir. At that point, the dreamer was too perplexed by the idea that as queen in heaven she must have usurped the position of Mary to seek clarification. He is now ready to ask her what sort of being this Lamb may be who has made her his bride (771–72). Her threefold answer draws on three scriptural sources which assert Christ's identity as a lamb in three different, and increasingly powerful, ways. The first, a passage from Isaiah interpreted prophetically by the church, takes the form of a simile: the meekness of the crucified Jesus resembles the meekness of a sheep when it is slaughtered or of a lamb when it is roughly handled by the shearer. In the second, a passage from the Gospel of John, the identification takes more intensely imagined form as a metaphor: on seeing Jesus, John the Baptist calls him the Lamb of God. In the third, a passage from Revelation, the symbolic animal displaces the human Christ. The symbol must be apprehended, not simply visualized; a mental picture of a lamb reading a book, like a creature in an animated cartoon, would hardly be an appropriate response. (An attempt to "see" the seven horns on the head of the Lamb in section 10 of *Pearl* and in Revelation 5:6, where the head is also said to have seven eyes, is similarly inappropriate, though medieval illuminators did sometimes represent these features. In the biblical source, the narrator turns immediately from the horns and eyes themselves to their significance: they are "the seven spirits of God, sent forth into all the earth.")

The three passages evoke a range of emotional responses. At one extreme, the familiar image of an appealing creature submitting to cruel or rough treatment arouses tenderness and pity; it has the sentimental quality exploited nowadays by pictures of curly-fleeced lambs on Christmas cards. At the opposite extreme, the vision of the divine Lamb presiding in majesty "inmydez the trone" (835) of heaven, evokes wonderment and awe verging on terror.

The maiden's language reflects these emotional values. In citing the first of the three passages, she describes Isaiah as speaking "pitously" (798), whereas in the third passage, she says that the heavenly hosts "con dare [cowered]" (839), that is, that they are overcome with dread, at the sight of the Lamb. (See *daren* v. sense 3 in *MED.*)

The story of Jesus and the children, the parable of the pearl, and the three passages describing the Lamb contain the major symbols of the poem, drawn from the gospel of Matthew and the Book of Revelation, and these now emerge in rich and complex interrelation. The children and the pearl are linked in that they share the key attribute of flawlessness, which is added by the poet to both his biblical sources. The pearl the maiden wears upon her breast now proves to "mean" the pearl described in the parable. The maiden further links it to the Lamb, telling the dreamer that it is he who has bestowed it upon her. The dreamer, in his inquiry about the nature of the Lamb, then refers to her reverently as "a makelez may and maskellez" (780), a peerless maiden and spotless. She acknowledges that she is "unblemished" (782) but says that she is not without peer, for she is one of a throng of maidens having equal status: the wives of the Lamb, seen by Saint John on Mount Sion (Revelation 14.1–5). She later describes the "flok" of wives as "wythouten flake" (947), echoing John's description of them as "sine macula" (5). Because this company is implicitly conceived of by the poet, in accordance with received Christian interpretation, as made up of the Holy Innocents, the "harmless" (725) and "spotless" (726) children whom Jesus gathered about him must be seen retrospectively as belonging to it. A last major symbol appears at the beginning of her answers to the dreamer's request that she explain the nature of the Lamb: she cannot do so, she says, without speaking about the city of Jerusalem (793–94).

The best-known biblical passage referring to a woman's flawlessness is surely Canticle of Canticles (Song of Songs) 4.7, where the lover says of his beloved, "There is not a spot in thee (macula non est in te)."[19] The church interpreted this book as portraying the love of Christ, either for the church or for the souls of the redeemed, and the latter is implied by the maiden's use of language from it when, replying to the dreamer's question about her divine attributes, she tells him how the Lamb invited her to come to him after her death:

> When I wente fro yor worlde wete,
> He calde me to hys bonerté:
> "Cum hyder to me, my lemman swete,
> For mote ne spot is non in the."
> [When I left your world of rain and sleet
> He called me in joy to join him there:
> "Come hither to me, my sweet beloved,
> For no speck or spot is in you.]" (761–64)

More important in relation to the poet's treatment of the theme, however, are the references to the crucified Christ as flawless, and the exhortations to communities of believers to emulate him, in the Epistles of Peter and Paul. In Hebrews 9.14, Paul says of Christ that he "semet ipsum obtulit inmaculatum Deo (offered himself unspotted unto God)." In 1 Peter 1.19, Christians are told that they have not been redeemed with things of material value, "sed pretioso sanguine quasi agni incontaminati et inmaculati Christi (but with the precious blood of Christ, as of a lamb unspotted and undefiled)."[20] The maiden herself refers to the Lamb as "that maskelez mayster" (900) and "the Lompe . . . wythouten spottez blake" (945).

The variety of the words the poet used in expressing the idea of flawlessness well exemplifies the verbal plenitude that enhances the multiplicity of *Pearl*. The idea is of course introduced in the opening stanza in the phrase "wythouten spot" (12), where a "real" pearl is the vehicle of a metaphor whose tenor is a person. It appears in passing in the dreamer's description of the maiden's attire, when he mentions the "wonder perle wythouten wemme" that was set upon her breast (221), and later in his reference to the phoenix, and to the Virgin Mary, of whom the phoenix is an emblem, as *frelez,* or "flawless" (429–32). The children invited by Jesus to come to him are said to be "wythouten mote other mascle of sulpande synne [without spot or speck of defiling sin]" (726), and the pearl the merchant is willing to sell all his goods to buy is *mascellez* (732). (The fact that the word *mascellez* is less common and more elevated as diction than the synonymous phrase "wythouten spot" in the opening stanza accords with the attribute's emerging spiritual significance.) Another synonym, *wemlez,* figures in the parable as one of the adjectives describing the pearl's properties (737). Three more, *mote, blot,* and *flake,* appear in the description of the children who gathered around Jesus (726), in the maiden's acknowledgment that she is indeed without flaw (782), and in her later reference to the "flock" that follows the Lamb (947). And the adjective *unblemyst,* which appears in the same line as the phrase "withouten blot," implies the noun *blemish.* Finally, the dreamer prefaces his request to see the city by praising the maiden as "gloryous wythouten galle" (915).

Of the major symbols brought together by the *Pearl*-poet, the celestial Jerusalem is the last to make its appearance in the poem. When the maiden, repudiating the dreamer's description of her as "peerless," speaks of Saint John's vision of the throng of brides accompanying the Lamb, she locates them on Mount Sion, as John did, and locates Mount Sion in "the nwe cyté o Jerusalem" (792), as John did not. She then tells the dreamer that she must speak of Jerusalem if she is to explain the Lamb's nature to him (793). In the first and second of the three biblical passages she proceeds to paraphrase, she refers to the historical Jerusalem where Jesus was judged and killed but makes no explicit transition from the new city to the old one. Only when the dreamer asks her later in their conversation about the "gret ceté" (927) in which she and her compeers must surely live does she explain the distinction between the two, describing the celestial Jerusalem, in terms of two medieval interpretations of its name, as the residence of the divinity whose occupants live in eternal peace. It is this description that impels him to make his final request, which the maiden grants in part: that he may be brought to the city and allowed to see her chamber within it. The next three sections of the poem present an account of the three phases of the ensuing vision. These resemble the maiden's three descriptions of the Lamb in that they elicit a range of emotional responses. But whereas the description of the Lamb began with human tenderness and ended in awe, the vision of the celestial Jerusalem moves in the opposite direction.

In its first phase, the dreamer sees the city abstractly, in what might be called a three-dimensional analogue of an architect's plan. Or rather, he apprehends it in and through the terms of the description in Revelation, to which the poet adds very little. There is, in fact, no clear distinction between the things he sees — the twelve precious stones, for example, that form the twelve layers of the city's foundation — and the names given them by John, which he had presumably seen "in writ" (997). A simile original with the poet compares the shining of the city's jasper walls to *glayre* (1026), a substance used to give a glossy finish to manuscript illuminations. This reinforces our sense that the content of the vision at this point and the words on the page that mediate it are virtually undistinguishable. The unreal, or surreal, nature of the experience is evident in the dreamer's statement that he "saw" the city's cubic shape:

> As John deuysed yet sagh I thare:
> Thise twelue degres wern brode and stayre;
> The cyté stod abof ful sware,
> As longe as brode as hyghe ful fayre;
> [As John had written so I was ware
> How broad and steep was each great tier;
> As long as broad as high foursquare
> The city towered on twelvefold pier.] 1021–24)

Human eyes cannot see a cube as such; we can see without distortion only one side of an object that we know has five other sides of the same width and height. Here again, the dimensions of the city are not so much seen as apprehended: he "saw" them as Saint John saw them measured (1032).

The vision's second phase likewise has its source in Revelation, though here the poet expands the biblical account somewhat. Whereas in the first phase, the structure and composition of the city were contemplated in terms of immutable substances and geometrical patterns, the dreamer now becomes aware of living presences within it: "the hyghe Godez self" (1054), seated on his throne, who presides over the perpetual sacrifice of the Lamb, the River of Life that flows through every street, the open gates through which spotless souls, and they alone, may pass; the trees along the river that bear fruit annually in a twelvefold cycle.

By the time this description of the city's interior comes to an end, the dreamer is overcome with awe. His mind's eye has been blinded by a metaphysical analogue of the blinding of the bodily eye when it gazes at the light of the sun:

> A rever of the trone ther ran outryghte
> Watz bryghter then bothe the sunne and mone. . . .
> And to even wyth that worthly lyght
> That schynez upon the brokez brym,
> The planetez arn in to pover a plyght,
> And the sel[vë] sun ful fer to dym.
> [A river therefrom ran fresh and free,
> More bright by far than sun or moon. . . .
> And to equal that wondrous light
> That shines upon the waters clear,
> The planets are in too poor a state,
> And the sun itself far too dim.] (1055–56, 1073–76)[21]

He stands motionless, rapt in amazement, all but unaware of his inner state. Then, "on a wonder wyse" (1095), his attention is attracted by the sudden appearance of a procession that fills the streets. The third, culminating phase of the vision begins, and stupefaction turns to delight. Though certain of the details of the third phase have their source in Revelation, the underlying conception is the poet's own. What the dreamer sees, in an experience of the utmost intensity, is the very "life" that he inquired about early in his conversation with the maiden. It takes the form of her presence in a procession led by the Lamb and made up of his 144,000 brides. In a communion with him symbolized by the church-administered sacrament of communion on earth, they follow him toward the throne at the city's center. But the phrase "toward the throne" implies earthly space, and the word "ongoing" implies earthly time, whereas the scene as the poet now imagines it is exempt from both. I have said elsewhere that "the rules of geometrical or positional space do not apply to the heavenly kingdom" in *Pearl* (see, in this volume, "*Pearl*'s Maynful Mone," p. 119). This statement holds true for time as well.

The image of the round moon at or approaching the full, which introduces the vision's final phase, is implicitly superimposed on the city, which is thus imagined as framed by a circle, though it was imagined earlier as a cube. The two shapes have equal symbolic validity, and the poem demands that we consider them equally "true."[22] The River of Life, described earlier as filling every street (1059), must thus flow outward in all directions from the throne of God (1055) as if along the radii of a circle. But every street is also filled by the procession (1096–1100), which moves inward along these same radii toward the central throne. Realistically, it cannot move "through" a bounded space that is already full, but in the transworldly realm, its motion takes place in a timeless continuity: one could say of it that at every moment it is departing, traversing its route, and arriving.[23] The straining of language to encompass the unimaginable enhances the emotional intensity that, in this final phase of the dreamer's experience, reaches its high point in the poem. The link-word of the passage, *delit*, signifies the emotion that dominates the scene and, in an abrupt and startling turn of events, brings the dream to an end.

The variety of emotional coloring in *Pearl* inheres partly in the difference between passages that are matter-of-fact in tone and passages that carry an emotional charge, and partly in differences among the emotions themselves — for example, between the poignancy of the lamb as described by Isaiah and its surreal magnificence as described by Saint John. I now want to look at the ways in which these differences are reflected in the stylistic variety of the poem, as manifested in features of language. I noted earlier, without describing it as such, a semantic or lexical marker of emotionally colored language: the evaluative or qualitative terms — terms implying moral or esthetic judgments — that may be added to the gist of a narrative or description. From the story of Jesus and the children, I cited the qualitative adverbs *fayr* and *swetely* and the qualitative adjectives *harmlez*, *trwe*, and *undefylde*, together with *mascellez* and its synonyms. Such terms may, of course, express disapproval as well as approval. Negative evaluation is implied by the noun *mascle* and its synonyms and by the adjective *sulpande* "defiling" (726). Qualitative language is a feature of style, not of content, in that its use is optional: the *Pearl*-poet could have formulated the line "Jesus thenne hem swetely sayde" (717) without the adverb and could have omitted the adjective from the line "Wythouten mote other mascle of sulpande synne" (726).

A less familiar but more interesting and important feature of language with respect to which passages of *Pearl* differ from one another is the grammatical corollary of a conceptual difference. The relevant grammatical terms are "stative" and "dynamic"; the relevant concepts are permanence and change. For those not familiar with the grammatical distinction, some examples will help to clarify it.[24] Finite verb-forms, that is, verbs having person and tense, can be either stative or dynamic.[25] In assertions of fact, such as "MS Cotton Nero A.X contains four poems thought to be by the *Pearl*-poet," the finite verb-form (*contains*) asserts a permanent relationship between two entities (the manuscript and the four poems) and is stative. In simple narrative statements, such as "I reread *Pearl* this morning," the finite verb *reread* locates the performance of an action in time and is dynamic. A sign of the stative character of a verb in a given context is the fact that if it is recast in the progressive aspect, the resultant sentence, that is, "MS Cotton Nero.A.X. is containing four poems," is no longer idiomatic. Dynamic verbs can survive this change intact: "I was rereading *Pearl* this morning, when . . ." Although in the above two examples, the stative verb happens to be in the present tense and the dynamic verb in the past tense, the difference between stative and dynamic is not tense-bound. A verb in the past tense would be interpreted as stative if the statement containing it were taken to signify a fact, as the statement "My grandfather spoke Norwegian" probably would be. It would be interpreted as dynamic if the statement were taken to signify an action located in time, as in "I loved to listen to my grandfather when he spoke/was speaking Norwegian." Stative verbs in the present tense are sometimes said to signify a "timeless present."[26]

A range between stative and dynamic is built into English grammar (and the grammars of related languages) in the classification of words into parts of speech. Among words of the four "open classes," that is, those whose members have lexical content, the nouns, which signify such entities as persons, things, and concepts, are inherently the most stative.[27] The finite forms of "full verbs," which signify relationships and actions, are inherently the most dynamic. The descriptive adjectives are "characteristically stative" but may have dynamic force in certain meanings. Those denoting "definitional" or permanent attributes tend naturally to be interpreted as stative, those denoting fluctuating or temporary ones as dynamic.[28] Thus, *English*, in the statement "He is English," is normally interpreted as stative, whereas *cautious*, in "He is cautious," is interpreted as dynamic. Among nonfinite verb-forms, the infinitives and gerunds function like nouns and are stative; the past participle functions like a stative adjective, and the present participle may have either stative or dynamic adjectival force. Compare "All the rooms in the hotel have running water," in which the participle has stative force, with "The running water made a pleasant sound," in which its force is dynamic. The latter statement can be recast in the progressive aspect: "The water was running, making a pleasant sound." Recasting the former results in a change of meaning: "The water is running in the next room."

Because the four major parts of speech differ among themselves in the ways I have described, it is possible to apply the stative/dynamic distinction not only to single words but to words in sequence, whether spontaneously uttered on everyday occasions or given form by an author. The language of one passage can be described as more stative than that of another if it contains a consistently higher proportion of nouns to the total number of words counted off seriatim. Conversely, the language of a passage in which the proportions of finite verb-forms are consistently higher than those in another can be described as the more dynamic of the two.[29] Needless to say, such differences are linked to differences in subject matter. We expect the language of a shopping list to be stative, that is, to consist largely of nouns, and that of an unembellished account of daily actions in a diary to be dynamic, that is, to contain a high proportion of verbs. The artistry of an accomplished poet, however, can teach us that subject matter in language is not destiny. Wallace Stevens imagines the redness of rubies as an event in process when he writes of "rubies reddened by rubies reddening," the present participle here having dynamic force. And Marianne Moore's penchant for fixity reveals itself in such freeze-frames as the phrase "a wave at the curl," in which an ongoing action is expressed by two nouns.

A more interesting correlation than that between grammar and subject matter is that between grammar and occasion, meaning by "occasion" the various contexts in which we use language, classified in terms of levels of formality.[30] These range from the informal extreme of spontaneous everyday talk to the formal extreme of advanced academic prose and literary works composed in traditional "high styles," with casual writings such as personal letters and (nowadays) emails and journalistic and fictional writings designed for general consumption occupying a middle ground. In general, the more formal, the more stative—our across-the-board experience of language confirms this generalization. The sentences first spoken by children are short, tending to have one verb per sentence and one adjective per noun, if that. At the formal extreme, academic prose is notorious, among other things, for its lack of verbs and the preponderance, among the verbs it does contain, of that most stative of verb-forms, *is*, whether standing singly or linked with past participles in the passive voice. Tabulations of sizeable bodies of language divided into sequences of 100 words bear out these observations. They also reveal statistical parameters: the language of tape-recorded stretches of recorded conversation proves to contain, on the average, 16 finite verb-forms or more per 100 words. Average counts of verbs in academic prose vary by author and by subject but may well fall below 10 finite verb-forms per 100 words, sometimes far lower.[31]

Variation from passage to passage on a range between stative and dynamic, as indicated by the comparative proportions of the major parts of speech, is worth observing in itself as an aspect of the variety of language in *Pearl*. But it has a more profound significance as well. I noted earlier that the stative/ dynamic opposition in grammar has a conceptual corollary in the opposition between permanence and change, which takes dramatic form in *Pearl* in the relation between heavenly and earthly realms. And this relationship in turn is one aspect of the opposition between singleness and multiplicity that pervades the poem.

Asked to identify the passage in *Pearl* whose content has the most to do with the passing of time, a reader might well choose the maiden's rendering of the vineyard parable in section 9. Not only is the symbolic subject of the parable a series of actions taking place in the course of a day, but the poet, as we learn from the interpretation that follows, conceives of the successive stages of the day as representing the successive stages of mortal life, equating hours spent in the vineyard with years spent on earth. The passage does, as we might expect, represent the dynamic extreme I referred to above, as measured by propor- tionate frequencies of finite verb-forms. It is 523 words long; its first five 100- word groups contain percentages of 18, 18, 18, 20, and 18 finite verbs, re- spectively; the 4 verbs in the final group of 23 words amount to slightly over 18 percent.

Is this syntactic feature simply a reflection of the language of the parable as it stands in the Bible? or does it also represent the handling of the narrative by the poet? A ready way of finding out is to compare the two. The parable in the Vulgate is less than half as long as the *Pearl*-poet's reworking of it. Each of its two complete 100-word passages contains 19 finite verbs; the final 32-word group contains 6 finite verbs, or almost 19 percent. There is thus a negligible difference of less than 1 percent between them. But in view of the much greater length of the parable as told in *Pearl*, the virtual equivalence of the two counts means that the language added by the poet to his version contains the same high proportion of finite verbs found in the Vulgate original. For example, the Vulgate says, referring to the workmen hired earliest by the lord of the vine- yard, "misit eos in vineam suam [he sent them into his vineyard]" (Matthew 20.2). The *Pearl*-poet says that the lord finds some workmen suitable for the task and enters into an agreement with them, whereupon

> forth thay gotz,
> Wrythen and worchen and don gret pyne,
> Kerven and caggen and man hit clos.
> [forth they go,
> Toil and work and take great pains
> Cut and tie and make it orderly.] (510–12)

The 17 words of this detail include 7 finite verbs.

The language of the parable as told in *Pearl* resembles that of the Vulgate version in another respect: it is virtually devoid of the qualitative terms that the poet adds *passim* to the story of Jesus and the children and the parable of the pearl of great price. Of the adjectives added by the poet to his Latin original, *stronge* in line 531 "He segh ther ydel men ful stronge," and *sobre* in 532 "And sade to hem wyth sobre soun," can be thought of as qualitative in that they signify praiseworthy attributes. *Dere* in line 504 "To labor vyne watz dere the date," is an all-purpose term of approval, here vaguely meaning "correct" or "appropriate," and *gret* in line 511 "Wrythen and worchen and don gret pyne," merely emphasizes the meaning of the noun it modifies. Three clearly qualitative terms appear in both versions: *resonabele* in line 523 "What resonabele hyre be naght be runne," for *iustum* (4), *lyther* in line 567 for *nequam* (15) in "Other ellez thyn yghe to lyther is lyfte [or else your eye is directed to evil]" and *goude* for *bonus* (15) in 568 "For I am goude and non byswykez [As I am good, to none untrue]." But their significance is not stylistic; each is part of the parable's content.

The proportionate frequencies of finite verbs in the language used by the maiden in her version of the vineyard parable reach, indeed exceed, the high extreme represented by the language of everyday speech (see above). Her language is thus dynamic in the grammatical sense. But it is far from dynamic in the more ordinary sense of the word. Rather, it sounds matter-of-fact, lacking in the emotional intensity that might have been added to it by logically superfluous qualitative language. Both its "dynamic" grammar and the plainness of its diction befit the parable: it tells of ordinary events in an everyday setting that signify the lives led by ordinary Christians on earth. The maiden's account of the actions and transactions involved in the tending of the vineyard differs, say, from her description of the Lamb and his company on Mount Sion somewhat as a film in black-and-white differs from a film in technicolor. The temporal world of the vineyard and the marketplace, as we see it portrayed in the parable, is "but blo [bleak] and blynde," as the dreamer thought the real world to be in comparison with the dream-landscape into which he first awakened.

In which passage in *Pearl* might we expect the proportionate frequencies of finite verbs to represent the low extreme of the stative/dynamic range, as versus the high extreme represented by the parable of the vineyard? Most readers would, I think, choose the first phase of the dreamer's vision of the celestial Jerusalem, in which he sees the immutable substances of which the city is composed and its geometrical design. A comparison between the poet's description and the corresponding description in the Vulgate shows, first of all, that in translating the biblical original, as in translating the parable of the vineyard, he also expanded it. The description in *Pearl* contains 313 words to the 110 in Revelation.[32] The language of the poem and that of its Vulgate source also prove, as expected, to be alike in containing low percentages of finite verb-forms, the Vulgate being even more stative, in this sense, than *Pearl*. The first three groups of 100 words in section 17 contain 8, 7, and 10 finite verbs; the single 100-word group in the corresponding verses of Revelation contains only 4. This difference is due partly to the fact that whereas John in his account mentions only one action of his own (*vidi* in Revelation 1.2), the *Pearl*-poet speaks of a number of John's actions (of seeing, naming, and so on) and adds corresponding actions on the part of the dreamer, who "sees" and "knows" by name the component materials of the city exactly as John saw and named them. And the language of the description figuratively ascribes actions to several of the twelve precious stones that make up the city's foundation, whereas the Vulgate simply names them: jasper "glente [gleamed] grene in the lowest hemme" (1001), sapphire "helde the secounde stale" (1002), and chalcedony "in the thryd[ë] table con purly pale [paled purely]" (1004). The qualitative terms that were absent in the parable of the vineyard are present throughout the passage in such phrases as "ryally dyght" (987), "gentyl gemmez" (991), "derely devysez [nobly describes]" (995), and "wythouten wemme [without blemish]" (1003).

I observed earlier that in the second phase of the dreamer's vision of the city animate presences begin to appear. The proportionate frequencies of finite verb-forms in section 18 are somewhat greater than those in section 17, with percentages of 12, 10, 11, and 12 averaging out to slightly over 11 percent versus the total of slightly over 8 percent in the preceding section. The vision's third and culminating phase (section 19) actually shows the dreamer the life of the blessed about which the pearl maiden has been instructing him. The proportionate frequencies of finite verb-forms again increase, averaging out to 11.5 percent; this includes a strikingly high total of 16 verbs in the passage's fourth group of 100 words, in which the dreamer's gaze moves from the Lamb to the maiden and he is impelled to wade into the stream. Qualitative language continues to be conspicuously present in both phases. The dreamer describes the "parfyt perle" (1038) of which each gate of the city was made, "the hyghe trone" (1051) on which sat the "hyghe Godez self" (1054), and the spotlessness of the River of Life, which "rushed (*swange*)," "wythouten fylthe other galle other glet," through every street (1059–60). Praiseworthy beyond all else is the city's brightness, which exceeds anything in earthly experience; the lines referring to it (1055–58, 1073–76) contain, in addition to *bryghter* (1056), the positive and negative qualitative terms *swete* (1057), *worthly* "worthy" (1073), *pouer* "poor" (1075), and *dym* (1076).

In the vision's final phase, the admiring stupefaction resulting from the dreamer's prolonged contemplation of supernal glory gives way to emotions signified by the qualitative term *delit*, which, as the link-word of section 19, appears again and again.

We can more clearly sense the imaginative impact of the three-act drama by shifting our attention from counts lumping verbs together to particular verbs and their meanings, including their stative or dynamic force as implied in context. What this reveals is the increasingly dynamic character of the verbs the dreamer uses in the course of the vision as a whole, when actions taking place within the city, rather than facts about it, move into the foreground. As is to be expected, stative verbs of factual import, such as (*con*) *nemme* "named" (997), *hyght* "was called" (999), *joyned* (1009), and, of course, forms of the verb *to be* (988, 989, 994, 1013, 1022, 1027), preponderate in the description of the city's plan and the materials composing it. The description also contains a number of stative verbs signifying perception as facts rather than as ongoing actions. In modern English, this class is exemplified by the verb *to see* in sentences like "You see Long Island Sound from the top of Sleeping Giant," where *see* does not admit of conversion into "are seeing."[33] In section 17 of *Pearl*, such verbs include *sygh(e)/sagh* (985, 986, 1021, 1032), *knew* (998, 1019), and (*con*) *wale* (1000, 1007). The description, as I noted earlier, does include a few verbs ascribing actions to the gemstones, notably *glent* "gleamed" in "He [jasper] glente grene in the lowest hemme" (1001; cf. 1026) and *schon* in "jasporye . . . that glysnande [glistening] schon" (1018). But the potential dynamic force that would be made explicit by translating them "was gleaming" and "was shining" is inhibited by the overwhelmingly definitional force of the description as a whole. Furthermore, everything in it, as I noted earlier, is mediated through the words of the Bible; it is the biblical statements about the precious substances, as much as the substances themselves, that the dreamer seems to "see."

In the second phase of the vision, the activity of the dreamer in viewing the city begins to change from "seeing" to "watching," and what he watches is motion actually taking place during the time signified by verb tense. We can thus construe his statement that the River of Life "swange thurgh uch a strete" (1059) as equivalent to the statement that it "was rushing through every street." And we can translate other verbs in similar fashion: "such light *was gleaming* in all the streets that they had no need of sun nor moon" (cf. 1043–44), "the city *was shining* brightly because of the brightness of the Lamb" (cf. 1048), and "the high God himself *was sitting* on the high throne" (cf. 1051, 1054). Activity, as opposed to scene, becomes even more important in the next section, and key verbs in that section have the same dynamic force.

The dreamer watches the maidens "gliding" (1105) along together in stately fashion, the lamb "moving" proudly at their head (1120), the elders "falling" prostrate when he approaches (2120), legions of angels "casting" incense (1122), and all the assembled company "singing" in praise of the Lamb (1124), from whose side blood is "gushing" (1137). To accept these translations as legitimate and to read the lines of the original as having the dynamic force they imply is to feel fully the impact of the poet's stunningly audacious conception.

The change I have just described is in a sense minor: a shift from one grammatical class of finite verbs to another. But it figures importantly in the movement of the dream toward its conclusion. The dreamer's request to see the city could not have come earlier in the poem. It is predicated on his new understanding of the maiden's otherworldly mode of existence and royal state, and, more important, on the love, now mingled with reverence, that he feels for her as a transfigured being. In the vision that follows, passive response to scriptural authority gives way to direct experience of increasing emotional intensity, and this in turn brings about an action that abruptly breaks off the dream. But the poem continues: the dreamer reflects on his dream, regrets that he did not learn more from it, and resigns himself to the continuation of his life as a Christian on earth.

The line traced by the narrative as a whole, including the sections that frame the dream, begins, as I have said, with the state of benighted despair and grief that engulfs the narrator before he falls asleep and ends with the state of comparative enlightenment and resignation in which he finds himself on wakening. But the trajectory of the dream within the narrative does not arrive at a similarly satisfactory conclusion. The narrator blames himself afterward for the fact that the dream broke off too early: had he not rushed into the stream separating him from the celestial city, more divine mysteries might have been revealed to him (1194). Though this disparity between endings must somehow reflect the design of the poem, we can hardly think of it as reflecting the collaborative design of the maiden and the Lamb in granting the narrator the vision within the dream. The dreamer's "mad" rush into the stream was not foreordained; it was an act of free will, like the act of Adam and Eve in tasting the forbidden fruit. Are we as readers supposed to deplore it, as the narrator does in the final section, and share his regret that he did not see more? If so, what more are we to think he might have seen?

These questions, I believe, are not frivolous; my attempt to answer them will hopefully lead to a more adequate understanding of the singleness underlying the multiplicity of *Pearl*. I begin it with an observation made by A. C. Spearing: that toward the end of the poem the symbols of the pearl and the Lamb show signs of merging into one.[34] I noted earlier that the attribute of flawlessness, signified in section 13 by the link-word *maskelez*, is added by the poet to the pearl in the parable and then transferred to the Lamb, when the maiden explains why spotless souls such as hers are fit to be his brides:[35]

> Thys Jerusalem Lombe hade neuer pechche
> Of other huee bot quyt jolyf
> That mot ne masklle moght on streche . . .
> Forthy uche soule that hade never teche
> Is to that Lombe a worthyly wyf;
> [This Jerusalem Lamb had never a fault
> Of other hue than gay white;
> That neither spot nor mark could appear on . . .
> And so each soul that never had a stain
> Is a worthy wife with the Lamb to dwell (841–43, 845–46)

She again describes the Lamb as flawless when she refers to him as "wythouten spottez blake" (945), in speaking of the New Jerusalem to which he has transported his company of brides. Another sign, noted by Spearing, of the incipient merging of the two symbols is the fact that the maiden calls the Lamb her "dere juelle" (795) when she responds to the dreamer's inquiry about his nature. The dreamer uses this same word in the final phase of his vision, when he sees, at the center of the city, how all present "songe to love [praise] that gay juelle" (1124). And the raiment of the Lamb at the head of the procession seems to him to resemble "praysed perlez" (1112).

The merging of these two symbolic values, initiated late but not completed, exemplifies an aspect of the poem's singleness or continuity that I have not had occasion so far to speak of: its every section points in some way toward Christ. God the creator-father is, of course, present in the poem as well—we interpret the linking phrase "the grace of God" in section 11, as applying to him, and the dreamer sees his throne at the center of the celestial city (1054). But appellations for the paternal and filial aspects of the diety are by no means wholly distinct in Middle English, and language in *Pearl* that we might take, at first glance, to refer to the Father often turns out, on consideration, to refer to the Son. (The two were conceived of as aspects of a single triune divinity—in the Gospel of John, for example, Christ says, "I and the Father are one" [10.30]. But this does not prevent the poet from emphasizing one more than the other.) God is in fact absent from the city in the final phase of the dreamer's vision of it except for his reference to the throne: only the angels and the elders receive the Lamb and his entourage when it arrives at the center.

A brief survey of the poem will show that Christ is latent in the narrator's consciousness throughout. In the first section, it is "the kynde [nature] of Kryst" (55) that intimates to the narrator the possibility of comfort. When the maiden, early in their conversation, rebukes his presumptuousness, she accuses him of ignoring the promise made him by "oure Lord," that he would be resurrected after the death of his body (304–06). Because she is alluding to words spoken by Jesus in the New Testament,[36] "oure Lord" must mean Christ. Later, educating the dreamer about heavenly courtesy, she paraphrases the teaching of Paul in 1 Corinthians 12, to the effect that "uch a Krysten sawle [is] A longande lym [limb belonging] to the Mayster of myste [the Master of mystery]" (461–62). The poet, like Paul, is saying that Christian souls belong to Christ. At the end of the parable of the vineyard, the name of Christ is substituted for an expected reference to the earthly lord who interprets the story in the Bible:

> "Thus schal I," quod Kryste, "hit skyfte:
> The laste schal be the fyrst that strykez."
> ["Thus," says Christ, "shall I shift it awry:
> The last shall be the first in the queue."] (569–70)

It is Christ who brings God's abounding grace to humankind: the blood shed on the cross "uus boght fro bale of helle And delyvered uus of the deth secounde [redeemed us from the pain of hell And delivered us from the second death]" (651–52). As a result (to echo the poem's rather tortuous syntax), no obstacle stands between us and the "blysse" of the heavenly kingdom that Christ did not remove (657–58). In arguing for the certain salvation of the innocent, the maiden quotes the Wisdom of Solomon, whose central figure, Lady Wisdom, was identified in medieval thought with Christ.[37] And the pearl of great price in the parable of the merchant, which represents the "blithe" kingdom (738) of the saved, is said by the maiden to be Christ's gift to her.

Even before the symbols of the Lamb and the pearl come to be described in overlapping terminology, they are seen in intimate interrelation, as the thing bought — the pearl-like eternal bliss of heaven — is related to the agency of the buyer — the lamb-like Son of God. In recounting the parable of the one great pearl, the maiden refers to its teller, Christ, as "the Fader of folde and flode" (736) (note sense 5b of *fader* n. in *MED*). The symbolic meaning of the celestial Jerusalem, which plays a major part in the last six sections of the dream, merges with the meanings of the other two symbols. The city is one form of the "reme of hevenesse clere [the realm of the bright heavens]" (735) that is also signified by the pearl. It bears the name of the earthly city in which Christ was crucified, and it is the dwelling place of his divinity, as revealed to Saint John in his vision.

Still other signs point toward Christ indirectly. Reading the poem's opening stanza, we infer from the narrator's words the metaphor whose vehicle is an earthly pearl and whose tenor is an earthly maiden. The pearl is precious in that its shining surface is free of visible flaws, and it is prized by worldly princes who like to have such jewels set in gold. But we also know, whether "we" are the poet's contemporaries or educated twentieth-century readers, that princes and pearls in Christian tradition have symbolized, respectively, the divine Prince who is the Son of God, and the single Pearl that is more precious than all other jewels — that is, Christ and the heavenly kingdom bought by his submission to death on the cross. These symbolic values, though they do not become explicit until later, are latent all along. The idea of an earthly prince and that of the Prince of Peace are joined retrospectively when the word *prince*, which had appeared in the first line of the poem, reappears in the linking phraseology of the final section. The latent symbolic value of the pearl of the opening metaphor is present also in the pearls strewn prodigally on the ground of the surreal landscape into which the dreamer first "wakes," grinding like gravel under his feet (81–82). In addition to the one immeasurably valuable pearl that the maiden wears upon her breast, lesser pearls decorate her garments and her crown in an abundance that may strike the modern reader as excessive.[38] Yet it is typical of this poet that he should imagine the splendor of her attire as excelling that of the most lavishly opulent garments worn by noblewomen in his time. The herbs in the first section have the same reality and potentially symbolic value as the pearls of the first and second: their fragrance, which lulls the narrator to sleep, is an attribute of the divine realm (cf. 1122), and their medicinal powers over the body portend the dreamer's progress toward spiritual health, which takes place under the auspices of the Lamb.[39] The second section's beryl banks of the stream and the emeralds and sapphires lying at the bottom reappear in section 17 among the precious stones making up the foundation of the celestial city which is the Lamb's dwelling place.

The presence of Christ underlies the changing content of the successive sections of *Pearl* as a ground bass in music underlies a series of changing melodies and harmonizations. I want now to consider the poet's references and allusions to him in relation to an important linguistic principle, first enunciated by Ferdinand de Saussure in his *Cours de linguistique générale*,[40] and an analogous principle of mental association, discussed in a foundational and still indispensable essay by Roman Jakobson entitled "Two Aspects of Language and Two Types of Aphasic Disturbances."[41] Saussure asserted the copresence in all utterance of two kinds of relationships among words, called syntagmatic and paradigmatic (originally associative). Syntagmatic relationships link words together in linear series. Paradigmatic relationships (or associations) link words together in groups of which only one member is made explicit at each point in a given series, the others remaining stored in the speaker's mind.[42] The two kinds of relationship can be diagrammed in spatial terms as a horizontal line (representing the syntagmatically linked terms in a series) and a vertical line (representing a particular term plus the implicitly present terms of the paradigm to which it belongs).[43] What is particularly relevant to the study of poetic language is Saussure's inclusion of similarities of sound-pattern, among other kinds of association, among paradigm determinants.[44] Every rhyme-word chosen by a poet can thus be thought of as one member of a paradigm consisting of all words in the language rhyming on the sound in question.

Jakobson was concerned with the divide in human thought between two kinds of link between ideas: similarity and contiguity or extension. (These correspond to the paradigmatic and syntagmatic relationships, respectively, posited by Saussure.)[45] Jakobson called associations based on similarity metaphorical, and those based on contiguity or extension metonymic. With each he associated a major trope, or kind of figurative language.[46] Figurative language based on similarity includes not only metaphor proper, in which similarity is implied, but simile, in which it is explicitly asserted. (Thus in *Pearl* 962, the maiden is metaphorically called a "lufly flor" rather than being said to resemble one, while in 178, the whiteness of her face is described in a simile: "Hyr vysayge whyt as playn yvore." The Middle English equivalent of "her ivory face" would have stated the same idea as a metaphor.) In metonymy, a term designating an attribute of a subject or something otherwise associated with it is substituted for an inclusive designation of the subject itself. Thus in *Pearl* 421, the dreamer addresses the maiden metonymically as "blysful," referring to her in terms of her state of blessèdness and thus bringing it to the foreground as one of her most important attributes. Descriptive details can acquire metonymic force without the figurative substitution of one term for another. In *Pearl*, the idea of the maiden's blessèdness, expressed by the metonymic appellation "blysful," is given additional saliency by the repeated appearance of the words *blys* and *blysful* in descriptive details pertaining to her and her surroundings. The attribute, so emphasized, takes on metonymic significance in itself.

Jakobson held that the language of poetry and that of prose tend toward the metaphoric and metonymic poles, respectively.[47] If we think more specifically of lyric and narrative, we can easily recognize the truth of this description. Metaphors and similes are a hallmark of lyric poetry. Furthermore, the phonic resemblances to one another of rhyme-words and lines having the same metrical pattern correspond, on the level of sound, to the resemblances in the world of ideas that inspire metaphors and similes. The events of a narrative, on the other hand, are naturally contiguous in time, and the details of a description are contiguous in space. A literary work such as *Pearl,* which is a narrative written in elaborately patterned verse, can be expected to be rich in both metaphoric and metonymic relationships. Harking back to the vertical and horizontal dimensions in terms of which the theories of Saussure and Jakobson can be expressed, we can think of the totality of the poem's 101 stanzas, identical in rhyme and meter, as overlaid or "stacked" on one another and thus as exemplifying the vertical line of paradigmatic and metaphoric equivalence. At the same time, the variety of rhyme-sounds and rhyming words which is a feature of the poem's language represents a complementary principle of expansion or amplification, thus exemplifying the horizontal line of syntagmatic and metonymic extension. The contents of the sections are similarly stacked, in that they reflect stages of a single spiritual progression toward a single goal, yet they too extend onward and outward in their discursive, narrative, and descriptive variety. Jakobson's often-quoted statement, that "the poetic function projects the principle of equivalence from the axis of selection into the axis of combination," might have been formulated with *Pearl* in mind.[48]

The metonymic presentation of Christ in *Pearl* consists chiefly, as might be expected, in references to the narrative of his life on earth. The dreamer alludes to his birth when he speaks of the Virgin:

> "We leven on Marye that grace of grewe,
> That ber a barne of vyrgyn flour."
> ["We believe in Mary, from whom grace derived,
> Who bore a child, flower of a virgin."] (425–26)

The story of Jesus and the children belongs to the course of his life as an itinerant preacher and teacher. The maiden makes a series of references to his death, which are couched in a variety of kinds of language. Her first reference to it is metonymic in that she speaks of the "ryche blod" and "wynne water" that "ran on rode so roghe" from a "brode wounde" (646–47, 650) without naming the being who was wounded or the manner of his execution. Her second reference is less oblique: she describes Christ as "he on rode that blody dyed, Delfully [grievously] thrugh hondez thryght [pierced]" (705–06). A little later, she calls Christ "My Lorde the Lombe, that schede hys blode" (741). In the first of the three biblical passages she cites in describing the Lamb to the dreamer in section 14, she refers to him metonymically as "that gloryous gyltlez that mon con quelle [killed] Withouten any sake [charge] of felonye" (799–800). (*Gyltlez* is a metonymic designation; the attribute it selects for expression is further emphasized by the relative clause that follows.) Her final account of the condemnation and crucifixion is detailed, emotional, and melodramatic:

> "In Jerusalem watz my lemman slayn
> And rent on rode wyth boyez bolde. . . .
> Wyth boffetez watz hys face flayn
> That watz so fayr on to byholde . . .
> For uus he lette hym flyghe and folde
> And brede upon a bostwys bem."
> ["In Jerusalem my true love died,
> Rent by rude hands with pain and woe; . . .
> His blessèd face, or ever he died,
> Was made to bleed by many a blow;
> For us he was beaten and bowed low
> And racked on the rood-tree rough and grim."] (805–06, 809–10, 813–14)

Among the metonymic references to Christ in *Pearl* must be included his personification in section 12 as a feminine being called, in a generally accepted emendation, *Coyntise,* that is, "wisdom." This personage was evidently derived by the poet from the Book of Wisdom, apocryphal in Protestant tradition but included in the Vulgate Bible as Liber Sapientia and interpreted by the church as signifying Christ as the Divine Wisdom (see above, p. 147). The portrayal in *Pearl* is metonymic in that it is based not on a resemblance, but on a single aspect of the personified being. Here we have neither verbal substitution nor the selection of a descriptive detail for emphasis, but something on the larger scale of symbolism: the entrance on the dramatic scene of a character who temporarily takes the place of another.

A survey of the metaphorical references to Christ in *Pearl* must include a number of expressions that had probably become "dead metaphors," largely devoid of their original force, by the *Pearl*-poet's time. Such metaphors were presumably devised to make the divine realm accessible to human understanding by describing it in terms drawn from earthly experience.[49] Such a term is *lord,* which affirms a resemblance between an earthly ruler's relation to his subjects and the relation of the divinity to mortal beings. This term appears many times in *Pearl* with reference to both God the father and God the Son. To it the maiden adds the synonym *Dryghtyn* (349), which according to *MED* (s.v. *Drihten* n.) was applied in Middle English to God and Christ alike. *Lord* takes on a double metaphorical meaning when the maiden refers to Christ as her lord (403), since the word meant "husband" as well as "sovereign" (*MED* senses 1 and 10). A third meaning, "property owner" (*MED* sense 1[b]), is called into play in the parable of the vineyard, where the "lord" allegorically signifies Christ. Other words for Christ expressing worldly sovereignty are *prince* (1, 1176, et al.) and the rarer *cheventayn* (605). As I pointed out earlier, the phrase "the Fader of folde and flode" (736) refers to Christ rather than to God. When he is implicitly represented as the body of which each faithful Christian is "a longande lym" (462), he is called "the Mayster of myste [master of (spiritual) mystery]" (ibid.). The maiden, alluding to the Song of Songs in explaining the relationship between them to the Dreamer, calls him her "lemman," or lover (763, 796, 805, 829).

Of the figurations of Christ in *Pearl* that should be classed as metaphorical in the broad sense of being based on similarity, the most important is surely the Lamb. Like the personification of Christ as Wisdom, this representation operates on a larger than verbal scale. It involves, not the displacement of a literal term by a figurative term, as in metaphor, or the explicit affirmation of a single resemblance, as in simile, but the substitution of one entity for another. The symbol of the Lamb begins to move toward the foreground of the narrative when the maiden tells the dreamer that the one pearl of the parable is in fact the pearl she wears on her breast, and that the Lamb has given it to her. She goes on to explain that she was vested with the supernatural attributes of beauty and power the dreamer sees in her when the Lamb took her as his bride. Then, in a passage I discussed earlier, she answers the dreamer's question about the nature of her divine husband by citing three scriptural passages expressing his identity as Lamb first in a simile, then metaphorically, and finally in a symbolic portrayal as a creature remote from the terms of human experience.

These various and sundry representations point, in one way or another, toward the final appearance of Christ in the penultimate section of the poem. They add up to a multilayered and dramatically powerful conception of the divine being whom the dreamer sees at last within the celestial Jerusalem. The breaking off of the dream, which occurs immediately afterward, is followed by the five stanzas of the final section. It is now time to reconsider the meaning of these two endings and the relationship between them. In the course of the dream, we have seen two forces pulling in opposite directions. One continually draws the dreamer toward the symbolic center which is the procession within the city; one continually delays his progress toward it. The hindering force is his mortal nature: his self-centeredness, which is temporarily dispelled in the course of the dream, and his habit of thinking in terms of relationships of space, time, and degree, which is not. The opposite, attracting force emanates from the maiden on whom the dreamer's heart is set. At first, he desires to possess her once more as he possessed her on earth. His realization that this is impossible does not dispel his longing for her; rather, it awakens in him a more spiritual kind of longing: to apprehend her in her transfigured state.[50]

She for her part, in guiding him toward the understanding he seeks, is motivated by what we must see, if not as love in the human sense, then as a benignity merging into the benignity of Christ. Persistently, if not always patiently, now adopting one tactic, now another, she counters his objections and corrects his misunderstandings. But the more fully she reveals herself to him, the more he must understand her in terms of her new "life" and its new setting. The Lamb is central to both. Though she is recognizably herself, she is also part of a throng of thousands upon thousands, whose members share their identity and dwelling-place as his brides. It is the Lamb who has invested her with transcendent beauty, courtesy, and wisdom, and it is he who has conferred upon her the pearl, a visible symbol of the eternal bliss of her union with him. The dream brings the dreamer ever closer to an apprehension of her, but in so doing it also brings him ever closer to her celestial bridegroom. If this movement were to be completed, his cupidinous desire for the maiden who was his earthly pearl would shift permanently to the heavenly pearl of which she has become an intrinsic part. Both pearls are uniquely valuable, but their "singleness" is of two quite different kinds. At the beginning of the poem, singleness (8) is a sign of human partiality: the fixation of the lover's desire on one irreplaceable person. The one pearl of the parable stands for the one truth proclaimed by Christian doctrine. Despite the fact that it adorns the breasts of thousands of maidens, it stands for one Redeemer, one salvation, one offer of eternal bliss that must be chosen in preference to everything else.

In the final phase of the dream, the dreamer is allowed to see what he has been hearing about, and his visionary experience of the eternal realm, as I tried to show earlier, more and more approximates experience in earthly time. It culminates in a virtual face-to-face encounter with the Lamb, so intensely imagined that its natural and supernatural aspects are scarcely distinguishable. The Lamb's awe-inspiring and poignant personae, presented separately earlier in the poem, are now brought together in a doubly affecting presence. The dreamer sees him first as the supernatural creature of Revelation, moving proudly at the head of the procession, his brow adorned with "hornez seven of red golde cler," his clothes as bright as "praysed perles" (1111–12). At his approach, the awestruck elders fall prostrate (1120). But immediately afterward, the dreamer sees him as the meek lamb whose coming was prophesied by Isaiah and affirmed by John the Baptist: he manifests a delight that is shared by all those who see him, his clothes are "worthly whyte," his glances transparently express his inner graciousness (1129–34). In this more appealing aspect, he bears the visible emblem of his earthly abasement in the wound on his side, from which the blood of redemption continually flows (1135–37). All this fills the dreamer with a responsive delight, with compassion, and with love. Fixing his attention on the Lamb, he finds him "best . . . blythest, and most to pryse" of anyone he has ever heard of, and the sight of the bleeding wound moves him to sorrow and indignation (1131–32, 1138–40). Then, as if an arrow could both hit and veer from the center of a target, his gaze moves away from the leader of the heavenly company to the company itself. When he sees, among the thousands upon thousands of queens, the one who is singularly "his" he is overcome by the kind of delight a mortal lover takes in his beloved and rushes into the stream.

He blames himself, of course, for having tried to cross it and for having been expelled, as a result, from the "fayre regioun" of the dream and "alle the syghtez so quyke and queme [living and pleasurable]" he had seen there. More mysteries, he thinks, might have been revealed to him had he not been so rash and willful (1167, 1189–94). But, to repeat my earlier question, what more might he have seen? The answer I propose is: nothing — that is, nothing, either in the symbolic vision of which the pearl is an intrinsic part, or in the didactic allegory of the workaday world in the parable of the vineyard, provides a basis for a deeper and more lasting apprehension of the Lamb than the dreamer experiences. In fact, he looks at the Lamb with an odd naiveté, as if what he saw were a real though preternaturally radiant creature adorned with pearls, and not an embodiment of the Redeemer. In particular, he has no idea what cruel person might have been responsible for the bleeding wound, or what it means.[51]

This ignorance on the part of a man we know to be a believing Christian, inexplicable in realistic terms, is an important sign of the constraints imposed on the poem by the poet's shaping conception. Though Christ is everywhere present in it, he enters it only in response to the dreamer's sustained attempts to possess the maiden, first physically, then imaginatively. When he does, he figures in it as the Redeemer, not of the human race in general, but of the maiden and the company to which she belongs, whose perfect number is to be apprehended not literally but symbolically. The fact that, conceived of in terms of worldly time, that company continuously grows larger (846–50) is irrelevant. So too is the spiritual status of the dreamer himself. True, the maiden implies that as a righteous Christian he may, by penitence, prayer, and God's grace, attain salvation and thus join her after death (661–64), but the words she speaks are not directed to him personally. It is thus not surprising that the inhabitants of the celestial city, when he sees them at last, prove to consist entirely of the Holy Innocents, even though, as conceived of in ecclesiastical tradition, these merely constitute a kind of elite corps within the entire population of the redeemed. Speaking momentarily with a naiveté similar to the dreamer's, one might say that there is no room in the procession for him because the streets of the city are already filled. The Lamb's "glentez gloryous glade" (1144), that is, his glorious and gracious glances, are directed, within the enclosing walls of jasper, toward those who follow him and await him. Though according to church doctrine, the blood that flows from his side was shed out of love for all humanity and cleanses of original sin all who believe in him, the dreamer, while still dreaming, does not and cannot respond to that sacrifice as made for him.

At this point, we should, I think, turn from the poem to its author, who imposed on it a design we can infer, without danger of lapsing into the "intentional fallacy," from its form. As we all know, the number of its lines, 1,212, repeats the number 12, which is exemplified in the celestial Jerusalem as described in Revelation, by the layers making up the city's foundations, by its dimensions, by the total of gates in its four walls, and by the twelve fruits of the tree of life that are renewed twelve times a year. Since the pearl-maiden dwells in it, the number 12 points to her as well. The square of 12, or 144, is her number in that she is one of the company of the Lamb's 144,000 brides. The numerical design of the poem thus both stands for and sets a limit on the action it dramatizes — the dreamer's sustained attempt to possess the maiden. We can now see the goal toward which he has been moving as the realization, based not on knowledge of doctrine but on experience, that she is one of the Holy Innocents, united with her fellows and with the bridegroom they share in eternal bliss. Once this imaginative goal has been reached, the dream can, and in a sense should, be broken off.

Perhaps we ought to think of the dreamer's foray into the stream as a kind of *felix culpa*, an act which, out of context, should be deplored, but which should also receive our gratitude in view of its happy consequences for *Pearl* as poetic drama. It gives the dream an ending that is startling, moving, and, on consideration, inevitable. Once the awakened dreamer has vented the grief that overcomes him on finding himself cast out of the visionary realm, its radiance fades into the light of common day. He remembers the maiden in her heavenly surroundings not as a blissful participant in a magnificent procession, but as part of a *garlande* (1186). Because this word, which has not previously appeared in the poem, can mean both "wreath of flowers" and "coronet" (*MED* s.v. *gerlond* senses 1[a] and 2[a]), it restates her identity as a "reken [praiseworthy] rose" and a queen, in language that lies outside the imagery of the dream. *Doel [grief]-doungoun*, the awakened dreamer's metaphorical name for the real world in which he lives, strikes me as an expression used in passing and devoid of genuine emotional charge, like "vale of tears."[52] Its presence in his statement that "all is well" with him need not prevent us from taking that statement seriously. This diminution of intensity in the poem's final section is attended by a change of verb tense, from the past, not only of the dream, but of the dreamer's reactions immediately on awakening, to the present of a mental life no longer caught up in a vision — the "time being" of W. H. Auden's Christmas oratorio. The speaker now presents himself to us as a member of a Christian congregation, one who knows Christ as both his divine Redeemer and his earthly "frende" (1204). He consigns to God the *lote*, or "utterance," he received while bowed down on the burial mound (I take this *lote* to be the poem),[53] and the lost child who inspired it, invoking Christ's blessing on them and adding his own. The last four lines hark back to the two major symbols of timelessness in the poem, the penny and the pearl, and associate these with the round wafer as well as the wine that become the sacrificial body and blood of Christ in the communion service. These symbols are now literally quotidian, shown by the priest every day to "uus" (1210), that is, to the poet and his fellow communicants, medieval and modern.[54]

As I read this concluding stanza, the words on the page seem to me no longer fictional. I hear in them the all but unmediated voice of a man who, in the late fourteenth century, grieving over the death of a beloved daughter, found comfort in poetic creation, lavishing his craftsmanship on a narrative in which he sent a surrogate self in search of her in a dream. The language dramatizing that search, though marked by the intellectual, modal, and stylistic contrasts and complementarities I have expounded here, repeats over and over again a single stanzaic pattern. "The one remains, the many change and pass." But the dreamer-narrator of *Pearl* does not, like the speaker of the last stanzas of Shelley's *Adonais*, triumphantly repudiate the earthly world in favor of the eternal. Rather, his vision of the one is grounded in and shaped throughout by mortal partiality. The many colors of *Pearl* are part of the brilliance that we, as "jewelers," perceive and admire; the limitations of the poet's singular vision give it the poignancy that has continued, through the centuries, to move us as human beings.

Appendix:
Rhyme-Sounds and Rhyme-Words in
Lines 1–120 of Pearl *and* Pety Job

The rhyme-scheme shared by *Pearl* and *Pety Job* calls for three different rhyme-sounds, with four instances of the A-rhyme, six instances of the B-rhyme, and two instances of the C-rhyme in each stanza. In *Pearl*, the A- and B-rhymes change from stanza to stanza; the C-rhyme remains constant in groups of five stanzas, but changes from section to section. In *Pety Job*, a single C-rhyme is used throughout: the twelfth line of every stanza is the refrain "Parce michi, domine," and the tenth line rhymes with it. There are thus 10 A-rhyme sequences and 10 B-rhyme sequences in the first 10 stanzas, or 120 lines, of each poem, or 20 A- and B-sequences in all. In the first 10 stanzas, or 2 sections, of *Pearl*, there are also 2 different C-rhyme sequences, with 10 instances of the rhyme-sound in each group of five stanzas. Since all the stanzas of *Pety Job* end in the same C-rhyme, the first 10 stanzas contain 20 instances of it. The numbers of rhyme-sounds in the first 120 lines of the two poems thus add up in *Pearl* to 20 + 2, or 22, and in *Pety Job* to 20 + 1, or 21. Theoretically, lines 1–120 of *Pearl* could contain 22 different rhyme-sounds, and lines 1–120 of *Pety Job* could contain 21.

It would be understandable if a medieval, or for that matter a modern, poet composing 10 or more stanzas in so demanding a rhyme-scheme were to fall back again and again on the stock of rhyme-words that evolved in English, once continental end-rhyme had replaced the native alliterating line. The words making up these groups were "common" in terms both of level of diction and frequency of occurrence in the language: words such as *day/way/say*, etc., *night/bright/light*, etc., *ought/sought/thought*, etc., among others. The rhyme-sounds in question would tend to appear more than once in the resultant poem, and repetition of sound would entail repetition of words. These two kinds of repetition do occur in both poems. But tabulations of rhyme-sounds and rhyme-words in the first 120 lines of each bear out the impression they make on their readers: that there is far less repetition in *Pearl* than there is in *Pety Job*. Lines 1–120 of *Pearl*, for example, contain 21 different rhyme-sounds out of a possible 22 (10 A-rhymes + 10 B-rhymes + 2 C-rhymes). Lines 1–120 of *Pety Job* contain 13 out of a possible 21 (10 A-rhymes + 10 B-rhymes + 1 C-rhyme). And whereas 20 of *Pearl's* 21 rhyme-sounds occur in only one sequence, the total of rhyme-sounds occurring in only one sequence in *Pety Job* is 9 out of 13.

Other figures could be cited to the same effect; I shall be selective. In *Pearl* 1–120, only one rhyme-sound occurs in more than one sequence, namely, *-ere*, which occurs twice. In *Pety Job* 1–120, one rhyme-sound occurs in 4 sequences, one in 3, three in 4, and two in 2.

As for the variety of rhyme-words, as distinct from rhyme-sounds, in the first 120 lines of the two poems, anyone examining comparatively this aspect of their language must take into account the fact that the design of *Pearl* calls for the fivefold reiteration of two link-words in the first two sections, whereas in *Pety Job* there is only one link-word, namely, *domine*, which occurs at the end of every stanza and thus appears ten times in the poem's first ten stanzas. Setting aside the formally prescribed reiterations in both poems, we find that the repetition of a given rhyme-sound entails less repetition of rhyming words in *Pearl* than it does in *Pety Job*. The most frequently used rhyme-sound in *Pearl* 1–120, for example, is *-ere*, which occurs ten times in two sequences: it is the B-rhyme of stanza 1 of section 1, occurring six times, and the A-rhyme of stanza 3 of section 2, occurring four times.[55] Nine different words, *clere* (line 2), *pere* "peer" (4), *were* (6, 87), *synglere* (8), *erbere* (9), *luf-daungere* (11), *dere* (85), (*in*) *fere* "together" (89) and *gyternere* (91) are used in these ten occurrences. In *Pety Job* 1–120, the most frequently used rhyme-sound is *-ay*, which occurs sixteen times in three sequences; it is the B-rhyme of stanza 2, occurring six times, the A-rhyme of stanza 6, occurring four times, and the B-rhyme of stanza 8, occurring six times. Seven different words, *alle-way* (14, 86), *ay* (18), *clay* (16, 65), *day* (20), *may* (24), *sey/say* (21, 63, 90), *away* (61), *nay* (67, 95), *display* (87), *domysday* (92), and *pray* (93), are used in these sixteen occurrences. (If *day* [20] and *-day* in *domysday* [92] are counted as two instances of the same word, then only six different words are used in the *-ay*-rhyme.)

These statistical differences between the two poems are reflected in differences in reader response. I venture to say that the reader (or auditor) of *Pearl* does not become conscious of repetitions of rhyme-sounds or rhyme-words other than those decreed by the poem's verbal design. For one thing, the repetitions that do occur fall too far apart for the inner (or outer) ear to become conscious of them. The first of the five rhyme-sequences on *-ere*, for example, occurs in the first stanza; this rhyme-sound is not repeated until the second stanza of section 2, so that its last occurrence in 1.1.B (line 85) is separated from its first occurrence in 2.3.A (line 11) by 74 lines. Moreover, though the word *were* appears in each of these two sequences (6, 87), their wording is otherwise different: *clere, pere, synglere, erbere, luf-daungere* appear in 1.1, *dere,* (*in*) *fere*, and *gyternere* in 2.3. Moreover, these rhyme-words vary in stylistic level and frequency of use. *Synglere*, as is shown by the citations in *MED* s.v. *singler(e)* adj., is of elevated quality, unlike *dere* and *clere*, and *gyternere*, again unlike *dere* and *clere*, is a word of rare occurrence; see *MED* s.v. *giterner(e)* n.. In contrast, a reader of *Pety Job* is likely to be struck by the "inartistic," that is, rhetorically pointless, repetition of sounds and words when, as happens a number of times, sequences of a given rhyme-sound, with repetition of rhyme-words as well, occur in close proximity. Sequences of rhymes on *-ay*, for example, occur in stanzas 6 and 8, with repetition of the words *nay* (67, 95) and *say* (63, 90). In addition to appearing twice in the C-rhyme of every stanza, rhymes on long *-e* appear in 8 sequences, including the A-sequences of stanzas 9 and 10, with repetition of the word *the(e)* "thee" (97, 115). The word *me* also appears twice in these two stanzas, in line 99 of stanza10 and in the C-rhyme of stanza 10 in line 118. Other similar details could be cited — there are repeated phrases, such as "clot off clay" 16, 65, as well as repeated words, in *Pety Job* — but the preceding examples should suffice to make the point: in *Pearl*, formal repetition of sounds and words is complemented by a variety achieved despite the severe constraints imposed by formal patterns.

To convey in visual terms the repetitiousness of rhymes and rhyme-sounds in *Pety Job*, I append here the first 120 lines of that poem, with repeated rhyme-sounds emphasized and repeated rhyme-words capitalized. I give the text as edited by C. Horstman from MS. Harley 1706, omitting the Latin passages preceding the stanzas that translate them. I have disregarded square brackets indicating emendations, and italicizations indicating letters (chiefly final *-e*) substituted for scribal flourishes and have modernized the Middle English alphabet as I have done elsewhere in this book. I have also changed initial *v* to *w* in *woundes* "wounds" 45.

Pety Job, *stanzas 1–10*

1	Parce michi, DOMINE[56]
	Lyff lorde, my soule thou SPARE;
	The soth I sey now sykerl*y*
	That my dayes nought they *are*;
5	For though I be bryght off bl*e*,
	The ffayrest man that ys ough-wh*are*,
	Yet schalle my ffayrnesse fade and fl*e*
	And I schall be but wormes w*are*,
	And whan my body ys alle b*are*
10	And on a bere brought shalle BE,
	I not what I may synge th*are*
	But *parce michi* DOMINE.

What ys a man, wete I wolde,
That magnyfyeth hym-self ALLE-WAY,

15   But a marke made in molde
      Off a clyngyng clot off CLAY?
      Thou shopest us ffor that we schulde
      Have bene in blysse ffor ever ande *ay*:
      But now allas bothe yong ande olde
20   Foryeten hit bothe nyght ande *day*.
      A, goode lorde, what shalle I SEY,
      I that stande in thys DEGRE?
      I wote no thyng that helpe m*ay*
      But *parce michi DOMINE.*

25   Or why puttist thou thyn herte ayenst MANE,
      That thou hast so dere bought?
      Thou vysytest hym ande art ffulle ffayne
      Sodenly to preve yeff he be ought.
      To longe in synne we have layne,
30   For synne hath so oure soule thorow-sought
      To helpe oure-selff have we no mayne,
      So moche woo hit hath us wrought.
      But to the pytt whene we be brought,
      Then men wylle wepe ffor the ande ME;
35   But certys, alle that helpeth nought,
      But *parce michi DOMINE.*

      O why so longe or thou wylt SPARE
      Me, in synne that depe dyve?
      Thou woldest suffere nevermore[57]
40   Me to swolowe my salyve?
      I have the gylt ande grevyde s*oore*,
      For synne wyth me hath ben to ryve:
      But, lorde, now lere me with thy l*ore*,
      That dedly synne fro me may dryve;
45   Ande, Ihesu, for thy woundes fyve,
      As thou be-cammest mane for ME,
      When I shalle passe oute off this lyve
      Than *parce michi DOMINE.*

      What shalle I doo unto THE,
50   O thou kepar off al mankende?
      Off suche a matere why madest thou ME
      To the ("thee") contrarious me for to FYNDE?
      O ffadere off hevene fayre ande FRE,
      As thou art bothe gode ande hende,

55   Yet be kynde, as thou hast BE,
      And spare me, lorde, that am unkynde;
      Thy ffrendesshyp, ffader, late me FYNDE,
      As thou art gode in trynyt*e;*
      Off thy mercy make me have mynde
60   Wyth *parce michi* DOMINE.

      Why takest thou nat my synne aw*ay,*
      A thou gode off al goodn*esse?*
      And why also, as I the s*ay,*
      Dost not awey my wykkedn*esse?*
65   Thou madest me off a clot off CLAY
      That breketh ofte thorough brotyl*nesse;*
      Ful brotylle I am, itt ys no NAY:
      That maketh me ofte to do am*ys.*
      But, good Ihesu, I pray the th*ys*
70   For thy grete benygnyt*e:*
      Thy mercy, lorde, late me not m*ysse,*
      But *parce michi* DOMINE.

      Loo, in poudere I shalle slepe,
      For oute of powdere ffyrst I cam;
75   Ande in to poudere must I crepe,
      For off that same kynde I AM.
      That I am poudere I may not threpe,
      For erthe I am as was Adame.
      And now my pytte is dolvene depe,
80   Though mene me seke ryght nought I AME.
      O thou ffadere Abrahame,
      For Mary love that mayde so FFREE
      In whos bloode thy sone swamme,
      So *parce michi* DOMINE.

85   Hit fforthynketh my soule I-w*ys*
      The lyff that I have ledde ALLEWAY,
      For now my speche ayenst me *ys,*
      Sothly my-self I shalle dyspl*ay,*
      In sorow ande in byttyrnesse
90   Off myne oune soule thus shalle I SAY:
      Now, goode Ihesu, kyng off bl*ysse,*
      Dampne me nat att domysday;
      Ande, goode Ihesu, to the I pr*ay*
      Telle how thus thow demest ME

95   Now yeve me mercy, & say not NAY
        Wyth *parce michi* DOMINE

        Semeth hit goode, lorde, unto THE
        To thryste me doune and me accuse?
        I am thy werke, thou madest ME;
100   Thyne onne handewerke thou nat refuse.
        Wythyne the close of chery*te*,
        Good god, thou me recluse,
        And yeff I gylte the in any DEGRE,
        With thy mercy thou me excuse,
105   Ne late me never off maters muse
        That fallene unto deshonest*e*.
        Thy prayer lord thou nat recuse,
        But *parce michi* DOMINE.

        Whethere thyn eyene fflesshly BE?
110   Or yeff thou seest as seeth a MANE?
        Nay fforsothe, butt only *we*
        Off outewarde thyngis beholdyng hane.
        But inwarde thyngis dost thou s*ee*
        That non other may se ne cane.
115   Therffor, lorde, I pray to THE
        Warne me whane I ame mys-tane,
        That I may fflee ffro fowle sathane
        That ys aboute to perysshe ME.
        Lese nat that thou ones wane,
120   But *parce michi* DOMINE.

8

Systematic Sound Symbolism in the Long Alliterative Line: Beowulf and Sir Gawain

In the second stanza of *Sir Gawain and the Green Knight*, a well-known allusion to narration in alliterative verse echoes in tantalizing fashion a similar passage in *Beowulf*. The *Gawain*-poet announces that he intends to recount an adventure, one of "Arthurez wonderez" (29), and that he will tell it as he himself has heard it told,

> As hit is stad and stoken
> In stori stif and stronge,
> With lel letteres loken,
> In londe so hatz ben longe.
> [As it is fashioned featly
> In tale of derring-do,
> And linked in measures meetly
> By letters tried and true.] (33–36)[1]

In *Beowulf*, after the hero has torn off Grendel's arm and sent him forth to die in his lair, we are told that the celebrations on the following morning included the narration of this exploit in verse by a thane who knew many traditional stories ("ealdgesegena / worn gemunde" [869–70]).[2] On this occasion, he "found other words [that is, new words], truly linked" ("word ōþer fand / sōðe gebunden" [870–71]). (Translations, unless otherwise specified, are my own.)

Both *lel* (a Middle English form of the word *loyal* which descends into modern Northern and Scottish English as *leal*) in *Sir Gawain* and *sōðe* ("truly") in *Beowulf* can, of course, be narrowly interpreted as referring to the technique of verse-composition: the alliterative links among metrical units in successive lines (the "letteres" of the *Gawain*-passage) are formally correct. But surely this is only part of their meaning — surely we may infer that such linkages, in addition to serving their metrical purposes, somehow enhance the "truth" (*sōðe*), or "faithfulness" (*lel*), of the unfolding story.

This effect of enhancement depends on an important aspect of the expressive values we instinctively attach to the sounds of words, especially in poetry. I call it systematic sound symbolism. Operating through chance similarities or identities on the level of sound, the magical, incantatory powers of language lend a validity to connections among words which is quite other than the kind of validity having to do with connections among meanings and aspects of subject matter. The influence of systematic sound symbolism is apparent in the everyday uses of language in the numerous proverbial expressions, set phrases, nursery rhymes, and the like in which alliterating or rhyming words enhance the "truth" of a generalization or a story. (In what follows, I shall limit my examples to alliterative combinations.) We feel, without stopping to think about it, that "fit as a fiddle" defines fitness more fittingly than "fit as a violin"; that the logical companion for a boy named Jack who goes to fetch a pail of water is a girl named Jill; that more than mere coincidence is at work in the alliteration of *pea* with *pod*; that the proverb "Early ripe, early rotten" carries more conviction than "Early ripe, early spoiled." (In this last example, systematic sound symbolism works ironically to sharpen a contrast between meanings, as it also does, to give but one additional example, in the expression "as different as chalk from cheese.")

The alliterating formulas of the verse tradition to which both *Beowulf* and *Sir Gawain*, despite the wide chronological gap that separates them, belong derive a part of their expressive power from the reinforcement of connections among meanings by connections among sounds. Systematic reinforcement of this sort is apparent in such combinations in Old and Middle English as "wigum ond wǣpnum" (*Beowulf* 2395; cf. *Gawain* 384, 1586); "heard under helme" (*Beowulf* 342, 404, 2539); "burne on blonk" (*Gawain* 785, 2024); and "lorde and . . . ledez" (*Gawain* 1231, 1413). The particular subject matter and cast of characters of a new narrative tend to generate new combinations on the old models. In *Sir Gawain*, for instance, "burne on blonk" underlies "the gome upon Gryngolet" (748), and formulas combining *kyng* and *court* (cf. 100, 1048) underlie "this kyng lay at Camylot" (37). Our sense of the natural affinities of warriors with weapons, helmets, and warhorses is confirmed by the existence of alliterative links among words having these meanings; the first letter of the name of Sir Gawain's horse makes it all the more suitable that he should belong to that particular knight; a castle whose name begins with the *k*-sound is a fit residence for a famous *king*.

When two or more words are linked both formally, by alliteration, and referentially, on the level of subject matter, and when they appear a number of times in each others' vicinity as designators of important elements of a narrative, the resultant sound-system may take on thematic importance. Such systems can be identified in *Beowulf* and in *Sir Gawain*. Though they are founded on the same expressive principle, they take different forms and produce different kinds of effects within their respective contexts. I am especially interested in the relationship between these differences and the differences in metrical structure between the two poems.

In the first part of the narrative of *Beowulf* (I shall arbitrarily define this as comprising Beowulf's journey to Denmark and his reception at Heorot), three important words alliterating on *g* signalize key aspects of the identity of the hero: his Geatish nationality, his prowess in battle (*gūð*), and, most important, his intrinsic worth, his goodness. When he enters the poem, having decided to seek out King Hrothgar and put an end to the persecution of the Danes by the monster Grendel, he is called, first, Hygelac's thane, then "good among the Geats" ("gōd mid Gēatum" [195]). He commands that a "good ship" be made ready ("hēt him ȳðlidan / gōdne gegyrwan" [198–99]), on which he will travel to Denmark to offer his services to that country's "battle-king" ("gūðcyning" [199]). He is "the good one" ("se gōda" [205]) who chooses "warriors from among the Geatish nation" ("Gēata lēoda / cempan" [205–06]) to accompany him. During the banquet in Heorot on the evening of his arrival, he assures the Danish king that the strength and courage of the Geats shall before long offer battle to Grendel: "him Gēata sceal / eafoð and ellen ungeāra nū / gūðe gebēodan" (601–3). The words *gōd* and *gūð* are associated with King Hrothgar as well. One of the first appellations bestowed on him is "nobleman good from of old" ("æðeling ærgōd" [130]). Beowulf, announcing himself at Heorot to the courtier Wulfgar, says that he and his men would like to greet Hrothgar, if he, "swā gōdne" (347), will grant them permission. (Talbot Donaldson translates this phrase "good as he is.")[3] Wulfgar replies that he will inquire and will report back the answer that "the good one" (355) gives him. *Gūð* appears in association with Hrothgar in the above-cited *gūðcyning* (199), and in his characterization, on hearing Beowulf's pledge to do battle with Grendel, as "grey-haired and renowned in battle" ("gamolfeax ond gūðrōf" [608]). And Beowulf speaks of Heorot, Hrothgar's royal seat, as a "battle-hall" ("gūðsele" [443]). To the g-system represented by *gōd* and *gūð* as it relates to Hrothgar, we should add a third word, one which expresses an important aspect of the Germanic concept of kingly magnanimity, namely, *gold*. Hrothgar is, among other things, a magnanimous ruler. He bestows on those who serve him the lavish rewards that are spoken of in the opening lines of the poem in the narrator's comment on the generosity of his ancestor King Scyld: a young man ought to bring it about by "goodness" (*gōde*), that is, by "splendid gifts" ("fromum feohgiftum"), that he will have loyal companions in his mature age (20–24). At the feast following Beowulf's victorious encounter with Grendel, the Danish queen, Wealhtheow, urging her husband to be gracious and generous toward the Geats, addresses him as "goldwine gumena," literally, "gold-friend of warriors" (1171). *Goldwine* alliterates with *Gēatum* in the same sentence, and with *Gēatas*, two lines later, in the sentence that follows; a link on the level of sound thus symbolizes the hoped-for link of friendship between the king of the Danes and Beowulf's people.[4]

In part 1 of *Sir Gawain and the Green Knight*, the "goodness" of the hero is underscored by systematic sound-symbolism as the poet takes advantage of the alliterative link between his name and the adjective *god*. He is called "gode Gawan" when he is first mentioned in the poem, at the head of a list of those seated at the high table at Arthur's New Year's feast: "There gode Gawan watz graythed Gwenore bisyde" (109). He is referred to when he tells the Green Knight his name and when he takes his place at table with King Arthur after the Green Knight's departure as "the go(o)de knyght" (381, 482). In part 2, the narrator's explanation of the five times fivefold symbolic values of the pentangle painted on his shield is prefaced by the statement that

> ay faythful in fyve and sere fyve sythez
> Gawan watz for gode knawen, and as golde pured.
> [ever faithful fivefold in fivefold ways
> Was Gawain in good works, as gold unalloyed] (632–33)

(The second of these lines links the two elements of the still-familiar alliterating simile "good as gold.")

We must not overlook the emphasis on reputation in the original language of this last statement: Sir Gawain was *"known for* his goodness" — specifically, for the mutually reinforcing set of virtues publicly proclaimed as his by the emblem displayed on his shield. From the outset, in fact, the adjective *god*, in appellations for Sir Gawain, is used as an epithet, that is, as signifying an attribute for which the person possessing it is widely known. ("Good Gawain" is paralleled in the line that immediately follows by another combination of proper name and well-known attribute, "Agravayn a la dure mayn" [110].) The phrase "the good knight" is used exclusively with reference to Gawain — it

is a "title that he has," just as "the Green Knight" is the title of the personage we will later come to know as Lord Bertilak. The adjective *god* is thus
part of the hero's unchanging identity in the imagined world of the poem. As
Odysseus, in the *Odyssey*, is always *polytropos*, a "man of many shifts,"
and Aeneas, in the *Aeneid*, is always *pius*, so Sir Gawain in *Sir Gawain and
the Green Knight*, is always "good." Or so we are assured as the story begins
to unfold.

Although, as I have said, the adjective *gōd* functions in *Beowulf* as one
element of a system of words alliterating on *g* which help define various aspects of the hero's identity, we do not construe it as an epithet as we do the
same adjective in *Sir Gawain*. In the first place, it cannot be linked by alliteration with the name Beowulf (indeed, that name remains unexpressed until the
hero identifies himself to the Danish coast guard [343]). Neither, though Beowulf is indeed referred to immediately after his entry on the scene as "se gōda,"
does that appellation serve as his particular title. For one thing, it appears side
by side with a number of other equally salient appellations and descriptive
statements. Immediately after Beowulf is introduced as "Hygelac's thane, /
good among the Geats," he is described as "the greatest in physical strength
among the human race at that time, noble and well-grown" ("se wæs mon-
cynnes mægenes strengest / on þæm dæge þysses lifes, / æþele ond ēacen"
[196–98]). And the wise men of the kingdom urge him to undertake the journey to Denmark because they see him to be one "valiant of spirit" ("higerōfne"
[204]). In addition, the adjective *gōd* is associated with persons other than
Beowulf. It sums up the virtues of Hrothgar's ancestor Scyld in the formulaic
half-line "þæt wæs gōd cyning" (11), and it appears several times, as I have
said, with reference to Hrothgar himself (see above).

When we compare the lines in which Beowulf and Sir Gawain are first called
"good," we sense, in little, a crucial difference in tone between the two poems
which depends in part on differences in meter. In "gōd mid Gēatum," *gōd*
takes up almost one-fourth of the line in which it appears. According to the
system of musical scansion applied to the poem by John C. Pope, it has the
temporal value of a dotted quarter-note or three-quarters of a measure, and it
receives the highest grade of stress the meter allows—"strong primary," in
Pope's terminology (p. 246).⁵ (For the classification of "gōd mid Gēatum"
as Type A.2, see the "Line Index to the Catalogue," p. 390; for the temporal
and stress patterns exhibited by half-lines of this type, see p. 248.) As a self-
contained appositive, the phrase is separated by pauses both from the line that
precedes it and the half-line that follows. The poet thus speaks deliberately
and with emphasis when he tells us that Beowulf is good among his people.
But in *Sir Gawain*, the *gode* of "gode Gawan" is rapid and comparatively

unemphatic. Because we understand the main thrust of the statement to be the introduction and identification of the hero, we subordinate the descriptive adjective metrically to the first syllable of the proper name that follows it, giving it less than primary stress. (In classical terminology, "There gode Ga-" would be described as an anapestic foot.)[6] The adjective can thus be thought of as extending the half-line, supplying it with a third "lexical" or content-signifying word which also contributes a third alliterating syllable. Metrical structure requires no such additional weight or alliteration; the simple or basic half-line "There Gawan watz graythed" would have been fully acceptable. Considered in relation to the noun and verb phrases which make up the basic version, the adjective *gode* is superfluous in terms of grammatical structure as well. This supererogatory character inevitably carries over into the realm of meaning. Gawain's goodness, it seems, goes without saying, can be taken for granted. By that same token, the adjective has an attenuated force or generality, comparable, in the realm of moral terminology, to that of a dead metaphor in the realm of figuration.

The two appearances, later in part 1, of the phrase "the go(o)de knyght" as an appellation for Sir Gawain are best discussed comparatively. When Sir Gawain tells the Green Knight his name, the poet writes,

> "In god fayth," quoth the goode knyght, "Gawan I hatte."
> ["In good faith," said the good knight, "Gawain am I."] (381)

When Sir Gawain and King Arthur take their places at table at the end of part 1, he writes,

> Thenne thay boghed to a borde thise burnes togeder,
> The kyng and the gode knyght, and kene men hem served
> Of alle dayntyez double, as derrest myght falle.
> [Then they turned toward the table, these two together,
> The good king and Gawain, and made great feast
> With all dainties double, dishes rare.] (481–83)

In lines 381 and 482 of the original poem, the phrase "the go(o)de knyght" occupies the same metrical position, immediately preceding the caesura at the end of an extended first half-line. It can and should be scanned in two different ways, however, on the basis of "rhetorical stress," that is, on the basis of the comparative importance of the meanings of adjective and noun in each line. The correctness of these differing scansions is borne out by the fact that each of them accords with the relation of the adjective to the alliterative pattern. In 381, we feel that the goodness of the good faith with which Gawain speaks and his own intrinsic goodness complement and reinforce each other; both are reinforced, in turn, by the alliterative link between the adjective and the proper name which appears in the second half-line. We thus read both instances of *god* as what I call major chief syllables, demoting *fayth* and *knyght* to minor chief rank. In 482, we understand the main point of the half-line to be the pairing of Sir Gawain with King Arthur. Accordingly, we subordinate the descriptive adjective to the noun it modifies, as in "There gode Gawan watz graythed" in line 109; metrical subordination again corresponds to lack of emphasis in the realm of meaning.[7]

The adjective thus has three different metrical roles in the three lines in which it refers to Sir Gawain in part 1: in 109, it is an alliterating minor chief syllable; in 381, it is an alliterating major chief syllable; in 482, it is a non-alliterating minor chief syllable. In 381, goodness is imputed to Sir Gawain as he performs an important and courageous action; rhetorical and metrical stress go hand in hand. In lines 109 and 482, in which he is said simply to occupy or take his place at the banquet table, he is called good in passing and without emphasis; the adjective is more an honorific than an accolade.

In *Beowulf*, by contrast, the adjective *gōd* always receives a high degree of stress (in Pope's terminology, either strong primary or strong secondary). With only one exception, it or, in inflected forms, its first syllable has the musical value of a quarter or dotted quarter-note, half or more of one of the two measures making up the half-line.[8] Nuances in the poet's use of it with reference to persons derive in part from relationships between the half-lines in which it appears and the sentences, typically drawn out over two or more lines by appositive phrases and other elaborative materials, in which these half-lines are in turn embedded. On a still larger scale, we may respond, as readers familiar with the poem, to connections among sentences in different parts of the story. Thus when Beowulf makes his entrance on the scene as "Higelaces þegn, / gōd mid Gēatum," he is linked first to his king and then, with the aid of systematic sound-symbolism, to the other warriors of his nation. The descriptive statement that follows places him, more generally, in the context of all the other male warriors of the human race whom he excels in size and strength. As "gōd mid Gēatum" and "se gōda," he is linked, across the scope of the poem as a whole, to the bygone time of the reign of King Scyld, to the present time of his youth in the reign of King Hrothgar, and to the future time of his old age as king of the Geats, through the thrice-repeated summary statement "þæt wæs gōd cyning," which refers to each of the three kings in the order of their reigns (11, 863, 2390).

Whether or not we are aware of these verbal linkages as such, we cannot fail, as we read the poem, to sense its all-important theme of continuity: the transmission through historical time, against all odds, of the values embodied by the good Germanic kings and the good thanes who serve them. In affirming these, the voice of the narrator is at all times solemn, emphatic, and unequivocal. The imagined world of the poem is one in which intrinsic goodness and evil manifest themselves clearly in good and evil actions. These in turn are made known through the dissemination of stories, including the story of *Beowulf* itself, in the course of which praise is bestowed on the former and blame on the latter by the poet-narrator.

In *Sir Gawain*, the bearing out of reputation by performance is by no means a foregone conclusion. The relation between the two is explicitly called into question (with relation not so much to virtue, it would seem, as to virility) by the lady in the first bedroom scene, when she complains that " 'So god as Gawayn gaynly is halden . . . Couth not lyghtly haf lenged so long wyth a lady, Bot he had craved a cosse' " (1297–1300). The narrator's account of the significance of the pentangle, which comes immediately before Sir Gawain leaves King Arthur's court in search of the Green Chapel, presents him as a paragon. We are told that he displays the emblem on his shield and coat-armor by right, "as tulk of tale most trwe" (638), and that his perfection consists in part of a set of five virtues which includes "fraunchyse," or generosity (652). When, at the end of the story, he bitterly reproaches himself for his "falssyng" (2378) and "covetyse" (2380), he is acknowledging, as we also must, that the reality of his behavior under severely trying conditions has fallen short of the ideal goodness imputed to him before the events at Castle Hautdesert and the Green Chapel have taken place.

In underscoring this theme of an uneasy relation between reputation and actuality, the poet avails himself of the numerous metrical options provided him by the late Middle English long alliterative line, including the possibility of extending the basic form of the line by the "gratuitous" addition of descriptive adjectives, including the adjective *god*. He also makes use of a second adjective belonging to the g-system, namely, *gay*, which makes its first appearance with reference to Sir Gawain immediately after the poet's account of the meaning of the pentangle:

> Now graythed is Gawain gay,
> And laght his launce ryght thore,
> And gef him alle goud day,
> He wende for evermore.
> [Now armed is Gawain gay,
> And bears his lance before,
> And soberly said good day,
> He thought forevermore.] (666–69)

The meanings and uses of the adjective *god* in Middle English, for all their variety and scope, include nothing disparaging. *Gay*, however, had not only its most common modern sense, "joyous, lighthearted, carefree," but a number of other senses which have not survived in modern English, some of them bordering on or actually encroaching on morally dubious territory. These include "wanton, . . . lascivious," "glittering," "showy," and "superficially pleasing, specious" (MED s.v. *gai* adj., senses 1, 2[a] and [b], and 3[c]). *God* and *gay*, as monosyllabic lexical adjectives, are interchangeable for metrical purposes,[9] and the poet's deployment within the long alliterating lines now of one, now of both, is of great interest.

God in *Sir Gawain* is associated almost exclusively with men, especially the hero, and *gay* with women, especially the lady of the castle.[10] As *god* becomes, in effect, an epithet for Sir Gawain, so *gay* becomes an epithet for the lady. At the moment when Gawain first sees her, the narrator refers to her as "that gay" (970); when she opens the dialogue in the first bedroom scene, and later in that same conversation, she is called "that/the gay lady" (1208, 1248); Gawain addresses her as "gay" (1213) in the first bedroom scene, and as "my gay" in the third (1822). But Gawain himself is also referred to as "gay" at moments when he is splendidly attired. I have already quoted the line "Now graythed is Gawan gay" (666). Attending the Christmas Eve service at Hautdesert in his fine new mantle, having feasted on fish and warmed himself with wine, he "glydez ful gay" toward his host and hostess (935). An ominous distinction between inner qualities of goodness and outer ones of gaiety or splendor would seem to be suggested when we are told that on the morning of the first hunt "Gawain the god mon in gay bed lygez" (1179). The two adjectives are grammatically superfluous, and they elaborate on, rather than figure in, the gist of the statement. Nonetheless, they are thrust on our attention by the chief metrical rank given them in a properly expressive reading.

The *g*-system I identified in the first five hundred lines of *Beowulf* as consisting of *Gēat*, *gūð*, *gōd*, and *gold* remains operative in part 2 of the poem, when the aged Beowulf, having reigned fifty years as king of the Geats, undertakes his final and fatal adventure. The all-important theme of the historical continuity of kingly and "thanely" virtues thus continues to be reinforced, in part, by systematic sound-symbolism. In particular, expressions containing the words *gūð*, *gōd*, and *gold* which in part 1 were used with reference to King Hrothgar reappear in later references to Beowulf as king of the Geats. The hero is referred to four times (2335, 2563, 2677, 3036) as a "gūðcyning," a title he himself, in part 1, had bestowed on Hrothgar (199); the narrator had also used it of Hygelac, who was king of the Geats in Beowulf's youth (1969).

Beowulf, like Hrothgar before him, is a "nobleman good of old," an "æþeling ǣrgod" (130, 2342). Whereas Hrothgar had been described as "gold-friend of warriors" ("goldwine gumena" [1171, 1602]), Beowulf is called "gold-friend of the Geats" ("goldwine Gēata" (2419, 2584). Among the endlessly varied appellations devised by the poet for his aged hero, there are of course a number in which the adjective *gōd* appears. Thus Beowulf is described, as he gazes on the fiery stream flowing from the dragon's cave, as "the one, good in accordance with manly virtues, who had survived many battles":

> se ðe worna fela
> gumcystum gōd gūðe gedīgde. (2542–43)

In part 1, the young Beowulf had used the phrase "gumcystum gōd" in praising King Hrothgar for his generosity toward him (1486).

The narrator's concept of the qualities that make kings and warriors worth celebrating remains unaltered to the end, and his belief in them remains unshaken. Nonetheless, a sea change has occurred. In the fatal venture against the marauding fire-dragon, the goodness of the hero is manifest still. But it now no longer prevails. In view of the poem's foregone conclusion, late references to Beowulf and his war-gear as good, though they remain unequivocal and emphatic, take on an ironic ring, especially when the adjective is linked with other words that have participated in the *g*-system: "The gold-friend of the Geats did not boast of victories in combat; the battle-sword failed, bared in hostility, as it should not have done, the iron good from of old."

> Hrēðsigora ne gealp
> goldwine Gēata; gūðbill geswāc,
> nacod at nīðe, swā hyt nō sceolde,
> īren ǣrgōd. (2583–86)[11]

When the word *gōd* makes its final appearance in the poem, the alliterative link in which it participates has tragic significance. Wiglaf orders that wood for the funeral pyre be carried to the body of the "good one" ("gōdum tōgēnes" [3114]); the alliterating word in the second half of the line is *glēd*, "fire."

As the plot of *Sir Gawain* approaches its denouement, the complexity of the relationship between "goodness" and "gaiety" (in the latter word's two Middle English senses of "visible splendor" and "showiness or speciousness") continues to be underscored by the appearance of the two relevant adjectives, singly or juxtaposed, in varying metrical positions and with varying degrees of metrical and rhetorical emphasis. After he has accepted the green girdle and promised to conceal the fact, Sir Gawain, awaiting his host's arrival, is blandly referred to as "Sir Gawayn the gode" (1926); the adjective receives full metrical emphasis in an unextended first half-line. Telling us how Gawain dressed himself for his visit to the Green Chapel the following morning, the poet assures us that he did not leave that magic talisman behind:

> Yet laft he not the lace, the ladiez gifte,
> That forgat not Gawayn for gode of hymselven. . . .
> Swythe swethled umbe his swange swetely that knyght
> The gordel of the grene silke, that gay wel bisemed,
> Upon that ryol red clothe that ryche watz to schewe.
> [Yet he left not his love-gift, the lady's girdle;
> Gawain, for his own good, forgot not that: . . . .
> Sweetly did he swathe him in that swatch of silk,
> That girdle of green so goodly to see,
> That against the gay red showed gorgeous bright.][12] (2030–31, 2034–36)

Here, *gode* has strategic rather than ethical significance, and "that gay" in line 2035 is unusual in that it refers to a man rather than a woman. The implications are obvious.

The adjective *good* figures several times in the scene at the Green Chapel. When Sir Gawain calls out to whoever is making an unconscionable racket up on the hill, he bestows the appellation "gode Gawayn" on himself, perhaps with feigned self-confidence: "now is gode Gawayn goande ryght here" (2214). A few moments afterward, when he has flinched from the first blow of the ax, his tormentor accuses him of being, not "good Gawain," but someone else:

> "Thou art not Gawayn," quoth the gome, "that is so goud halden,
> That never arghed for no here by hille ne be vale."
> ["You are not Gawain the glorious," the green man said,
> "That never fell back on field in the face of the foe."] (2270–71)

After all has been revealed, of course, the Green Knight speaks more kindly, saying, among other things, that

> "As perle bi the quite pese is of prys more,
> So is Gawayn, in god fayth, bi other gay knyghtez."
> ["As pearls to white peas, more precious and prized,
> So is Gawain, in good faith, to other gay knights."] (2364–65)

In the second of these lines, *other* is a major chief syllable, *gay* being subordinated to minor chief rank.[13] We are to understand that Gawain is intrinsically good, whereas other knights are outwardly gay, or perhaps that Gawain, unlike other knights, is one in whom praiseworthy outward and inward qualities coincide.

When the hero reappears at Camelot at last, he is joyfully received:

> Ther wakened wele in that wone when wyst the grete
> That gode Gawayn watz commen; gayn hit hym thoght.
> [Bliss abounded in hall when the high-born heard
> That good Gawain was come; glad tidings they thought it.] (2490–91)

What are we to make of this ascription of goodness to the hero, now that he has shown his true colors? I have no space here to address the endlessly debated questions of moral judgment raised by the poem, but I shall make one further observation founded in part on metrical analysis: the matter of Gawain's goodness, as alluded to on his return to the court, is of no great moment. We can see this if we return to line 109, "There gode Gawan watz graythed Gwenore bisyde," where the hero is first mentioned and at the same time the adjective is first used with reference to him. The phrase "gode Gawan" in that line and the same phrase in line 2491 stand in identical positions and have identical metrical values. And the adjective in the two lines is equally lightweight, both metrically and in meaning (see the discussion of line 109 above, pp. 166, 167–68). It is almost as if the aristocratic members of King Arthur's court ("the grete") had learned that Gawain, "that good fellow," or even "good old Gawain," was once again among them.

Fred C. Robinson has well said that "in reading *Beowulf*, as in reading all great poetry, we have the sense that the author's genius has been happily merged with the one style and language which alone could convey his poetic apprehension of his subject."[14] To this I would add "and the one metrical form." The rapid, voluble long lines of *Sir Gawain* and the slow-paced, stately measures of *Beowulf* seem alike suited to the stories these poems have to tell and to the meanings of those stories, locked by two superbly skilled poets in letters tried and true.

PART III

Philological

Reading Sir Gawain and the Green Knight *Aloud*

In the play of its constantly varying rhythms and repeated sounds, *Sir Gawain and the Green Knight* is a delight to the ear as well as to the imagination, and if we neglect this dimension of the poem in our teaching, our students' experience will be sadly diminished. They should hear it read aloud, and they should be made to try reading passages of it themselves. Neither they nor we should refrain from reading the poem aloud for fear of mispronouncing the words or on the ground that "we cannot know for certain how the poet's spoken English sounded." *Gawain* was literally made to be performed, and any rendition, whether fully accurate philologically or not, gives it the life of the voice and moves its aural designs from the visible script into the domain of audible reality.

I began by speaking of play: the description of the meter that I present below can be thought of simply as a set of rules, resembling those of a game. The value of any set of game rules is tested by the pleasure of playing the game, and the value of any set of metrical rules is tested in part by the pleasure of reading in accordance with them. I happen to believe that my rules also form a true description of the way the poet read his poem, but that is another — and a far more complicated — story.

My first two rules deal with syllable count. Once they have been applied, the metrical patterns of the wheels will be readily understood, and after presenting them I shall limit my discussion to the long alliterative line.[1]

Many students who read *Gawain* in the original will have read the *Canterbury Tales*, and Chaucer's verse in the *Tales* is a good place to start. Traditionally, the Chaucerian line has been analyzed as decasyllabic, that is, made up of ten syllables, except that it may have nine syllables when there is neither an unstressed syllable nor a trochaic reversed foot at the beginning of the line and eleven when an unstressed syllable is added to the normal ten-syllable sequence to make a feminine ending. The letter *-e* at the ends of words is frequently sounded to make up these sequences, and it is always sounded, where present, in rhyming words. But *-e* was already well on its way to becoming silent, as it is in modern English, in the Southeast Midland dialect of Chaucer's London, and philologists agree that this change to modern usage had occurred well before Chaucer's time in the Northwest Midland dialect area that was the home of the *Gawain*-poet. The sounding of final *-e* in the verse of *Gawain* would therefore be an archaism, necessitated somehow by the metrical form. But the metrical form of the long alliterative line, whatever it is, is obviously quite different from that of Chaucer's decasyllabic line. In my view, no rules for the sounding of *-e* can be deduced for that form as the *Gawain*-poet used it, and therefore I have proposed that the long lines of *Gawain* should be read aloud without sounding of *-e* within the line. I concede the possibility that *-e* may have been sounded in words final in the line, provided that it was present in their ancestral forms. Such sounding would be a metrically decreed archaism like the (infrequent) sounding of *-e* in the rhyming lines of *Sir Gawain*, as also in *Pearl*, inherited from an earlier time when all the long lines had "feminine endings."[2]

There are, however, two inflectional syllables of frequent occurrence that seem to have been sounded more often than not in the verse of *Gawain*, as also in Chaucer: the ending of the plurals of nouns and the third-person singular present indicative of verbs (spelled *-es* or [modernized] *-ez*) and the ending of the past tense forms and past participles of weak verbs (spelled *-ed*).

Here is a typical passage of Chaucerian verse, scanned in the traditional way. It contains examples of sounded *-e*, *-es*, and *-ed*:

> Whan Zephirus eek with his sweetë breeth
> Inspirëd hath in every holt and heeth
> The tendre croppës, and the yongë sonnë
> Hath in the Ram his halvë cours yronnë (I[A], 5–8)

And here is a typical passage from *Sir Gawain*, read in accordance with my proposed method of syllable count (silent final *-e*'s are emphasized):

After the sesoun of somer wyth the soft wyndëz
Quen Zeferus syflez hymself on sedëz and erbëz,
Wela wynne is the wort that waxes theroute,
When the donkande dewe dropëz of the leuëz,
To bide a blysful blusch of the bryght sunne.
[And then the season of summer with the soft winds,
When Zephyr sighs low over seeds and shoots:
Glad is the green plant growing abroad,
When the dew at dawn drops from the leaves,
To get a gracious glance from the golden sun.] (516–20)

It should be noted that *soft* and *bryght,* in similar phrases in Chaucerian verse, would be spelled and in all likelihood pronounced with final *-e*.

I suggest that the form of the long alliterative line — or rather the variety of its forms — should be studied in two separate stages, the alliterative patterns of the line being considered first, the metrical patterns thereafter.

In looking at the alliterative patterns, we must take into account the division of each long line into two half-lines at some point of phrasal or clausal demarcation. We may call this break a caesura if we wish, but it need not involve a pause calling for a punctuation mark. In the first line of the poem, "Sithen the sege and the assaut watz sesed at Troye," for instance, the dividing point comes between subject and predicate, and the line flows without interruption.

The basic alliterative pattern of the long line requires that at least one syllable in the second half-line should alliterate with one or more syllables in the first; the two halves of the line are thus formally linked. Usually the first half-line has two alliterating syllables, though there may be only one; the second half-line rarely contains more than one, and this single alliteration does not as a rule fall on the last important word in the line. (The groups *sp*, *st*, and *sk* alliterate as if they were single consonants, and words beginning with vowels may alliterate with words beginning with other vowels and with *h*. The long line has a variant form containing two different alliterating sounds: one word beginning with each sound will normally appear in each half of the line. Such lines differ from those having single alliteration, in that the last important word usually does participate in the alliterative pattern.)

A good way of studying the various patterns exhibited by the long lines is to mark them schematically. In my system of notation, the caesura, or point of division between half-lines, is indicated by a slash below the line. Alliterating sounds are marked *a* (or, where two sounds are present, *a* and *b*), and the initial sound of the last important word in the line, assuming that it does not alliterate, is marked *x*. I give a few examples, taking them, as I shall take all my examples from now on, from a single long-line sequence in *Gawain*, lines 203–26:

1. Ne no pysan ne no plate that pented to armes
      a   a   /   a   x
[Nor plate, nor appurtenance appending to arms]
2. Ne no schafte ne no schelde to schwve ne to smyte
      a   a   / a   x
[Nor shaft pointed sharp, nor shield for defense]
3. That is grattest in grene when grevez ar bare
         a   a   /   a   x
[That is goodliest in green when groves are bare]
4. And an ax in his other, a hoge and unmete
         a   a / a   x
[And an ax in his other, a huge and immense]
5. That watz wounden wyth yrn to the wandez ende[3]
      (a) a   (a) b /   a   b
[That was wound all with iron to the weapon's end]

In line 4, the alliteration falls on two different vowels and *h*. Given the possibility of vowel-*h* alliteration, line 5 must be analyzed as having two alliterating sounds. "Watz" and "wyth" in 5 have been marked (a) to indicate that their initial *w*'s are superfluous to the alliterative pattern. Their presence can be thought of as accidental in the sense that they do not contribute to the lexical content of the line. Although its superfluous alliterating words are less conspicuous, line 4 presents the same problem.

Turning now to meter, as distinct from alliteration, in the long lines, I shall begin by describing the basic pattern. I concede that the pattern I denote thus is at times honored more in the breach than in the observance, but I believe that it can in fact be seen as the basis, or point of departure, for the other metrical patterns found in the poem.

In lines conforming to the basic metrical pattern, there are four syllables — two in each half-line — that clearly predominate in stress over syllables adjacent to them. I call them chief syllables, and I call the other syllables in the line intermediate. Readers and listeners familiar with the form will feel that the chief syllables of the basic line fall at temporally equivalent (though not *equal*) intervals of time, rather like the first notes of successive measures in a waltz played rubato. Whereas in Chaucer's decasyllabic verse stressed syllables are usually separated by single intermediate syllables, chief syllables in the long alliterative line may be separated by two, three, or, rarely, more than three intermediate syllables. And they may be juxtaposed; this happens more often in the second half line than in the first.

I illustrate the basic pattern from a group of lines that have four clearly predominant syllables, and no more. These chief syllables should be marked with a capital C above the line; as a way of reviewing rules of syllable count, intermediate syllables may at first be marked *x*; the alliterative pattern of each line should be indicated by notation below it, as before.

```
        x  x  Cx  x  x   C    x   Cx  xC   x
    1. Ne no pysan ne no plate that pented to armes
            a        a   /  a       x
```

```
        x  x   C  x x   C   x   C    x x   C
    2. Ne no schafte ne no schelde to schwve ne to smyte
            a          a   / a          x
```

Examples in which only chief syllables are marked:

```
            C         C        C     C
    3. That is grattest in grene when grevez ar bare
            a        a   /    a       x
```

```
            C     C     C        C
    4. And an ax in his other, a hoge and unmete
            a        a   / a         x
```

```
              C         C       C   C
    5. That watz wounden wyth yrn to the wandez ende
          (a)    a      (a)  b  /   a      b
```

These examples show something of the range in the number of intermediate syllables found between chief syllables. In line 1, there are three between *pys-* and *plate*, but only one between *plate* and *pent-*. If we were to divide the lines into metrical feet and call them by their traditional names, the most common foot by far would be the anapest, the next most common, the iamb. In musical terms, triple time would seem to be the norm of the verse.

Lines like those above are self-explanatory, and rules for reading them would be superfluous. What is needed, rather, is a way of reading sequences in which lines having the basic metrical pattern of four chief syllables and only four appear in company with heavier lines. To this end, I have two rules to offer, and with them my account of the game of reading *Gawain* aloud will be complete. First, the metrical patterns of the lines, though linked with the alliterative patterns, are not wholly governed by them; the meter must be allowed to define itself independently. Second, in lines having heavy syllables above and beyond the basic four, there are nonetheless four syllables that predominate. I call these major chief syllables. Heavy syllables other than major chief I call minor chief. I thus interpret the long line as a structure invariably consisting of four metrical units, each containing one major chief syllable, some containing minor chief syllables as well.

Evidence for my first rule is provided by lines in which the all-important single alliterating syllable in the second half-line can be stressed only if we distort the natural patterns decreed by part-of-speech relations. A clear example is offered by line 987. "Lord Bertilak has just offered his hood to whomever makes the greatest contribution to the Christmas merriment at Hautdesert; he says he will compete with the best of his guests before he will lose the prize — " Er ["before"] me wont ["is lacking to me"] the wede ["the garment," that is, the hood], with help of my frendez." The alliterating letter is *w*, but the preposition "with" (the sole alliterating word in the second half-line) must be accentually subordinate to the noun that follows. Perhaps more important is the rhetorical emphasis that a dramatically expressive reading will allot, in the first half-line, to "me." The lord is saying, "I'll compete with the best of them before *I* lose the prize!"

As for my second rule, a trial reading of any sequence of long lines based on the assumption that there are no more than four major chief syllables to the line will find its biggest stumbling block in those lines that contain more than four syllables belonging to the major parts of speech: the nouns, the lexical adjectives, the verbs, and the lexical adverbs. This is true especially when, as often happens, all these syllables alliterate. In lines 203–26, we can without distortion subordinate the conjunctive adverb *whether* "however" in 203, and the preposition "in" and the colorless verb "hade" in 206. If we do so, we get a reading of the first six lines of the passage that exemplifies the basic metrical pattern:[4]

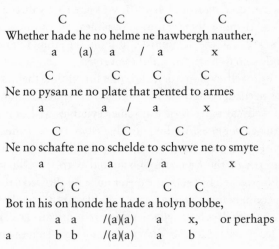

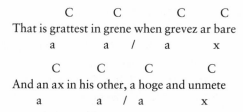

C   C   C   C
That is grattest in grene when grevez ar bare
    a   a   /   a   x

C   C   C   C
And an ax in his other, a hoge and unmete
    a   a   / a   x

But now comes "A spetos sparthe to expoun in spelle, quoso myght," in which a lexical adjective, the noun it modifies, and an infinitive all alliterate in the first half-line. In this phrase, as in many others in long lines containing the sequence "lexical adjective + noun," a reading with two major chief syllables finds its justification in the genius of the English language itself, which forbids the placement of primary stress on both components of such a sequence in a single phrase. Where adjective and noun are followed, as here, by an infinitive that goes with the adjective (the half-line could be reduced to "Spetos to expoun"), it is natural to make the adjective predominate over the noun. Thus we say "a *long* row to hoe" and "a *hard* act to follow" rather than "a long *row*," "a hard *act*." If we read the phrase "a spetos sparthe to expoun" this way, we are giving *spet-* and the second syllable of *expoun* major chief status and reading *sparthe* as minor chief. Marking *sparthe* with a lowercase *c*, we can schematize the line thus:

C   c   C   C   C
A spetos sparthe to expoun in spelle, quoso myght
    a   a   a   / a   x

In other adjective-noun sequences, we have the option, as we do in the spoken language, of emphasizing either the signified attribute or its possessor. Thus in the sentence "Gloria is a good girl," we can place primary stress on either "good" or "girl"; either reading is "correct." In deciding between minor chief and major chief status for this or that adjective in the half-lines of *Gawain*, we seem sometimes to be given a clue by the alliterative pattern. It is natural, for instance, to read "grene stele" (211) and "bryght grene" (220) with major emphasis on the alliterating adjective. But in "stif staf" (214) and "tryed tasselez" (219), it seems possible to signalize either the thing or the attribute; either way, an acceptable reading results. And the independence of the metrical pattern from the alliterative pattern is shown in this passage by the fact that in a dramatically expressive reading of line 224, "fyrst," which does not alliterate, requires more emphasis than "word," which does.

If it is right to read phrases like "A spetos sparthe to expoun" and "the fyrst word that he warp" — and to these let me add "the bit burnyst bryght" (212) — as sequences in which a minor chief syllable falls between two major chief syllables, then the meter of the long line of *Gawain* has important affinites with the meters of nursery rhymes and verses chanted in action games. The same sequence appears in "Pease porridge hot," "Ding, dong, bell," and other familiar lines. The latter differs from the slower, more emphatic sequence "Break, break, break" in Tennyson's poem, where each word is in effect a monosyllabic metrical unit, and the three stresses have equal status. And Tennyson's line could itself, in a different setting, be read somewhat faster, with the middle word demoted to minor chief status:

$$C \quad c \quad C$$
Break, break, break
$$C \quad c \quad C$$
An egg to bake a cake.

In nursery rhymes and game chants, such alternation is present throughout the verse; in *Gawain*, however, heavier sequences containing minor as well as major chief syllables are continually juxtaposed with — and, so to speak, reined in by — lighter sequences. It is as if "Pease porridge hot," read as we read it in nursery rhyme, were to appear in some such context as the following: "They were civilly seated and served at once / With pease porridge hot, the plainest of fare." In fact, the alliterative and metrical patterns that these lines exemplify appear again and again in the verse of *Sir Gawain*.

I believe that in a sustained reading of the poem, if it is fluent and expressive, the kinds of patterns I have been arguing for will in fact emerge, more and more clearly as the cumulative swing of the meter establishes itself. One obstacle to such a reading, of course, is the alien and difficult language of the poem. But there is nothing to be gained by approaching that language with reverential timidity. Despite its unfamiliar letters and uncouth Norse words, the metrical patterns into which the poet wrought it have fewer affinities with the verse of Shakespeare and Milton than with poems we have always known, poems whose cadences are as natural to us as breathing.

10

A Cipher in Hamlet

Throughout the play, Hamlet shows himself as quick and apt at speech as he is slow and inept at revenge.[1] We see him expatiating with ironic eloquence on the glory of man (2.2.286–90), declaiming from memory, in the person of Aeneas, "with good accent and good discretion" (2.2.408–25), affecting the idiom of antifeminist satire in conversation with Ophelia (3.1.137–40), discoursing to the players on elocution and gesture (3.2.1–12), making a deeply felt and high-minded declaration of devotion to his stoical friend Horatio (3.2.44–64), and, in the graveyard scene, indulging in fancifully macabre speculations on buried bones (5.1.64–99). All this, in addition to the series of soliloquies in which he unpacks his heart.

Shortly before the action of the play moves to its conclusion, Shakespeare seems to have provided his hero one more occasion for verbal display. I refer to an exchange of words with "young Osric,"[2] the courtier who informs Hamlet, in language of offensive preciosity, that the king wishes to back him in a fencing match with Laertes. In a passage which appears in the Second Quarto but was apparently cut in the Folio version, Hamlet counters Osric's "extolment" of Laertes (5.2.100–05) with an encomium of his own (106–12). This latter speech, which seems simply parodic in its extreme verbal elaboration and density, is in fact a complicated amphibology (to adapt an Elizabethan term),[3] covertly disparaging what it purports to praise.

It is characteristic of Hamlet that in speaking with those he has reason to distrust, he hides himself behind his words, using them to vent his hostility and rage while at the same time protecting himself from the possible consequences of overt self-expression. His feelings toward Claudius are unmistakably intimated in the first words he utters, well before his suspicions have been confirmed by the words of his father's ghost. The cryptic aside "A little more than kin, and less than kind" (1.2.65) is an ironic comment on Claudius's ostensibly loving designation of him as "my cousin . . . and my son" (1.2.64).[4] Immediately afterward, he responds to Claudius's question, "How is it that the clouds still hang on thee?" by perversely taking the metaphor literally: "Not so my lord, I am too much i'th'sun" (67). Here the homonymy of *sun* and *son* makes possible a veiled repudiation of the king's proffered fatherhood. Once he has put an antic disposition on, Hamlet can safely insult those he despises or hates in the language of his supposed madness, as when he accuses Polonius of being dishonest, that is, hypocritical, and gives in his presence a detailed description of physical and mental senility (2.2.170–77, 193–96). When, in act 4, Claudius informs him that he is being sent to England, he deliberately miscalls him "dear mother" in saying farewell. Claudius corrects him, and he replies "My mother. Father and mother is man and wife, man and wife is one flesh, and so, my mother" (4.3.48–49). This choplogic enables him to allude once more to the incestuous sexual relations that obsess him, relations which, in the preceding scene, he has described to Gertrude, taking her breath away with the savagery of his words.

In act 5, scene 2, Osric's entrance immediately follows the returned Hamlet's account to Horatio of how he foiled Claudius's design to have him executed in England and sent Rosencrantz and Guildenstern "to't" in his place. After an exchange of greetings, Hamlet, speaking aside to Horatio, describes Osric as a "water fly" and a "chough," or jackdaw, that is, as a gaudy, insignificant chatterer.[5] Osric owes his position at court, Hamlet tells his friend, to the fact that he is a landholder of some importance, or, in Hamlet's words, one "spacious in the possession of durt" (5.2.87). This last phrase is a kind of oxymoron, meaning in effect "possessing a great deal of what is not worth possessing."[6] As such, it presages what is to come. After some further dialogue in which Hamlet protests against Osric's insistence on speaking with hat in hand, Osric launches into his pretentious encomium on Laertes. Hamlet responds immediately, effortlessly, and in kind:

> Sir, his definement suffers no perdition in you, though I know to devide him
> inventorially, would dosie th'arithmaticke of memory, and yet but yaw nei-
> ther in respect of his quick saile, but in the veritie of extolment, I take him to

be a soule of great article, & his infusion of such dearth and rareness, as[,] to make true dixion of him, his semblable is his mirrour, & who els would trace him, his umbrage, nothing more. (112–20)

Throughout this speech, Hamlet does indeed parody Osric's affected and inflated language.[7] Indeed, he outsoars Osric in high-flown praise, as he had outdone Laertes in hyperbolic "ranting" in the preceding scene, and, continuing in the same vein, reduces him to virtual stupefaction. But in the second of the two parts into which the speech divides, beginning with "I take him to be a soul of great article," he gives expression, as earlier in the play, to hostility cloaked in verbal obscurity. The remainder of the description is a double-edged sword, consisting of a series of phrases that simultaneously express opposite meanings. I shall give two paraphrases of it, then present lexical evidence for my twofold interpretation, postponing discussion of the phrase "of great article" until the end:

> I take him to be a soul of great article, and his admixture of innate faculties to be of so rare and precious a quality that, to speak truly of him, there is no one like him save his own mirror image, and those who seek to emulate him can be nothing more than a faint representation of him.
>
> I take him to be a soul of great article, and his admixture of innate faculties so insubstantial and diluted that, to speak truly of him, he resembles nothing so much as a reflection of himself in the mirror, and only his shadow has any desire to follow in his footsteps.

1. "his infusion of such dearth and rareness"

The verb *infuse*, literally "to pour in," was formed, like many other verbs which came directly from Latin into early modern English, from the past participle rather than the infinitive: *infusus* rather than *infundere*.[8] Hamlet uses the noun *infusion* in an extension of its established figurative meaning, "the action of infusing some principle, quality, or idea into the . . . soul" (sense 2). Laertes' "infusion" is the admixture of psychic faculties or qualities native to him (*OED*, citing only this line, supplies the nonce definition "infused temperament" [sense 2c]). The action of infusing in the figurative sense was often attributed to divine grace, and this association forms part of the expressive value of the word in the laudatory aspect of the phrase. *Dearth* and *rareness*, too, have laudatory meanings which are called into play, namely, "dearness, costliness" (s.v. *dearth* sb. sense 2) and "unusual or exceptional character, esp. in respect of excellence" (sense 4 of *rarity*, with which sense 4 of *rareness* is identified).

But *dearth* and *rareness* also had meanings of a nonlaudatory or even a derogatory sort. That of *dearth* is the word's most familiar modern sense, "scarcity of anything, material or immaterial . . . want or lack of a quality" (sense 4, cited as early as the mid–fourteenth century). *Rareness* had two such meanings in Shakespeare's time, namely, "thinness; fewness, scantiness" (sense 1, cited from 1588 to 1610) and "of substance . . . Thinness of composition or texture" (sense 2 of *rarity*, as above, cited from 1614 on). In conjunction with these, *infusion* should be taken in its concrete sense, "a dilute liquid extract obtained from a substance by . . . steeping it in . . . water" (4b). Laertes' temperament, described figuratively in these terms, is lacking in vital qualities, like a watery soup.

2. "his semblable is his mirror"

The word *mirror* must be used here in a metonymically transferred meaning, "image reflected by a mirror," not listed in *OED*. Another figurative meaning, "of persons: A model of excellence" (5b), contributes to the laudatory aspect of the phrase (see the prologue's reference to Harry, in *Henry V* act 2, as "the mirror of all Christian kings"), which I interpret as follows: "The only one like him is his reflection in the mirror — that is, he is unique, a paragon."[9] On the derogatory side, it is merely a tautology: "His reflection in the mirror looks just like him," with perhaps the additional implication that he is more an image of a fine man than the reality.

3. "who else would trace him, his umbrage, nothing more"

Who functions here as a compound relative pronoun, meaning "anyone that, whoever" (*OED* s.v. sense II. 6). *Trace* takes on a figurative meaning "to emulate" derived from the meaning "to follow the footprints or traces of; . . . hence, to pursue" (*OED* s.v. *trace* v.[1] II. 5; cf. *trace* sb.[1] sense 4, "*pl.* The series . . . of footprints left by an animal"). The word *umbrage*, too, is used figuratively; this line is cited in *OED* s.v. *umbrage* sb. sense 3 "a semblance . . . or faint representation." But the literal meanings of *trace* and *umbrage* (that is, "shadow," cited in *OED*, s.v. sense 1, until 1687) figure in the derogatory interpretation of the speech I have given above.

Throughout Hamlet's words in their derogatory aspect, there appear images of lack, insubstantiality, vacuity. What of the opening statement, "I take him to be a soul of great article"? I must confess that I had until recently assumed that the word *article* played no part in the system of amphibologies I detected in the passage. Viewed as part of a speech of praise, it presents no particular lexical difficulty. It is glossed "theme; matter for an inventory" by Jenkins; Edwards paraphrases "there would be many articles to list in his inventory." Both apparently rely on *OED*'s sense 10, "A particular piece of business, a matter, . . . a subject," under heading IV, "A separate thing (immaterial or material)," taking these in conjunction with Hamlet's reference to dividing Laertes "inventorially." *OED* itself cites the phrase "of great article" under this same sense, but supplies what seems to me a better definition, namely, "of great moment, of importance."

The word *article* had, however, another meaning in Shakespeare's time which nicely corresponds to the covert negative force of Hamlet's description, a meaning which had evidently died out by the middle of the eighteenth century and hence is adduced neither by Johnson nor by any of his successors. As I checked the *OED* entry, my eye was caught by heading V, "In *Arithmetic*." The definition that follows (sense 15) is, "The number 10; each of the tens, or round numbers between units . . . and hundreds." A citation from Trevisa (1398) is followed by citations from two sixteenth-century works, namely, the first edition of Robert Recorde's *Grounde of Artes* (1543),[10] and Thomas Blundevil's *Exercise* (1594); the definition quoted from Blundevil is "Article is any number ending in a Cypher." I have since checked the discussion of the term in Recorde. His *The Grounde of Artes, Teaching the works and practice of Arithmetike* . . . , was the first such textbook printed in English; it continued in print, in a series of editions, for more than 150 years and was in all probability used in school when Shakespeare studied the subject as a boy.[11] In a discussion of kinds of number, Recorde first defines a digit as any number under 10 and then distinguishes between articles, which are numbers divisible by 10, and mixed numbers, which contain "at the least one article and a diget, as 12, 16, 19, 21, 38, 107, 1005, and so forth."[12] He adds, "for the more ease of understanding and remembrance," that "the article and the myxt numbers are ever written with more than one figure: and thus thei differ, that the article hath evermore this cypher o, in his first place [that is, counting from the right], and the myxte numbre hath ever there some digite."[13] In view of the series of double entendres in Hamlet's language linking substance and vacuity (not to mention his reference to "th'arithmaticke of memory" in the preceding sentence), it seems clear that the application to Laertes' character of the word *article* should be interpreted as simultaneously imputing to his soul the positive value of a digit and the negative value of a cipher. Shakespeare does not use the word *article* in this sense elsewhere, but he alludes to the concept in *Winter's Tale* 1.2.6–8, when Polixenes, having said that no amount of time would be adequate for full expression of his gratitude for Leontes' hospitality, continues, "And therefore, like a cipher, Yet standing in rich place, I multiply With one 'We thank you' many thousands moe That go before it." Laertes, like the extensively landed Osric, "stands in rich place" at the right hand of King Claudius, regardless of his intrinsic worth.

After Osric departs, now wearing his hat, Horatio satirically calls him a "lapwing" that "runs away with the shell on his head." Hamlet responds that he is one of "many more of the same bevy" whom "the drossy age dotes on."

The language of such men makes a favorable impression in social encounters by virtue of "a kind of yesty collection . . . and do but blow them to their trial, the bubbles are out" (165–70). At this moment, a lord enters, sent by Claudius to ask Hamlet if he wishes the match to take place now or later, and Hamlet replies that he is ready.

In act 3, scene 2, after Polonius has summoned him to his mother's closet, Hamlet recalls the cautionary words of his father and resolves to "speak daggers to her but use none" (357). And Gertrude does indeed cry out, in anguished protestation against Hamlet's graphic description of her lovemaking with Claudius "in the rank sweat of an enseamed bed," "These words like daggers enter in my ears" (3.4.93, 95). Elsewhere, however, we see Hamlet resorting to words when real daggers would be more appropriate to his mandate, channeling into outbursts of language, directed at times against himself, at times against others, energies that might otherwise have impelled him to conclusive action. In the penultimate scene of the play, he engages in a brief verbal skirmish with Osric, vanquishing him with a summary virtuosity whose full force has hitherto gone unrecognized. Perhaps, as those responsible for the Folio text of the play must have thought, this blowing away of froth to reveal the emptiness of mind of a member of the royal retinue, which in any case is over before a reader can say "one," is of no great consequence. Osric's discomfiture is momentary only, and Hamlet and Horatio dismiss him immediately from their thoughts. A few minutes later, Hamlet, lending himself passively to the machinations of Claudius the poisoner, proceeds to his almost inadvertent revenge and then falls silent. Until, once again, we open the play.

Notes

Chapter 1. Dimensions of Judgment in the Canterbury Tales

1. I am indebted to Traugott Lawler, who read a considerable portion of this essay at an early stage, for saving me from a number of errors of wording and content, especially in part 2; to Wayne A. Meeks, for generously allowing me to avail myself of the breadth and depth of his knowledge of the Bible and the early history of Christianity; and to Sherry Reames for her trenchant, meticulous, and sympathetic critique of the penultimate version.

2. " 'Whan She Translated Was': A Chaucerian Critique of the Petrarchan Academy," in *Literary Practice and Social Change in Britain, 1380–1530*, ed. Lee Patterson (Berkeley: University of California Press, 1990), pp. 156–215.

3. For a recent and full account of Richard's deteriorating relationship with Parliament, see Nigel Saul, *Richard II* (New Haven: Yale University Press, 1997), esp. chap. 8, "Humiliation and Constraint, 1386–87," pp. 148–75.

4. "The Summoner and the Abominable Anatomy of Antichrist," *Studies in the Age of Chaucer* 18 (1996): 91–117. Though the essay's innovative analysis of partisan materials in the tale would seem to imply a Chaucer more personally involved in the radical side of the controversy between orthodoxy and Lollardy than had previously been supposed, Fletcher stops short of this conclusion: "If anything is to be salvaged of Chaucer the author from all this, what does seem irreducibly true is that he was better acquainted with Lollard thought than has been suspected, a none too surprising conclusion given the place and time of his writing" (pp. 111–12). The idea that there are Wycliffite affinities in the *Canterbury Tales* goes back at least eighty years; for citations, see the addendum that

follows this essay. I summarize below the facts about Wyclif's life that imply, if not personal acquaintance with him on Chaucer's part, at least knowledge of his career and his doctrines (pp. 26–27, 30). For details of Fletcher's findings concerning the *Summoner's Tale,* see note 121, below.

5. I have used the text of the *Canterbury Tales* in *The Riverside Chaucer,* 3d ed., ed. Larry Benson et al. (Boston: Houghton Mifflin, 1987), referred to hereinafter as "Riverside."

6. The best account I know of the intertwined lives of Chaucer the civil servant and Chaucer the poet is Derek Pearsall's *The Life of Geoffrey Chaucer, A Critical Biography* (Oxford: Blackwell, 1992). I quote one pertinent statement among many: "Chaucer kept a low profile in the political conflicts of his day, steering clear of potential trouble in his public life and never mentioning anything controversial in his poetry. In this way, with the instinct of the artist, he kept secure his poetic career" (p. 96).

7. Subtitled *The Literature of Social Classes and the General Prologue to the Canterbury Tales* (Cambridge: Cambridge University Press, 1973).

8. See, for example, her discussion of the word *worthy* in the portraits of the Knight (I[A] 43, 47, 50, 64, 68), the Friar (243), the Merchant (283) and the Franklin (360), pp. 195–206.

9. To these, the expression "fair langage" should be added. *MED,* s.v. *fair* adj. sense 7(b) "of speech . . . deceptively agreeable," cites the *Parson's Tale* 1022, "Thow shalt nat eek peynte thy confessioun by faire subtile wordes."

10. 1 Corinthians, chap. 13. The final verse reads, "And now there remain faith, hope, and charity, these three: but the greatest of them is charity (Nunc autem manet fides, spes, caritas, tria haec: maior autem his est caritas)." Here and elsewhere, I quote the Vulgate from *Biblia Sacra iuxta Vulgatam Versionem,* 4th ed. (Stuttgart: Deutsche Bibelgesellschaft, 1994). I quote the Bible in English from the Douay-Rheims version of 1899, *The Holy Bible Translated from the Latin Vulgate* (photographic reproduction, Rockford, Ill.: Tan Books and Publishers, 1971). I add punctuation and capitalization to the Latin, which has neither, in accordance with Douay-Rheims.

11. Line 142 in the portrait of the Prioress is the earliest citation given in *MED* for *conscience* in the meaning it takes on retroactively in that line (sense 4), "tenderness . . . , solicitude; anxiety." The meaning we expect the word to have pertains to the rigorous scrutiny of one's own actions and motives that is especially important in the life of a religious; the most pertinent definition in *MED* is sense 2(a), "The faculty of knowing what is right, esp. with reference to Christian ethics." The Christian meaning of *charity* is spelled out in *MED* s.v. *charite* n. sense 1a (a), "The supreme virtue of Love or Charity according to Christian doctrine"; for the secular meaning, see sense 3 (a) "Loving kindness, affection." See also *pitous* adj. senses 1 (a) "merciful, compassionate" and 3 "godly, righteous, reverent, devout, pious." *Pité* and *pitous* had not yet become wholly distinct in Chaucer's time from *pieté* and *pietous(e),* modern "piety" and "pious."

12. For the theological meanings of *grace,* see *MED* s.v. sense 1; for the meaning "good fortune, a stroke of good luck," see sense 3(c). The passage in Matthew reads, in full, "Lay not up to yourselves treasures on earth: where the rust, and moth consume, and where thieves break through and steal. But lay up to yourselves treasures in heaven: where neither the rust nor moth doth consume, and where thieves do not break through,

nor steal (Nolite thesaurizare vobis thesauros in terra, ubi erugo et tinea demolitur, ubi fures effodiunt et furantur. Thesaurizate autem vobis thesauros in caelo, ubi neque erugo neque tinea demolitur, et ubi fures non effodiunt nec furantur)."

13. In an essay entitled "The Wife of Bath's Lenten Observance" (*Papers in Language and Literature* 7 [1971]: 293–97), James Finn Cotter takes the Robertsonian hard line. Noting the allusion in the Wife's boast about the good condition of her clothes to Matthew 6:20, Cotter points out that that text is read during the Mass of Ash Wednesday at the beginning of Lent, the season when the Wife liked to walk abroad. The same Gospel passage includes a warning against being anxious about one's clothing (6:25), a warning "she has heard, but . . . has not understood" (p. 296). The double meaning of *grace* in line 553 "mirrors the clash between divine and human values" in the Prologue as a whole (p. 294). Even the "seemingly innocuous oath," "upon my peril" with which she emphasizes her assertion implies a "risk of eternal punishment" that she does not perceive (p. 296).

14. See Bernard S. Levy, "Biblical Parody in the *Summoner's Tale* ," *Tennessee Studies in Literature* 11 (1966): 45–60, and Alan Levitan, "The Parody of Pentecost in Chaucer's Summoner's Tale," *University of Toronto Quarterly* 40 (1971): 236–46. The note in Riverside to *Summoner's Tale* 2255 ff. endorses their interpretation and refers to Levitan's essay, among others.

15. In an essay entitled "Chaucer's Wheel of False Religion: Theology and Obscenity in the Summoner's Tale" (in *The Centre and Its Compass: Studies in Medieval Literature in Honor of Professor John Leyerle* [Kalamazoo, Mich., 1993], pp. 265–96), V. A. Kolve proposed what he considered a more likely model for the cartwheel in a pair of twelfth-century diagrams illustrating a treatise entitled "Concerning the Wheel of True and of False Religion," by the Augustinian canon Hugh of Fouilloy (pp. 274–87). Kolve did not claim more than a "possible" acquaintance with the work either on Chaucer's part or on the part of the original readers or audiences of the *Summoner's Tale*. But he found the close fit between Hugh's wheels and Chaucer's inescapably suggestive in view of the fact that "no wholly convincing source [other than Hugh's treatise] ha[d] yet been proposed for Jankyn's twelve-spoke, fart-dividing wheel" (p. 289). In a note to this passage, he accepted a connection between the gift of the fart itself and the gift of the Holy Spirit at Pentecost but maintained that the medieval iconography of the wheel, adduced by Levitan, was "completely overshadowed by the more standard iconography" ("The Parody of Pentecost," pp. 289–90).

16. *Studies in the Age of Chaucer* 21 (1999): 209–45.

17. *The Canterbury Tales* (London: George Allen & Unwin), p. 228.

18. Ibid. In his essay "The *Canterbury Tales* II: Comedy," in *The Cambridge Chaucer Companion* (ed. Piero Boitani and Jill Mann [Cambridge University Press, 1986]), Pearsall expresses this view at greater length: "All our memory of the quarrel between the Friar and the Summoner, all possibility of morally based satire on the friar, seem swallowed up in the conclusion of the story, in the posing of the puzzle of the divided fart and its fantastically imaginative solution. Humour gets the better of satire, and Chaucer, as often, seems to prefer complicity with the world of his creatures to moral criticism" (p. 141).

19. See *The Literary Context of Chaucer's Fabliaux*, ed. Larry D. Benson and Theodore M. Andersson (Indianapolis and New York: Bobbs-Merrill, 1971), p. 340; the tale is

printed in the original and in the editors' translation on pp. 344–59. Benson and Andersson note the probable existence of "a great many versions of [the *Summoner's Tale*]" and include a story from *Til Eulenspiegel* among the analogues they print, on the ground that despite the late date of the latter, "the stories it contains are probably older" (p. 340).

20. The most complete account of the learned and literary works embodying the antifraternal tradition is Penn R. Szittya's *The Antifraternal Tradition in Medieval Literature* (Princeton: Princeton University Press, 1986), which I have relied on heavily in this part of my essay. In addition, Szittya's study includes chapters entitled "The English Poetic Tradition" (with an account of "French forerunners"), "Chaucer and Antifraternal Exegesis: The False Apostle of the *Summoner's Tale*," and "The Friars and the End of *Piers Plowman*." The first scholar to identify St. Amour, FitzRalph, and Wyclif as the most important representatives of the antifraternal tradition in its learned aspect was Arnold Williams. His essay "Chaucer and the Friars" (*Speculum* 28 [1953]: 499–513) predates Szittya's study by more than thirty years but continues to have value as a succinct and clear summary of the main points. Williams wrote to correct what he saw as a prevalent but erroneous opinion: that the particularly intense hostility toward friars displayed by Chaucer in the *Canterbury Tales* was grounded in personal experience. His consultation of the editions of St. Amour and FitzRalph that had recently become available convinced him that "the true genesis . . . of Chaucer's attack" was literature rather than life (p. 500). In fact, neither of these sources need exclude the other.

21. Szittya, in the chapter entitled "Chaucer and Antifraternal Exegesis: The False Apostle of the *Summoner's Tale*," largely disregards the *Roman* as a source for the tale, the possibility that Chaucer's antifraternal satire was shaped by its being brought in only as a kind of last resort: "Even if [Chaucer] knew no Latin tracts at all, he would have encountered the apostolic debate in the poetry of his contemporaries . . . and in the *Roman de la rose*, which he read and probably translated" (p. 242).

22. Arnold Williams accords the *Roman* an importance equal to that of William of St. Amour and Richard FitzRalph as a Chaucerian source; the antifraternal satire of the *Summoner's Tale* "derive[s] ultimately from the charges made by the principal opponents of the friars," as is apparent if we "compare point by point Chaucer's work with the chief documents in the attack. From an examination of manuscript resources it is easy to say that these documents were William of St. Amour's *De periculis*, much of which was repeated in Jean de Meun's portion of the *Roman de la rose*, and the various works of FitzRalph" (p. 505).For reasons he does not make clear, however, Williams finds "no evidence of the peculiarly Wycliffite point of view in Chaucer's jabs at the friars; . . . it is certainly a mistake to use Wycliffite documents to illustrate Chaucer's friar" (p. 504). Fleming, in an essay entitled "The Antifraternalism of the *Summoner's Tale*" (*Journal of English and Germanic Philosophy* 65 [1966]: 688–700), identifies three kinds of antifraternal literature current in the fourteenth century: "There was in the first place the formal theological dissertation, carrying on directly in the tradition of William of Saint-Amour [and including the writings of Richard FitzRalph as well as Wyclif]. . . . Next, there is the body of primarily vernacular antimendicant satire itself . . . the best known examples of which are the Faussemblant 'chapters' from the *Roman de la rose*" (pp. 690–91). For the third type, the "left-wing propaganda" written by the friars themselves (p. 691), to which Fleming devotes most of his essay, see p. 24 and n. 64, below.

23. For the account of William's career that follows, see Szittya, *Antifraternal Tradition,* chap. 1 ("William of St. Amour and the Perils of the Last Times"), pp. 11–17. I have used the edition of the *De Periculis* printed in the second volume (*Appendix . . . sive Tomus Secundus*) of *Fasciculus Rerum Expetendarum & Fugiendarum . . . .* ," edited by Edward Brown after Orthwin Gratius (London: Richard Chiswell, 1690), pp. 18–41. Here it is entitled *Scriptum Scholæ Parisiensis de periculis Ecclesiæ*; it is assigned the dates 1339 and 1380, both erroneous, the first in the table of contents, the second following the title on p. 18. The text is repetitive and gives the impression of being somewhat garbled; it breaks off at the end with the phrase "if anyone should object (si quis objecerit)." This same volume also contains two antifraternal sermons in Latin, preached by William in 1256. I shall refer to these as "Sermon I" and "Sermon II." Sermon I is discussed by Szittya as edited in William's *Opera Omnia* (1632), where it has the title *De Phariseo* (see Szittya, *Antifraternal Tradition,* n. 28, pp. 17–18, 34–40). Part of the last chapter of *De Periculis,* translated into English by the editor, is included, with a short account of William's life and work, in *Chaucer: Sources and Backgrounds,* ed. Robert P. Miller (New York: Oxford University Press, 1977), pp. 245–50.

24. See Szittya, *Antifraternal Tradition,* p. 18: "Considering their reputation as polemical attacks, the most startling feature of all [William's] works is the almost total absence of any references to the friars themselves. When he was summoned before a synod of bishops, shortly after the appearance of the *De periculis,* to answer charges of defamation brought by the friars, he said he had never attacked any order approved by the church. The *De periculis* was not about the friars, but rather a treatise about the 'perils of the last times' predicted in Scripture."

25. For William's constant recourse to the *Glossa Ordinaria,* see Miller, *Chaucer: Sources and Backgrounds,* p. 245. Cf. Szittya, *Antifraternal Tradition,* p. 19: "William was . . . using the normal tools of his trade, and . . . wrote in the genre of his profession: not polemic but Biblical exegesis."

26. Each chapter opens with a question, e.g., "Through whom will the aforesaid dangers come about (per quos instabunt dicta pericula)?" (chap. 2), "What and of what sort will the dangers to the church be, that the aforesaid seducers will bring about (quæ & cujusmodi erunt pericula ecclesiæ, quæ inducunt seductores prædicti)?" (chap. 4), and "Whose responsibility is it to inquire about and foresee and repel the aforesaid dangers (quorum est inquirere & prævidere, & repellere dicta pericula)?" (chap.9). (William's answer to this last question is the "prelates [prælati]," i.e. the high-ranking members of the secular clergy.) (Translations from the *De periculis* and William's sermons are my own.)

27. At the beginning of chap. 2, William lists sixteen of the vices named in 2 Timothy 3 as signs whereby the dangerous men of his own times can be known. They are "lovers of themselves, covetous, haughty, proud, blasphemers, disobedient to parents [interpreted by William as the officials of the established church], ungrateful, wicked, without affection, . . . slanderers, incontinent [William adds "in gluttony or lust"], . . . without kindness, traitors, stubborn, puffed up, and lovers of pleasures more than of God (se ipsos amantes, cupidi, elati, superbi, blasphemi, parentibus inoboedientes, ingrati, scelesti, sine affectione, . . . criminatores, incontinentes, . . . sine benignitate, proditores, protervi, tumidi, voluptatum amatores magis quam Dei)" (2 Timothy 3.2–4; *De periculis,* p. 20).

28. Matthew 23 is quoted in the *De periculis* in connection with William's explanation of the thirteenth of the thirty-nine signs he lists in chap. 14, by which true apostles can be distinguished from false ones: that true apostles do not deceive (p. 37). Sermons I and II make extensive use of 2 Timothy 3 and Matthew 23, respectively; each also contains an allusion to the other biblical passage (see Sermon I, p. 44, Sermon II, p. 53). Apropos of the frequent use of Matthew 23 in antifraternal criticism, Mann points out that "the . . . passage had long afforded material for satire on intellectual arrogance: Jerome applied it to heretics, and later satirists to scholars in general. . . . The hint for its application to friars comes from St Francis himself, who exhorted his followers that they should not be called masters" (*Cambridge Chaucer Companion,* p. 39).

29. Thus in 2 Timothy 3:2–5, the men of the last days, in addition to being "covetous (*cupidi*)" and lovers of pleasures more than of God are described as "having an appearance indeed of godliness, but denying the power thereof (habentes speciem quidem pietatis, virtutem autem eius abnegantes)" (2, 4–5). In Matthew 23, Jesus accuses the scribes and pharisees of doing "all their works . . . for to be seen of men (omnia vero opera sua faciunt ut videantur ab hominibus)" (5); "you make clean the outside of the cup and of the dish, but within . . . are full of rapine and uncleanness (mundatis quod de foris est calicis et parapsidis, intus autem pleni estis rapina et immunditia)" (25). They are "like to whited sepulchres, which outwardly appear to men beautiful, but within are full of dead men's bones, and of all filthiness (similes . . . sepulchris dealbatis, quae a foris parent hominibus speciosa, intus vero plena sunt ossibus mortuorum et omni spurcitia)" (27). At the beginning of chap. 3, William interprets 2 Timothy 3:5, "Having an appearance indeed of godliness, but denying the power thereof (habentes speciem quidem pietatis, virtutem autem eius abnegantes)" with the aid of the *Glossa Ordinaria*, as "denying charity, not with words but with deeds (charitatem abnegantes non verbis, sed factis)." He expands on this interpretation with reference to Paul's extended description of charity in 1 Corinthians 13, arguing that in taking over the duties of priests, the friars deny charity with their deeds, because charity "is not ambitious (non est ambitiosa)" (5), and in resenting correction, because charity "endureth all things (omnia sustinet)" (p. 23).

30. "With the justified aim of making themselves fit to act as spiritual guides the friars . . . devoted themselves to studies' with the glorious result that at the end of the thirteenth century the mendicants not only crowded the benches of the students but also occupied the chairs of the professors; indeed, it may safely be stated that from shortly after the middle of the thirteenth century and until the time of the Great Schism, learning and the universities were dominated by the mendicants" (L. L. Hammerich, *The Beginning of the Strife between Richard FitzRalph and the Mendicants, with an Edition of his Autobiographical Prayer and his Proposition Unusquisque* [*Det Kgl. Danske Videnskabernes Selskab., Historisk-filologiske Meddelelser* 26.3 (Copenhagen: Levin and Munksgaard, 1938)]).

31. "Who the penetrators of houses are, the *Glossa Ordinaria* explains thus: on the literal level, those who penetrate houses are those who enter the houses of people whose souls it does not pertain to them to care for, and [keep] prying into private matters, that is, their secrets; which cannot be accomplished unless they insinuate themselves into hearing the confessions of their sins: this is to penetrate the houses of the sins of men, that is, to investigate their consciences, which are called their houses (Qui autem sunt penetrantes

domos, exponit Glossa sic: Illi penetrant domos, qui ad literam ingrediuntur domos illorum, quorum regimen animarum ad eos non pertinet, & rimantes proprietates, id est, secreta eorum: quod non potest fieri, nisi ingerant se ad audiendum confessiones peccatorum eorum: hoc enim est penetrare domos hominum peccatorum, scilicet rimari conscientias eorum, quæ eorum domus appellantur)" (pp. 20–21). The action of "penetrating houses" is referred to again and again in the course of the treatise and is the first of the signs distinguishing false apostles from true ones listed in the final chapter (p. 35). The statement in the *Summoner's Tale* that "in every house [Friar John] gan to poure and prye [i.e., gaze intently and inquisitively]" (1738) is surely reminiscent of this phrase.

32. "Non missi," with or without a citation from Paul, is one of the phrases William applied most frequently to the friars. Lack of a proper "mission" is the sixth of the signs distinguishing a false apostle from a true one in the last chapter (p. 36). See also Sermon II, p. 50: "They are false apostles, and [persons] who will preach without having been sent: because thus says the Apostle [Paul]: How will they preach, unless they are sent? (Isti sunt falsi Apostoli, & qui prædicabunt non missi: quia sicut dicit Apostolus: Quomodo prædicabunt, nisi mittantur)?"

33. In this connection William cites 1 Corinthians 9:14, "So also the Lord ordained that they who preach the gospel, should live by the gospel (Ita et Dominus ordinavit his qui evangelium adnuntiant de evangelio vivere)" (*De periculis*, p. 22).

34. "As in the twelve apostles is the form of the bishops, so in the seventy-two disciples is the form of priests, . . . nor are more degrees constituted for the ruling of the church (Sicut in duodecim Apostolis est forma Episcoporum: sic in Septuaginta duobus discipulis forma est Presbyterorum, . . . nec plures sunt in Ecclesia gradus ad regendum Ecclesiam constituti)" (*De periculis*, p. 21).

35. "Neither did we eat any man's bread for nothing, but in labour and in toil we worked day and night (neque gratis panem manducavimus ab aliquo, sed in labore et fatigatione nocte et die operantes)" (2 Thessalonians 3.8; *De periculis*, p. 31). In addition, the wording of the statement that "the workman is worthy of his food ["meat" in Douay Rheims] (dignus enim est operarius cibo sua)," made by Jesus in Matthew 10:10 and, with a slight difference, in Luke 10:7, was considered by William to imply that what the apostles and disciples received was remuneration and not alms.

36. Matthew 10:11; Luke 10:7; *De periculis*, pp. 21, 32, 39. William cites Luke 10.7 in corroboration of the twenty-fourth sign by which to know a false apostle from a true one, "namely, that true apostles are content with the food and drink offered them, not asking for sumptuous food but eating and drinking whatever their hosts have on hand (edentes & bibentes quae apud illos sunt)," *De periculis*, p. 39. Matthew 10.11 is cited in the discussion of the twenty-sixth sign, that true apostles seek out, not "splendid lodgings (hospitia opulentiora)," but those that are "fitting" or "honourable (honestiora)" (ibid.).

37. Acts 20:33, 2 Corinthians 14; *De periculis*, pp. 27, 37, 38.

38. 2 Corinthians 12:10,12; *De periculis*, pp. 20, 35.

39. 2 Thessalonians 3.6.

40. *De periculis*, p. 31; cf. Sermon I, p. 44. A statement of Paul's in 2 Timothy is cited, to the same effect: "No man, being a soldier to God, entangleth himself with secular businesses (Nemo militans inplicit se negotiis saecularibus)" (2 Timothy 2:4; *De periculis*, p. 31).

41. "Now I beseech you . . . to mark them who make dissensions and offenses contrary to the doctrine which you have learned (Rogo autem vos . . . ut observetis eos qui dissensiones et offendicula praeter doctrinam quam vos didicistis faciunt)" (Romans 16:17–18; *De periculis*, pp. 31, 35).

42. Corinthians 11:6; *De periculis*, pp. 34–35, 37; cf. Sermon I, p. 45. "These seducers of Christ will be found, therefore, among Christians, appearing pious, ever devoted to the study of letters, artful and dabbling in knowledge, notorious for offering advice (Invenientur ergo seductores Christi isti inter Christianos, apparentes pii, studio literarum semper dediti, astuti & scioli, in consiliis dandis famosi" (*De periculis*, p. 35).

43. Fleming, in "The Antifraternalism of the *Summoner's Tale*," notes St. Francis's insistence that "the friars' churches be small, and their buildings made of wood and mud" and cites the above-quoted comment of William's from his *Opera* (pp. 696–97).

44. In addition to Szittya's account, see the notes in the edition of *Le roman de la rose* by Langlois cited in note 46, below (Langlois, 3, 319–21). The popularity of the *De periculis* is shown by the fact that the ecclesiastical authorities thought it necessary to condemn it again in 1257 and in 1260 (ibid., 320–21).

45. See Szittya, *Antifraternal Tradition,* chap. 2, "William of St. Amour in England: Circulation and Dissemination," pp. 62–122. Manuscripts of English provenance survive in cathedral, monastic, and university libraries, including four in Oxford, and recorded lists of books indicate the existence of copies which have since disappeared. Szittya shows that extensive passages from William's works were included, with or without attribution, in what he terms *summas*, i.e., compendia on various subjects consisting largely of excerpts, some lengthy, from standard authories (ibid, p. 112). An antifraternal tract written by the monk Uthred de Boldon during the 1360s used William's language, themes, and biblical texts, including 2 Timothy 3 (ibid., pp. 102–12).

46. In the following discussion of the antifraternal material in Jean's part of the *Roman,* I cite, wherever possible, "Fragment C" of the incomplete Middle English translation of the poem entitled the *Romaunt of the Rose,* as printed by Riverside from the single extant manuscript. Though this may not be Chaucer's work, it is close to Chaucer in time, place, and language. Citations from the *Romaunt* are followed by the corresponding passages in Old French, as edited by Ronald Sutherland from the manuscript of the *Roman* whose wording he found closest to that of the Middle English version, with occasional emendations from related manuscripts (*The Romaunt of the Rose and Le Roman de la Rose: A Parallel-Text Edition* [Oxford: Basil Blackwell, 1968]). I have silently omitted the marks in Sutherland indicating that full forms have been supplied for abbreviated ones, and that words have been taken from manuscripts other than the base, and I have occasionally revised Sutherland's punctuation in conformity with that of the *Romaunt* in Riverside. Of the three extant fragments of the *Romaunt,* only the first, which breaks off well before Jean de Meun's continuation begins, can with any likelihood be assigned to Chaucer. See Alfred David's discussion of the linguistic evidence in the explanatory notes in Riverside (pp. 1103–04), and his prefatory remarks to the textual notes (pp. 1198–99). But the importance for Chaucer of the *Roman,* whether or not he translated any part of it, is generally recognized; thus Larry Benson's introductory remarks to the *Romaunt* in Riverside, pp. 685–86, include the statement that "Chaucer

was more deeply influenced by the *Roman de la rose* than by any other French or English work" (p. 685). I cite passages of the *Roman* not included in the *Romaunt* from *Guillaume de Lorris et Jean de Meun, Le roman de la rose*, ed. Félix Lecoy, 3 vols. (Paris: Librairie Honoré Champion, 1965–70), adding modern prose translations from Charles Dahlberg, *The Romance of the Rose by Guillaume de Lorris and Jean de Meun* (Hanover and London: University Press of New England, 1983). I have also consulted the comprehensive scholarly apparatus in Ernest Langlois, *Le roman de la rose, par Guillaume de Lorris et Jean de Meun*, 5 vols. (Paris: Firmin-Didot et cie., 1914–24). The edition of William's "Sermon II" in *Fasciculus Rerum* referred to above (see n. 23) provides an interesting piece of evidence that a connection between William and Chaucer via the *Roman* was recognized at the end of the seventeenth century. On p. 51, there appears a marginal note to a reference in the sermon to "that book which is called the Eternal Gospel (librum illum qui vocatur Evangelium sempiternum)," reading in part as follows: "Concerning which . . . our Chaucer also in his poem *The Romance of the Rose*, . . . has some things worth reading (De quo . . . Chaucerus etiam nostras [*sic*] in poemate suo Romantio [*sic*] de Rosa . . . aliqua habet lectu digna)."

47. See Dahlberg, p. 2: "[Jean] was undoubtedly connected in one way or another with the University of Paris." Dahlberg's suggested date for the completion of the poem is approximately 1275 (ibid., p. 2), Langlois's, between 1275 and 1280 (1, 19), and Lecoy's, 1278 (1, viii). William died in 1372 (see Langlois, 3, 320).

48. I give the name as it appears in the *Romaunt*. Lecoy's text has "Faus Semblant," that of Langlois, "Faus Semblanz," and that of Sutherland "Faus Samblant." Dahlberg translates the name as "False Seeming."

49. "Fragment C" of the *Romaunt*, following a gap in the translation of some 5,520 lines, begins over 150 lines after the beginning of the Fals-Semblant episode in the *Roman*, at a point corresponding to line 10561 in Lecoy's edition and line 10679 in Sutherland's French text. Fals-Semblant's father is Baraz (10437), his mother, Ypocrisie (10439). (The former name, translated "Fraud" by Dahlberg, appears as "Gile" in *Romaunt* 6112.)

50. From this point on, line numbers cited for the French text are those in Sutherland.

51. Full wel I can my clothis chaunge,
    Take oon, and make another straunge. . . .
    Somtyme a wommans cloth take I;
    Now am I a mayde, now lady. (6325–26, 6345–46 [11187–88, 11207–8])

52. Alan J. Fletcher, in "The Topical Hypocrisy of Chaucer's Pardoner" (*Chaucer Review* 25 [1990]: 110–26), cites a passage from an anti-Lollard poem in Latin which is tantalizingly similar in wording to the Pardoner's description of himself as a serpent in lines 421–22 of his *Prologue*. He argues that the Latin poem was probably part of "the battery of anti-Lollard polemic which was being put about in London during the last two decades of the fourteenth century," and that Chaucer may well have read it (p. 111–12).

53. Thou hooly chirche, thou maist be wailed!
    Sith that thy citee is assayled
    Thorugh knyghtis of thyne owne table,
    God wot thi lordship is doutable!

If thei enforce hem it to wynne
That shulde defende it fro withynne,
Who myght defense ayens hem make? (6271–77 [11135–41])

54. Similar catalogues appear in Fals-Semblant's list of his disguises, referred to above and in lines 6859–76, where he tells of the "emperesses and duchesses, . . . queenes, and eke countesses" and others of similarly high station whom he likes best to serve as confessor.

55. The condemnation in the *Pardoner's Tale* of the elaborate efforts made by cooks to stimulate the appetite of the glutton seems to echo line 7046 of the *Romaunt*: "they caste noght awey That may go through the golet softe and swoote" (542–43), since the text of the *Romaunt* differs in meaning from what seems to have been the French original of line 11748, literally, "with which we stimulate (literally, "strike") our gullets."

56. In the *Romaunt*, the cat is called "Gibbe" (6204) — "a common name for a tomcat," according to the note in Riverside; the sheep and wolf remain nameless (6259–60).

57. For the prayer in Proverbs, see 6529–43; 11276–92; cf. *De periculis*, p.32. For Paul's instructions, see 6661–65; 11383–88, and p. 16 and n. 35, above.

58. *Romaunt* 6544–50; 1193–99; *De periculis*, p. 33. A list of the circumstances in which begging by the able-bodied is justified, explicitly attributed to William by Jean (*Romaunt* 6705–6770; 11425–95), closely follows a passage in the *Responsiones*, William's defense of the *De periculis* against a commission of cardinals investigating his views (Szittya, *Antifraternal Tradition*, p. 17). The passage is quoted in the notes to the French editions; see Langlois, 3:318 and Lecoy, 2:285.

59. William had identified the dangerous men of the last days with Anticrist (*De periculis*, p.19); in the *Roman*, Jean has Fals-Semblant identify himself and his compeers similarly: "Thus, Antecrist abiden we, For we ben alle of his meyne" (*Romaunt*, 7155–56).

60. "Nat ful cleane" corresponds to "Toutes fretelees de crottes," i.e., "All ornamented with daubs of mud," or possibly "turds," in the next line of the French.

61. The image of a dog returning to its vomit appears in Proverbs 26:11. It is alluded to in 2 Peter 2:22.

62. I cannot share Szittya's scepticism regarding Chaucer's knowledge of the doctrines of Gerard of Borgo San Donnino. In arguing against the possibility of their transmission — "Gerard had almost no following, and . . . the Summoner's friar says nothing that bears the slightest resemblance to Gerard's Joachimist doctrines" (*Antifraternal Tradition*, p. 236) — he ignores what Chaucer would have learned from Fals-Semblant's discourse (in which, to be sure, Gerard is not named).

63. My account of FitzRalph's career and writings is indebted to Szittya, *Antifraternal Tradition*, chap. 3, "The Antifraternal Ecclesiology of Archbishop Richard FitzRalph" (pp. 123–151), to Katherine Walsh, *A Fourteenth-Century Scholar and Primate: Richard FitzRalph in Oxford, Avignon, and Armagh* (Oxford: Clarendon Press, 1981), to Hammerich, *The Beginning of the Strife*, and to James Doyne Dawson's essay "Richard Fitz-Ralph and the Fourteenth-Century Poverty Controversies," *Journal of Ecclesiastical History* 34 (1983): 315–44. Arnold Williams gives a brief account of FitzRalph's career in "Chaucer and the Friars," pp. 503–04. There is an excerpt in modern English from the *Defensio Curatorum*, with a prefatory note on FitzRalph, in Miller, *Chaucer: Sources*

and Backgrounds, pp. 255–58. I have relied on Szittya, Hammerich, and Dawson in discussing works of FitzRalph's other than *Unusquisque*, books 1–4 of *De pauperie Salvatoris*, and the *Defensio Curatorum*. *Unusquisque* is edited in Hammerich, *The Beginning of the Strife*, pp. 53–73. Books 1–4 of *De pauperie Salvatoris* are appended by Reginald Lane Poole to his edition of Wyclif's *De dominio divino* (London: Wyclif Society, 1890), pp. 257–476. The Latin original of the *Defensio Curatorum* was edited by Melchior Goldast in *Monarchia S. Romani Imperii* (Frankfurt: Conrad Biermann, 1614; repr. Graz: Akademische Druck- u. Verlagsanstalt, 1960), 2:1391–1410 (referred to hereinafter as "Goldast"). In quoting the *Defensio*, I cite first the late fourteenth-century translation into Middle English attributed to John Trevisa. See *Dialogus inter Militem et Clericum, Richard FitzRalph's Sermon: "Defensio Curatorum," and Methodius: 'The Bygynnyng of the world and the Ende of Worldes*, ed. Aaron Jenkins Perry (London: EETS 167, 1925) (referred to hereinafter as "Trevisa"). I then give the Latin text as it appears in Goldast.

64. See Fleming, "Antifraternalism," pp. 688–700. Fleming identifies the writings of the Spiritual Franciscans as a "third kind of antifraternal literature" (691) and maintains that in the *Summoner's Tale*, Chaucer shows his knowledge of the Franciscan Rule and of Spiritualist propaganda (pp. 693–94). According to Dawson, FitzRalph in the *Unusquisque* "was . . . consciously reviving a favourite argument of the Spiritual Franciscans, who by mid-century appeared to have been utterly defeated. . . . Primitive Franciscanism had found a new and improbable defender" ("FitzRalph and the Fourteenth-Century Poverty Controversies," p. 333).

65. For a detailed discussion, see Hammerich, *The Beginning of the Strife*, pp. 30–41.

66. For the sake of clarity and brevity, I disregard distinctions among the different fraternal orders in the wording of this and other statements. Walsh points out that it was the Franciscans in particular who had failed to establish "a comfortable compromise . . . [enabling] them to combine, for the most part without undue tension, the ideal of poverty with the academic and pastoral concerns which soon came to characterize the friars' role in later medieval society" (*A Fourteenth-Century Scholar and Primate*, p. 351). (Cf. the reference to the "Spiritual Franciscans," above.) According to Dawson, FitzRalph habitually "spoke of all mendicants while using terms that properly applied to the Franciscans alone" ("FitzRalph and the Fourteenth-Century Poverty Controversies," pp. 332–33).

67. See Dawson, "FitzRalph and the Fourteenth-Century Poverty Controversies," p. 330. *Unusquisque* is also known by its longer title, as the *Proposicio ex parte prelatorum et omnium curatorum totius ecclesie*, i.e., *Proposition on Behalf of the Prelates and All the Curates of the Church as a Whole*. The title *Unusquisque* is the first word of a general statement in 1 Corinthians 7, the epistle on which FitzRalph based his argument: "Let every man, wherein he was called, therein abide with God (Unusquisque in qua vocatione vocatus est in ea permaneant)" (20).

68. "We, then, the major and minor prelates of the church, have been called as having prepuces, because we dispense the temporal goods of our mother the church militant. . . . The friars, however, are called in circumcision: professing in their perfection the holy and devout state of highest poverty, they are circumcised with respect to temporal [goods] (Nos autem ecclesiarum prelati maiores atque minores in prepucio sumus vocati, quia temporalia bona matris nostre militantis ecclesie dispensamus. . . . Fratres vero . . . sunt in

circumcisione vocati: sanctam enim atque deuotam paupertatem altissimam profitentes ex sua perfeccione sunt temporalibus . . . circumcisi" (pp. 54–55). Translations from *Unusquisque* are my own.

69. "He deserves to lose power who has abused the power conceded to him. . . . The friars of these four orders *abuse* in diocese after diocese both the office of preaching and absolving, and the office of burying, and also other privileges conceded to them, as my lords here present and others bear witness (potestatem meretur amittere qui sibi concessa abutitur potestate . . . . Tam facultate predicandi et absoluendi quam facultate sepeliendi et alijs eciam priuilegijs eis concessis fratres istorum iiij ordinum in singulis diocesibus *abutuntur*, vt domini mei presentes et alij contestantur)" (p. 72). The emphasis is Fitz-Ralph's.

70. For the genesis of the *De Pauperie*, see Poole, *De dominio divino,* preface, p. xxxv. An analytical summary of its contents is presented by Dawson, "FitzRalph and the Fourteenth-Century Poverty Controversies," pp. 333–41.

71. Walsh identifies FitzRalph as one of the two Oxford theologians (the other being Thomas Bradwardine) to whom Wyclif acknowledged his greatest intellectual indebtedness. "Most obvious of all, a comparison of the texts of [Wyclif's] *De Dominio Divino* and parts of *De Civili Dominio* with FitzRalph's dialogue [i.e., the *De pauperie*] indicate the fact all too clearly — not merely did Wyclif take the germ of the idea from his predecessor but often repeated lengthy passages of his arguments" (*A Fourteenth-Century Scholar and Primate,* p. 378). In Dawson's view, "the ideas FitzRalph had spread [in the *De pauperie*] were more dangerous to his own side than to his opponents. He had implied, in however confused a fashion, that natural lordship ideally meant the total renunciation of civil jurisdiction and that this was an ideal binding on the whole church. . . . [Wyclif] turned this doctrine into a call for the compulsory disendowment of the Church, thereby returning it to the apostolic simplicity of its original state" ("FitzRalph and the Fourteenth-Century Poverty Controversies," p. 343).

72. See Szittya, *Antifraternal Tradition,* pp. 126–31, and Dawson, "FitzRalph and the Fourteenth-Century Poverty Controversies," pp. 341–42.

73. His personal resentment of the friars resonates in complaints such as the following: "In my diocesy Armacan, y trowe y have two thusand sugettes, mansleers, comyn theves, incendiaries that settith houses afyre, & other evel doeres, that beth acursed by sentence evereche yere, of the whiche vnnethe [scarcely] cometh to me & to my penitaunsers, fourty a yere, & siche fongeth [and such men receive] the sacramentis as other men doth; & me trowith [it is believed], that thei beth assoyled, & by noon other than by freres, with-oute drede, for noon other men assoileth hem (Ego enim in mea diœcesi Armachana, vt puto, habeo duo milia subditorum, qui singulis annis per sentencias excommunicacionis latas [through sweeping sentences of excommunication] contra homicidas voluntarios, fures publicos, incendiarios & istis consimiles sunt excommunicationis sententiis inuoluti: de quibus vix veniunt ad me seu pœnitentiarios meos quadraginta in anno: & recipiunt sacramenta omnes tales, vt cæteri, & absoluuntur vel absoluti dicuntur, nec per alios quam per Fratres. Non dubium, cum nulli alii ipsos absoluunt, absoluti creduntur [they are thought to be absolved])" (p. 45).

74. "One has the impression that the *De Pauperie salvatoris* was a long detour between two bouts of not very original anti-mendicant preaching" (Dawson, "FitzRalph and the Fourteenth-Century Poverty Controversies," p. 342).

75. See Walsh, "Epilogue: Lollard saint and the cult of 'St. Richard of Dundalk,'" *A Fourteenth-Century Scholar and Primate*, pp. 452–55. She quotes the line about Fitz-Ralph in English on p. 455 and refers to the original Latin version in *Political Poems and Songs*, ed. Thomas Wright (2 vols., Rolls Series, 14, London, 1859–61), 1:259. The quatrain is quoted in Hammerich, *The Beginning of the Strife*, pp. 11–12.

76. In addition to Herbert B. Workman's comprehensive and authoritative biography, *John Wyclif: A Study of the English Medieval Church*, 2 vols. (Oxford: Clarendon Press, 1926), I am indebted to the succinct but substantial biographical essay (s.v. Wycliffe, John) in *The Oxford Dictionary of the Christian Church*, and to chap. 2, "The Establishment of the Wycliffite Movement," in Anne Hudson, *The Premature Reformation* (Oxford: Clarendon Press, 1988), pp. 60–119. I have also drawn on the account of Wyclif's career and of Lollard influences at the court of Richard II in Saul, *Richard II*, pp. 293–300, and on William Mallard's essay, "Clarity and Dilemma: The *Forty Sermons* of John Wyclif," in *Contemporary Reflections on the Medieval Christian Tradition: Essays in Honor of Ray C. Petry*, ed. George H. Shriver (Durham, N.C.: Duke University Press, 1974), pp. 19–38. There is a full "Chronology of Wyclif's Life" (extending beyond his death in 1384 to the burning of his bones in 1428) in Workman, *John Wyclif*, 1:xxxvii–xl.

77. See Hudson, *The Premature Reformation*, p. 65 and n. 33, and Mallard, "Clarity and Dilemma."

78. Workman summarizes "the 'two truths' with which [*De Civili Dominio*] opens: one that no man in mortal sin can hold *dominium* or lordship: the other that every one in a state of grace has real lordship over the whole universe. Civil lordship can only be ascribed to the wicked by an abuse of language, for such lordship is . . . incompatible with the perfection which must belong to all gifts of God" (*John Wyclif*, 1:261). Writing shortly after the death of the Black Prince in 1376, Wyclif attacked the "prelates and rich clergy," claiming that "by their wealth and worldliness and their consequent neglect of their spiritual duties" they were "ruining the land and robbing the poor of their rights" (*John Wyclif*, 1:287). "[Gaunt] made Wyclif's scheme of disendowment . . . peculiarly his own, untrammeled by Wyclif's social aims or spiritual desires . . . He saw his chance of doubling his estates and of gaining over a greedy baronage by the prospect of spoil. So for a few years John of Gaunt and his clique made use of the Reformer and his pen, while Wyclif, either too high-souled to see the selfish aims of his allies, or else so intent on the realization of his ideals that he was willing to avail himself of every weapon that fell into his hands, used their protection to push his doctrines" (*John Wyclif*, 1:278).

79. Workman, *John Wyclif*, 2:294. "Though in later years the alliance [between John of Gaunt and Wyclif] was dissolved, [Gaunt] would not allow the church to take its revenge against his former associate. Through his protection, Wyclif was neither imprisoned nor martyred, but died in peace at Lutterworth" (1:279). Cf. 2:294–97. See also Hudson, *The Premature Reformation*, pp. 110–11; she argues that "the apparent absence of any attempt to pursue Wyclif in Lutterworth [after the Blackfriars Council], despite the evident hostility of the diocesan John Buckingham and the metropolitan William Courtenay, and despite the stream of writings that continued to come with no concealment from his pen, seems to require the assumption of powerful political protection."

80. A precipitating event in Wyclif's break with the friars was the publication in 1379 of his theoretical treatise concerning eucharistic transubstantiation, *De eucharistia*.

Theologians belonging to the fraternal orders, most notably Thomas Aquinas and Duns Scotus, had arrived at an explanation, widely accepted by Wyclif's time, of the paradoxical fact that the host, when consecrated, became the body of Christ while remaining outwardly unchanged. Using the Aristotelean distinction between substance, or underlying identity, and accidents, or perceptible qualities, they maintained that the substance of the bread was replaced by the substance of Christ's body, but the accidents remained. This, Wyclif maintained, entailed the clearly false idea that a set of accidents could exist without an underlying substance. He based his counterargument, characteristically, on a commonsense, literal reading of scripture. In saying, at the last supper, "This is my body (Hoc est corpus meum)" (Matthew 26:26, Mark 14:22, Luke 22:19), Jesus must have meant by "this" the bread he was holding in his hands, since otherwise the statement would have been redundant. But he also must have meant what he said, affirming that the bread *was* his body. It is thus incumbent on the Christian to believe that during the mass, the wafer continues to have the real identity it had before it was consecrated, while also assuming the equally real identity of the body of Christ. This duality, like the duality of the human and divine natures of Christ, is beyond human understanding; attempts to rationalize it in philosophic terms are accordingly misguided. See Workman, *John Wyclif,* 2:31–33, and Szittya, *Antifraternal Tradition,* pp. 156–58. In what follows, I undertake no further analysis of this aspect of Wyclif's thought, since the ethical aspects of his antifraternalism make a more important contribution than the doctrinal aspects to the intellectual background of the *Summoner's Tale.* However, see below, note 93.

81. Of the works I have found useful as illustrating the characteristic themes and rhetoric of Wyclif's antifraternalism, some are in English and some in Latin. Among the former, I have not attempted to distinguish between writings by Wyclif himself and writings by his followers in which his views are expressed. F. D. Matthew, in a prefatory comment on the English treatise "De Officio Pastorali" (see below), notes that there exists a Latin tract with this same title, and that the two are essentially the same; he concludes that Wyclif sometimes published English translations of writings composed in Latin, in order to reach a wider audience (p. 405). In the discussion that follows, I quote from the following works: (in English) *De Blasphemia contra fratres,* in *Select English Works of John Wyclif,* ed. Thomas Arnold (Oxford: Clarendon Press, 1871), 3:402–29; *The Church and Her Members,* in Arnold, 3:338–65; a sermon on Matthew 23 entitled by its editor "The Ecclesiastical Hierarchy," in *Selections from English Wycliffite Writings,* ed. Anne Hudson (Cambridge University Press, 1978), pp.75–83 (also in Arnold, 2:379–89, where it is entitled "Vae Octuplex"); "Fifty Heresies and Errors of Friars," Arnold, 3:366–401; *De officio pastorali,* in *The English Works of Wyclif, Hitherto Unprinted,* ed. F. D. Matthew, EETS 74 (London, 1880), pp. 405–57; and "Sermons on the Gospels for Sundays and Festivals" in Arnold, *Select English Works,* l, *passim* ; (in Latin) *De fundatione sectarum,* in *John Wiclif's Polemical Works in Latin,* ed. Rudolf Buddensieg (London: Wyclif Society, 1883), 1:13–80; *De ordinatione fratrum,* in *Polemical Works,* 1:83–106; *De quattuor sectis novellis,* in *Polemical Works,* 1:233–90; *Exposicio textus Matthei XXIII,* in *Opera minora,* ed. Johann Loserth "with English Side-Notes by F. D. Matthew," 313–53 (London: Wyclif Society, 1913); *Purgatorium sectae Christi,* in *Polemical Works,* 1:291–316; *Tractatus de apostasia,* ed. Michael Henry Dziewicki (London: Wyclif Society, 1889); and *Tractatus de blasphemia,* ed. Michael Henry Dziewicki (London: Wyclif Society, 1893).

82. In chapter 2 of *De ordinatione fratrum*, for example, Wyclif says that he is not the first to inveigh against these sects, since "the blessed Richard, Bishop of Armagh, had recently labored to purge the church of the crimes newly introduced by the orders of friars, and William of St. Amour did the same thing after the friars had been founded (Nec sumus nos primi, qui invehimus contra ipsos, sed recenter beatus Richardus, Armacanus episcopus, laboravit ad purgacionem ecclesie de criminibus per sectas fratrum noviter introductis. . . . Et idem f[e]cit Willelmus de Sancto Amore . . . postquam fratres inceperant)" (pp. 91–92). See also *De apostasia*, p. 36, *De blasphemia contra fratres*, p. 412, and *Tractatus de blasphemia*. The latter includes a long extract from one of Fitz-Ralph's sermons (pp. 232 ff.; see above, p. 25 and n. 71).

83. In addition to the *Expositio textus Matthei XXIII*, see chaps. 7–8 of *De fundatione sectarum*, in which Paul's accusations in 2 Timothy 3 are explicated in detail. For Matthew 23, see also *De Apostasia*, pp. 26, 29, and 36, and the sermon entitled "The Ecclesiastical Hierarchy" or "Vae Octuplex." For the figurative identification of the friars with wolves preying on sheep, see, *inter alia*, "Sermons on the Gospels," ##8, 48, and 64.

84. "It is said, in accordance with the evidence from which our faith is derived, that since Christ did not authorize these new traditions, and since he is most powerful, most wise, and most loving of his spouse [i.e., the Christian church], in omitting mention of these traditions he teaches that they profit his church little or nothing (Dictum est secundum evidencias dantes fidem, quod, cum Cristus non auctorizat istas tradiciones novas et sit summe potens, summe sapiens et summe diligens sponsam suam, in dimittendo istas tradiciones docet, quod nichil aut modicum prosunt sue ecclesie)" (*Purgatorium Sectae Christi*, p. 298).

85. "And since sect derives from 'sequor,' it appears that all the faithful must be of the Christian sect, as is said in Acts 11. The founder of this sect is the Lord Jesus Christ, and his rule is the Catholic faith, that is, the evangelical law. And it is also plain that no other sect can be better or more general than this. . . . And it appears that no private sects other than this common sect are approved by God (Et cum secta a 'sequor' dicitur, patet, quod cuncti fideles debent esse de secta cristiana, ut dicitur Act. ll. Patronus autem huius secte est dominus Iesus Cristus, et regula sua est fides catholica, scilicet lex ewangelica. Et patet, quod ista secta nulla melior vel generalior potest esse. . . . Et videtur, quod nulle private secte preter sectam istam communem sunt a domino approbate)" (*De fundatione sectarum*, p. 22). *OED*, s.v. *sect* n.[1], says that sense 1b. "a religious order" properly derives from sense 1 "a class or kind (of persons)," but that "Wyclif affects to take it in sense 4 ["a religious following; adherence to a particular religious teacher or faith"], as if the orders (esp. the mendicant orders) were new religions, competing with the 'sect' of Christianity."

86. "And here we takun as bileve that ech member of holi Churche shal be saved with Crist, as eche member of the fend is dampned; and so the while we fighten here and witen not where ("whether") we schal be saaf, we witen not where we ben membris of holi Church . . . But as ech man shal hope that he schal be saaf in blisse, so he shulde suppose that he be lyme ("a limb") of holi Chirch" (*The Church and Her Members*, p. 339). Cf. *De Officio Pastorali*, p. 422. In *The Ecclesiastical Hierarchy*, Wyclif maintains that if even the pope or his prelates fail to follow Christ, we must consider them "the fiend's synagogue" (p. 82).

87. The *Tractatus* is for the most part devoted, chapter by chapter, to the ways in which

the sinful occupants of twelve positions in the church, from popes to questors (i.e., pardoners), blasphemously contravene the teachings of Christ. The portion of the treatise that deals with the friars is three times as long as any other. The English treatise *De Blasphemia contra fratres* deals with three major blasphemies by which the friars "blind the people": what Wyclif saw as their heresy concerning the eucharist (pp. 402–10; see above, note 80), their claim that Christ begged as they do (pp. 410–19), and their supposed grant of spiritual aid to those to whom they sell letters of fraternity (pp. 420–29).

88. Wyclif reasons that in saying they are like the apostles, the friars are implicitly saying that the apostles, who represented God on earth, were like them. This false claim exemplifies the first of the three kinds of blasphemy defined by Wyclif at the beginning of the *Tractatus de Blasphemia* as *insipiens detraccio honoris domini*, a foolish detraction from God's honor, namely, the unjust ascription of attributes to God.

89. "To such a degree have the aforesaid sects slipped in the direction of the world, led by the devil, that their patriarchs would be able to utter the saying in Matthew 25[:12], 'Amen I say to you, I know you not.' . . . What, therefore, if Christ should come in his human person to the dwellings of the possessioners or the friars, and should find in both the ownership of sumptuous houses, worldly furnishings, and a treasury? Can we believe that he would recognize them as his sons, who so blaspheme against him [as to say] that they live just like him? (Ad tantum quidem secte predicte sunt ducatu diaboli lapse ad seculum, quod patriarche eorum possent dicere illud Matth. 25 *Amen dico vobis, nescio vos* . . . . Quid ergo si cristus veniat in humanitate ad domicilia possessionatorum aut fratrum, et inveniat utriusque domus proprias sumptuosas, utensilia secularia et thesaurum? Numquid credimus quod recognoscet istos eius filios, qui tantum blasfemant in eum, quod vivunt sibi simillime?)" (pp. 222–23).

90. "Et cum sectas suas tantum magnificant super Cristum, patet quod sunt blasphemi. Cristus enim noluit habere nisi duodecim apostolos, sed isti audent multos conventus colligere sub uno patrono vel capitaneo notabili peccatore. Quis, rogo, foret blasphemus si non ille, qui excedit Cristum et non justificat suum excessum?" (p. 39).

91. "Ista secta . . . per dyabolum introducta seducat multos per callidiores cautelas et specialiter per ypocrisim, in qua ista secta habundat ex meandris mendacibus patris sui. Fundatur enim super isto mendacio blasphemo, quod Cristus taliter mendicavit; et . . . superaddunt aliud blasphemum mendacium, quod religio et vita eorum sit perfeccior quam religio apostolorum ; et tercio fingunt . . . quod habitus eorum, litere fraternitatis et alia opera meritoria sint perfecciora et magis necessaria, quam illa que in aliis ordinibus prefuerunt . . . Et quarto menciuntur blaspheme, quod sua specialis oracio plus prodest populo quam oracio dominica, sicut forma sue predicacionis, eciam facte ex frivolis, singulariter sit laudanda" (p. 252).

92. Tatlock, in "Chaucer and Wyclif," states that "it is hardly credible that [Chaucer] was not very familiar with Wyclif's views and even with the man himself." (See the addendum, p. 49.)

93. A passage in the *Pardoner's Tale* seems to involve a joke about the conflict between Lollard and orthodox views on transubstantiation. The Pardoner inveighs against those cooks who, laboring to gratify men's gluttonous desires, "stampe, and streyne, and grynde, And turnen substaunce into accident" VI [C] (538–39). Riverside's note quotes the passage in the *De miseria condicionis humane* of Innocent III of which 539 is a

translation. It also cites F. N. Robinson's earlier edition to the effect that "Chaucer could hardly have failed to relate this to the controversy over transubstantiation, a lively topic in Chaucer's time, and to have been reminded of Wyclif's facetious remark that the faithful should forbid friars to enter their cellars lest the wine be transubstantiated into nothing." Paul Strohm (in "Chaucer's Lollard Joke: History and the Textual Unconscious," presented as a Biennial Chaucer Lecture and published by the New Chaucer Society in *Studies in the Age of Chaucer* 17 [1995]: 23–42), expresses the view that the passage in the *De miseria* alluded, when it was published in 1195, to the "newly fashionable terms" of Aristotelean theory (p. 26). With reference to Chaucer's echoing of Innocent's statement, he points out that "the relation between the substance of Christ's body and the accidents of bread" had come to be used after 1382 as "the crucial litmus by which the errant Lollard was to be separated from the orthodox fold. . . . In the heated controversial climate surrounding Chaucer's retelling, this same joke could not *help* but be perceived as eucharistic" (p. 28). He goes on to say that "The presence of some Lollard sympathies in Chaucer's audience by no means reduces, and may even enhance, a valence in which Lollards are twitted as obtuse and stubborn about accidents. By the same token, though, its audience situation confers a kind of 'in-house' quality, one which . . . suggests that nobody needs to be very discombobulated about it all" (p. 34).

94. For Chaucer's life, I have used Derek Pearsall's recent biography (see above, n. 6) to supplement the account in Riverside by Martin M. Crow and Virginia E. Leland (pp. xv–xxvi).

95. See Pearsall, *A Critical Biography,* pp. 130–31, 180–83, K. B. McFarlane, *Lancastrian Kings and Lollard Knights* (Oxford University Press, 1972), and J. Anthony Tuck, "Carthusian Monks and Lollard Knights: Religious Attitude at the Court of Richard II" (*Studies in the Age of Chaucer: Proceedings* 1 [1984]: 149–61). Tuck's views usefully counterbalance those set forth in McFarlane's study. He argues that the Lollard sympathies of the knights in question were more limited than McFarlane had maintained. He also adduces evidence of widespread interest on the part of lay Christians, including Richard II himself, in the Carthusian order, the devotion of whose members was marked by "individuality and asceticism. . . . The interest in the Carthusians . . . is an important, if seldom discussed, aspect of the lay piety of the late fourteenth century. . . . It is also consistent with some of the spiritual attitudes of the group of [Lollard] knights" (pp. 159–60). See also the introduction and notes to V. J. Scattergood's edition of *The Works of John Clanvowe* (Cambridge, England: D. S. Brewer Ltd. and Totowa, N.J., Rowman and Littlefield, 1975).

96. Cf. Saul, *Richard II,* p. 298: "The general character of [the] personal religion [of the Lollard knights] seems clear: it was informed by the same moralistic, anti-clerical, and possibly anti-papal sentiments as that of the other leading *dévots* of the day."

97. There is another link between the lives of Chaucer and Wyclif in the form of their friendship with the man addressed as "philosophical Strode" at the end of *Troilus and Criseide* (v.1857). According to the explanatory notes in Riverside, this person probably was the Radulphus Strode who was a fellow of Merton College, Oxford; he was the author, among other works, of a treatise on logic (no longer extant). Two essays of Wyclif's seem to have been written in reply to communications from him (see "Responsiones ad argumenta Radulfi Strode" and "Responsio ad decem questiones magistri

Ricardi [?read *Radulfi*] Strode" in *Opera Minora*, ed. Johann Loserth and F. D. Matthew [London: Wyclif Society, 1913], pp. 175–200, 398–414, respectively). The first of these deals in part with the problem of predestination: a subject on which Troilus declaims at tortuous length in his despair at the prospect of losing Criseide (IV.958–1078). Martin M. Crow and Clair C. Olson, in *Chaucer Life-Records* (Oxford: Clarendon Press, 1966), reprint a document dated 1381 according to which Chaucer, Radulphus Strode, and two others figure as guarantors that a certain John Hend, a London draper, will keep the peace. Crow and Olson believe that this Strode and the Oxford philosopher were one and the same (pp. 281–84).

98. In his essay, "The Rise of the Medieval Fabliau" (*Romanische Forschungen* 85 [1973]: 275–97), Peter Dronke cites Joseph Bédier's discovery that only a small number of the themes of the Old French fabliaux can be traced back to the orient. "As for the rest — the vast majority — they are, to borrow Wordsworth's phrase, 'the genuine progeny of common humanity.' They can be found in that world-wide range of anecdotes, ribald jokes, stories for the tavern and suchlike that are seldom given a *literary* form, but survive for long periods orally or are improvised afresh" (p. 276).

99. The *Prologue* anecdote belongs to the branch of popular literature consisting of anonymous parodies of sacred or otherwise revered texts; a modern example would be the lyrics set to the tune of "The Stars and Stripes Forever" beginning "Be kind to your web-footed friends." Its extant literary sources, of which the earliest is a Cistercian monk's account of the vision, vouchsafed to him by the Virgin in heaven, of his deceased brothers reposing under her mantle, are discussed in John Fleming's "The Summoner's Prologue: An Iconographic Adjustment" (*Chaucer Review* 2 [1967]: 95–107). The trick played on Friar John in the tale has been identified by Roy J. Pearcy, in "Structural Models for the Fabliaux and the Summoner's Tale Analogues" (*Fabula* 15 [1974]: 103–13), as exemplifyng a variation on the folktale "theme of the 'satiric legacy,' in which an acquisitive character is persuaded that something valueless or even disgusting is precious and highly desirable" (p. 104). This theme is also represented by a story in the late fifteenth-century Low German *Adventures of Til Eulenspiegel*: the hero deceives a priest whom he knows to be avaricious and deceitful by giving him a pot half-filled with turds and strewn on top with money, into which the priest greedily plunges his hand (Pearcy quotes the relevant passage from an early sixteenth-century English translation of the tale [ibid.], which is given in full in Benson and Andersson, *Literary Context of Chaucer's Fabliaux*, pp. 360–61). A story told in the sixteenth century about Jean de Meun exemplifies the same theme with an antifraternal twist and demonstrates the affinities of popular stories with real life. It is summarized as follows by Benson and Andersson: "Jean de Meun . . . left a heavy chest to the Jacobin friars in Paris on condition that they bury him in their church and not open the coffer until after his burial. The friars, thinking Jean had repented for the many insulting things he had written about them . . . rushed to open the coffer as soon as Jean's burial service was finished. When they opened it, they found it was filled with lead" (*Literary Context of Chaucer's Fabliaux*, p. 339). There is a version of this story, too, in *Til Eulenspiegel* (ibid., p. 340).

100. "Flen, flyys, and freris populum domini male cædunt, Thystlis and breris crescentia gramina lædunt; Christe . . . Destrue per terras breris, flen, flyyes, and freris . . . For non that her ys lovit flen, flyyes, ne freris (Fleas, flies, and friars grievously afflict the

people of god; Thistles and briars harm the growing seeds; Christ, . . . Destroy throughout the earth briars, fleas, flies, and friars, . . . for none that is here loves fleas, flies, and friars);" "Fratres Carmeli . . . Non sunt in cœli, quia [fuccant wivys of heli] . . . Fratres cum knyvys goth about and [swivyt mennis wyvis] (Carmelite brothers are not in heaven, because they fuck the women of Ely . . . Friars with knives [to give away or sell; cf. *General Prologue,* 233–34] go about and fornicate with men's wives"). (The incorrect form *cœli* may have been substituted for *cœlis* for the sake of the rhyme with *heli*.) The words I have put in brackets are spelled in cipher in the manuscript. See "Carmina Jocosa," in *Reliquiæ Antiquæ: Scraps from Ancient Manuscripts Illustrating Chiefly Early English Literature and the English Language,* ed. Thomas Wright and James Orchard Halliwell (London: John Russel Smith, 1845), 1:91. Incidentally, the word *fuck* is recorded in English in this passage (albeit in veiled form) for the first time. The editors point out that a corrupted version of the first two lines of the second passage is "still popular among school-boys."

101. The manuscripts are dated a1450, c1450, and a1500 by *MED,* s.v. *skulk(e* n. sense (b). We may, of course, owe the expression "a skulk of friars" to the wit of a single compiler (though his choice of the word is still significant); *OED,* s.v. *skulk* n. sense 2, cautions that the terms in such lists had "at no time much real currency."

102. It is cited, along with the proverb referred to above, in *MED, loc. cit.,* and is included in B. J. Whiting's collection of proverbs. In *De Apostasia,* Wyclif quotes two rhyming lines which he calls a "common proverb (commune proverbium)":

Dum peccatum regnat
in secretis cameris bursa fratrum pregnat;

("while sin reigns, in secret rooms the purse of the friars grows heavy") (p. 42). And the late fourteenth-century chronicler Thomas Walsingham reports that "in these days there is a good argument in everyone's mouth . . . 'This is a friar, therefore a liar' (in diebus istis in ore cujuslibet bonum sit argumentum . . . 'Hic est Frater, ergo mendax')" (*Chronica Monasterii S. Albani,* ed. Henry Thomas Riley [London, 1864, Kraus Reprint, 1965], 2 (A.D.1381–1422), 13.

103. Pictorial evidence for the existence of a "lecherous friar" stereotype is furnished by a drawing at the bottom of a leaf of the Taymouth Hours, reproduced in *Chaucer: Sources and Backgrounds,* p. 239, which shows a friar using what the editor describes as "the 'Nicholas approach' " on a woman outside a tavern. The seemingly irrelevant text inscribed on the leaf is Psalm 42 (A.V. 43):1–4, which begins, "Judge me, O God, and distinguish my cause from the nation that is not holy (Iudica me, Deus, et discerne causam meam a gente non sancta)." A partly illegible inscription below the drawing contains the word "lecherie."

104. In the words of Derek Brewer, "Although Chaucer's writing is not realistic in the way that we have become used to, there is no doubt that it penetrates and is penetrated by life, to an extent that more realistic writing often fails to achieve" (*Chaucer in His Time* [London: Thomas Nelson and Sons, 1963]), p. 236.

105. In 1972, R. E. Kaske wrote that the *Summoner's Prologue and Tale,* formerly thought "a pair of lame and rather shallow anecdotes," has more recently "been taking form as a skilfully managed and richly packed piece of antifraternal literature, with its

meaning carried largely by allusion to the popular themes of antifraternal controversy as well as to the great common images of medieval Christianity [including the Pentecostal image parodied by the squire's cartwheel]" ("Horn and Ivory in the *Summoner's Tale*" [*Neophilologische Mitteilungen* 73 (1972): 122–26]). In addition to the writings of Fletcher, Kolve, Levitan, and Levy cited above, I am much indebted, as the notes to my discussion of the *Prologue* and *Tale* will show, to the previously published scholarship. The observations made and conclusions reached in the published essays I have seen inevitably overlap, and it has not been possible to document fully my indebtedness to them, or my disagreement on specific points. Among them, the one that struck me as most illuminating, though I did not discover it until I had written the penultimate version of this essay, is John Fleming's "Anticlerical Satire as Theological Essay: Chaucer's *Summoner's Tale*" (*Thalia* 6 [1983]: 5–22). Fleming's assessment of the tale as at once comic and deeply serious accords fully with my own, and I found his discussion of the medieval religious background a valuable supplement to the observations of other scholars. I part company with him, however, as to the implied damnation of the Wife of Bath (see pp. 46–47), and I see the themes of penance and wrath as ancillary to a central theme of Wycliffite provenance not identified in his essay.

106. Mary Carruthers discusses the similarity between the two tales in terms of their common concern with "glossing," i.e., the interpretation of language ("Letter and Gloss in the Friar's and Summoner's Tales," *The Journal of Narrative Technique* 2 (1972): 208–14). She points out that glossing can involve either the discovery of the "spiritual or true meaning . . . beneath the literal surface" or the "cover[ing] over [of] meaning in a disingenuous way. . . . The tales of those unholy twins, the Friar and the Summoner, use the ambiguity of the word 'gloss' to explore the question of true meaning in far-reaching ways . . . . The Friar seeks to deny the letter, the Summoner to deny the gloss" (p. 209).

107. "The insult Thomas will visit upon this friar will be, for all its physical grossness, a piece of poetic justice, a return of flatulence for flatulence" (Earle Birney, "Structural Irony within the *Summoner's Tale*," *Anglia* 78 [1960]: 204–18), p. 212. "If the arguments from iconography are right, the harmonious balance of fraternal virtues becomes the equal sharing of a nasty smell, and the Pentecostal inspiration of the Holy Spirit the breathing in of the most crudely physical stink" (Helen Cooper, "The Summoner's Tale," in *The Canterbury Tales, Oxford Guides to Chaucer*, [Oxford: Clarendon Press, 1989], pp. 176–83), p. 179. According to John A. Alford ("Scriptural Testament in *The Canterbury Tales*: The Letter Takes Its Revenge," *Chaucer and Scriptural Tradition*, ed. David Lyle Jeffrey [Ottawa: University of Ottawa Press, 1984], pp. 197–203), Thomas repays the friar by giving "*crepitus* for *crepitus*." He cites two meanings of the word *crepitus* in classical Latin: "noise, prattle, boasting" and "a breaking wind." The resultant ambiguity was punned on by Plautus (p. 200 and n. 7).

108. Roy J. Pearcy has shown that in making the lord of the manor refer to the task set by Thomas as "an impossible" (2231), Chaucer is alluding satirically to the university studies that have enabled Friar John to claim the title of Master (" 'No maister, sire,' quod he, 'but servitour, Thogh I have had in scole that honour'" [2185–86]). See "Chaucer's 'An Impossible' ('Summoner's Tale' III, 2231)", *Notes and Queries*, n.s. 14, 322–25. Pearcy explains the Latin term underlying the lord's English word as designating "a class of exercises used in late medieval scholastic teaching" (322). He observes that "a general

connexion with the university is first established by the friar" in lines 2185–86, and that the appearance of "polysyllabic technical terms (*reverberacioun, perturbynge*)" in the passage that follows enhances the parodic resemblance between the squire's presentation and an academic *disputatio*, "a public event, the master proposing and defending his sophistical arguments before a critical audience of students, or . . . other members of the university intellectual élite" (323).

109. Szittya points out that, parody aside, there was a "natural association of the friars with Pentecost" (which Chaucer would presumably have known about) because "the general chapter of the Franciscans — the only time when the missionary *fratres minores* sent all over the world gathered together as a group — was held approximately every third year at the feast of Pentecost. . . . Francis chose the date for the general chapter primarily because of its symbolic connection with the apostles, whose life he strove so devoutly to imitate, and because of its commemoration of the beginning of their missionary journeys and the beginning of the preaching of the Gospel" (*Antifraternal Tradition*, pp. 237–38). This relationship confirms the parodic connection implicit in the tale.

110. Roy Peter Clark ("Doubting Thomas in Chaucer's *Summoner's Tale*," *Chaucer Review* 11 [1976]: 164–78) shows that *grope*, which appears once in the tale with reference to confessional inquisition and twice with reference to Friar John's reaching for Thomas's gift, is also the standard English word in medieval descriptions of the probing of Christ's wounds by Doubting Thomas (pp. 171–72). He also cites the account of Thomas's later apostolic mission to India and other remote nations in the *Legenda Aurea*, concluding that the contrast between Thomas's selfless assiduity in spreading the word of Christ and the self-serving "mission" of Friar John is "bitterly ironic" (pp. 168–69).

111. The Wycliffite view on this matter is expressed in typical fashion in the following passage: "[Christ] bad his apostils preche . . . to eche mon tho gospel; . . . . Bot thei schulden not preche cronyclis of tho world, as tho batel of Troye, ne oper nyse fablis, . . . ffor Crist biddes his clerkes preche tho gospel, and by that thei wan tho world and scounfitiden ('discomfited') tho fende" (*De officio pastorali*, p. 147).

112. For a detailed analysis of "the comic incoherence and inconsistency of the sermon, and the moral and intellectual obtuseness [the *exempla*] reveal," see Paul N. Zietlow ("In Defense of the Summoner," *Chaucer Review* 1 [1966]: 4–19), pp. 9–13. Zietlow maintains that, even granted the appropriateness of their use in preference to biblical materials, the Senecan examples lack point, since their original meanings are obscured in the friar's retelling (pp. 12–13).

113. For discussions of plays on words and their significance particularly in the *Summoner's Tale*, see Janette Richardson ("The *Summoner's Tale*," in *Blameth Nat Me: A Study of Imagery in Chaucer's Fabliaux* [The Hague and Paris: Mouton, 1970], pp. 153–57), Carruthers, "Letter and Gloss in the Friar's and Summoner's Tales," p. 213, and Cooper, "The Summoner's Tale," pp. 179–80. Cooper remarks that "language is as slippery here as anywhere in the Canterbury sequence. Friar John's own readiness to pervert the Word of God is itself parodied by a series of puns appropriate to the nature of Thomas's gift" (ibid., p. 179).

114. Thomas D. Cooke, in the chapter on "Chaucer's Fabliaux" in *The Old French and Chaucerian Fabliaux: A Study of Their Comic Climax* (Columbia: University of Missouri Press, 1978), pp. 170–94, makes the standard classification, counting the *Miller's Tale*,

the *Reeve's Tale*, the *Friar's Tale*, and *Summoner's Tale*, the *Merchant's Tale*, and the *Shipman's Tale*, along with the fragmentary *Cook's Tale*, as representing the genre, as does Derek Brewer, in "The Fabliaux," *Companion to Chaucer Studies*, ed. Beryl Rowland, rev. ed. (New York and Oxford: Oxford University Press, 1979), pp. 296–325. Pearsall considers the *Friar's Tale* and the *Summoner's Tale* to be "satiric anecdotes" rather than fabliaux (*The Canterbury Tales*, p. 166; cf. "The Canterbury Tales II," p. 139). Cooper includes the *Summoner's Tale* among the fabliaux (*The Canterbury Tales*, p. 176) but considers the *Friar's Tale* an "extended exemplum" (ibid., p. 168).

115. "The Fabliaux," pp. 296–97.

116. Comments on the Friar's greeting of Thomas's wife that hint at the nature of the relationship between the two but do not spell it out include the following: "[the Friar] 'leads captive' Thomas's wife with outrageous flattery and a kiss which is certainly suspicious when judged by the canons of clerical seemliness" (Fleming, "Antifraternalism," p. 693); "[the Friar's] greeting ... displays a sensuality hardly in accord with his words on the subject" (Richardson, *Blameth Nat Me,* p. 150); "[the Friar] deals adroitly with the social niceties—asking after Thomas's wife, greeting her with something more than the conventional kiss" (Pearsall, *Canterbury Tales*, p. 224); "the courtesy he shows is certainly not the religious sort ... and how far the tightness of his embrace and the sweetness of the kiss go beyond polite form is indicated by the simile of the proverbially lecherous sparrow" (Cooper, "The Summoner's Tale," p. 182). Szittya states flatly that "this friar is out to lead astray this wife" (*Antifraternal Tradition,* p. 245), but the fact is that he has done so already.

117. Bernard F. Huppé ("The Friar-Summoner Quarrel," in *A Reading of the Canterbury Tales*, rev. ed. [State University of New York, 1967], pp. 194–209) notes, apropos of the opening reference to Thomas's house in line 1767, that "the Wife of Bath's spectacular word-play on 'refresshed' tends to remain on one's mind," but then hedges: "the way the friar greets Thomas' wife seems to suggest not only his accord with the wife, but the presence of hanky-panky" (p. 203). The Wife of Bath (whose Prologue connects forward with the Summoner's *Prologue* and *Tale*) uses the word twice. Envying the happiness that must have come to Solomon from "alle his wyvys," she wishes she might "be refresshed half so ofte as he" (III [D] 35–39). (*MED* defines the phrase "ben refreshed" as "to take a new spouse," citing only the Wife's allusion to Solomon [s.v. *refreshen* v. sense l(f)], but the inadequacy of this definition is surely obvious.) Later, acknowledging that, as a married woman, she is not "white bread," but "barley bread," she alludes wittily to the miracle of the loaves and fishes: "And yet with barly-breed, Mark telle kan, Oure Lord Jhesu refresshed many a man" (145–46). She thus implies that the miracle of the loaves and fishes, in Huppé's words, "authorizes her exercise of plenitude in sexual gratification" (p. 117). David Leon Higdon, in "The Wife of Bath and Refreshment Sunday" (*Papers on Language and Literature* 8 [1972]: 199–201), describes the Wife's use of the word *refreshment* similarly, as "typical of [her] generally euphemistic rhetoric" (p.199). He makes the interesting observation that the story of the loaves and fishes forms the Gospel for *Dominica Refectionis*, or Mid-Lent Sunday, which "has long been known in England as Refreshment Sunday" (p. 200). "The traditions associated with Refreshment Sunday are ... peculiarly appropriate to the Wife of Bath. On this day, Lenten discipline was relaxed, and the Church enjoyed a pause from the rigors of abstinence and sorrow"

(pp. 200–01). Higdon notes that though "the *OED* records no overtly sexual meaning for 'refreshment,' . . . 'refection' [Latin *refectio*], which was used interchangeably with 'refreshment' during the fourteenth century, did carry such a sense." To this I would add an equally important Latin equivalent for *refreshment*, namely, *refrigerium*, which in several biblical passages signifies spiritual fulfillment and joy. It appears, for example, in Jeremiah 6:16, the Latin epigraph of the *Parson's Tale*: "State super vias, . . . et interrogate de viis antiquis que sit via bona . . . ; et invenietis refrigerium animabus vestris" (X [I] 73); in the English version that follows, *refrigerium* is translated "refresshynge." Cf. Isaiah 28:12 and Psalm 65 (AV 66):12. Like *grace*, *refresshen* in the language of the Wife of Bath's Prologue takes on contrasting or complementary meanings in profane and sacred spheres and can point toward the latter when used ostensibly with reference to the former. Though, as Higdon notes, no such meaning as the Wife of Bath's for *refreshment* is listed in the *OED*, the euphemistic development is natural. Charles Muscatine, in *The Old French Fabliaux* (New Haven: Yale University Press, 1986), lists, as one of the expressions referring to the sexual act in the language of the fabliaux, "to be restored or eased or satisfied (*aasiez*)" (p. 112). The Wife of Bath uses the corresponding English word *ese* (127) in the same way.

118. These include—*mutatis mutandis*—not only the wife of the merchant in the *Shipman's Tale* (a tale originally intended for the Wife), but the Alison of the *Miller's Tale*, and Pertelote in the *Nun's Priest's Tale*. One might even add the "Alison" the Wife remembers affectionately in her Prologue (529 ff.), who was her confidante and, presumably, behaved much like her.

119. Muscatine, *The Old French Fabliaux*, p. 131. Fleming, in "Anticlerical Satire as Theological Essay" (*Thalia* 6 [1983]: 5–22), observes that the cast of characters of the tale form "the classic menage of medieval farce: the rich old man, the sexy wife, the slippery cleric" (p. 12). But he dismisses the relationship between the friar and the wife as "a brief flirtation" that interrupts the friar in his pursuit of a money gift from John (*ib.*).

120. See, e.g., Birney, "Structural Irony within the *Summoner's Tale*," p. 216: "On the instant [when Thomas has let the fart], Master John, that most eloquent preacher against wrath, starts up wrathful as 'a wood leoun,' swearing revenge," and Huppé, "The Friar-Summoner Quarrel," p. 208: "His gift causes the friar to illustrate his own sermon; . . . . He goes off in a boiling rage to the 'lord of that village'."

121. As my brief history of the tradition has shown, many, if not most, of the charges against friars implicit in the *Summoner's Tale* date back to the original antifraternal treatise of William of St. Amour and were duly repeated by Jean de Meun, FitzRalph, and Wyclif. But the charge of blasphemy, which was central in Wycliffite polemic, does not, so far as I have observed, figure in the writings of Wyclif's precursors. It thus joins the specific links with Wycliffite antifraternalism which Alan J. Fletcher, in the essay I referred to at the outset, identified in the tale. One of these is the letter of fraternity binding Thomas and his wife to Friar John's convent: the accusation of fraud directed against the "sale" of such letters was, according to Fletcher, "a centerpiece . . . in the Lollard attack on the detested friars" ("The *Summoner's Tale* and the Abominable Anatomy of Antichrist," p. 101), but is absent from the antifraternal writings of William of St. Amour and Richard FitzRalph. In the tale, the letter seems to have been arranged for by Thomas's wife rather than by Thomas himself, and Thomas's private

estimate of its value seems to underlie his decision to give the friar a blatantly insulting gift:

> "Ye sey me thus, how that I am youre brother?"
> "Ye, certes," quod the frere, "trusteth weel.
> I took oure dame oure lettre with oure seel."
> "Now wel," quod he, "and somewhat shal I yive
> Unto youre hooly covent whil I lyve;
> And in thyn hand thou shalt it have anon." (2126–31)

(Birney exclaims, "How valuable, in the sardonic structure of the tale, is this device of the lay brother!" ["Structural Irony within the *Summoner's Tale*," p. 215].) The trentals whose efficacy Friar John extols in his sermon at the beginning of the tale are singled out by Fletcher as another sore point with the Lollards in particular, as was the claim made by the mendicants, and repeated by Friar John in his sermon, that the prayers of friars were especially efficacious in delivering souls from purgatory (*SumT* 1724–26, 1729–32; cf. Fletcher, "The Summoner and the Abominable Anatomy of Antichrist," pp. 102–05). I discuss later in another connection a further affinity noted in Fletcher's essay: the bringing in, toward the end of the tale, of the biblical text "Ye are the salt of the earth," which is quoted by the lord of the manor; this text was a staple of Wycliffite antimendicant criticism (*SumT* 2196; see p. 40 and n. 130).

122. This false claim is discussed, and relevant details from the tale are cited, by Szittya, *Antifraternal Tradition*, pp. 239–46. In an earlier chapter, Szittya notes the importance of an episode in the life of St. Francis in which the saint heard the instructions of Jesus to the apostles read aloud. He quotes in translation Bonaventura's account in the *Legenda major*: "When Francis heard that they were not to provide gold or silver or copper to fill their purses, that they were not to have a wallet for the journey or . . . shoes or staff, he was overjoyed. . . . There and then he took off his shoes and laid aside his staff . . . . The whole desire of his heart was to put what he had heard into practice and conform to the rule of life given to the Apostles in everything" (pp. 43–44). Kaske, citing Szittya, sees "no reason why the friar of the *Summoner's Tale* may not be intended as an antithesis both of the fraternal ideal and of Christ's instructions in the Gospels; and the Gospels themselves seem clearly enough established as a deliberate frame of reference" ("Horn and Ivory," p. 123).

123. William cites 1 Peter once (p. 38) and 2 Peter twice (pp. 35, 41). The former provides a scriptural basis for the nineteenth of his signs by which to know true apostles: that they suffer tribulation in patience (2.23). 2 Peter 2 is devoted in its entirety to a denunciation of the "lying teachers (magistri mendaces)" (1) who will infiltrate the congregation of the faithful. A number of the vices ascribed to them, including blasphemy and adultery, are conspicuously exhibited by the friar in the *Summoner's Tale*. The impostors are said to "walk . . . in the lust of uncleanness (in concupiscentia immunditiae ambulant);" they "fear not to bring in sects, blaspheming, . . . having eyes full of adultery (sectas non metuunt introducere blasphemantes, . . . oculos habentes plenos adulterii)" (10, 14). These parallels are striking and, once pointed out, seem relevant, but did Chaucer expect his readers to be mindful of them? Perhaps we should envisage a small audience of the elite, capable of recognizing scriptural allusiveness in full, and a larger

audience comparable, say, to the groundlings at Shakespeare's Globe. This larger audience would find much to entertain them in a tale such as the Summoner's, but many of its more subtle nuances would go unappreciated, as caviar to the general. It seems reasonable, for example, to suppose that Chaucer's friends among the Lollard knights (see p. 44, above), who, like him, knew the Bible very well indeed, would have understood the ironic significance of Friar John's references to the epistles of Peter, would have been aware of the denunciation of false teachers in 2 Peter 2, and might even have recognized the relevance of certain of its details.

124. It was evidently Tatlock, in an essay published in 1914, who first pointed out that Friar John's statement that no bells were rung in his convent to mark the occasion of the child's death serves the purpose of explaining away the otherwise suspicious circumstance that no bells were heard at the time (cited by Birney, "Structural Irony within the *Summoner's Tale*," p. 211, n. 1, and Richardson, *Blameth Nat Me*, p. 149, n. 4). Cf. Pearsall, *Chaucer Companion*, p. 140. Fleming, in "Anticlerical Satire as Theological Essay," cites an interesting analogue to the friar's false claim in the form of the "self-serving prophetic visions which formed almost a distinct genre among mendicant letters in the late Middle Ages" (ibid.).

125. "What has been inexorably taking shape in the tale is a working out of poetic justice against the corrupters of apostolic spirit and Holy Spirit" (Levitan, "The Parody of Pentecost," p. 240).

126. Lawrence Besserman, in his comprehensive study *Chaucer and the Bible: A Critical Review of Research, Indexes, and Bibliography* (New York: Garland, 1988), says that though "Chaucer's 'biblical poetics' and seemingly 'biblical' world view came to him in part by way of . . . [earlier] writers and their works . . . this does not invalidate the very obvious counter-proposition that Chaucer's poetry is steeped in biblical language, imagery, and ideas, and that the Bible . . . is the most important and most pervasive of all those works out of which he made original poetry and prose" (p. 45).

127. P. M. Kean has pointed out the affinities of the Pardoner with the "self-revealing and self-describing vice figures common in allegorical writing," particularly Fals-Semblant. Such a figure, being "a self-contained, self-conditioned entity, operating according to the laws of its nature with perfect self-satisfaction," has the simplicity of an abstraction rather than the complexity of a human being. She sees Jean de Meun as presenting, through the agency of Fals-Semblant, "a body of material which . . . includes the topical question of new and dangerous beliefs and movements among the so-called Béguins and Joachimite Friars, as well as much general criticism of hypocrisy, with special, though not exclusive, reference to the clergy," but feels that Chaucer has little interest in this purpose (*Chaucer and the Making of English Poetry* [London and Boston: Routledge and Kegan Paul, 1972], 2:98). I believe, on the contrary, that Chaucer was vividly aware of and deeply concerned about the relevance to his own time of Fals-Semblant's monologue, and that it is as important a source for the *Summoner's Tale* as it is for the *Pardoner's Prologue*, though its influence operates in the former more indirectly.

128. Among those who have written about the tale, Levy and Fleming in particular have taken Friar John's sinfulness seriously in my sense. For Levy, "the point of the Summoner's attack . . . is that the Friar is not specially inspired by the Holy Ghost, as he apparently pretends, but rather that all his speech and actions have a fundamentally

diabolic inspiration" ("Biblical Parody in the *Summoner's Tale*," p. 56). Fleming, in "Anticlerical Satire as Theological Essay," speaks to the matter more at length: "the *Summoner's Tale* plunges deeper [into the question of penance than the *Friar's Tale*] and raises more frightening questions about the very practicability of penance administered by 'vessels of mercy' who are really vessels of wrath, and who blasphemously adorn the filthiest of wrath's 'stinking engendrures' with the outward forms of the sublimest mysteries of divine grace." Taking issue with a statement in "a recent book" to the effect that in the *Summoner's Tale*, Chaucer could be said to be pronouncing a "moral condemnation . . . if the word evil were not too portentous for comedy and for Chaucer's comedy in particular," Fleming goes on to make a statement of his own which I find both eloquent and definitive: "I see no way of talking about the *Summoner's Tale* without talking about evil, nor do I find that the urgency of the *sentence* compromises the brilliant triumph of the *solas*" (p. 19).

129. Sanctity is linked with fragrance in the *Tales* in the "soote savour" of the crowns of roses and lilies given by the angel to Cecilie and her newly converted husband Valerian in the *Second Nun's Tale*, which penetrates the heart of Tiburce and converts him as well (VIII [G] 218–59). Levy points out that "Confirmation, which derives from Pentecost, has as its main outward sign the anointing with 'chrism,' the perfumed holy oil." In this connection, he quotes Jean Daniélou's statement, in *The Bible and the Liturgy*, that "the perfume . . . constitutes the essence of the symbol" ("Biblical Parody in the *Summoner's Tale*," p. 60, n. 17). Alford cites 2 Corinthians 2:15–16, "Now thanks be to God, who . . . manifesteth the odour of his knowledge by us in every place. For we are the good odour of Christ (Deo autem gratias, qui . . . odorem notitiae suae manifestat per nos in omni loco: quia Christi bonus odor sumus Deo)" ("Scriptural Testament in *The Canterbury Tales*," p. 199). Cf. Philippians 4:18. Richard H. Osberg, in "A Voice for the Prioress: The Context of English Devotional Prose" (*Studies in the Age of Chaucer* 18 [1996]: 25–54), notes, with reference to the casting of the *clergeon*'s body into a privy, the frequent references, in medieval sermons and theological writings, to "excrement or to the evacuation of faeces as an image for mortal sin" (p. 49).

130. "'Savour,' Chaucer's *Summoner's Tale*, and Matthew 5:13," *English Language Notes* 31 (1994): 25–29. For the meanings "agreeable smell, perfume, aroma" and "disagreeable odor, offensive smell; the stench of a dead body," see *MED* s.v. *savour* n. senses 2b (c) and (e). Fletcher, in "The *Summoner's Tale* and the Abominable Anatomy of Antichrist" (see above, n. 4), points out that this particular text, though not cited by William of St. Amour or FitzRalph, was a favorite of the Wycliffites, found by them to be "convenient for reminding the clergy of their dominical commission and for reproving those who were lapsing" (pp. 105–07).

131. Kolve presents abundant pictorial evidence to justify his observation that obscenity (specifically, scatology) was located, for the literate medieval Christian, "within a metaphysical framework authorized by God himself" ("Chaucer's Wheel of False Religion," p. 268). His illustrations include a reproduction of the frontispiece of an early fourteenth-century English manuscript, showing God enthroned in heaven in the upper half and Lucifer in hell in the lower. Lucifer is shown "squatting above Hell Mouth in a posture unmistakably suggestive of farting or defecation—an anal orientation familiar to Chaucer's early audiences from the cycle plays as well, where devils frequently made their

exits farting" (pp. 268–69). He also reproduces a drawing similar in import at the bottom of a page of the Luttrell Psalter, an early fourteenth-century English manuscript, of a two-legged grotesque whose front end rises into the upper torso of a man playing a bagpipe, and whose rear end is a human head with a trumpet in its mouth (pp. 271–73). Readers of the *Inferno* will remember how, at the end of canto 21, Barbariccia, leader of a troop of demons, "has made a trumpet of his rear (avea del cul fatto trombetta)" (trans. John D. Sinclair in *The Divine Comedy of Dante Alighiere* [New York: Oxford University Press, 1961]).

132. With reference to the friar's choice of delicacies, Chauncey Wood notes, in addition to 1 Corinthians 6:13, a number of passages from the New Testament in which Christians are exhorted to value spiritual over fleshly nourishment, e.g., Matthew 4:4, "Not in bread alone doth man live, but in every word that proceedeth from the mouth of God (Non in solo pane vivit homo, sed in omni verbo, quod procedit de ore Dei)." Though these have no specific echoes in the wording of the passage, the idea signified by the biblical texts in question was well known and implicitly undercuts the friar's self-congratulation. See Wood, "Artistic Intention and Chaucer's Uses of Scriptural Allusion," *Chaucer and Scriptural Tradition* (Ottawa: University of Ottawa Press, 1984), pp. 35–46.

133. Riverside's note on this passage states that the view of Tatlock (that the narrator's statement has a Wycliffite thrust) "is now generally accepted."

134. I thus agree only in part with Pearsall's assessment: "There is much to take delight in here [i.e., in the persuasive rhetoric trained by the friar on Thomas]. . . . The artistic and dramatic power of the lines almost overwhelms our moral consciousness, as Chaucer, in a characteristic vein, draws us to a delighted assent in the vitality of his creations, in the teeth of our objections to their vicious greed and hypocrisy" (*Canterbury Tales,* p. 226). I believe that a twofold response such as I describe with relation to the *Summoner's Prologue* and *Tale* is elicited by Chaplin's film *The Great Dictator* (1940). In addition to farcical scenes in which Chaplin and Jack Oakie impersonate Hitler and Mussolini, the film includes melodramatic episodes involving victims of Nazi persecution (Chaplin also plays a Jewish barber).

135. Pearsall, having spoken of the detail of the cat, goes on to say that the friar's actions on entering Thomas's house "have the easy and insinuating assumption of privilege. . . . His mastery of the situation is complete. His manner is easy and affable, and he deals adroitly with the social niceties" (*Canterbury Tales,* p. 224).

136. In the *Epistola contra Jovinianum*, which is Chaucer's source for this and much else in the *Prologue*, St. Jerome cites the parable of the Samaritan woman at the well in connection with his discussion of the legitimacy of marriage — in particular, of remarriage for widows as preferable to promiscuity. For him, the crucial point is not the difference between four husbands and five, or five husbands and six, but the difference between one husband and two or more. He takes Jesus' statement about the sixth man as meaning that any husband other than the first is not, properly speaking, a husband at all. I quote the English translation by Philip Schaff and Henry Wace in *St. Jerome: Letters and Select Works, A Select Library of Nicene and Post-Nicene Fathers of the Christian Church,* 2nd Series, 6 (New York: Christian Literature C., 1893), p. 358, and Jerome's Latin from Bartlett J. Whiting, "The Wife of Bath's Prologue," *Sources and Analogues of Chaucer's*

Canterbury Tales, ed. W. F. Bryan and Germaine Dempster (Chicago: University of Chicago Press, 1941), p. 209: "For it is better to know a single husband, though he be a second or third, than to have many paramours: that is, it is more tolerable for a woman to prostitute herself to one man than to many. At all events this is so if the Samaritan woman in John's Gospel who said she had her sixth husband [actually she did not say this; cf. John 4:17] was reproved by the Lord because he was not her husband. For where there are more husbands than one the proper idea of a husband, who is a single person, is destroyed (Melius est enim licit alterum et tertium, unum virum nosse, quam plurimos: id est, tolerabilius est uni homini prostitutam esse, quam multis. Siquidem et illa in Evangelio Joannis Samaritana, sextum se maritum habere dicens, arguitur a Domino, quod non sit vir ejus. . . . Ubi enim numerus maritorum est, ibi vir, qui proprie unus est, esse desiit)." Long before I had read Chaucer, I heard a joke about a woman who had had four children and was afraid to have another because she had been told that every fifth child born into the world was Chinese. I find it significant that both the misunderstanding in this joke and the false interpretation of the biblical story imposed on the Wife of Bath have an antifeminist thrust, as becomes obvious if one tries to substitute a man for the woman as the protagonist of either one. I take it that Jankin the clerk is also responsible for the antifeminist version of the story of Midas and his ass's ears that the Wife has learned; her airy instruction to the company to "read Ovid" to learn the rest of the story masks her own inability to read.

137. While he offers an interpretation of the Wife's monologue from which mine diverges in certain specific respects (see above), Lee Patterson finds, as I do, that the Wife of Bath represents a *tertium quid*, a way of life differing equally from the evildoing of a Friar John and the saintliness of a Constance: "By introducing a rhetoric that is at once carnal and moral . . . the Wife of Bath ameliorates the harsh polarizations of Augustinian theory and opens up a space in which what we have come to call literature can find its home" ("'For the Wyves love of Bathe': Feminine Rhetoric and Poetic Resolution in the *Roman de la Rose* and the *Canterbury Tales*" (*Speculum* 58 [1983]: 656–95). Alcuin Blamires, in "The Wife of Bath and Lollardy" (*Medium Ævum* 58 [1989]: 224–42), argues persuasively for some degree of what he calls "convergence" between the the Wife of Bath's *Prologue* and Wycliffite controversy. The issues raised by the Wife at the beginning would have been of heightened topical interest toward the end the fourteenth century: of the *Twelve Conclusions* published by the Lollards in 1395, one opposed priestly celibacy and another recommended that widows remarry. A favorite text of the Wife's, the injunction "Increase and multiply (crescite et multiplicamini)" in Genesis 9:1 (cf. *Prologue* 28), was used in the early fifteenth century in the interrogation of Margery Kempe and "may have functioned as a touchstone for detecting Lollard 'error' well before [her] time" (233). Given a presumption of allusiveness, "Jankyn's nightly readings to [the Wife] from a 'book of wikked wyves' would amount to a parody of the practice in Lollard cells whereby heretical doctrine characteristically passed around 'through domestic, familial introductions,'" and the enforced burning of the book by Jankin would similarly allude to the fact that "much Lollard literature went up in flames" (235). Blamires concludes that there is reason for reconsidering "the extent of Chaucer's involvement with . . . principles stridently advanced by this controversial pressure-group that gathered strength as his literary career developed" (p. 236).

138. The story of an altercation between Chaucer and a friar in London postdates his death by about two hundred years. It was told by Thomas Speght in his biography of Chaucer (1598); the relevant passage reads as follows: "Not many years since, Master Buckley did see a record in [the Inner Temple], where Geoffrey Chaucer was fined two shillings for beating a Franciscane fryer in Fleetstreete" (see *Chaucer Life-Records*, ed. Martin M. Crow and Clair C. Olson [Oxford: Clarendon Press, 1966], p. 12, n. 5). No such record has been found, nor has the incident been otherwise confirmed; nevertheless, the idea sticks in one's mind.

139. An instance of Chaucer's "caution" at the beginning of his career was cogently analyzed as early as 1952 by Bertrand Bronson ("The *Book of the Duchess* Re-opened," *PMLA* 67: 863–81). What is involved in this poem is simple deference toward a social superior rather than reluctance to give offence by offering distasteful criticism to those in authority. The counsel the young poet addresses to his patron, John of Gaunt, is clear and forceful: he must cease his fruitless mourning, accept the finality of death, and get on with his life. But it is buried in a story told early in the poem, where it is conveyed to Queen Alcyone by the supposed ghost of her husband, King Seys, and thus distanced from the narrator himself. Chaucer's decision to limit the response of the narrator, at the end of the dialogue with the Man in Black, to an exclamation of pity was explained by Bronson as follows: "He well knew that the best advice in the world would be inappropriate when served up to his patron as the last word in such a conversation, on such a topic. It would be socially impudent and out of place, as well as ineffectual. . . . The true conclusion has had to be thrown forward from the end to an inconspicuous point where it can insinuate its meaning unobtrusively and without risk of antagonizing, carried as it is not by the poet but by a third spokesman, the figure of Ceyx" (pp. 880–81). Lee Patterson's " 'No Man His Reson Herde': Peasant Consciousness, Chaucer's Miller, and the Structure of the *Canterbury Tales*, in *Literary Practice and Social Change*, pp. 134–55, describes Chaucer's search "for an ideological posture by means of which to distance himself from the cultic and increasingly caste-defined aristocratic culture of his time" (p. 146). Alan Fletcher, in "The Topical Hypocrisy of Chaucer's Pardoner," notes that the theme of religious hypocrisy was especially prominent in the orthodox versus Lollard debate of the 1380s and finds that the "distinctive emphasis" on that theme in the *Pardoner's Prologue and Tale*, and "even some of the very words and phrases used to express it," were colored by that ongoing debate (p. 116). Chaucer's assignment of that part of the *Canterbury Tales* to a pardoner rather than a friar "can be interpreted as a strategy of political and literary tact . . . . it lets Chaucer hide behind a character traditionally corrupt yet into whom he can safely introduce the resonance of the most urgent and topical theological argument of his day" (p. 119). Sherry Reames, arguing from Chaucer's choice among possible source-texts for the second half of the *Second Nun's Tale*, as well as from "the ways in which Chaucer adds emphasis to Cecilia's trial, and more particularly to her ridicule of Almachius," finds it "reasonable to conclude that he designed the second half of the SNT as a satiric commentary on a contemporary ruler or rulers whom he saw as re-enacting the sins of such ancient Roman persecutors" ("Artistry, Decorum, and Purpose in Three Middle English Retellings of the Cecilia Legend," in *The Endless Knot: Essays on Old and Middle English in Honor of Marie Borroff*, ed. M. Teresa Tavormina and R. F. Yeager [Cambridge, England: D. S. Brewer, 1995], pp. 177–99); see p. 198. Among

ecclesiastical rulers whom Chaucer might have had in mind, "one thinks first of the English church authorities who condemned Wyclif and started persecuting his followers in the 1380s. Although there is a certain oddity about the idea of Chaucer's using a saint's legend on behalf of the Wycliffites, who objected on principle to most aspects of the cult of the saints, this hypothesis would make sense of the tale's strong emphasis on the folly of worshipping graven images" (p. 198).

140. "Chaucer and Ricardian Politics," *The Chaucer Review* 22 (1988): 84–184; see p. 182.

Chapter 2. Silent Retribution in Chaucer

1. Cambridge: Cambridge University Press, 1991.

2. This can safely be called the minority view. It is stated most unequivocally in Carol Everest's "'Paradis or Helle': Procreation and Pleasure in Chaucer's *Merchant's Tale*," which I discuss in note 8, below, and in Milton Miller's "The Heir in the *Merchant's Tale*" (*Philological Quarterly* 29 [1950]: 437–40). Miller cites the references made by the narrator and January himself to the begetting of children and points out that the *Miroir de mariage* "makes a good deal of the argument of legitimate heirs as a reason . . . to marry" (p. 439). For Miller, what is central to the tale is the thematic relationship between deception and self-deception; he evidently believes, wrongly in my view, that January has no legitimate reason for thinking he can impregnate May (he refers to January's "lack of conjugal competence" [ibid.]). He concludes that "the irony of both the deception and the self-deception is obvious; whatever [May's] *plit* was before ascending the pear-tree, it may well now be what she said it was then" (440). Winthrop Wetherbee argues that the bringing of Proserpine into the story implies the possibility of May's becoming pregnant: "as Proserpine's own role as fertility goddess depends on her separating herself from her husband for a season each year, so May . . . may grow fertile in the arms of Damyan" (*Geoffrey Chaucer: The Canterbury Tales* [Cambridge: Cambridge University Press, 1990], p. 73).

3. See, e. g., Crane's statement in his introduction to Crane et al., *Critics and Criticism, Ancient and Modern* (Chicago: University of Chicago Press, 1952): "The form or 'power' of a poem [viewed as a product of mimesis] is determined primarily by the poet's representation of humanly significant or moving actions, characters, or thoughts. . . . the form exists for our contemplation or edification . . . as it is realized in the succession of the poet's words in ways conditioned by his choice of manner or technique" (p. 21). See also Crane's account of "five groups of critical questions" that can be brought to bear on literary works, in "Questions and Answers in the Teaching of Literary Texts," in *The Idea of the Humanities and Other Essays, Critical and Historical* (Chicago: University of Chicago Press, 1967), 2:181–88. In the second of these groups—questions pertaining to the "criticism of structure or form"—the "basic structural parts of a literary work" are taken to be "its language and content. . . . [The work] may be the representation of a human experience of some sort, for the sake of its effects on our emotions and the beauty of its rendering, in which case the other parts are such things as thought, character, plot, . . . and the various technical expedients by which thought, character, emotion, situation, action are brought before us" (p. 184). What Crane calls "beauty" I prefer to

call "power"; I conceive of mimetic power, in turn, as deriving from the interaction of features present at verbal and subverbal levels of form. See note 5, below.

4. In *The Rhetoric of Fiction*, 2d ed. (Chicago: University of Chicago Press, 1983), Booth distinguishes between the narrator, who, as "speaker in the work . . . is after all only one of the elements created by the implied author," and goes on to say that "our sense of the implied author includes not only the extractable meanings [of a work of fiction] but also the moral and emotional content of each bit of action and suffering of all the characters. It includes, in short, the intuitive apprehension of a completed artistic whole" (p. 73). To designate this most comprehensive agency, Booth posits our need for "a term that is as broad as the work itself but still capable of calling attention to that work as the product of a choosing, evaluating person rather than as a self-existing thing. The 'implied author' chooses, consciously or unconsciously, what we read; we infer him as an ideal, literary, created version of the real man; he is the sum of his own choices" (pp. 74–75).

5. In *Language and the Poet* (University of Chicago Press, 1979), I argue that "there is no single form-content opposition in [literary] language; rather, there are various 'levels' of form at which the critic may engage the literary text, from the most local and particular to the most broad and general" (p. 21). I distinguish there between two levels close to the surface of language, namely, "formulation" and "verbalization." I define formulation as those aspects of form that remain constant in a translation from one language to another kindred language, say, from English to French, or vice versa — chiefly lexical meaning and syntax. I define "verbalization" as consisting in the values, usually untranslatable, of the particular words of the original language, including values as diction, values resulting from emotional and other associations, and values dependent on phonetic qualities. I also identify two deeper levels of form, namely, "development," perceived as the realization of basic material or "gist" in successive parts or episodes, and the "conception" underlying the whole (ibid.).

6. "The Effect of the Merchant's Tale," *Speaking of Chaucer* (New York: W. W. Norton, 1970), pp. 30–45. In his discussion of the passage, Donaldson remarks, "This construction ['bad God sholde hem blesse'] seems to me to reflect the disgusted disillusion of the narrator, who here reduces, with a contempt bred of familiarity, Christian ritual to perfunctory hocus-pocus" (p. 41). If the Monk were the original narrator of the tale, Donaldson's comment would be even more apropos; see p. 69 and n.33, below.

7. I quote the translation of the *Ameto* by Judith Serafini-Sauli (New York: Garland Publishing, 1985), p. 89. I have consulted the original in the edition of Nicola Bruscoli, Giovanni Boccaccio, *Opere*, 5: *L'Ameto. Lettere. Il Corbaccio*, 5 (Bari: Giuseppe Laterza & Figli, 1940), pp. 3–152.

8. See Danielle Jacquart and Claude Thomasset, *Sexuality and Medicine in the Middle Ages*, trans. Matthew Adamson (Princeton: Princeton University Press, 1988). The theory of "female seed" and its corollary concerning pregnancy rested on no less an authority than Galen, though it contradicted the views of Aristotle, who denied that the fluid emitted by women during intercourse was seminal (pp. 61–66). Among the medieval authorities whose views on female sexuality accorded with those of Galen was Avicenna, whose *Book of the Canon of Medicine* Chaucer alludes to twice, first in the portrait of the Physician (I [A] 432) and second in the description of the death of the three sinners by

poison at the end of the *Pardoner's Tale* (VI [C] 889–94). Jacquart and Thomasset refer to the opinion of Avicenna that "when the woman does not emit any sperm, conception cannot take place" (p. 130). The generally shared belief in female seed and other aspects of medieval ideas about sexuality are adduced as arguments for May's pregnancy after her encounter in the tree with Damian in Carol Everest's comprehensive treatment of the question in "'Paradys or Helle': Pleasure and Procreation in Chaucer's 'Merchant's Tale'" (in *Sovereign Lady: Essays on Women in Middle English Literature*, ed. Muriel Whitaker [New York and London: Garland Publishing, 1995], pp. 63–84). Everest cites two passages in the *Parson's Tale* (X 575–76 and 965) in which reference is made to female as well as male emissions (p. 67). She further notes that the action in the pear tree takes place at a time near the summer solstice (p. 74) and alludes to the narrator's description of the warm sunny weather on that day in lines 2220–24: "The greenness and beauty of January's private playground suggest the lush fecundity of 'nature naturing' under the engendering warmth of Phoebus' golden rays" (p. 75). See also Margaret Hallissy, *Clean Maids, True Wives, Steadfast Widows: Chaucer's Women and Medieval Codes of Conduct* (Westport, Conn.: Greenwood Press, 1993), pp. 157–60. Hallissy sees May as unwisely risking pregnancy in the tree but does not infer that she in fact becomes pregnant. She does infer from the doctrine of the two seeds that January cannot impregnate May (pp. 157–59). But she sees May, along with January, as comically victimized at the end of the poem. She notes that after the two enter the garden on the fateful day, January assures May of his intention to give her "al [his] heritage, toun and tour" (2172). "In order to inherit 'al,'" unencumbered by an heir, May should avoid pregnancy," but, "too lusty to scheme, she risks all the advantages of childless widowhood for an interlude of pleasure. Thus Chaucer uses contemporary . . . medical beliefs to make his May look just as foolish as his Januarie" (pp. 159–60). My reading of the poem differs from Hallissy's with regard to what might be called its emotional form: I see its punitive force as concentrated on January throughout, and with particular intensity at the end.

9. I have substituted *limp* for Serafini-Sauli's *loose* in translating Boccaccio's *lenta* (p. 95).

10. See John Bugge, "Damyan's Wanton *Clyket* and an Ironic New *Twiste* to the *Merchant's Tale*," *Annuale Mediaevale* 14 (1973): 53–62.

11. Quoted by Mann, "Apologies to Women," p. 33, n. 15.

12. "The Morality of *The Merchant's Tale*," *The Yearbook of English Studies* 6 (1976): 16–25; I quote from p. 17.

13. See chapter 1 above.

14. Howard describes this as "an artistry which we cannot realistically attribute to the teller. . . . [It] is the author's, though selected features of the pilgrim's dialect, argot, or manner may still be impersonated" (*The Idea of the Canterbury Tales* [Berkeley: University of California Press, 1976], p. 231).

15. M. Copland, in "The *Reeve's Tale*: Harlotrie or Sermonyng?" (*Medium Ævum* 31 [1962]: 14–32), reminds us that "Chaucer devotes more than sixty lines to [the social background and pretensions of Simkin and his family] in a very short tale. Nor, as might appear on a cursory reading, do they remain mere unfunctional decoration nor are they there simply to increase our belief in the characters" (p. 19). Rather, they are "summoned back with a powerful rush" toward the end of the tale.

16. Glending Olson, "The *Reeve's Tale* as a Fabliau," *Modern Language Quarterly* 35 (1974): 219–30, p. 220, n. 3. Olson dismisses the idea, espoused in some of the published criticism of the tale, that it has a morally serious dimension — that Simkin, for example, is "an exemplification of Pride, the greatest of the sins" (pp. 219–22). I too find such interpretations inappropriately heavy-handed, given the conventions of the genre to which the tale obviously belongs. But the narrator's comment, in lines 3983–86, on the parson's plans for disposing of his property seems to me to be spoken in a voice that comes from outside the cynical world of the fabliau genre. And the note it sounds has reverberations, for ears attuned to them, that enlarge our understanding of the punishments inflicted on Simkin's family at the end.

17. The verb *devoure* is particularly powerful. The action it signifies is predicated in Middle English chiefly of fire, as in Isaiah 29.6, "A visitation shall come from the Lord of hosts in thunder . . . and with the flame of devouring fire (et flammae ignis devorantis)," and wild beasts, as in 1 Peter 5.8, "The devil, as a roaring lion, goeth about seeking whom he may devour (quaerens quem devoret)." (See *devouren* v. in *MED*.) The narrator's words are reminiscent in tone of Fals-Semblant's description, in the *Romaunt of the Rose*, of the endangerment of the church by its enemies within:

> "Thou hooly chirche, thou maist be wailed!
> Sith that thy citee is assayled
> Thourgh knyghtis of thyne owne table,
> God wot thi lordship is doutable!
> If thei enforce [hem] it to wynne
> That shulde defende it fro withynne,
> Who myght defense ayens hem make?" (6271–77)

Cf. chapter 1, pp. 20–22.

18. According to the predictably austere view of Wyclif on this matter, the prayers of priests who cohabited with concubines were invalid, and such priests ought not to officiate at mass. See, for example, "De precationibus sacris" in *Select English Works of John Wyclif*, ed. Thomas Arnold (Oxford: Clarendon Press, 1871), 3:224–25: "The pope comaundith in his lawe, that no man here the masse of that prest, whanne he whot withouten doute that he hath a concubine or lemman" (p. 224).

19. Copland observes that Simkin's outburst is both "unexpectedly and outrageously in character." He also see it — rightly in my opinion — as "the key to the moral coherence of the tale" ("The *Reeve's Tale*," p. 21).

20. D. W. Robertson, Jr., points out that the Pardoner "tempts his listeners by assuring them that the proper application of his 'relics' will multiply the 'beestes' and the 'stoor' of his customers, cause them to be unconcerned about the marital infidelities of their spouses, and bring about a 'multiplying' of grain. In other words, he appeals to their cupidity and encourages it, at the same time seeking to satisfy his own" (*A Preface to Chaucer: Studies in Medieval Perspectives* [Princeton: Princeton University Press, 1962], pp. 332–33).

21. One of the best accounts of the dramatic power peculiar to the tale is A. C. Spearing's, in the introduction to his edition of *The Pardoner's Prologue and Tale* (Cambridge: Cambridge University Press, 1965): the tale "is told with a shattering intensity,

and the emotion it arouses helps to convey a profound significance. . . . We see the actors not simply judged by an outraged deity, but recklessly damning themselves, throwing themselves headlong upon their fate" (p. 1; cf. p. 30). Spearing's edition is also valuable for its full account of the office of pardoner, or *quaestor*, as sanctioned by the church, and of efforts on the part of the ecclesiastical hierarchy in Chaucer's time to reform its abuses (pp. 5–12). See also Spearing's essay on the *Pardoner's Tale* in *The Cambridge Chaucer Companion*, ed. Piero Boitani and Jill Mann (Cambridge: Cambridge University Press, 1986), pp. 165 ff.

22. In addition to the ironic allusions to Christian doctrine I have mentioned, two figures point from within the infernal world of the tale toward salvation, though both are contemptuously disregarded by its sinful protagonists. The first of these is a child—a "knave" in the service of one of the rioters. He brings to mind the children spoken of as types of innocence in the Bible: the "little child" of the Book of Isaiah 11.6, who is to lead the beasts in the Peaceable Kingdom, and the child spoken of by Jesus in Mark 10.15 ("whosoever shall not receive the kingdom of God as a little child, shall not enter into it"). In warning his master to be ready *everemoore* to meet Death (683), he echoes the counsel given to the faithful Christian by the church (cf. Matthew 25.13, "Watch ye therefore, because you know not the day nor the hour"). The "dame" who taught him this precept may thus be Lady Holy Church herself. The second figure is the old man, whose significance has been variously explained. I suggest that he personifies death-in-life, the ever-deteriorating state of the physical body which must last as long as mortality lasts and which is spoken of as "this corruptible" by Paul in 1 Corinthians 15.53–54: "For this corruptible must put on incorruption . . . then shall be brought to pass the saying that is written: Death is swallowed up in victory." Life so conceived, in the words given by Chaucer to Scipio Africanus in the *Parliament of Fowls*, "nis but a maner deth, what wey we trace" (54); it must be endured by all human beings until the end of time as foretold in Christian doctrine.

23. Cited in part by Warren Ginsberg in "Preaching and Avarice in the *Pardoner's Tale*" (*Mediævalia* 2 [1976]: 77–99), p. 85. Ginsberg makes the point that pride and avarice are "inseparably linked" in medieval thought (ibid.). Eric W. Stockton, "The Deadliest Sin in the *Pardoner's Tale*" (*Tennessee Studies in Literature* 6 [1961]: 47–59), identifies pride as latent, but of major importance, in the tale. But in arguing that the three rioters are "chiefly" guilty of pride, he plays down the relationship between sinfulness generally and death (physical and spiritual) that I see as fundamental to Chaucer's conception.

24. "The rioters . . . cannot respond to spiritual meanings—they are all literalists whose interpretations are governed entirely by material reality" (Martin Stevens and Kathleen Falvey, "Substance, Accident, and Transformations: A Reading of the *Pardoner's Tale*" [*Chaucer Review* 17 (1982): 142–58], p. 147). Spearing notes the "sinful materialism" of the Pardoner's world (*Companion*, p. 167).

25. They are in the habit of swearing blasphemous oaths, a vice discussed in the *Parson's Tale* under the heading of anger (X [I] 586–95). The Pardoner's complaint that the rioters tear apart the body of Christ as if the Jews had not torn it enough (474–75) is paralleled in *Parson's Tale* (590).

26. One of the "twigges" (390) of Pride listed in the *Parson's Tale* is irreverence, manifested "whan men do nat honour there as hem oghte to doon" (403).

27. "The *Pardoner's Tale* and the Quest for Death" (*Essays in Criticism* 24 [1974]: 107–23). Pittock introduces the distinction with relation to a play by Max Frisch (pp. 107–08) and goes on to apply it to the allegorical play *Everyman*. Everyman "knows (but does not know) from the start that 'on mourra seul,' that kindred and friends cannot die for one, or possessions accompany one to the grave; nor are the doctrines of the Church about the proper way to die, which are presented to Everyman as if they were new ideas to him, really unfamiliar. . . . The play dramatises the way in which emotional alienation from the reality of death turns into acceptance of it, by presenting notional awareness in terms of literal ignorance and intellectual confusion" (p. 108). The Pardoner's "notional awareness" of the damnation in store for him never undergoes such a change.

28. An early, often-quoted interpretation of the statement was offered by George Lyman Kittredge, who thought that the Pardoner experienced at this point, out of the blue, "a paroxysm of agonized sincerity" (quoted in John Halverson, "Chaucer's Pardoner and the Progress of Criticism," *Chaucer Review* 4 [1970]: 184–202, p. 189). Dewey R. Faulkner argues that according to medieval thought on evil, "the Pardoner exists, therefore he cannot be totally evil, therefore some good must be in him, and in lines 916–18, pure and untainted, there it is" ("Introduction," *Twentieth-Century Interpretations of The Pardoner's Tale* [Englewood Cliffs: Prentice-Hall, 1973]), p. 11. Stockton, in "The Deadliest Sin," takes exactly the opposite line: "This closing formula is surely not the one sincere moment of repentance, as Kittredge would have it, but his crowning infamy. For the Pardoner does not believe . . . that Jesus Christ is our souls' physician, nor does he truly pray for Christ to save anyone" (p. 56). The disparity among interpretations of the speech (to those I have cited, others could be added), bears out my own contention concerning the speech, for which see below.

29. I find the Host an especially appropriate adversary for the Pardoner because he is so obviously endowed with the virility the Pardoner lacks: the narrator says of him in the *General Prologue* that "of manhod hym lakkede right noght" (I [A] 756). I suspect that *synne*, in the Pardoner's snide remark, has its specific sexual meaning; see *sinne* n. in *MED*, sense 2 (c).

30. Though we differ as to its dramatic motivation (or lack thereof), I find strikingly apt what Harold Bloom says about the Pardoner's benediction, and the passage leading up to it, in the introduction to his collection, *Geoffrey Chaucer's The Pardoner's Tale* (Modern Critical Interpretations series [New York: Chelsea House, 1988]), p. 9: "Moved by the extraordinary intensity of his own tale-telling, the Pardoner achieves a kind of vertigo that mixes pride in his own swindling with something dangerously authentic out of the supernatural order of grace." It is not surprising that the concept of grace appears as one of the many elements of Christian doctrine parodied in the tale. When the "worste" of the rioters suggests that he and his two companions should wait until night to carry away the treasure and in the meantime cast lots to see which of them is to fetch food and drink, he prefaces his scheme by exclaiming "Ey, Goddes precious dignitee! Who wende / To-day that we sholde han so fair a grace?" (782–83).

31. In the Wycliffite tract, "How the office of curatis Is ordeyned of god," one of the faults ascribed to priests is allowing pardoners to preach to their congregations (*The English Works of Wyclif*, ed. F. D. Matthew [London: Early English Text Society, O.S. 74, 1880, pp. 143–63], p. 154). Though the writer first speaks of "a pardoner with stollen

bullis & false relekis," that is, one who, like Chaucer's Pardoner, is dishonest, he soon makes clear his scepticism about official pardons generally, since the church, in authorizing them, claims for itself "more power than euere crist grauntid to petir or poul or ony apostle" (ibid.). See chapter 1 above, "Dimensions of Judgment in Chaucer," p. 29.

32. The word appears at the beginning of the Monk's portrait (166) and is glossed in the 1987 Riverside edition of Chaucer as "hunting." In addition, *prikyng* (191) is glossed as "tracking," and *prikasour* (189) as "horseman, hunter on horseback." The author of the explanatory notes to the portrait disputes Paull Baum's interpretation of these words as puns alluding to sexual activity, pointing out that *OED* does not record a sexual meaning for *venerie* until 1497, and that the earliest lexical evidence for a sexual meaning for *prick* (the noun, not the verb) dates from 1592. But the potential suggestiveness of *venerie* need not, and does not, derive solely from the English meanings of the word. On the contrary, it is translinguistic, reaching out beyond English to two languages well known to Chaucer, medieval Latin and Italian. (The Italian name of the goddess Venus, which appears repeatedly in the *Ameto*, is *Venere*.) And as for a clearly implied, though lexically unrecorded, metaphorical meaning of the verb *to prick*, one need look no further than the *Reeve's Tale*. John, one of the two young Cambridge students from Cambridge who are staying with the larcenous miller, invades his host's wife's bed during the night; once arrived there, as the narrator puts it, "He priketh harde and depe as he were mad" (4231). (Furthermore, it is difficult to understand how anyone can fail to grasp the ironic sexual implications of the verb *prick* when it is used by the narrator no fewer than five times in twenty-nine lines in describing the peregrinations of the ethereally lovelorn Sir Thopas.) For the refreshment received by Friar John at the house of Thomas, see chapter 1 above, p. 34 and n. 117.

33. More than seven decades ago, this commonsensical view was strongly hinted at, if not definitely espoused, by John Matthews Manly, in his edition of the *Canterbury Tales* (New York: Henry Holt, 1928): "[The *Merchant's Tale*] was originally intended for another narrator.... Can it have been the Monk, retaliating for the satire on monks in the *Wife of Bath's Tale* (now assigned to the Shipman)?" (p. 624). Manly cites line 1251, with its reference to "thise fooles that been seculeer," along with other indications that "the narrator was a member of a religious order" (ibid.). More recently, J. D. Burnley, seeing little relationship between the tale and the Merchant, has described its narrator, as implied by his language, in terms that irresistibly suggest the monk, without, however, explicitly mentioning him. Quoting an article by Norman T. Harrington, Burnley calls the narrator "cool, controlled, acidulous" and goes on to speak of his "chilling air of superiority" reflecting "supercilious intellectualism" ("The Morality of the *Merchant's Tale*," p. 16). Burnley also finds in the tale "a deliberate system of allusion" to "the liturgy of the Nuptial Mass" which "brings the shocking and amoral events of the tale into inevitable juxtaposition with an idealized conception of marriage" (p. 19); the same purpose is served by the later allusions to the Song of Songs (pp. 23–24). Familiarity with the liturgy and the Bible is something we should of course expect from the Monk, but such familiarity need not rule out a cynical view of what marriage is actually like. In writing the tale, Chaucer devised a "deliberate scheme of association by which the significance of marriage in Christian doctrine is juxtaposed with its reality" (p. 23).

34. "The *Canterbury Tales* as a whole . . . is a kind of meta-fabliau in which certain tales and pairs of tales, and certain links, are the matter for the acting out of similar professional clashes among the pilgrims described at the beginning. Thus the whole conflict between the Friar and the Summoner, in both the headlinks and their tales, is a 'fabliau' introduced by their respective descriptions in the General Prologue. . . . The Miller and the Reeve are opposed in a similar fabliau-like conflict. . . . Other fabliau-like professional clashes, not fully developed . . . occur between the Host and the pardoner; the Shipman and the Merchant; the Host, the Cook, and the Manciple; the Pardoner, the Friar, and the Wife, and between the Clerk and the Wife" (*The One and the Many in the Canterbury Tales* [Hamden, Conn.: Archon Books, 1980], pp. 39–40).

Chapter 3. *"Love's Hete"* in the Prioress's Prologue and Tale

1. The phrasing of her allusion to Saint Nicholas, early in her tale, implies that she is in the habit of meditating on this miracle of the Virgin and its associations:

But ay, whan I remembre on this mateere,
Seint Nicholas stant evere in my presence. (513–14)

2. Sumner Ferris, in "The Mariology of the *Prioress's Tale*" (*American Benedictine Review* 32 [1981]: 232–54), shows that in both *Prologue* and tale, Chaucer consistently represents the Virgin's place in the supernatural order in accordance with Catholic doctrine. She is "supreme among God's creatures" yet, in that she herself is one of those creatures, she is "infinitely inferior to [God]. . . . [She] does not share in the kind of worship reserved for him" (235). He notes that in the *Prologue* God literally takes precedence over the Virgin (234), and that in describing the Virgin as "the roote Of bountee," Chaucer, in the person of the Prioress, adds "next hir Sone" (465–66). As for the tale itself, "although this is by genre a Miracle of the Blessed Virgin, the words of the narrator and of the (Christian) characters in the Tale acknowledge, without exception, that the power and glory belong to God" (242). Ferris further quotes lines 652–55, from the martyred boy's speech to the abbot, to show that "even [he] respects and observes the proper order of precedence" (243).

3. For the Latin text, see the notes to lines 36–56 in *The Works of Geoffrey Chaucer*, ed. F. N. Robinson, 2d ed. (Boston: Houghton Mifflin, 1957), p. 757. *The Riverside Chaucer* substitutes a modern translation: "The womb (*claustrum*) of Mary bears Him, ruling the threefold fabric (*trinam machinam*), Whom earth, stars, sea, honor, worship, proclaim."

4. The word *labour*, which occurs earlier in the Prologue ("To telle a storie I wol do my labour" [463]), carries an additional suggestion of the theme of pregnancy which, I am arguing, is implied in lines 481–83. In Chaucer's English, the noun had not yet come to signify, in independent use, "the pains and efforts of childbirth" (see sense 6a of *labour* n. in *OED*, first cited from Spenser). But the cognate verb, in sense 16, "Of women: To suffer the pains of childbirth," is cited by *OED* from the *Paston Letters* (1454). These meanings do not appear in *MED*, but the phrase "labour of birthe" is cited s.v. *labour* n. sense 4 and "labouren of child" s.v. *labouren* v. sense 3[a].

5. Donald Fritz, in "The Prioress's Avowal of Ineptitude" (*Chaucer Review* 9 [1974]:

174–79), sees the Prioress's professed inability to "declare" the worthiness of the Virgin as having its source in the "inexpressibility topos." He does not associate her comparison of herself to an infant, capable of praising the Virgin only through the intercession of the Virgin herself, with the miraculous spreading of God's praise by infants suckling at the breast.

6. See Robert Worth Frank, Jr., "The *Canterbury Tales* III: Pathos," in *The Cambridge Chaucer Companion*, ed. Piero Boitani and Jill Mann (Cambridge: Cambridge University Press, 1986), pp. 143–47, 153–54. According to Frank, the *Prioress's Tale*, among others, exemplifies a mode of religious pathos which "in fourteenth- and fifteenth-century literature and art . . . was powerful and persuasive" (144). Frank emphasizes the absence of irony and complexity in Chaucer's "tales of pathos;" his "principal artistic concern [in these tales] is to produce a strong emotional effect" (p. 143). Alfred David, in "An ABC to the Style of the Prioress" (in *Acts of Interpretation*, ed. Mary J. Carruthers and Elizabeth D. Kirk [Norman, Okla.: Pilgrim Books, 1982], pp. 147–57), remarks on the "pervasive emotionalism," associated with "the clash of opposites: good and evil, innocence and cruelty, the hope of salvation and the fear of damnation," characteristic of late fourteenth-century works of courtly and religious art (p. 152). John C. Hirsh, in "Reopening the *Prioress's Tale*" (*Chaucer Review* 10, #1 [1975]: 30–45), finds a "non-biblical source for [the *Prioress's Tale*] . . . which is of utmost importance," namely, "the background of affective piety which informs the tale throughout" (37). He quotes from a modern description, applicable to medieval devotional practice, of "affective prayer" as characterized by the predominance of emotion over "argument," by the substitution of intuition for logical deduction, and, to a greater or lesser degree, by "simplification" of the soul (pp. 35–36). Hirsh also argues that "the Prioress's own allegations against the Jews are more restricted than is usually assumed." He notes that the Provost puts to death "only those Jews 'that of this mordre wiste'" (1820), and that "neither the Provost nor the Prioress institutes a pogrom," citing Thomas Aquinas's distinctions among the rulers of the Jews, the Jews of lesser rank, and the soldiers who carried out the execution as deserving of greater and lesser blame for the crucifixion of Jesus (39–40). But it is exactly such distinctions, I should argue, that are ruled out by the affective or pathetic simplicity pervading the narration of the tale. It is "the Jews" of the ghetto generally, not a small high-ranking group, who are incited by Satan to have the boy killed (565–66) and who therefore, we must assume, knew of the murder.

7. Sister Nicholas Maltman, O.P., in her essay "The Divine Granary, or the End of the Prioress's 'Greyn'" (*Chaucer Review* 17 [1982]: 163–70), convincingly argues that the "greyn" laid upon the boy's tongue by the Virgin has its source in a responsory and versicle and a prosa, or extension of the responsory, used in the second vespers of that Feast. The latter, which she quotes in full, includes the following lines: "The marble pavement of Christ's sanctuary is rubied with the stream of holy blood. The martyr, given the laurel wreath of life, is, like the grain purged from the chaff, transported into divine granaries" (Sister Nicholas's translation). Though she does not mention the image of the marble stones specifically, I take its appearance in the prosa in conjunction with the ruby (and the grain) as evidence that the marble in Chaucer's poem is a further echo of the liturgical passage.

8. The dungheap is more than a gratuitously sensational detail; it acquires symbolic

resonance in opposition to the marble sepulcher in which the "litel body sweete" of the martyr is appropriately entombed. The dungheap suggests the medieval denigration of the bodies of sinful men that we hear in the *Pardoner's Tale*: "O wombe! O bely! O stynkyng cod, / Fulfilled of dong and of corrupcioun!" (VI 534–35); the sepulcher represents the incorruption and splendor of the heavenly realm to which the soul of the martyred "innocent," whose virgin body was likewise pure, has been translated. See also the preceding note.

9. For Fritz, both "song" in the *Prioress's Prologue and Tale* and the Latin of the *Alma redemptoris* convey a "reality . . . different in *kind* from the reality of the world of the young boys [and, presumably, that of the Canterbury pilgrimage]," thus contrasting with "the vernacular language . . . [of] ordinary communications" (p. 173). The difficulty, for the Prioress, of finding language adequate for devotional praise, and the difficulty, for the little boy, of understanding Latin, point toward "a belief that God always transcends anything man can think or say of him" (pp. 173–74).

Chapter 4. Chaucer's English Rhymes

1. A comprehensive essay on rhyme, written mainly by T. V. F. Brogan, with sections entitled "Definition," "Taxonomy," "Terminology," "Analogues," "Functions," "Language and Art," "Data," and "Origin and History," as well as numerous cross-references and a large bibliography, may be found in *The New Princeton Encyclopedia of Poetry and Poetics*, ed. Alex Preminger, T. V. F. Brogan, et al. (Princeton: Princeton University Press, 1993), pp. 1052–64. Brogan endorses the view that "rhyme . . . is a natural linguistic structure which can arise in any language having the right set of features" and goes on to point out that "there is considerable evidence that children manufacture rhymes spontaneously as one basic form of sound permutation; conspicuous too is rhyme in the chants and charms of many primitive cultures" (p. 1061). However, "it is a thundering fact that most of the world's 4,000 languages lack rhyme in their poetries altogether" (ibid.).

2. Michael McKie, in "The Origins and Early Development of Rhyme in English Verse" (*Modern Language Review* 92 [1997]: 817–31), sees the development whereby rhyme came to be a prevailing feature of English verse as having had three stages, "each of which is marked by the impact of another culture upon English verse. Initially, rhyme was imported from Church Latin by Anglo-Saxon versifiers steeped in the culture of the Church. . . . In the second stage, under the pressure of linguistic changes brought about by the Conquest, narrative verse in rhymed couplets emerged. . . . In the final stage, poetry and music moved to a closer union, and the simplicity of couplet-rhyme was overtaken by the more highly prized complexity of stanzaic rhyme-patterns" (p. 829).

3. See the preliminary discussion of the varieties of sound symbolism in my essay "Sound Symbolism as Drama in the Poetry of Robert Frost," *PMLA* 107 (1992): 131–44.

4. In *The Verbal Icon: Studies in the Meaning of Poetry* (Lexington: University of Kentucky Press, 1954), pp. 153–66.

5. See, for example, the categories discussed in the opening pages of P. Rickard, "Semantic Implications of Old French Identical Rhyme," *Neuphilologische Mitteilungen* 66 (1965): 355–401.

6. My examples and statistics derive from a detailed study of two passages of the part written by Guillaume de Lorris: lines 1–128 and lines 524–74 (the description of Oiseuse). Citations and line numbers refer to *"The Romaunt of the Rose" and "Le Roman de la Rose": A Parallel-Text Edition*, ed. Ronald Sutherland (Oxford: Blackwell, 1968). I have silently deleted the parentheses and italics whereby Sutherland indicates departures from his base manuscript and expansions of scribal abbreviations. I have also consulted the text of the *Roman* as edited by Félix Lecoy, *Guillaume de Lorris et Jean de Meun, Le Roman de la Rose*, 3 vols. (Paris: Honoré Champion, 1965–70). For the French terminology, see Brogan, "Rhyme," part 3, p. 1059.

7. In "simple rhyme," the eighth syllable of the line may or may not be followed by a syllable containing the weakly stressed vowel which is spelled *e* and pronounced like the *a* in *tuba*, as in *peirë/feirë*, above, *songës/mensongës* (1–2), and *kalandrë/entendrë* (77–78).

8. The term *rime léonine* is also used in French of rhymes of types (4) and (5) in my classification.

9. The triple rhymes of Old French poetry differ from rhymes in English verse like *tenderly/slenderly*, in that the second and third syllables of the latter are normally extrametrical, coming after the "chief syllable" of the final foot. A rhyme in English pentameter between *dare to die* and *ne'er to die*, in which *dare* and *ne'er* were the fourth chief syllables of their respective lines and *die* was the fifth, would correspond to a triple rhyme in French, but I can think of no examples. If others know of any such, I would be happy to have them drawn to my attention.

10. I have rounded off the third decimal place in several of these figures.

11. Many of the simple rhymes of the *Roman* are also "interesting" in Wimsatt's sense. I shall limit my examples, however, to the categories of more or less elaborate rich rhymes that I have identified above. I do this partly for reasons of space, partly also because the kinds of tension between phonic identity and disparities of other sorts that interested Wimsatt are obviously enhanced when phonic identity, as in rich rhyme, is more than usually conspicuous.

12. Modern translations of the *Roman* are taken from *The Romance of the Rose by Guillaume de Lorris and Jean de Meun*, trans. Charles Dahlberg (Hanover: University Press of New England, 1983).

13. There is a brief discussion of rich rhyme, called "echo rime," in Paull F. Baum, *Chaucer's Verse* (Durham: Duke University Press, 1961), pp. 37–38. Baum finds such rhyming "fairly common" in Chaucer; he cites *heere* "here" / *heere* "hear," from "An ABC" 26, 31 and *herte* "hurt" / *herte* "heart," from the *Book of the Duchess* 883–84 as chronologically early examples, and *seke* "seek" / *seke* "sick" in lines 17–18 of the *General Prologue* as an especially familiar one.

14. Caroline D. Eckhardt, in "The Art of Translation in *The Romaunt of the Rose*" (in *Studies in the Age of Chaucer* [1984], pp. 41–63), states that "the most obvious quality of the *Romaunt* as a translation is certainly its very high degree of literal reproduction of its source" (p. 46); "overall, the primary principle of translation is that of near-minimal change" (p. 48).

15. The lines in the *Romaunt* corresponding to those I tabulated in the *Roman* are l–134 and 537–84.

16. *Oon* "one" rhymes, irregularly for Chaucer, with *don* in 39–40, with *anoon* in

105–06, 237–38, and with *noon* "none" in 983–84; *goon* rhymes, again irregularly, with *doon* in 187–88 and 193–94; also with *anoon* in 355–56 and 395–96. *Ought* rhymes with *nought* in 459–60 and with *thought* in 523–24 and 537–38; *noght* rhymes with *thoght* in 3–4, 503–04, 509–10, 691–92, 705–06, 789–90, 843–44, 885–86, 1109–10, 1133–34, 1149–50, and 1185–86; *thoght* rhymes with *ykaught* in 837–38, and *nought* rhymes with *wrought* in 89–90, for a total of seventeen occurrences.

17. Baum (*Chaucer's Verse*) discusses repetitive rhyming in Chaucer on pp. 43–47. After expressing some scepticism as to the artistic merits of a series of more or less adjacent echoes in the *General Prologue*, including "the cheap rimes in *-ly* 105–06 and 123–24," and the sequence *-ly* / *-ly* / *-ye* / *-ye* in 761–64, he goes on to defend such repeated linkages in the *Knight's Tale* as *brother* / *oother*, *cold* / *old*, and *lyf* / *wyf* on the ground that "that is a long poem with recurrent motifs and something now and then that savors of epic repetition" (42).

18. A spot check will serve to bear this out. Of the first 100 rhyming words in the *Roman*, 46 contain suffixes; of the first 100 in the *Romaunt*, 21; of the first 100 in *BD*, 10. One reason for the difference is obvious. Although there were more suffixes in Middle English that could be stressed, and therefore could rhyme, than there are in Modern English, both native (*-ly*, *-ing*, *-ness*) and Romance (*-aunt*, *-oun*, *-ure*), there were fewer such suffixes in Middle English than in Old French. An important case in point is the ending of the infinitive, which in Middle English was an unstressed *-e(n)*. In Old French, the corresponding ending *-(i)er* of most verbs could appear in rhyming position as the eighth syllable of the line; virtually any infinitive could thus rhyme with any other. Chaucer's notorious reference, at the end of "The Complaint of Venus," to the "skarsete" of rhyme in English, and his difficulty in following the "curiosity" of the French poet Oton de Grandson, whose poems he is translating, may, as the notes in Riverside suggest (p. 1081), be disingenuous. But it may also refer to the lack in English of some of the suffixes found useful for rhyming purposes by the French poets. It is noteworthy, in this connection, that the French originals of two of the three 24-line ballades making up the group contain ten rhyming infinitives apiece.

19. Among the words that occur with greatest frequency in the approximately four thousand lines of de Lorris's part of the *Roman*, some do appear in rhyming position a number of times, and more than once in combination with one and the same rhyme-word, but these repetitions are distributed over a far wider compass than those I have observed in the *Romaunt* and *BD*, and are comparatively few. To refine my generalization about the comparative dearth of repetition in French, I checked 25 of the lexical words that appear 20 times or more in *Roman* 1–4028, as cited in appendix II, "A Word-frequency List, Arranged in Descending Order of Frequency," in *A Concordance to the Roman de la rose of Guillaume de Lorris*, by Joseph R. Danos (Chapel Hill: UNC Department of Romance Languages, 1975), pp. 273 ff. The patterns I found most reminiscent of the English tradition were those presented by the words *faire* and *bele*. *Faire*, which occurs 75 times in all, rhymes 22 times: 4 times with *treire*, 3 times with *plere* and *contreire*, 2 times with *portraire* and *peire*, and once with eight other words. *Bele* occurs 23 times in all, and rhymes 8 times: 4 times with *novele* and once with four other words. More typical are the words *joie* and *chose*: each occurs 7 times out of 35 in rhyming position; *joie* rhymes with six different words, and *chose* with five.

20. Of the first 100 couplets of Chrétien's *Yvain* and Machaut's *Le Dit dou lyon*, 42

and 58, respectively, are linked by rich rhymes (*Yvain: Le chevalier au lion*, ed. T. B. W. Reid [Manchester University Press, 1942]; *Oeuvres de Guillaume de Machaut*, ed. Ernest Hoepffner [Paris: Firmin Didot, 1911], 2:159–237). For an analysis of a specimen passage of Froissart, see below. In view of these practices, Brogan's statement, in the article "Rich Rhyme" in *The New Princeton Encyclopedia of Poetry and Poetics*, that "rich rhyme first appears in French poetry in quantity in the 15th century" (p. 1070) stands in need of revision.

21. There is naturally a considerable amount of repetition of common suffixes, and even a certain amount of repetition of rhyming words and rhyming pairs, from poem to poem and from poet to poet, in the body of Old French poetry as a whole, though this network of relationships lies beyond the scope of my expertise. The *Roman*'s opening rhyme *songe / mençonge*, for example, occurs in *Yvain* 171–72, and for all I know de Lorris may have taken it, consciously or unconsciously, from Chrétien. Here, as also with regard to repeated rhyme-words and rhyming pairs, my judgment is comparative, my point being that repetition is a feature — one might say an accepted convenience — of the English rhyming tradition as it is not in the French.

22. I can do no more than mention two additional aspects of Middle English rhymed verse that differentiate it from Old French verse. The first of these is the regular alternation between heavier and lighter stress in what I call chief and intermediate syllables, meaning by the former the even-numbered and by the latter the odd-numbered syllables of the eight-syllable line. The second is the linking of stressed chief syllables by alliteration. Lines in *BD* like "My windowes werë shette echon, And throgh the glas the sonnë shon Upon my bed with bryghtë bemës, With many gladë gildë stremës" (336–38) and "My lyf, my lustës, be me loothë For al welfare and I be wroothë" (581–82) display Chaucer's command of a repertoire not only of rhymes, but of cadences of rhythm and sound that are quintessentially English.

23. Twenty-three words rhyme on *-ight* in the first 100 lines of *Degravant*, and the disproportion continues throughout. For the expressions cited, see lines 11, 24, 28, 102, 198, 235, etc. (*The Romance of Sir Degravant: A Parallel-Text Edition from MSS. Lincoln Cathedral A.5.2 and Cambridge University Ff. I.6*, ed. L. F. Casson, EETS, 221 [London: Oxford University Press, 1949]).

24. I am indebted to Professor Daniel Poirion for help with this part of my essay.

25. See the comparative observations on the two passages in Derek Brewer's essay, "The Relationship of Chaucer to the English and European Traditions," in *Chaucer and Chaucerians: Critical Studies in Middle English Literature*, ed. Brewer (University of Alabama Press, 1966), pp. 1–38; I quote pp. 2–3. Brewer's account of the blending of native and continental sources in the formation of the style of Chaucer's verse applies, on a smaller scale, to my account of his rhyming in the *Romaunt* and *BD*: "In respect of language, therefore, Chaucer grafts on to his basic English style, found in the romances, a new diction, more elaborate, learned and formal, though also colloquial. This new diction signalises Chaucer's progressive immersion in European literary culture, first in the poetry of the leading poet of his day, Machaut, and in the dominant poetic influence of his day, *Le Roman de la Rose*" (p. 27).

26. Brewer analyzes "be this lyght" as a variant of the common asseveration "by my truth" and goes on to make the following interesting observations: "It looks common-

place enough, but the earliest quotation in the *MED* is from an interlude of 1510. . . . The later quotations of *by this light* are from colloquial contexts, and this example . . . suggests that Chaucer was more colloquial on occasion than even his earliest masters, the romance-writers" (p. 6). A citation from *Firumbras* which perhaps antedates Chaucer's use of the expression was published in *MED* after the appearance of Brewer's essay; significantly, it occurs in dialogue (s.v. *light* n. sense 1b[c]). The wording of the oath may in fact have some relevance to the poem and its bookish narrator, since light in Chaucer is associated with the activity of reading (cf. *The Parliament of Fowls,* 85–87: "The day gan faylen, and the derke nyght, That reveth bestes from here besynesse, Berafte me my bok for lak of lyght").

27. See chap. 1, "Ricardian Style," of *Ricardian Poetry: Chaucer, Gower, Langland and the "Gawain" Poet* (New Haven: Yale University Press, 1971), esp. pp. 16–18. Burrow observes that Chaucer accommodated "a rather limited and fundamentally sim-ple inherited idiom to more complex and sophisticated purposes" (p. 18). Cf. Eckhardt's description of "patterns of departure from the original *Roman* [in the *Romaunt*]," includ-ing "the expansion that leads to an informality of tone" and "the deviations from *cour-toisie* toward colloquialism," that "tend to impart to the *Romaunt* a fresh new narrative voice." Eckhardt cautions, however, against "overestimat[ing] the extent to which the mature Chaucerian voice is present in . . . a rather early literary effort" (pp. 60–61).

28. Baum's discussion of "recurrent motifs" expressed by rhymes such as *brother / oother* in the *Knight's Tale* is referred to in note 17, above. Baum remarks on "the continual repetition of *Troye / joie* [in *Troilus and Criseyde*] — thirty times, beginning in the very first stanza and running like a pedal point throughout the poem," and notes that the same rhyme also appears three times in *BD*, and elsewhere in Chaucer (pp. 46–47 and n. 4).

29. *Trowthe / rowthe* is also a thematic rhyme in *Troilus and Criseide*, where it occurs 17 times (not counting one instance of *untrowthe / rowthe*). There, its meaning is some-what different, since *rowthe* comes to signify "compassion" in the specific, indeed almost technical sense of Criseide's willingness to accept Troilus as her lover. This latter idea is expressed in *BD* by the word *mercy* ("My lady yaf me al hooly The noble yifte of hir mercy" [1269–70]). The relationship between "fidelity" and "mercy" in *Troilus* is defini-tively expressed by Criseide in book 4, when she tells Troilus that "moral vertu, grounded upon trouthe — That was the cause I first hadde on yow routhe!" (1672–73).

30. I have arrived, by a different route, at an account of Chaucer's rhymes that has many affinities with that presented by Charles A. Owen, Jr., in his comprehensive and insightful essay, "Thy Drasty Rymyng . . . ," *Studies in Philology* 63 (1966): 533–64. Owen says of rhyme in *Troilus and Criseyde* that "it both surprises and delights us to find seemingly natural speech falling into measures of rhythm and rhyme" (p. 545). Rhyme "has been given a structural as well as a decorative role [in *Troilus*]. . . . It reinforces the meaning. It remains for the most part unobtrusive" (p. 554). In general, Chaucer "subor-dinated rhyme, . . . eschewing the more difficult and self-conscious exercises so dear to his French contemporaries. The result was a freeing of the sound pattern to . . . support . . . the interest in human personality as it revealed itself in speech, characteristic of his poetry" (p. 564). For Owen's observations on repetitiveness in Chaucer's rhymes, see p. 538 (*Anelida and Arcite,* "The Complaint unto Pity," and "The Complaint of Mars") and

542 (Sir Thopas). "Thematic emphasis" in the repeated rhyme *freres / preyeres* in the *Summoner's Tale* is discussed on pp. 561–62.

Chapter 5. Sir Gawain and the Green Knight: *The Passing of Judgment*

1. *A Reading of "Sir Gawain and the Green Knight"* (London: Routledge and Kegan Paul, 1965), pp. 127–33. The references to "a pretend, secular confession" and "a real, sacramental one" occur on p. 133; the "absolution" is discussed on pp. 131–32.

2. Burrow observes that "the poet does not allow Ber[t]ilak to use the proper clerical term 'assoil'" (ibid., p.132).

3. This view is best known as presented by John Speirs: "The Green Knight whose head is chopped off at his own request and who is yet as miraculously or magically alive as ever . . . can be no other than a recrudescence in poetry of the Green Man . . . . [The Green Man] is surely a descendant of the Vegetation or Nature god of almost universal and immemorial tradition . . . whose death and resurrection are the myth-and-ritual counterpart of the annual death and rebirth of nature" (*Medieval English Poetry: The Non-Chaucerian Tradition* [London: Faber and Faber, 1957], p. 219).

4. Cf. Hans Schnyder, *"Sir Gawain and the Green Knight," An Essay in Interpretation* (Bern: Francke, 1961), p. 41: "In the context of our story the appearance of the Green Knight would consequently herald the manifestation of divine interference in the course of worldly events . . . . His behaviour is . . . that of a benevolent though severe father who deems it necessary to admonish unruly children."

5. "It is . . . clear that [the Green Knight] is not an ordinary executioner but a supernatural, an immortal one, in fact, the only deathless executioner known, namely Death itself . . . . The mysterious Green Knight is none other than the Lord of Hades, who comes to challenge to a beheading game the heroes sitting round the fire" (A. H. Krappe, "Who *Was* the Green Knight?" *Speculum* 13 [1938]: 206–15; cf. 208, 215). Krappe views the Green Chapel as a version of the motif, common in Celtic legend, of "the fairy hill or elfin knoll, the abode of the dead ancestors" (p. 213).

6. Dale B. J. Randall, in "Was the Green Knight a Fiend?" (*Studies in Philology* 67 [1960]: 479–91), argues that *Sir Gawain and the Green Knight* "achieved part of its impact on a medieval audience by means of its demonic overtones" (486). The Green Knight's appearance and behavior are "fiend-like" in a number of respects (479–85), and "the grim setting in which Gawain meets Bercilak," which he, like Krappe, associates with the fairy hill of Celtic legend, "may be regarded as hellish" (489). He does not, however, "insist that the Green Knight is *de facto* a fiend" (485); cf. the final paragraph of the essay (491).

7. "The Green Knight, enacting the role of the Challenger, does so with all the gusto of an accomplished mummer. . . . Later, at the Green Chapel, . . . he drops on the instant his role of magic horror and becomes again the gallant, benevolent Bercilak, full of warm goodwill" (Laura Hibbard Loomis, "Gawain and the Green Knight," pp. 19–20, in *Critical Studies of "Sir Gawain and the Green Knight,"* ed. Donald R. Howard and Christian K. Zacher [Notre Dame: University of Notre Dame Press, 1968], pp. 3–23). Loomis's essay originally appeared in Roger Sherman Loomis, ed., *Arthurian Literature in the Middle Ages: A Collaborative History,* (Oxford: Oxford University Press, 1959),

pp. 528–40. Martin Puhvel sees the poem as keeping its readers "teetering on the brink of recognising a long train of supernatural elements" which prove on examination to be "magic shadows not cast by solid objects" ("Art and the Supernatural in *Sir Gawain and the Green Knight*," *Arthurian Literature* 5 (1985): 1–69; see p. 67). In Fitt I, the Green Knight "may have been fitted out with an artificial, detachable head" (p. 17), which could have been made to move its eyes and to seem to speak by trickery and ventriloquism (p. 18).

8. A complex and paradoxical answer to the question of the Green Knight's identity, incorporating most of the above-mentioned interpretations, has recently been presented in chap. 3, "The Greenness of the Green Knight," of Piotr Sadowski, *The Knight on His Quest: Symbolic Patterns of Transition in "Sir Gawain and the Green Knight"* (Newark: University of Delaware Press, 1996), pp. 78–108. Analyzing all the associations of greenness in the poet's time and taking into consideration the "semantic scatter [over many subjects of reference]" of the word *grene* as exhibited in *MED*, Sadowski develops a "working hypothesis . . . that the Green Knight embodies comprehensively features of *all* worlds. . . . he is a personified synthesis . . . uniting in himself the negative, fiendish elements associated with the underworld; death and decay; the elements of nature and the cyclicity of life processes; human, worldly affairs . . . ; and finally the divine, heavenly forces that act upon the lower regions ensuring the continuity of life through the possibility of rebirth" (pp. 84–85). Because in alchemy greenness had two forms, a *benedicta viriditas* under which aspect it was closely related to the perfection of gold and the *verdigris*, or impure stain or rust, characteristic of unrefined metal (pp. 99–102), the combination of gold and green stessed in the poet's description of the Green Knight's attire represents a paradox which the "dialectical minds" of original audiences of the poem would have been "well prepared to accept and comprehend" (p. 102); they would have perceived the Green Knight as "a 'complete' figure, partaking simultaneously of fiendish, natural, and divine realms, as such epitomizing man's crucial metaphysical anxieties in relation to life, death, and the hereafter" (p. 103). Though none of these associations can be categorically ruled out, the comprehensive analytical response Sadowski invokes seems to me to involve an improbable detachment from the action of the poem as it unfolds for the reader or hearer—in particular, the significant change in the Green Knight as perceived, first in Fitt I, then in Fitt IV. Actually, once he has presented the above-summarized analysis, Sadowski zeroes in on the role of the Green Knight as an agent of the divine powers, offering a corrective to the childish self-indulgence and disregard of the true meaning of Christmas displayed in the feasting at Camelot that opens the poem (p. 145). In the end, only Sir Gawain acquires the knowledge of his own sinfulness that is a prerequisite for salvation, "taking on himself, Christlike, the sins that afflict . . . the guardians and 'heads' of the social order" to which he belongs (p. 213). The fact that the court responds to Gawain's story with laughter signifies their unfortunate failure to acquire this knowledge for themselves.

9. A major rift divides those readers of *Sir Gawain and the Green Knight* who see the poet as sympathetic toward secular "reality," finding in human actions and institutions qualities of goodness and splendor commensurate with those of the divine realm, and those who see him as implicitly condemning human institutions and actions, however good or splendid they may seem, in terms of the eternal "reality" and absolute moral

standards mediated on earth by the Catholic Church. The former view (with which I associate myself) was definitively stated by Derek Brewer, in "The *Gawain*-Poet: A General Appreciation of Four Poems" (*Essays in Criticism* 17 [1967]: 130–42): "[The poet] admits that much of reality goes against the grain, but he is also passionately convinced of [its] ultimate beauty and joy" (p. 131). For a clear, forceful statement of the latter view, see Derek W. Hughes, "The Problem of Reality in *Sir Gawain and the Green Knight*" (*University of Toronto Quarterly* 40 [1971]: 217–35). Hughes, having identified in the poem a "cluster" of four kinds of images of artifice, including "a translation of life into overtly fictional or theatrical terms so as to stress its distance from reality" (p. 217), goes on to say that "all these ideas can also be found in other writings of the period, their normal function being to measure devotion to false, temporal good against the realities of eternity" (ibid.). Interpretations of the court at Camelot as innocent or culpable stem from an adherence to one or the other of these two views. To put it another way, critics such as Brewer assume that for the *Gawain*-poet, human and divine values, however greatly they may differ in degree, are the same in kind (in which case they are related metonymically, by underlying identity and contiguity); critics such as Hughes assume that human and divine values, however closely they may appear to resemble each other, are radically different (in which case, they are related metaphorically, by similarity and disjunction). See also note 12, below.

10. The translation (unpublished) is my own.

11. At least, without a figurative allusion to pork. In the alliterative *Morte Arthure*, the giant killed by the king is said to be "greesse-growen as a galte" (1102), i.e., as a swine (*The Alliterative Morte Arthure: A Critical Edition*, ed. Valerie Krishna [New York: Burt Franklin, 1976]); I follow *MED*, s.v. *gres(e* n., in treating *greesse growen* as a compound. In *The "Gest Hystoriale" of the Destruction of Troy* 3838, Polidarius, one of the kings of Greece, is said to be "as a porke fate, / ffull grete in the grippe, all of grese hoge" (ed. George A. Panton and David Donaldson, 2 vols., EETS, 39, 56 [1869, 1894]).

12. Hughes, in "The Problem of Reality," notes "the strong awareness of the flesh of the deer and boar" in the first two hunting episodes (229). I agree, though, as I have already intimated, I do not follow Hughes in seeing a contrast between the world of the hunting scenes and the "artificial," game-oriented world of Arthur's court (cf. 219). For an eloquent statement of the opposing view, see A. C. Spearing, *The "Gawain"-Poet: A Critical Study* (Cambridge: Cambridge University Press, 1970), p. 181: "The Camelot of this poem is a young Camelot, a place of gaiety and elegance, where a 'fayre folk in her first age' (54) is ruled over by a 'childgered' king (86), who cannot bear to do any one thing for long. . . . It is a delightful place, an innocent version of the ideal aimed at by any of the great courts of Western Europe in the later Middle Ages."

13. *A Reading*, p. 94.

14. In view of this encompassing concern, I suggest that "the naked" in line 2002 refers to the unclothed bodies of animals as well as the exposed flesh of human beings.

15. The phrase is cited from the poem by *MED*, s.v. *heigh* adj. sense 6b, "full, complete, total," and translated "mature age."

16. My count is based on descriptive and narrative material only, including *inquits* interpolated in passages of dialogue when the subject of these is the Green Knight. In "quoth that other thenne" (2444), for example, the poet might have used an appellation

mentioning his color. The word *green* does occur twice in passages of dialogue between lines 2296 and 2478, once when the Green Knight says the girdle is as green as his gown (2396), once when he refers to "the chaunce of the grene chapel" (2399).

17. Here too the word *green* occurs twice in dialogue. It is used by the Knight both times in the phrase "the Green Chapel" (451, 454).

18. The poet does not say that the new ax the Green Knight wields at the Chapel is green. He describes it simply as "a felle weppen, / A denez ax nwe dyght . . . / With a borelych bytte bende by the halme" and a "lace that lemed ful bryght" (2222–26). The *grayn* of the original ax (Davis's gloss, "blade," seems preferable to *MED*'s "spike" [s.v. *grein* n. sense 1(c), "the edge of a horn, the spike of a gisarme"]) had been "al of grene stele and of golde hewen" (211).

19. Puhvel, in "Art and the Supernatural," points out that the green girdle evidently has lost its supposed magical properties in Fitt IV, since both men speak only of "its various material attributes" (p. 44). For him, this means that the girdle is and has been "a fake object" (ibid.). For me, this change is part of the fading away of wondrousness generally that takes place in the last part of the poem.

20. I quote from "The Master of Game," the early fifteenth-century translation of Gaston's *Livre de Chasse* by Edward, Duke of York. See Douglas Gray, ed., *The Oxford Book of Late Medieval Verse and Prose* (Oxford: Oxford University Press, 1985).

21. *Style and Consciousness in Middle English Narrative* (Princeton: Princeton University Press, 1983), p. 60.

22. As has often been noted, there are clear signs, especially in Fitt I, of a "generation gap" between the Green Knight and the court. Arthur and his knights and ladies are said to be "in their first age" (54), Arthur is described as *child-gered* (86), the Green Knight scornfully calls the knights of the Round Table "beardless children" (280), and so on. Beardedness, in fact, becomes recognizable in the poem as a motif, a sign of full physical maturity. The details of the description of the Green Knight include "a beard as big as a bush" (182), and his beard is mentioned twice in the action that follows (306, 334); when Bertilak is introduced, the narrator devotes a full line to his "broad, bright" beard; and when the Green Knight reappears, he looks as he had looked at first, "flesh and legs, locks and beard" (2228). There are other, more subtle touches as well: for example, the "bristly brows" of the Green Knight (305) are characteristic not of a youth but of an older person.

23. If it is essential to the meaning of the poem that we should experience vicariously Gawain's surprise, bewilderment, discomfiture, and fear, and should thus find ourselves in accord with the lenient interpretation we see placed upon his lapse of loyalty at the end, then the Green Knight must be presented in such a way as to elicit these emotions with maximum force. I believe that the "overdetermined" character of his portrayal, its multiple symbolic suggestiveness, can be understood in this light. Supporting evidence in the form of descriptive detail and wording can be and has been adduced for each of the identifications of the Green Knight which I listed on p. 99, above. He does seem to speak with a kind of supernatural severity, he does seem demonic, he does seem to embody the vitality of vegetative nature, he does seem to have the implacable and irresistible summoning power of death itself. He even seems, in retrospect, to be Lord Bertilak dressed up in mummer's costume, come to court to frighten it with a terrifying feat of stage magic! Derek Brewer has said that the poet "presents his material entirely from Gawain's point

of view" ("The *Gawain* Poet," p. 137), and I take this to mean, among other things, that we cannot ask who the Green Knight, or Bertilak, "really is." Either of them is whatever Gawain thinks or feels him to be at a given point in the poem.

24. In identifying maturation as the underlying theme of *Sir Gawain and the Green Knight,* my reading of the poem aligns itself with that in Derek Brewer, *Symbolic Stories* (Totowa, N.J.: Rowman and Littlefield, 1980), a book I was unaware of when I wrote this essay. Its scope includes the Bible, Chaucer, Malory, Shakespeare, Austen, and Dickens as well as *Sir Gawain*; all these are analyzed as "family dramas," concerned, literally or symbolically, with "the basic human experience of growing up" (pp. 7–8). Brewer's in-depth analysis of *Sir Gawain* identifies all who figure in the narrative, including the Virgin Mary, with members of the archetypal cast of characters. The Green Knight's praise of Sir Gawain at the end is predicated on the independence the hero has gained; he "can now . . . afford through the father-image to praise himself a little, to feel he has not done too badly, all things considered, though he need not feel conceited" (p. 91). Christopher Wrigley, in *"Sir Gawain and the Green Knight:* The Underlying Myth" (*Studies in Medieval English Romances: Some New Approaches,* ed. Derek Brewer [Cambridge, England, and Wolfeboro, N.H.: Boydell and Brewer, 1988], pp. 113–28), accepts Brewer's interpretation, while applying "the concepts of anthropological and psychoanalytical folkloric study" to the poem. He formulates its underlying subject as "the transition from childhood to the duties and privileges of adult life" (p. 117), attended, specifically, by mock threats of death and tests of sexual maturity. The themes of threatened loss of life and sexual temptation are joined in this process in African and European myths, in the story of the Fall of Genesis, in primitive puberty ceremonies, and in Arthurian literature, including *Sir Gawain.*

25. In its portrayal of Lord Bertilak as a man older but not yet elderly , supervising the progress of the youthful central figure of the poem toward a more mature view of life, *Sir Gawain and the Green Knight* is "Ricardian" in the sense established by John Burrow's important and well-known study, *Ricardian Poetry: Chaucer, Gower, Langland and the "Gawain" Poet* (New Haven: Yale University Press, 1971). Burrow argues that characters like Theseus, Harry Bailey, and Bertilak "embody an image of man which is not heroic, not romantic, and not at all 'monkish.' It is an image of 'high eld' which stands at the centre of Ricardian poetry, an ideal 'mesure' which involves [a] sober acceptance of things as they are" (p. 126).

26. David Aers, in a chapter on *Sir Gawain* in *Community, Gender, and Individual Identity: English Writing 1360–1430* (London: Routledge, 1988), finds in the poem "no signs . . . of the way in which for well over two centuries . . . English military organization had depended on money" (p. 154). The nobles of the late fourteenth century recruited military companies for cash, and knights served in these companies as mercenaries rather than as vassals fulfilling their feudal obligation (ibid.). Cf. Maurice Keen's observation in *Chivalry* (New Haven: Yale University Press, 1984) that "there was [in late medieval times] an attraction for rulers about employing companies of rootless, mercenary soldiers, in that their employer's obligations towards them ceased, at the end of a campaign, when he paid them off. For them, reciprocally, there was an attraction in service, which offered the prospects not only of pay but of loot as well" (p. 229). Even Chaucer, in portraying an idealized representative of knighthood, evidently felt that he could include

without disparagement the detail that the Knight had fought for one heathen against another, presumably for pay (I[A] 64–66).

27. "*Sir Gawain:* Pentangle, *Luf-lace,* Numerical Structure," in Alastair Fowler, ed. *Silent Poetry: Essays in Numerological Analysis* (London: Routledge and Kegan Paul, 1970), pp. 122–23.

28. I share the view finely and fully argued by P. J. C. Field, in "A Rereading of *Sir Gawain and the Green Knight*" (*Studies in Philology* 68 [1971]: 255–69), that the poet presents Gawain's act in withholding the green girdle from Bertilak as a venial rather than a mortal sin. "Gawain's lapse," Field concludes, "is real but minor: he has won but he has not triumphed. . . . And the court to which Gawain returns must be taken as giving the judgment of humanity" (269).

Chapter 6. Pearl's *"Maynful Mone"*

1. The members of the procession are evidently the 144,000 virgins who appear in the company of the Lamb on Mount Sion in Rev. 14.1–5. This event is described to the dreamer by the Pearl maiden in sec. 15, stanzas 3ff., in language which closely follows the biblical source. The account of the activity at the center of the city after the procession has reached it is based in large part on Rev. 5.8ff. There the elders, having harps and vials full of odors, are said to prostrate themselves before the Lamb. The angels around the throne, the four beasts, and the elders join in praise; the Vulgate text adds, "et erat numerus eorum milia millium" (5.11; cf. *Pearl*, line 1107, "Hundreth thowsande I wot ther were"). To this chorus are added the voices of all creatures in heaven, on earth, and under the earth (5.13; cf. *Pearl*, lines 1125–26, "The steven moght stryke thurgh the urthe to helle That the Vertues of heven of joye endyte [The sound could pierce through the earth to hell When the powers of heaven in song unite]").

2. *MED*, s.v. *glem* n. sense 1(a). *Day-glem* in *Pearl* is cited s.v. sense 1(e) "the light of day or dawn." The compound is erroneously translated "the morning glow, dawn" s.v. *dai* n. sense 13(b), where the line in *Pearl* is the only example given. In view of this meaning, *heven-glem* in *Purity* 946, "Erly, er any heven-glem, thay to a hil comen" would seem to mean simply "light in heaven"; *MED*'s definition "the light of dawn" (s.v. *heven* n. sense 7, "In combinations and compounds"), for which only *Purity* 946 is cited, is influenced by the context.

3. *MED* s.v. *driven* v. sense 7b(a). Citations include "quen it [is] drevyen to the derke & the day fynyst" from *Wars of Alexander,* and "Or this dredfull day was drif to nyght, there was slayn many a doughty knyght" from the *The Song of Roland.* A similar idiom may have been used in the original version of line 1999 of *Sir Gawain and the Green Knight,* where the poet tells of the coming of dawn on the day when Sir Gawain must leave the castle. The manuscript reads, "The day dryvez to the derk, as Dryghtyn biddez." The first half-line makes perfectly good sense; it is translated "Daylight comes up on the darkness" in Norman Davis's revision of the Tolkien and Gordon edition (1967). But it is possible that the poet wrote "the derk dryvez to the day" and that the two words were reversed in accordance with the more usual sequence by the scribe.

4. Peter Comester, in his discussion of the work of the fourth day in Gen. 1 in the *Historia scholastica,* remarks, with regard to the creation of the moon, that "quod autem

luna in plenilunio facta sit ex alia perpenditur translatione, quae habit: *Et luminare minus in inchoatione noctis*. In principio enim noctis non oritur luna nisi panselenos [i.e., 'pleni-lunar'], id est *rotunda*. . . . Inde perpenditur, quod sol factus est mane in oriente, et facto vespere luna facta est in initio noctis, similiter in oriente. Volunt tamen quidam quod mane simul facti sint, sol in oriente, luna in occidente, et sole occidente, luna sub terra rediit ad orientem in inchoatione noctis" (*Patrologia Latina* 198, col. 1061). ["It is considered by another version that the moon was created at the beginning of the full; (this version) reads 'And the lesser luminary (was made) at the beginning of the night.' For at the beginning of night, the moon rises only when it is full, that is, *round*. . . . Whence it is thought that the sun was made in the morning in the east, and when evening had come, the moon was created at the beginning of the night, likewise in the east. However, some argue that both were made at the same time, the sun in the east, and the moon in the west, and by the time the sun was setting in the west, the moon had returned under the earth to the east at the beginning of the night."] I am grateful to Rosemarie Potz McGerr for providing me with this reference.

5. *Maynful* is clearly one word, separated by a space from *mone*, in the facsimile of the manuscript (ed. I. Gollancz, EETS 162 [Oxford University Press, 1923; reprint, 1971] 54r). But the manuscript is not a holograph, and a scribe could have rewritten an original *mayn ful* as *maynful*. Moreover, word division is sometimes irregular according to modern standards (as one would expect). Without looking for examples, I noted *aldoun* and *wernalle* in lines adjacent to the moon simile; modern editors silently rewrite as *al doun* and *wern alle*. The adjective *mayn* does not appear elsewhere in *Pearl*, or in *Patience* or *Purity*, but it is used four times in *Sir Gawain and the Green Knight*, once with reference to Gawain's horse, and thus with implications of large size as well as strength. *Maynful* is used once in *Purity* in the phrase "maynful gode," i.e., "almighty God" (1730). See Barnet Kottler and Alan M. Markman, *A Concordance to Five Middle English Poems* (Pittsburgh: University of Pittsburgh Press, 1966). The possibility that the original wording was *mayn ful mone* cannot be ruled out on metrical grounds, since, though sequences of three heavy syllables are exceptional in *Pearl,* they do occur. Examples I have noted include "holtwodez bryght" (line 75), where the plural ending *-ez* is probably syncopated, "fyldor fyne" (106), "cler quyt perle" (line 207), "schorne golde schyr" (213), "schyr wod-schawez" (284), and "brende golde bryght" (989). Of these, "cler quyt perle," with its sequence of two descriptive adjectives plus noun, is closest to "mayn ful mone" in structure.

6. Rabanus Maurus, in the *Allegoriae in sacram scripturam,* begins the entry for *Oriens* as follows: "*Oriens* est Christus, ut in Zacharia: 'Visitavit nos oriens ex{alto},' id est, 'venit ad nos Christus de coelo' " (*PL* 112, col. 1012). The reference is to the words of Zacharias, father of John the Baptist, in Luke 1:78. Cf. the antiphon "O Oriens" in the series of "Antiphonae Majores" or "Great O's" that figure in the liturgy of Advent and were used as source materials by the author of the Old English "Advent Lyrics." In this antiphon Christ is addressed both as "Oriens," i.e., "rising" or "east," and "Sol," i.e., "sun": "O Oriens, splendor lucis aeternae, et Sol justitiae: / veni, et illumina sedentes in tenebris et umbra mortis [O Orient, splendor of eternal light, and sun of justice: / come and enlighten those sitting in darkness, and in the shadow of death]" (quoted and translated by Robert B. Burlin in *The Old English Advent: A Typological Commentary* [New

Haven, Conn.: Yale University Press, 1968], p. 41). Burlin notes that " 'the Orient' figured in several prophetic utterances which were to lend substance to later Messianic and Christian symbolism" and cites, from the Old Testament, Ezek. 43.2, the text of which in the Vulgate is "Et ecce gloria Dei Israel ingrediebatur per viam orientalem [And behold the glory of the God of Israel came in by the way of the east]"; he also refers to the interpretation of Rabanus Maurus mentioned above (pp. 100–01). The wording of the "O Oriens" antiphon seems specifically reminiscent of Isaiah 9.2: "Populus qui ambulabat in tenebris, Vidit lucem magnam; Habitantibus in regione umbrae mortis, Lux orta est eis [The people that walked in darkness, have seen a great light: to them that dwelt in the region of the shadow, light is risen]."

7. See *MED* s.v. *ende* n. (1), senses 1 and 14.

8. Thus the thirty-fourth homily of the series entitled *Opus Imperfectum in Matthaeum*, a work of uncertain authorship attributed in early times to Saint John Chrysostom, first explains the prediction in temporal terms as signifying, *inter alia*, that the Jews, who were called before the Gentiles, are to be saved after them. The homily continues, "aut ideo primos dicit novissimos futuros, et novissimos primos, non ut novissimi digniores sint quam primi, sed ut coaequentur" (*Patrologia Graeca* 56, col. 822). ["Or, he says that the first shall be last and the last shall be first, not because the last are to be more honored than the first, but because they are to be made equal."] Pseudo-Chrysostom goes on to cite Isaiah 28.5 and 62.5, where the Lord and the redeemed Jerusalem, respectively, are likened to a crown, and interprets these verses in a way directly relevant to my argument: "Sicut enim in corona, cum sit rotunda, nihil invenies quod videatur esse initium aut finis: sic inter sanctos, quantum ad tempus in illo saeculo, nemo novissimus dicitur, nemo primus" (ibid.). ["For as in a crown, since it is round, you will find nothing which seems to be the beginning or the end, so among the saints, so far as time in that realm is concerned, no one is called last, no one first."] The two interpretations of the dictum that the first shall be last and the last shall be first are given, with pseudo-Chrysostom explicitly acknowledged as a source, by Saint Thomas Aquinas in his interpretation of the parable. See *In Matthaei Evangelium* in the *Caterna aurea, Opera omnia*, ed. Fretté (Paris: Vives, 1876), 16:344, and *Commentarium super Matthaeum, idem*, 19:523. Cf. the *Expositio in Matthaeum* of Saint Paschasius Radbertus, *PL* 120, col. 683. Paschasius adds the image of a revolving wheel. I am grateful to M. Teresa Tavormina for her assistance in this aspect of my research.

9. See *MED* s.v. *gerlond* n., senses 2(a) "a chaplet or coronet of gold, etc." and 2(b). "a crown or headband symbolizing office."

10. A late Middle English text of interest in this connection is discussed by Laurence Eldredge in "Imagery of Roundness in William Woodford's 'De Sacramento Altaris' and Its Possible Relevance to the Middle English 'Pearl' " (*Notes and Queries*, n.s. 24, no. 1 [1978]: 3–5). In the *dubia,* or division, of the treatise which Eldredge edits, Woodford argues that roundness of shape is appropriate for the communion wafer because roundness symbolizes perfection, spotlessness, and simplicity and because it reflects the shape of the penny paid to the workers in the parable of the vineyard. According to Robert W. Ackerman ("The *Pearl*-Maiden and the Penny," *Romance Philology* 17 [1964]: 615–23), "The association of the daily bread in the Lord's Prayer with the gift of salvation and also the Eucharist is standard in medieval scriptural commentary" (pp. 620–21). Ackerman

shows that the daily bread was identified with the penny paid the workers in the parable by Friar Lorens, in his popular late thirteenth-century didactic treatise *Le Somme des Vices et des vertues,* which may have been known to Chaucer. Lorens's interpretation is also found in the *Ayenbite of Inwit,* a Middle English translation of the treatise by Dan Michel of Northgate.

11. *MED,* s.v. *hīl* n., cites only *Pearl* 41 and 1205; the etymology given is "prob. OE **hygel* hillock." *Hylle* in line 1172 may thus represent a scribal rewriting of an original *huyle* or *hyul.* However, the Middle English ancestor of the modern word *hill,* derived from OE *hyll,* overlaps with *huyle/hyul* in meaning. See *MED* s.v. *hil(le* n. sense 2 (a) "A manmade hill or mound." *Pearl* is not cited for this sense.

12. "I raxled" is translated as "I stretched myself" in both Gordon's edition and A. C. Cawley, *Pearl, Sir Gawain and the Green Knight,* Everyman's Library, no. 346 (London, 1962). *MED,* however, s.v. *raxlen* v., cites *Pearl* 1174 under the definition "To stretch, esp. on awaking from sleep; stretch out (one's arms)" sense (a). The stretching out of one of the awakened dreamer's arms would exactly parallel "Bifore that spot my honde I spenned" (49).

13. See "Design and Its Significance" in my introduction to *Pearl* in *Sir Gawain and the Green Knight, Patience, and Pearl: New Verse Translations* (New York: W. W. Norton, 2001), pp. 120–22.

14. See "Symbolism and Theme," ibid., pp. 115–18.

15. See *MED* s.v. *mōn(e* n. (1), sense 1(b), "the moon as the cosmological divider between the earth and the heavens." Citations for this sense include *The Pricke of Conscience,* line 992, "the hegher [world] reaches fra tha mon even Til the heghest of the sterned heven."

16. These and other phrases may be found in *MED* under the definition cited in the preceding note.

17. Cf. Chaucer's *Clerk's Tale,* E 995, 997–98: "O stormy people! unsad and evere untrewe! . . . . Delitynge ever in rumbul that is newe, For lyk the moone ay wexe ye and wane!" William Caxton, complaining of the inconsistencies of the English language in a well-known passage in the Prologue to his *Eneydos,* wrote, "For we englysshe men ben borne under the domynacyon of the mone, whiche is never stedfaste, but ever waverynge, wexynge one season, and waneth & dyscreaseth another season" (quoted, with punctuation modernized, from *The Prologues and Epilogues of William Caxton,* ed. W. J. B. Crotch [EETS 176, Oxford University Press, 1928; reprint, 1956], p. 108).

18. A quotation from the vernacular encyclopedic poem *Cursor Mundi* in *MED,* s.v. *mōn(e* n. (1), suggests an association in medieval tradition between the full moon and the Passion: "He [Christ] wald for uus martered bee / that time when the moyn wor ful."

19. See *MED* s.v. *brun* adj. sense 1(a) "dark, dull," and cf. sense 1(b) "cheerless, . . . gloomy." The gloss "fuscus, subniger" is cited s.v. sense 1(a) from the fifteenth-century *Promptorium parvulorum.*

Chapter 7. The Many and the One

1. The debt of this essay to the published literature on *Pearl* is so deeply pervasive that I have been unable to document it fully. Nonetheless, my account of the poem differs in purpose and draws different conclusions from previous accounts. Many of the observations presented here have been made before, but they have not, I think, been put to the

same use. Among those who have written about *Pearl*, it is A. C. Spearing, notably in *The Gawain-Poet: A Critical Study* (Cambridge: Cambridge University Press, 1970), who has most helped me to understand the poem as a work of art whose intricacies of structure uniquely enhance its power as a human drama. The sections on the poem in Spearing's *Medieval Dream-Poetry* (Cambridge: Cambridge University Press, 1976) and *Readings in Medieval Poetry* (Cambridge: Cambridge University Press, 1987) repeat in part, but also supplement, his earlier account. In his essay "Poetic Identity" in *A Companion to the Gawain-Poet*, ed. Derek Brewer and Jonathan Gibson (Cambridge, England: D. S. Brewer, 1997), pp. 35–52, Spearing revises his earlier reading of *Pearl*, in which he saw an ironic contrast between two equally fictional narrators: the inept "I" who figures in the dream and the "I" who narrates it from a later, morally superior vantage point. The latter, Spearing now maintains, is merely "a textual effect of the narrative *énonciation* by which these events are revealed to us"; it "is never given a fictive existence of any kind in the present" (50). But surely the speaker's act of blaming himself for the dream's abrupt termination is "fictive" simply in that it is part of the versified narrative. The final section seems to me to be part of that narrative, and not an appendage to it in the sense in which (in my view) the motto of the Garter is an appendage to *Sir Gawain and the Green Knight* and Chaucer's Retractation is an appendage to the *Canterbury Tales*.

2. Spearing, finding an artistic affinity between *Pearl* and the mid-fourteenth-century Lady Chapel at Ely Cathedral as described by Nikolaus Pevsner, says that in both, "richly detailed variables play like flames over a rigid framework" (*The Gawain-Poet*, p. 98). The project represented by this essay can be described in large part as an attempt to apply this statement to *Pearl* in full and literal detail.

3. *Yorkshire Writers: Richard Rolle of Hampole and His Followers*, ed. C. Horstman, 2 (London: Swan Sonnenschein and New York: Macmillan, 1896), no. 5, pp. 380–89.

4. For a somewhat different list of main and subsidiary genres in *Pearl*, see Ian Bishop, *Pearl in Its Setting: A Critical Study of the Structure and Meaning of the Middle English Poem* (New York: Barnes and Noble, 1968), pp. 13–14. Bishop identifies the story of the vineyard as an "exemplum" and points out the influence of the "verse lapidary" tradition in stanza 1 (p. 14).

5. David Aers, "The Self Mourning: Reflections on *Pearl*" (*Speculum* 68 [1993]: 54–73), p. 70. See below, pp. 155–56.

6. In the first section of the poem, the narrator has what Malcolm Pittock would call "notional awareness" of Christianity, as distinguished from "substantial knowledge." Pittock makes this distinction and applies it to the Pardoner in "The *Pardoner's Tale* and the Quest for Death" (*Essays in Criticism* 24 [1974]: 107–23). See, in this volume, chapter 1, "Silent Retribution in Chaucer."

7. "At the beginning of his vision [the dreamer] finds himself propelled, like a knight in medieval romance, 'In aventure ther mervaylez meven'" (Spearing, *The Gawain-Poet*, p. 105, quoting *Pearl* 64). Cf. Lawrence M. Clopper, "Pearl and the Consolation of Scripture," *Viator* 23 (1992): 231–45: "When the Dreamer awakes in a landscape of higher awareness, he imagines himself to be in some exotic romance world. . . . He uses romance vocabulary and style to describe his 'aventure'" (p. 243).

8. *Sir Gawain and the Green Knight*, ed. J. R. R. Tolkien and E. V. Gordon, 2d ed., rev. Norman Davis (Oxford: Clarendon Press, 1967).

9. I follow *MED* in reading *scherez* as an instance of *sheren* "to cut" (cf. modern

shear), and interpret it in *Pearl* 107 as meaning "makes a division (cf. sense 5[a]." They cite *Pearl* 107 under an extended sense 5(c) "to move, glide." *OED* (s.v. *sheer* v.1) associates it rather with *sheer* a. sense 3 ". . . of water . . . clear and pure." But the idea of separating or dividing is central to the poet's conception of the stream.

10. Spearing's description (referring to the poem as a whole) of "a verbal effect as bejewelled as the other world it describes" is particularly apposite here (*The Gawain-Poet*, p. 98).

11. No other interpretation of the maiden's relationship to the dreamer within the poem seems plausible in view of the fact that she was closer to him than an aunt or a niece when she was not yet two years old (233, 483). Whether we should understand her to have been the daughter of the man who wrote *Pearl*, a daughter who really died less than two years after she was born, is a different, and disputed, question. Nicholas Watson has recently argued that the author of *Pearl* could not have had a child if (as seems probable) he also wrote *Cleanness* and *Patience* because these poems "must surely be the work of a celibate cleric" ("The *Gawain*-Poet as a Vernacular Theologian," *Companion to the Gawain-Poet*, pp. 293–313; I quote p. 299). But John M. Bowers, in *The Politics of Pearl* (Cambridge, England: D. S. Brewer, 2001), makes the more plausible suggestion that the poet may have been "a married cleric who had remained in lower orders" (p. 60). Bowers cites, in support of his view, an article on *Pearl* by G. G. Coulton referring to the "vast host of ecclesiastics in lower orders [in the late fourteenth century] who not only might, but commonly did marry" (*ibid.*).

12. At the beginning of "The Self Mourning," Aers describes the love of Troilus for Criseide in Chaucer's poem, speaking of "his idealized image of her, an idealization that has been one of the traditional ways of controlling women in the interests of masculine self-identity" (p. 55). He goes on to speak of the opening of *Pearl*, which "presents a narrator identified as a mourner, his language one of intimate feelings. As a host of critics have demonstrated, this language is the conventional language of the courtly poetry of love evolved over the preceding two centuries. . . . In this familiar courtly language the lost object fulfills the traditional feminine role of nurturing life source." The narrator's language also identifies him socially; "indeed, he can only be identified as belonging to a particular kind of community by his language, the language of a courtly elite" (p. 57). Later, telling the maiden who has appeared to him in his dream that he has "concealed much longing for her since she slipped away into the grass," that he is "pensive, sees her in bliss while he is still suffering," he seeks to "frame the present relationship in a way that will allow him to continue the familiar masculine role that combines rhetoric of worship with the practice of controlling female identity to fit the idealizations and demands of male language" (p. 62).

13. Asserting that "there can be no doubt that secular love . . . is an important element in the powerful current of feeling that flows between the Dreamer and the Maiden," Spearing cites the narrator's early reference to the *luf-daungere* that wounds him (11) and translates the word "frustration in love." The narrator's frustration is intensified in the dream by "the transfiguration she, but not he, has undergone" (*The Gawain-Poet*, pp. 120–21).

14. A change in the proportionate frequencies of the more intimate and more formal second person pronouns in this episode is perhaps significant, though it must be remem-

bered that the scribe may on occasion have altered the poet's original wording. In his first three speeches to the maiden (241–52, 279–88, 325–36) the dreamer uses the intimate forms *thou* (241, 245, 280, 325) and *thee* (244), with one exception, *yow* in 287. After she has rebuked him, the forms *your* (369, 389, 392) and *ye* (371, 373, 381, 387, 390, 391) predominate in his apology and explanation (362–95), though *thou* appears in 375 and *thee* in 385. In the two speeches he addresses to her after she has told the parables of the vineyard and the merchant (745–56, 769–80), the forms *thee, thy,* and *thou,* which he uses consistently, take on the reverential value they have retained in present-day English.

15. Another variant with *en-* exemplifying a similar pattern of derivation is *enurned* "adorned" (*Pearl* 1026; cf. *Gawain* 634, 2037). OED explains this verb as an altered form of *anorn,* which in turn was an "erroneous" expansion of OFr. *aourner,* from Latin *adornare* (s.vv. *enorn* v. and *anorn* v.).

16. "The Dreamer apologizes to God—'Ne worthe no wraththe unto my Lorde' (362)—and shows a new humility towards the Maiden" (Spearing, *The Gawain-Poet*, p. 154).

17. I disagree here with Aers, who sees the dreamer's attitude toward the maiden as remaining essentially unchanged throughout their conversation. He cites lines 745–46 ("O maskelez perle in perlez pure, That berez . . . the perle of prys") as reflecting the dreamer's insistence "on maintaining his courtly figurations, ones in which he can remain in the comforting security of his familiar identity as courtly poet of love, keeping her in the equally reassuring and equally familiar role of unavailable love object" (p. 66). In so doing, he disregards the difference between the dreamer's earthly, comparative way of thinking, which does not change, and his conception of the maiden's identity, which does.

18. In a chapter entitled "The Maiden as an Innocent" (pp. 104–12), Ian Bishop cites Elizabeth Hart's observation that the description of the 144,000 virgins in Revelation occurred in the Missal as the Epistle for Holy Innocents' Day (p. 104) and provides further details: "At Vespers on St. John's Day (the Vigil of the Feast in question) a *responsorium* beginning with the words 'Centum quadraginta . . .' is chanted; this versicle and other portions of the Epistle recur in every office for the day itself and upon its octave" (p. 105). The major link between the narrator's child and the Innocents is the fact that both she and they died soon after baptism, the baptism of the Innocents, according to contemporary doctrine, having been effected by their martyrdom. Quoting Langland's description of different kinds of baptism, Bishop explains that "the difference between the two instances is simply that, whereas [the Innocents] suffered 'fullyng [baptism] in blode-schedynge', the [narrator's child] received 'fullyng of fonte [that is, in the church]'" (pp. 108–09).

19. In medieval typology, this was taken to be a prophetic description of the Virgin Mary (the source of *mascle,* one of the *Pearl*-poet's synonyms for "spot," is an Old French derivative of *macula*). She was thought by some medieval theologians to have been unique in that her conception was "immaculate," free of original sin; later, this belief was promulgated as church dogma (see *The Oxford Dictionary of the Christian Church*, ed. F. L. Cross, 3d ed., ed. E. A. Livingstone [Oxford University Press, 1997], s.v. "Immaculate Conception of the BVM").

20. Cf. 1 Timothy 6.14 and 2 Peter 3.14.

21. I differ from Gordon in interpreting line 1072, "What schulde the mone ther compas clym," as a question complete in itself, and reading the line that follows as connected by anticipation with lines 1075–76: "The planetez arn in to pover a plyght, And the sel[vë] sunne ful fer to dym . . . to even wyth that worthly lyght [The planets are in too poor a state, And the sun itself is far too dim]." I emend *self* in 1076 to dissyllabic *selvë* on metrical grounds.

22. See Sarah Stanbury's reference to representations of the celestial Jerusalem as circular in some Apocalypse manuscripts, p. 123 of "*Pearl* and the Idea of Jerusalem," *Medievalia et Humanistica*, n.s. 16 (1988): 117–31. I discuss in more detail the disparities between space as we experience it and space in the vision in chapter 6 of this volume, "*Pearl*'s 'Maynful Mone.' "

23. Readers of the poetry of T. S. Eliot will be reminded of the Chinese jar that, in "Burnt Norton," "moves perpetually in its stillness" (*Four Quartets* [New York: Harcourt Brace, 1943], p. 7).

24. The grammatical terminology and distinctions I use in this chapter are taken from *A Comprehensive Grammar of the English Language*, by Randolph Quirk, Sidney Greenbaum, Geoffrey Leech, and Jan Svartvik (London and New York: Longman, 1985), hereafter cited by paragraph numbers and referred to as "Quirk et al." General observations about "the 'notional' approach to word classes" will be found in § 2.43, "Word classes in relation to meaning." I have discussed the distinction between stative and dynamic, and compared the grammatically stative language of Marianne Moore with the more dynamic language of Robert Frost and Wallace Stevens, in *Language and the Poet* (University of Chicago Press, 1979). See chap. 5, "Marianne Moore's Promotional Prose: The Uses of Syntax," esp. pp. 90–99.

25. For treatment in more detail, with additional examples, see, in Quirk et al., §4.4, "Situation types: stative and dynamic verb senses," and §§4.27–28, "Situation types" and "Stative types *A* and *B*: qualities and states."

26. See Quirk et al., §4.5 "Meanings of the simple present tense with reference to present time:" "The STATE PRESENT, as we may call this category, includes general timeless statements, or so-called 'eternal truths.' " Examples include "Honesty *is* the best policy" and "The earth *moves* round the sun."

27. See Quirk et al., §2.34(b-d), where the "open classes" are said to consist of the noun, the adjective, the full verb, and the adverb, with two "lesser categories," numerals and interjections. "Full verbs" are distinguished from modals, which are always used as auxiliaries, and from the three "primary" verbs *be*, *have*, and *do*. For the inherent differences among the open classes with relation to "stative" and "dynamic" force, see the general discussion under "Word classes in relation to meaning" cited in n. 24, above.

28. See, in Quirk et al., §7.41 "Stative/dynamic" under the heading "Semantic subclassification of adjectives."

29. I used counts of finite verb forms in *Language and the Poet* to show that Marianne Moore's poetic language was more stative than the poetic languages of Robert Frost and Wallace Stevens. See pp. 95–96 and the tabulations in appendix A, pp. 137–53. The summary on p. 154 gives the average of finite verb counts in the tabulated passages of Moore, Frost, and Stevens as 8.1, 10.9, and 11.4, respectively. More than thirty 100-word passages were selected for tabulation from the poetry of each.

30. Ibid., pp. 92–95 and notes 18–19.

31. Ibid., p. 95 and note 22.

32. I use the more familiar title Revelation rather than the Vulgate's and Douay-Rheims's Apocalypse.

33. Quirk et al., in §4.29, list "states of perception (e.g. *see* . . .)" among the "private states" denoted by stative verbs. All the examples that follow (§4.30, [1a]–[5a]) contain the modal verb *can*; I should argue, however, that in the statement "You see Long Island Sound from the top of Sleeping Giant," *see* is equivalent in meaning to "can see." So too in the dreamer's statements that he "saw" this or that in the celestial Jerusalem described by John; conversion into "was seeing" would sound unidiomatic.

34. Noting that the term *juele* is applied to the Lamb himself (1124) in the final phase of the dreamer's vision of the celestial city, Spearing goes on to say that "other key qualities of the pearl are also found in him . . . when the Dreamer actually sees the Lamb for the first time, he perceives [his] whiteness explicitly as pearl-like. Surely we have here a pointer towards the potential culmination of the visionary experience, in which the pearl would be identified with the Lamb" (*Medieval Dream-Poetry*, pp. 127–28). P. M. Kean cites evidence, from medieval prose and poetry, including the writings of Saint Augustine, that the pearl was a symbol of Christ (*The Pearl: An Interpretation* [New York: Barnes and Noble, 1967], p. 150).

35. In fact, she has already applied it to the Lamb, if I am right in thinking that *makelez*, the manuscript reading of line 757, should be emended to *maskelez*. Since *makelez* and *maskelez* are not homonyms, the substitution of the former for the latter would not be justified as is the substitution of *now* in 613 for *innoghe*, the link-word of section 11, or *mote* "castle" for *mote* "spot" in section 16. In fact, the words *maskelez* and *makelez* are emphatically differentiated by the maiden (781–84). It also seems a little odd that a derivative of the noun *make*, which in Middle English primarily means "mate," should be used to refer to a being who is also described as the husband of 144,000 brides.

36. Cf. the words spoken by Jesus in John 6.40: "Every one who seeth the Son, and believeth in him, may have life everlasting, and I will raise him up in the last day." The poet may be alluding to this verse specifically, as the figure of Saint John as author not only of the fourth Gospel but (supposedly) of the Book of Revelation is of major importance in the poem. It is significant in this connection that the dreamer, repenting his arrogance, throws himself on "Crystes mercy and Mary and Jon" (383).

37. See *The Oxford Dictionary of the Christian Church* s.v. "Wisdom of Solomon": "In later writers the terms used of the Divine Wisdom are freely applied to Christ and so passed into the vocabulary of Christian theology." Editors of the poem like E. V. Gordon, Malcolm Andrew, and Ronald Waldron are surely right in emending line 690 by inserting the name *Koyntise*, meaning "wisdom."

38. This is the thesis of Felicity Riddy's essay, "Jewels in *Pearl*," in *A Companion to the Gawain-Poet*, pp. 143–56.

39. See, in *MED*, the citations from pharmaceutical recipes s.v. *gingivere* n., *gromilioun* and *gromil* n., and *pione* n. Of the herbs the poet lists, only *gilofre*, or gillyflower, seems to have been valued as a source of fragrance and flavor rather than as a medicine (ibid.).

40. Published posthumously in French as a book compiled from lecture-notes taken by

his students, and in English as *Course in General Linguistics*, ed. Charles Bally et al., and trans. Roy Harris (London: Duckworth, 1983), hereinafter referred to as *Course*.

41. It was reprinted in *Roman Jakobson: Selected Writings*, II (The Hague and Paris: Mouton, 1971), pp. 239–59. See also Jakobson, "Closing Statement: Linguistics and Poetics," in *Style in Language*, ed. Thomas A. Sebeok (Cambridge: M.I.T. Press, 1960), pp. 350–77.

42. "Syntagmatic relations hold *in praesentia*. They hold between two or more terms co-present in a sequence. Associative relations, on the contrary, hold *in absentia*. They hold between terms constituting a mnemonic group" (*Course*, p. 122).

43. See the discussion of Jakobson's theory of the two axes, with an accompanying diagram, in Kirsten Malmkjær's essay "Structuralist Linguistics," in *The Linguistics Encyclopedia*, ed. Malmkjær and James M. Anderson (London and New York: Routledge, 1991), p. 437

44. "[The association among members of a paradigm] may be based just on similarity of sound patterns" (*Course*, p. 124). But see also Saussure's cautionary footnote, ibid.

45. The diagram representing Saussure's syntagmatic and paradigmatic axes reappears in Malmkjær's account of Jakobson's theories in his essay "Stylistics" in *The Linguistics Encyclopedia* (p. 441).

46. A helpful explanation (and, in part, a critique) of Jakobson's theory is presented in part 2, "Metaphor and Metonymy," of *The Modes of Modern Writing: Metaphor, Metonymy, and the Typology of Modern Literature* by David Lodge (Ithaca: Cornell University Press, 1977), pp. 73–124. Lodge analyzes a variety of poems and fictional narratives in terms of the distinction. See also the essays on metaphor and metonymy in *The New Princeton Encyclopedia of Poetry and Poetics*, ed. Alex Preminger and T. V. F. Brogan (Princeton: Princeton University Press, 1993), pp. 760–66, 783–85.

47. See Lodge's recapitulation, "Metaphor and Metonymy," pp. 79–81. In the two-column scheme on p. 81, "Poetry" and "Lyric" are listed under the heading of metaphor, "Prose" and "Epic" under that of metonymy.

48. In "Closing Statement: Linguistics and Poetics," p. 358. See note 41, above.

49. In his discussion of *Pearl* in *Medieval Dream-Poetry*, Spearing makes the important point that metaphors and symbols, even in a *veray avysyoun* such as the awakened dreamer thinks he has had, do not represent the highest kind of mystical experience, "because the highest 'visions' of this kind do not really take the form of things seen. St. Augustine, for instance, had assumed that as a preliminary to genuine mystical experience, 'all dreams and revelations that come by imagery' would disappear" (p. 116). See my discussion of the dreamer's vision of the Lamb in the celestial city, pp. 153–54.

50. Elizabeth Kirk has well said that "it is of the very essence of human nature to experience *caritas* and *cupiditas*, relations of love and relations of power, as inextricably entwined, fueled by each other's energies like the different kinds of *vertu* whose connection and tension Chaucer's *General Prologue* so splendidly portrays" ("The Anatomy of a Mourning: Reflections on the *Pearl* Dreamer," in *The Endless Knot: Essays on Old and Middle English in Honor of Marie Borroff*, ed. M. Teresa Tavormina and R. F. Yeager [Cambridge, England: D. S. Brewer, 1995]), pp. 215–25; see p. 222. In my view, the dreamer's desire to grasp the maiden mentally, which replaces his desire to cross the stream and grasp her physically, represents a shift from *cupiditas* toward *caritas*.

51. See Sarah Stanbury, "*Pearl* and the Idea of Jerusalem," cited in n. 22, above: "In

contrast [to the exegetes who have written on the Apocalypse], the *Pearl* dreamer is an observer rather than a commentator. . . . The question [Who did that spyt?] . . . illustrates his own subjective placement in this vision, suspended from history, Scripture, and an exegetical tradition that tells the Christian [the answer] again and again" (p. 121).

52. Cf. the phrase "dale of dole," s.v. *dol* n.(2) [a] in *MED*, and Theseus's reference to "this foule prisoun of this lyf" in the *Knight's Tale* 3061, in a speech in which he also exhorts his audience to be merry and recommends the union of Palamon and Emily in "o parfit joye, lastynge everemo" (3072).

53. That is, I differ from both Gordon and Andrew and Waldron in taking *lote* 1205 to be an instance of *lot(e* n. in *MED* rather than of *lot* n.(1). The former can mean "a word, speech, talk" (sense 3[b]); the latter means "what is allotted" (sense 2[a]). The referent of *hit* in 1207 may be the words, or the pearl of 1206, or, conceivably, both.

54. As Spearing says, the "narrator's closing thoughts" are "not of himself (as they were in the opening section) but of the whole body of his fellow-Christians, as he wishes that not only his own pearl but all of them may be members of God's household and precious pearls to him" (*Medieval Dream-Poetry*, p. 129).

55. I do not distinguish, in tabulating rhymes in the two poems, between rhymes containing "long close *e*" and rhymes containing "long open -*e*." An attempt to do so would necessitate the invoking of philological details about the dialects of the two poems, or poets, that would not affect the comparatively simple point I am illustrating: that there is considerably more variety of rhyme-sounds in *Pearl* than in *Pety Job*.

56. "Parce michi, domine" is the twelfth line of every stanza of the poem and is printed by Horstman in italics. The poet also uses it as the first line of the poem (in which position Horstman does not italicize it), presumably to tie the end of the poem back to its beginning in phonic "circularity." (In *Pearl*, too, the end of the poem echoes its beginning: the C-rhyme of the twentieth and final section is -*ay* and the reiterated link-word of the section is *pay*, echoing the rhyme-word of line 1 of the poem, "Perle, plesaunte to prynces paye.") The C-rhyme of every stanza of *Pety Job* is thus -*e*, which sound appears in line 10 as well as line 12. Because *domine* is the rhyme-word of line 1, -*e* is the A-rhyme of the first stanza. The poet also uses it as the A-rhyme of stanzas 5, 9, and 10. This repetition of rhyme-sound is attended by reiteration of the rhyme-words *be*, *degre*, *me*, and *the* "thee."

57. I consider the A-rhyme of this stanza identical in sound (though not always in quantity) with the A-rhyme of stanza 1, on the assumption that the poet intended the rhyme-words of lines 39, 41, and 43, -*more*, *soore*, and *lore*, whose ancestors in Old English had long *a*, to be sounded with the *a* of the Northern dialect of Middle English despite the fact that we see them spelled (by the scribe) with the Midland and Southern *o*. There is a "Northern" rhyme in stanza 29 between *ware* (in *be ware*, OE *wær*) and *mare* "more;" spelling here corresponds to sound. There is also a Midland or Southern rhyme in stanza 25, in which *more*, *sore*, and *lore* are linked with *bore* "born" (OE *boren*).

Chapter 8. Systematic Sound Symbolism in the Long Alliterative Line:
Beowulf *and* Sir Gawain

1. The word *loken*, in the line "with lel letteres loken" is worth pausing over for a moment. It means, not "secured with a key," but simply "fastened together." Later in the

poem, other forms of this same verb (*louken* in Middle English) refer to the intertwining of the five lines of the pentangle, or "endless knot," and to the tieing of the green girdle, first around the lady's sides (1830), then under Sir Gawain's left arm (2487). Its use to signify the linkages among "letters" that form the long alliterative line thus introduces a theme of knottings or attachment — the invulnerable perfection of the pentangle knot and the ambiguousness or duplicity of human relationships — that runs through the narrative and contributes to its meaning.

2. I quote the original throughout from *Beowulf: An Edition with Relevant Shorter Texts*, ed. Bruce Mitchell and Fred C. Robinson (Oxford, U.K. and Malden, Mass., 1998). I retain the Old English letters, and the editorial marks indicating vowel-quantity, except in proper names such as *Beowulf, Hrothgar.*

3. E. Talbot Donaldson, *Beowulf: A New Prose Translation* (New York: W. W. Norton and Company, 1966), p. 7.

4. Mariann Reinhard, in *On the Semantic Relevance of the Alliterative Collocations in "Beowulf"* (Bern: A. Francke A. G. Verlag, 1976) presents comprehensive lists of "Basic Collocations" in which lexically congruent words are joined, including, among others, collocations whose members begin with the letter *g* (see p. 39 *et alibi*). Space forbids my discussing a "counter-system" in which the name *Grendel* alliterates, not only with adjectives denoting monstrous attributes, such as *grimm* and *grædig* (121), but with *guðræft* (127), a word signifying the human arts of war that are wholly unknown to such a creature. See Reinhard, p. 58, for the link between *Grendel* and *guð*; also p. 195, where *go(o)d, Gēatum,* and *Grendles* are listed among "Contrastive" word-groups; and p. 152, where a "Grendel-gold motif" is discussed (Grendel is the "opponent of all the values represented by gold").

5. John Collins Pope, *The Rhythm of Beowulf: An Interpretation of the Normal and Hypermetric Verse-Forms in Old English Poetry*, rev. ed. (New Haven: Yale University Press, 1966). The revised edition is identical, except for page-size, with the first, except that Pope has added a "Line Index to the Catalogue" (pp. 389–409) in which the two halves of each successive line of the poem are identified in accordance with his system of metrical nomenclature.

6. The fact that the second syllable is heavy does not rule out this description. So-called "anapestic" verses in English may contain feet whose first or second syllables, or both, receive considerable stress, as in "Not a word to each other; we kept *the great pace*," and "Till over by Dalhem a dome-*spire sprang white*," in Browning's "How They Brought the Good News from Ghent to Aix."

7. See Borroff, *Sir Gawain and the Green Knight: A Stylistic and Metrical Study* (London and New Haven: Yale University Press, 1962), especially pp. 173–75 and 192–98. The poetry of Chaucer provides evidence for alternative scansions, in the iambic pentameter line, of similar phrases, such that either the adjective or the noun is assigned chief rank; I confine myself to a single example of each. In *Troilus* 2.162 "'In good feith, em,' quod she, 'that liketh me,'" *good* is a chief syllable; in *The Parliament of Fowls* 24 "And out of olde bokes, in good feyth," it is an intermediate syllable. The scansion of Chaucerian lines in which *good* modifies words referring to persons is complicated by the fact that the adjective is usually disyllabic when declined weak or used in apostrophes. But cf. *Troilus* 2.309, "Now, good em, for Goddes love I preye" (a "headless" line) and

2.499 "Til at the laste, 'O goode em,' quod she tho." Here a dissyllabic pronunciation (as in *Clerk's Tale* 852 "O goodë God, how gentil and how kynde") is ruled out by elision. The two instances of *goodë* in *Troilus* 2.309 and 2.499 have intermediate and chief rank, respectively.

8. *God* appears in the first 400 lines of the poem in lines 11, 195, 199, 205, 269, 279, 347, 355, and 384; for scansions of these, see the "Line Index to the Catalogue" in Pope, pp. 389–409. The first syllable of *gōdan* is scanned by Pope as an eighth note in 384 "Ic þæm gōdan sceal" (p. 334, Type B1.2).

9. I am scanning the alliterating lines of *Sir Gawain* in accordance with my own theory that the final -*e* of monosyllabic adjectives is not sounded, except perhaps at the end of the line, in phrases in which it would be sounded in Chaucer's decasyllabic verse. See Borroff, *op. cit.*, pp. 154–60, 182–89; see also, in this volume, p. 178. Syllabication, in this line or that of the poem, may or may not be reflected in spelling (compare, e.g., the plural forms in "goude ladyez" 1625 and "goud chepez" 1939).

10. *Gay* is used only once of persons in Part I of the poem, with reference to Guenevere. Thereafter, it refers to Gawain and the lady of the castle (but not to Lord Bertilak). *God* refers to masculine persons seventeen times, to feminine persons only once ("the goude ladyez were geten, and gedered the meyny" [1625]). I suspect that the "gode halghez" of line 2122 are exclusively masculine.

11. In his pathbreaking essay, "Poetic Language and Old English Metre," *Early English and Norse Studies, Presented to Hugh Smith in Honour of His Sixtieth Birthday*, ed. Arthur Brown and Peter Foote (London: Methuen and Co., 1963, pp. 150–71), Randolph Quirk showed that the appellation "goldwine" takes on a poignant, rather than an exalted resonance when, late in the poem, it is linked with "geōmor" ("sad") (p. 160). I would add that such effects are not produced exclusively by the juxtaposition of terms of contrasting emotional value; the tried and true combinations themselves may take on tragic force.

12. Davis construes the last half-line of the original as a relative clause with the pronominal head unexpressed, and translates "which well suited that handsome man." "Splendidly dressed" would translate *gay* equally well.

13. A dramatically expressive reading of the line produces this metrical pattern, even though *gay* alliterates and *other* does not. For other similar examples in the poem, see Borroff, *op. cit.*, pp. 171 and 202.

14. *Beowulf and the Appositive Style* (Knoxville: University of Tennessee Press, 1985), p. 80.

Chapter 9. *Reading* Sir Gawain and the Green Knight *Aloud*

1. Anyone interested in trying to read *Sir Gawain* aloud in the original will probably be familiar with the values of the late Middle English long and short vowels, as explained in the introductory apparatus of any standard edition of Chaucer. The following recapitulates the standard view in condensed form. As a fairly reliable rule of thumb, we can assume that the vowel of a Middle English word is long if its descendent form has one of the so-called "long vowels" in modern English, exemplified by the words *mate, meat, meet, mite, moat, moot*, and *amount*. If the vowel of the modern descendant is "short," as

in *mat, met, mitt, Mott,* and *book,* the vowel of the Middle English word was probably short also. All the Middle English long vowels were literally long, i.e., prolonged in time. "Long *a*" in Middle English was pronounced like the *a* in modern English *father.* Examples from *Sir Gawain: tale, grace.* There were two kinds of long *e* and long *o,* called "open" and "close." "Long open *e,*" found in words whose modern descendants usually are spelled with *ea,* was pronounced like the *e* of met. Examples: *ded* "dead," *hede* "head." "Long close *e,*" found in words whose modern descendants usually are spelled with *ee* or *ie,* was pronounced like the *a* of ate. Examples: *dede* "deed," *fle* "to flee," *gref* "grief." "Long *i*" was pronounced like the *ee* of *meet.* Examples: *pine* "pain," *side.* "Long open *o,*" found in words whose descendants usually are spelled with *oa* or *o* plus consonant plus *e,* was pronounced like the *ou* of *ought.* Examples: *fole* "foal, horse," *stone,* *hom* "home." "Long close *o,*" found in words whose descendants usually are spelled with *oo,* was pronounced like the *o* of *note.* Examples: *flod* "flood," *mon(e)* "moon." "Long *u,*" whose descendants usually are pronounced with the *ou* of *mount,* was pronounced like the *oo* of *moot.* Examples: *croun* "crown," *browe.* The short vowels in Middle English were pronounced and spelled much as they are today, except that *y* and *i* are interchangeable, "short *u*" is spelled either with *u* or with *o* as in modern English, and "short *u*" always has the vowel of modern *put,* never that of *cut.* Examples: *gras, met, synne, fox, son/sun* "son,"*sunne* "sun."

2. Final *-e* is sounded in the wheels of *Sir Gawain,* and in *Pearl,* where a syllable is needed to make up minimal sequences of alternating stressed and unstressed syllables, as in "Wyth rychë cote-armure" (*Gawain* 586) and "Thenne nwë note me com on honde" (*Pearl* 135). It is also sounded in certain rhymes in *Sir Gawain* in which one of the rhyming components is a phrase, as in "to the" ("to thee") and "forsothe" ("forsooth") (413, 415). Complete lists will be found in my *Sir Gawain and the Green Knight: A Stylistic and Metrical Study* (New Haven and London: Yale University Press, 1962), pp. 159–60.

3. In these excerpts, my modern versions exemplify the same alliterative patterns as the original lines. But see the note that follows.

4. In translating the alliterative verse of the *Gawain*-poet, I use, in all their variety, the metrical patterns I have identified in the original. But, as detailed comparisons between the Middle English passages and the translations quoted in this essay will show, I make no attempt to duplicate the patterns of individual lines.

Chapter 10. A Cipher in Hamlet

1. I am indebted to Harvey Rosenberg for assistance in the research preparatory to the writing of this essay.

2. After 5.2.80, the Folio reads "Enter young Osricke"; Q2 has "Enter a Courtier." The Quarto reading is given in *Hamlet, Prince of Denmark,* ed. Philip Edwards (Cambridge: Cambridge University Press, 1985); I quote from this edition except for the dialogue between Hamlet and Osric, 5.2.81–112, for which I have used a copy of Q2 in the library of the Elizabethan Club at Yale University (listed as EC 168, with a full description, in Stephen Parks, *The Elizabethan Club of Yale University and Its Library* [New Haven and London: Yale University Press, 1986], p. 202). I am grateful to Stephen

Parks, the librarian of the club, for his kindness in making this copy available to me. I have also made use of *Hamlet*, ed. Harold Jenkins (London: Methuen, 1982) and have consulted C. T. Onions, *A Shakespeare Glossary*, rev. Robert D. Eagleson (Oxford: Clarendon Press, 1986). For plays other than *Hamlet*, I quote from *The Complete Works of Shakespeare*, ed. George Lyman Kittredge (Boston: Ginn and Company, 1936).

3. George Puttenham, in *The Arte of English Poesie*, published in 1589, lists *Amphibologia* as a vice of speech which manifests itself "when we speake or write doubtfully and that the sence may be taken two wayes," and counsels "our maker" to "avoyde all such ambiguous speaches unlesse it be when he doth it for the nonce and for some purpose" (Facsimile Reproduction of the 1906 reprint, ed. Edward Arber, introd. by Baxter Hathaway [Kent, Ohio: Kent State University Press, 1970], p. 267).

4. However one may wish to explicate this line, the force of the phrase "less than kind" surely includes the now-obsolete meaning "nature" of the word *kind* (*OED* s.v. *kind* sb. sense 4, cited, inter alia, from *The Merchant of Venice,* 1.3.86 in the phrase "the deed of kind," i.e., sexual intercourse). The meaning "natural" of the adjective (*OED* s.v. *kind* a. sense 1, cited as late as 1579), along with its usual modern meaning, is probably evoked as well. Hamlet views Gertrude's marriage to Claudius as unnatural in that it is incestuous and in that it has resulted from the abandonment of her human faculty of reasonable judgment: "O God, a beast that wants discourse of reason / Would have mourned longer. . . . Oh most wicked speed, to post / With such dexterity to incestuous sheets" (1.2.150–51, 155–56). Cf. the wording of the Ghost's revelation: "If thou didst ever thy dear father love . . . Revenge his foul and most unnatural murder" (1.5.23,25), and the lines that follow almost immediately: "Murder most foul, as in the best it is, But this most foul, strange, and unnatural" (27–28). A thematic opposition between the natural and the unnatural runs through the play; its last reverberation sounds in Horatio's reference, after the entrance of Fortinbras and the English ambassadors, to "carnal, bloody, and unnatural acts" (5.2.360).

5. Jenkins, in his "Longer Notes," p. 558, quotes the definitive comment of Dr. Johnson on the former word: "A water-fly skips up and down upon the surface of the water, without any apparent purpose or reason, and is thence the proper emblem of a busy trifler," adding that "Shakespeare appears to have envisaged an insect . . . with brightly flapping wings." *Chough* is interpreted by Jenkins (note to line 88) as a variant spelling of *chuff*; he glosses it "rustic, churl." Such a spelling is certainly conceivable in Elizabethan English, though given by *OED* only as eighteenth century (s.v. *chuff* sb.[1]). But the interpretation implies a fleshy, hearty solidity which seems inappropriate to the water-fly-like Osric. Cf. the homonyms meaning "a cheek swollen or puffed with fat" (*chuff* sb.[2]) and "swollen or puffed with fat; chubby" (*chuff* a.[1]), both cited in *OED* from Shakespeare's time, and note the phrase "fat chuffs" in *Henry the Fourth, Part I*, 2.2.94.

6. Cf. the citations in *OED* s.v. *spacious* a., senses 1 "Of lands, etc. . . . extensive" and 4 "Great . . . ample," and *dirt* sb. senses 1 "ordure" and 1b "As the type of anything worthless."

7. The first part of the speech, through the phrase "quick saile," amusingly enacts its own description, veering with dizzying speed from heavily Latinate language, including the affected substitution of *perdition* for *loss* and the polysyllabic neologism *inventorially*, doubly derived by Shakespeare from *inventory* (see *OED* s.v. *inventorial*), to native

diction (except for *respect*), shifting at one and the same time from a legal to a nautical image. The contrast is heightened in the latter part by a colloquial idiom, "but . . . neither"; cf. "But a trifle neither," spoken by the Clown in *All's Well that Ends Well*, 2.2.36, and "that is but a kind of bastard hope neither," spoken by Lancelot Gobbo in *The Merchant of Venice*, 3.5.9.

8. The earliest citation for *infuse* v. in *OED* is dated c1420, the earliest for *infusion* c1450. A synonymous verb *infund* is cited from 1514 to 1611.

9. There is a tantalizing echo here of a bit of Senecan fustian, line 84 of *Hercules Furens*: "Quaeris Alcidae parem? / Nemo est nisi ipse." Pope satirized Theobald's adaptation of this conceit as "None but thyself can be thy parallel," in *The Dunciad*. See G. K. Hunter, *Dramatic Identities and Cultural Tradition: Studies in Shakespeare and His Contemporaries* (New York: Barnes and Noble, 1978), p. 207.

10. This edition is dated 1543 in *A Short-Title Catalogue of Books Printed in England, Scotland, and Ireland . . . 1475–1640*, 2d ed. (London: Bibliographical Society, 1976), 2:269. George A. Plimpton, in *The Education of Shakespeare Illustrated from the Schoolbooks in Use in His Time* (London: Oxford University Press, 1933), says, without further explanation, that "the first edition was probably printed in 1542" (p. 71). See note 12, below.

11. "Shakespeare probably learned his arithmetic from *The Ground of Artes*, by Robert Recorde" (Plimpton, *The Education of Shakespeare*, p. 71).

12. Facsimile of a copy of the first edition in the Bodleian Library at Oxford, published by Da Capo Press, Theatrum Orbis Terrarum Ltd. (Amsterdam/New York, 2969), no pagination; sig. Cii. The facsimile is incorrectly dated 1542. I am grateful to Jane Phillips for consulting this facsimile and a copy of the 1549 edition in the library of the University of Cambridge; the latter expresses the difference between articles and mixed numbers in identical wording.

13. Ibid.

Bibliography of Works Cited

Compiled by Curtis M. Perrin

Ackerman, Robert W. "The *Pearl*-Maiden and the Penny." *Romance Philology* 17 (1964): 615–23.

Aers, David. "Christianity for Courtly Subjects: Reflections on the *Gawain*-Poet." In *A Companion to the "Gawain"-Poet,* edited by Derek Brewer and Jonathan Gibson, Arthurian Studies 38, 91–101. Cambridge, Eng.; Rochester, N.Y.: D. S. Brewer, 1997.

———. *Community, Gender, and Individual Identity: English Writing, 1360–1430.* London: Routledge, 1988.

———. "The Self Mourning: Reflections on *Pearl.*" *Speculum* 68 (1993): 54–73.

Alford, John A. "Scriptural Testament in the *Canterbury Tales:* The Letter Takes Its Revenge." In *Chaucer and Scriptural Tradition,* edited by David Lyle, 197–203. Ottawa: University of Ottawa Press, 1984.

Amundesham, Johannes. *Annales Monasterii S. Albani, a Johanne Amundesham, monacho, ut videtur, conscripti, (A.D. 1421–1440). Quibus praefigitur Chronicon rerum gestarum in Monasterio S. Albani, (A.D. 1422–1431), a quodam auctore ignoto compilatum.* Edited by Henry T. Riley. 2 vols. London: Longmans, Green, and Co., 1870–71. Reprint, Wiesbaden: Kraus Reprint, 1965.

Andrew, Malcolm, and Ronald Waldron, eds. *The Poems of the Pearl Manuscript: Pearl, Cleanness, Patience, Sir Gawain and the Green Knight.* York Medieval Texts, 2d ser. Berkeley: University of California Press, 1982.

Auden, W. H. "For the Time Being." In *Collected Poems,* edited by Edward Mendelson, 347–400. London: Faber and Faber, 1991.

Baum, Paull F. "Chaucer's Puns." *PMLA* 71 (1956): 225–46.

———. *Chaucer's Verse*. Durham, N.C.: Duke University Press, 1961.

Benson, Larry Dean, and Theodore Murdock Andersson. *The Literary Context of Chaucer's Fabliaux*. Indianapolis: Bobbs-Merrill, 1971.

Besserman, Lawrence L. *Chaucer and the Bible: A Critical Review of Research, Indexes, and Bibliography*. New York: Garland, 1988.

Birney, Earle. "Structural Irony within the *Summoner's Tale*." *Anglia* 78 (1960): 204–18.

Bishop, Ian. *"Pearl" in Its Setting: A Critical Study of the Structure and Meaning of the Middle English Poem*. New York: Barnes and Noble, 1968.

Blamires, Alcuin. "The Wife of Bath and Lollardy." *Medium Aevum* 58 (1989): 224–42.

Bloom, Harold, ed. *Geoffrey Chaucer's "The Pardoner's Tale."* Modern Critical Interpretations. New York: Chelsea House Publishers, 1988.

Boccaccio, Giovanni. *L'Ameto*. Translated by Judith Powers Serafini-Sauli. New York: Garland Publishing, 1985.

———. "L'Ameto." In *L'Ameto; Lettere; Il Corbaccio*, edited by Nicola Bruscoli, Opere di Giovanni Boccaccio, vol. 5, Scrittori d'Italia, no. 182, 3–152. Bari: Giuseppe Laterze and Figli, 1940.

Boitani, Piero, and Jill Mann, eds. *The Cambridge Chaucer Companion*. Cambridge: Cambridge University Press, 1986.

Booth, Wayne C. *The Rhetoric of Fiction*. 2d ed. Chicago: University of Chicago Press, 1983.

Borroff, Marie. *Language and the Poet: Verbal Artistry in Frost, Stevens, and Moore*. Chicago: University of Chicago Press, 1979.

———. *"Sir Gawain and the Green Knight": A Stylistic and Metrical Study*. Yale Studies in English, no. 152. New Haven: Yale University Press, 1962.

———. *Sir Gawain and the Green Knight, Patience, and Pearl: Verse Translations*. New York: W. W. Norton, 2000.

———. "Sound Symbolism as Drama in the Poetry of Robert Frost." *PMLA* 107 (1992): 131–44.

Bowers, John M. *The Politics of "Pearl": Court Poetry in the Age of Richard II*. Cambridge; Rochester, N.Y.: D. S. Brewer, 2001.

Brewer, Derek. *Chaucer in His Time*. London: T. Nelson, 1963.

———. "The Fabliaux." In *Companion to Chaucer Studies*, edited by Beryl Rowland, rev. ed., 296–325. New York: Oxford University Press, 1979.

———. "The *Gawain*-Poet: A General Appreciation of Four Poems." *Essays in Criticism* 17 (1967): 130–42.

———. "The Relationship of Chaucer to the English and European Traditions." In *Chaucer and Chaucerians: Critical Studies in Middle English Literature*, 1–38. University: University of Alabama Press, 1966.

———. *Symbolic Stories: Traditional Narratives of the Family Drama in English Literature*. Cambridge, England: D. S. Brewer; Totowa, N.J.: Rowman & Littlefield, 1980.

Bronson, Bertrand. "*The Book of the Duchess* Re-Opened." *PMLA* 67 (1952): 863–81.

Browning, Robert. "How They Brought the Good News from Ghent to Aix." In *The Complete Works of Robert Browning, With Variant Readings & Annotations*, edited by Roma A. King et al., 4:161–63. Athens: Ohio University Press, 1969.

Bugge, John. "Damyan's Wanton *Clyket* and an Ironic New *Twiste* to the *Merchant's Tale*." *Annuale Mediaevale* 14 (1973): 53–62.

Burlin, Robert B. *The Old English Advent*. Yale Studies in English, no. 168. New Haven: Yale University Press, 1968.

Burnley, J. D. "The Morality of the *Merchant's Tale*." *Yearbook of English Studies* 6 (1976): 16–25.

Burrow, J. A. *A Reading of "Sir Gawain and the Green Knight."* London: Routledge and Kegan Paul, 1966.

——. *Ricardian Poetry: Chaucer, Gower, Langland and the "Gawain" Poet*. New Haven: Yale University Press, 1971.

Carruthers, Mary. "Letter and Gloss in the Friar's and Summoner's Tales." *Journal of Narrative Technique* 2 (1972): 208–14.

Casson, L. F., ed. *The Romance of Sir Degrevant: A Parallel-Text Edition from MSS. Lincoln Cathedral A.5.2 and Cambridge University Ff.1.6,* EETS 221. London: Oxford University Press, 1949.

Cawley, A. C., ed. *Pearl; Sir Gawain and the Green Knight*. Everyman's Library 346. London: J. M. Dent, 1962.

Caxton, William. *The Prologues and Epilogues of William Caxton*. Edited by W. J. B. Crotch. EETS 176. London: Pub. for the Early English Text Society by H. Milford, Oxford University Press, 1928. Reprint, 1956.

Challoner, Richard, ed. *The Holy Bible, Translated from the Latin Vulgate: Diligently Compared with the Hebrew, Greek, and Other Editions in Divers Languages*. Rockford, Ill.: Tan Books and Publishers, 1989. Originally published, Baltimore: John Murphy Company, 1899.

Chaucer, Geoffrey. *Canterbury Tales*. Edited by John Matthews Manly. New York: Henry Holt and Company, 1928.

——. *The "Pardoner's Prologue & Tale," From the "Canterbury Tales."* Edited by A. C. Spearing, *Selected Tales from Chaucer*. Cambridge: Cambridge University Press, 1965.

——. *The Riverside Chaucer*. Edited by Larry Dean Benson. 3d ed. Boston: Houghton Mifflin, 1987.

——. *The Works of Geoffrey Chaucer*. Edited by F. N. Robinson. 2d ed. Boston: Houghton Mifflin, 1957.

Chaucer, Geoffrey, Guillaume de Lorris, and Jean de Meun. *The "Romaunt of the Rose" and "Le Roman de la Rose": A Parallel-Text Edition*. Edited by Ronald Sutherland. Oxford: Blackwell, 1968.

Chrétien de Troyes. *Yvain (Le Chevalier au lion)*. Edited by Wendelin Foerster and T. B. W. Reid. Manchester: Manchester University Press, 1942.

Clark, Roy Peter. "Doubting Thomas in Chaucer's *Summoner's Tale*." *Chaucer Review* 11 (1976): 164–78.

Clopper, Lawrence M. "*Pearl* and the Consolation of Scripture." *Viator* 23 (1992): 231–45.

Cooke, Thomas Darlington. *The Old French and Chaucerian Fabliaux: A Study of Their Comic Climax*. Columbia: University of Missouri Press, 1978.

Cooper, Helen. "The *Summoner's Tale*." In *The Canterbury Tales*, 2d ed., Oxford Guides to Chaucer, 176–83. Oxford: Oxford University Press, 1996.

Copland, M. "The *Reeve's Tale:* Harlotrie or Sermonyng?" *Medium Ævum* 31 (1962): 14–32.

Cotter, James Finn. "The Wife of Bath's Lenten Observance." *Papers on Language and Literature* 7 (1971): 293–97.

Crane, Ronald Salmon. *Critics and Criticism, Ancient and Modern.* Chicago: University of Chicago Press, 1952.

———. "Questions and Answers in the Teaching of Literary Texts." In *The Idea of the Humanities, and Other Essays Critical and Historical* 2:181–88. Chicago: University of Chicago Press, 1967.

Cross, F. L., and Elizabeth A. Livingstone, eds. *The Oxford Dictionary of the Christian Church.* 3d ed. Oxford: Oxford University Press, 1997.

Crow, Martin M., Clair Colby Olson, and John Matthews Manly, eds. *Chaucer Life-Records.* Oxford: Clarendon Press, 1966.

Danos, Joseph R. *A Concordance to the "Roman de la Rose" of Guillaume de Lorris.* North Carolina Studies in the Romance Languages and Literatures: Texts, Textual Studies, and Translations, no. 3. Chapel Hill, N.C.: U.N.C. Dept. of Romance Languages; Portland, Or.: Distributed by International Scholarly Book Service, 1975.

Dante Alighiere. *The Divine Comedy.* Translated by John D. Sinclair. 3 vols. New York: Oxford University Press, 1961.

Dawson, James Doyne. "Richard FitzRalph and the Fourteenth-Century Poverty Controversies." *Journal of Ecclesiastical History* 34 (1983): 315–44.

Donaldson, E. Talbot. *Beowulf: A New Prose Translation.* New York: W. W. Norton, 1966.

———. "The Effect of the *Merchant's Tale.*" In *Speaking of Chaucer,* 30–45. New York: W. W. Norton, 1970.

Dronke, Peter. "The Rise of the Medieval Fabliau." *Romanische Forschungen* 85 (1973): 275–97.

Eckhardt, Caroline. "The Art of Translation in *The Romaunt of the Rose.*" *Studies in the Age of Chaucer* 6 (1984): 41–63.

Edward, Duke of York. "The Master of Game (Translation of Gaston Phoebus' *Livre de Chasse).*" In *The Oxford Book of Late Medieval Verse and Prose,* edited by Douglas Gray, 145–48. Oxford: Clarendon Press, 1985.

Eldredge, Laurence. "Imagery of Roundness in William Woodford's *De Sacramento Altaris* and Its Possible Relevance to the Middle English *Pearl.*" *Notes and Queries* n.s. 24 (1978): 3–5.

Eliot, T. S. *Four Quartets.* New York: Harcourt Brace, 1943.

Everest, Carol. " 'Paradys or Helle': Pleasure and Procreation in Chaucer's *Merchant's Tale.*" In *Sovereign Lady: Essays on Women in Middle English Literature,* edited by Muriel A. Whitaker, 63–84. New York: Garland Publishing, 1995.

Faulkner, Dewey R., ed. *Twentieth Century Interpretations of the "Pardoner's Tale": A Collection of Critical Essays.* Englewood Cliffs, N.J.: Prentice-Hall, 1973.

Ferris, Sumner. "The Mariology of the *Prioress's Tale.*" *American Benedictine Review* 32 (1981): 232–54.

Field, P. J. C. "A Rereading of *Sir Gawain and the Green Knight.*" *Studies in Philology* 68 (1971): 255–69.

Fischer, Bonifatius, and Robert Weber, eds. *Biblia sacra iuxta Vulgatam versionem.* 4th ed. Stuttgart: Deutsche Bibelgesellschaft, 1994.

FitzRalph, Richard. "De pauperie salvatoris." In *Iohannis Wycliffe "De dominio divino libri tres"; To Which Are Added the First Four Books of the Treatise "De pauperie salvatoris,"* edited by Reginald Lane Poole, Wyclif's Latin Works, 257–476. London: Published for the Wyclif Society by Trübner, 1890.

——. "Defensio curatorum." In *Monarchia S. Romani Imperii,* edited by Melchior Goldast, 2:1391–410. Frankfurt: Conrad Biermann, 1614. Reprint, Graz: Akademische Druck- u. Verlagsanstalt, 1960.

——. "Defensio curatorum." In *Dialogus inter militem et clericum, Richard FitzRalph's sermon: 'Defensio curatorum' and Methodius: 'The bygynnyng of the world and the ende of worldes,'* edited by Aaron Jenkins Perry, translated by John Trevisa, EETS 167. London: Pub. for the Early English Text Society by H. Milford, Oxford University Press, 1925.

Fleming, John V. "Anticlerical Satire as Theological Essay: Chaucer's *Summoner's Tale.*" *Thalia* 6 (1983): 5–22.

——. "The Antifraternalism of the *Summoner's Tale.*" *JEGP* 65 (1966): 688–700.

——. "The Summoner's Prologue: An Iconographic Adjustment." *Chaucer Review* 2 (1967): 95–107.

Fletcher, Alan J. "The Summoner and the Abominable Anatomy of Antichrist." *Studies in the Age of Chaucer* 18 (1996): 91–117.

——. "The Topical Hypocrisy of Chaucer's Pardoner." *Chaucer Review* 25 (1990): 110–26.

Frank, Robert Worth, Jr. "The *Canterbury Tales* III: Pathos." In *The Cambridge Chaucer Companion,* edited by Piero Boitani and Jill Mann, 143–47, 53–54. Cambridge: Cambridge University Press, 1986.

Fritz, Donald. "The Prioress's Avowal of Ineptitude." *Chaucer Review* 9 (1974): 174–79.

Ganim, John M. *Style and Consciousness in Middle English Narrative.* Princeton: Princeton University Press, 1983.

Ginsberg, Warren. "Preaching and Avarice in the *Pardoner's Tale.*" *Mediaevalia* 2 (1976): 77–99.

Gollancz, Israel, ed. *Pearl, Cleanness, Patience, and Sir Gawain,* EETS 162. London: Published for the Early English Text Society by Oxford University Press, 1923. Reprint, 1971.

Gordon, E. V., ed. *Pearl.* Oxford: Clarendon Press, 1953.

Guillaume de Lorris, and Jean de Meun. *Le Roman de la Rose.* Edited by Ernest Langlois. 5 vols. Paris: Firmin-Didot, 1914–24.

——. *Roman de la Rose.* Edited by Félix Lecoy. 3 vols. Paris: H. Champion, 1965–70.

——. *The Romance of the Rose.* Translated by Charles Dahlberg. Princeton: Princeton University Press, 1995.

Hammerich, L. L. "The Beginning of the Strife between Richard FitzRalph and the Mendicants, with an Edition of His Autobiographical Prayer and His Proposition *Unusquisque.*" *Historisk-Filologiske Meddelelser: Det Kongelige Danske Didenskabernes Selskab* 26:3 (1917).

Hanks, D. Thomas, Jr. "'Savor,' Chaucer's *Summoner's Tale,* and Matthew 5:13." *English Language Notes* 31:3 (1994): 25–29.

Hasenfratz, Robert. "The Science of Flatulence: Possible Sources for the *Summoner's Tale.*" *Chaucer Review* 30 (1996): 241–61.

Hieatt, Kent. "*Sir Gawain:* Pentangle, *Luf-lace,* Numerical Structure." In *Silent Poetry: Essays in Numerological Analysis,* edited by Alastair Fowler, 116–40. London: Routledge and Kegan Paul, 1970.

Higdon, David Leon. "The Wife of Bath and Refreshment Sunday." *Papers on Language and Literature* 8 (1972): 199–201.

Hirsh, John C. "Reopening the *Prioress's Tale.*" *Chaucer Review* 10 (1975): 30–45.

Horstmann, Carl, ed. "Pety Job." In *Yorkshire Writers: Richard Rolle of Hampole, an English Father of the Church, and His Followers,* Library of Early English Writers 1–2, vol. 2, 381–89. London: Swan Sonnenschein; New York: Macmillan, 1895. Reprint, *Yorkshire Writers: Richard Rolle of Hampole and His Followers,* Rochester, N.Y.: D. S. Brewer, 1999.

Howard, Donald Roy. *The Idea of the "Canterbury Tales."* Berkeley: University of California Press, 1976.

Hudson, Anne. *The Premature Reformation: Wycliffite Texts and Lollard History.* Oxford: Clarendon Press, 1988.

Hughes, Derek W. "The Problem of Reality in *Sir Gawain and the Green Knight.*" *University of Toronto Quarterly* 40 (1971): 217–35.

Hughes, Ted. "Hawk Roosting." In *Selected Poems, 1957–1981,* 43. London: Faber and Faber, 1982.

Hunter, G. K. *Dramatic Identities and Cultural Tradition: Studies in Shakespeare and His Contemporaries: Critical Essays.* New York: Barnes and Noble Books, 1978.

Huppé, Bernard Felix. "The Friar-Summoner Quarrel." In *A Reading of the "Canterbury Tales,"* rev. ed., 194–209. Albany: State University of New York, 1967.

Jacquart, Danielle, and Claude Alexandre Thomasset. *Sexuality and Medicine in the Middle Ages.* Translated by Matthew Adamson. Cambridge, England: Polity Press, 1988.

Jakobson, Roman. "Closing Statement: Linguistics and Poetics." In *Style in Language,* edited by Thomas Albert Sebeok, 350–77. Cambridge: MIT Press, 1960.

———. "Two Aspects of Language and Two Types of Aphasic Disturbances." In *Selected Writings,* 2d ed., 2:239–59. The Hague: Mouton, 1971.

Jerome, Saint. "Against Jovinianus [Epistola contra Jovinianum]." In *A Select Library of Nicene and Post-Nicene Fathers of the Christian Church,* 2d Series, edited by Philip Schaff and Henry Wace, vol. 6, *St. Jerome: Letters and Select Works,* 346–416. New York: Christian Literature Company, 1893.

Kaske, R. E. "Horn and Ivory in the *Summoner's Tale.*" *Neuphilologische Mitteilungen* 73 (1972): 122–26.

Kean, P. M. *"The Pearl": An Interpretation.* New York: Barnes and Noble, 1967.

Kean, Patricia M. *Chaucer and the Making of English Poetry.* 2 vols. London: Routledge and Kegan Paul, 1972.

Keen, Maurice Hugh. *Chivalry.* New Haven: Yale University Press, 1984.

Kirk, Elizabeth. "The Anatomy of a Mourning: Reflections on the *Pearl* Dreamer." In *The Endless Knot: Essays on Old and Middle English in Honor of Marie Borroff*, edited by M. Teresa Tavormina and Robert F. Yeager, 215–25. Cambridge, England: D. S. Brewer; Rochester, N.Y.: Boydell and Brewer, 1995.

Kolve, V. A. "Chaucer's Wheel of False Religion: Theology and Obscenity in the *Summoner's Tale*." In *The Centre and Its Compass: Studies in Medieval Literature in Honor of Professor John Leyerle*, edited by Robert A. Taylor, 265–96. Kalamazoo: Medieval Institute Publications, Western Michigan University, 1993.

Kottler, Barnet, and Alan M. Markman. *A Concordance to Five Middle English Poems: Cleanness, St. Erkenwald, Sir Gawain and the Green Knight, Patience, Pearl.* Pittsburgh: University of Pittsburgh Press, 1966.

Krappe, A. H. "Who *Was* the Green Knight?" *Speculum* 13 (1938): 206–15.

Krishna, Valerie, ed. *The Alliterative Morte Arthure: A Critical Edition.* New York: Burt Franklin, 1976.

Kurath, Hans, and Sherman M. Kuhn, eds. *Middle English Dictionary.* Ann Arbor: University of Michigan Press, 1952–2001.

Levitan, Alan. "The Parody of Pentecost in Chaucer's *Summoner's Tale*." *University of Toronto Quarterly* 40 (1971): 236–46.

Levy, Bernard S. "Biblical Parody in the *Summoner's Tale*." *Tennessee Studies in Literature* 11 (1966): 45–60.

Lodge, David. *The Modes of Modern Writing: Metaphor, Metonymy, and the Typology of Modern Literature.* Ithaca: Cornell University Press, 1977.

Loomis, Laura Hibbard. "Gawain and the Green Knight." In *Critical Studies of "Sir Gawain and the Green Knight,"* edited by Donald Roy Howard and Christian K. Zacher, 3–23. Notre Dame: University of Notre Dame Press, 1968. Originally published, Roger Sherman Loomis, ed., *Arthurian Literature in the Middle Ages: A Collaborative History,* 528–40. Oxford: Oxford University Press, 1959.

Loomis, Roger. "Was Chaucer a Laodicean?" In *Essays and Studies in Honor of Carleton Brown,* 129–48. New York: New York University Press; London: H. Milford, Oxford University Press, 1940.

Mallard, William. "Clarity and Dilemma: The *Forty Sermons* of John Wyclif." In *Contemporary Reflections on the Medieval Christian Tradition: Essays in Honor of Ray C. Petry,* edited by George H. Shriver, 19–38. Durham: Duke University Press, 1974.

Malmkjær, Kirsten, and James Maxwell Anderson, eds. *The Linguistics Encyclopedia.* London: Routledge, 1991.

Maltman, Sister Nicholas, O.P. "The Divine Granary, or the End of the Prioress's 'Greyn.'" *Chaucer Review* 17 (1982): 163–70.

Mann, Jill. *Apologies to Women: Inaugural Lecture Delivered 20th November 1990.* Cambridge: Cambridge University Press, 1991.

———. *Chaucer and Medieval Estates Satire: The Literature of Social Classes and the "General Prologue" to the "Canterbury Tales."* Cambridge: Cambridge University Press, 1973.

McFarlane, K. B. *Lancastrian Kings and Lollard Knights.* Oxford: Oxford University Press, 1972.

Migne, J. P., ed. *Patrologiae cursus completus. Series Graeca.* 161 vols. in 166 vols. Paris: Migne, 1857–66.

Migne, J. P., and A. G. Hamman, eds. *Patrologiae cursus completus. Series Latina.* 221 vols. Paris, 1844–64.

Miller, Milton. "The Heir in the *Merchant's Tale.*" *Philological Quarterly* 29 (1950): 437–40.

Miller, Robert Parsons. *Chaucer: Sources and Backgrounds.* New York: Oxford University Press, 1977.

Mitchell, Bruce, and Fred C. Robinson, eds. *Beowulf: An Edition with Relevant Shorter Texts.* Oxford: Blackwell Publishers, 1998.

Moore, Marianne. "Like a Wave at the Curl." *The New Yorker,* Nov. 29, 1969, 50.

Muscatine, Charles. *The Old French Fabliaux.* New Haven: Yale University Press, 1986.

Olson, Glending. "The End of the *Summoner's Tale* and the Uses of Pentecost." *Studies in the Age of Chaucer* 21 (1999): 209–45.

———. "The *Reeve's Tale* as a Fabliau." *Modern Language Quarterly* 35 (1974): 219–30.

Olson, Paul A. "Summoner Wrath on Friar Perfection: The Apostolate of Friar John and Lay Brother Thomas." In *The "Canterbury Tales" and the Good Society,* 214–34. Princeton: Princeton University Press, 1986.

Onions, C. T. *A Shakespeare Glossary.* Revised by Robert D. Eagleson. Oxford: Clarendon Press, 1986.

Osberg, Richard H. "A Voice for the Prioress: The Context of English Devotional Prose." *Studies in the Age of Chaucer* 18 (1996): 25–54.

Owen, Charles A., Jr. "Thy Drasty Rymyng. . . ." *Studies in Philology* 63 (1966): 533–64.

Panton, George A., and David Donaldson, eds. *The "Gest Hystoriale" of the Destruction of Troy: An Alliterative Romance tr. from Guido de Colonna's "Hystoria troiana."* 2 vols, EETS 39, 56. London: Pub. for the Early English Text Society by N. Trübner, 1869, 1894.

Parks, Stephen. *The Elizabethan Club of Yale University and Its Library.* New Haven: Published for the Elizabethan Club by Yale University Press, 1986.

Patterson, Lee. " 'For the Wyves love of Bathe': Feminine Rhetoric and Poetic Resolution in the *Roman de la Rose* and the *Canterbury Tales.*" *Speculum* 58 (1983): 656–95.

———. " 'No Man His Reson Herde': Peasant Consciousness, Chaucer's Miller, and the Structure of the *Canterbury Tales.*" In *Literary Practice and Social Change in Britain, 1380–1530,* edited by Lee Patterson, 113–55. Berkeley: University of California Press, 1990.

Pearcy, Roy J. "Chaucer's 'An Impossible' (*Summoner's Tale* III, 2231)." *Notes and Queries* n.s. 14 (1967): 322–25.

———. "Structural Models for the Fabliaux and the *Summoner's Tale* Analogues." *Fabula* 15 (1974): 103–13.

Pearsall, Derek Albert. "The *Canterbury Tales* II: Comedy." In *The Cambridge Chaucer Companion,* edited by Piero Boitani and Jill Mann, 125–42. Cambridge: Cambridge University Press, 1986.

———. *The Life of Geoffrey Chaucer: A Critical Biography.* Oxford: Blackwell, 1992.

———. "The Summoner's Tale." In *The Canterbury Tales,* 222–28. London: G. Allen and Unwin, 1985.

Pittock, Malcolm. "The *Pardoner's Tale* and the Quest for Death." *Essays in Criticism* 24 (1974): 107–23.

Plimpton, George A. *The Education of Shakespeare Illustrated from the Schoolbooks in Use in His Time.* London: Oxford University Press, 1933.

Pollard, Alfred W., G. R. Redgrave, William A. Jackson, F. S. Ferguson, Katharine F. Pantzer, and Philip R. Rider. *A Short-Title Catalogue of Books Printed in England, Scotland, & Ireland and of English Books Printed Abroad, 1475–1640.* 2d ed. 3 vols. London: Bibliographical Society, 1976.

Pope, John Collins. *The Rhythm of "Beowulf": An Interpretation of the Normal and Hypermetric Verse-Forms in Old English Poetry.* Rev. ed. New Haven: Yale University Press, 1966.

Preminger, Alex, and T. V. F. Brogan, eds. *The New Princeton Encyclopedia of Poetry and Poetics.* Rev. ed. Princeton, N.J.: Princeton University Press, 1993.

Puhvel, Martin. "Art and the Supernatural in *Sir Gawain and the Green Knight.*" *Arthurian Literature* 5 (1985): 1–69.

Puttenham, George. *The Arte of English Poesie: Contrived into Three Bookes: The First of Poets and Poesie, the Second of Proportion, the Third of Ornament.* Kent, Ohio: Kent State University Press, 1970. Originally published, 1906, edited by Edward Arber.

Quirk, Randolph. "Poetic Language and Old English Metre." In *Early English and Norse Studies, Presented to Hugh Smith in Honour of His Sixtieth Birthday,* edited by Arthur Brown and Peter Godfrey Foote, 150–71. London: Methuen, 1963.

Quirk, Randolph, Sidney Greenbaum, Geoffrey Leech, and Jan Svartvik. *A Comprehensive Grammar of the English Language.* London: Longman, 1985.

Randall, Dale B. J. "Was the Green Knight a Fiend?" *Studies in Philology* 57 (1960): 479–91.

Reames, Sherry. "Artistry, Decorum, and Purpose in Three Middle English Retellings of the Cecilia Legend." In *The Endless Knot: Essays on Old and Middle English in Honor of Marie Borroff,* edited by M. Teresa Tavormina and Robert F. Yeager, 177–99. Cambridge, England: D. S. Brewer; Rochester, N.Y.: Boydell & Brewer, 1995.

Record, Robert. *The Grounde of Artes.* English Series: The English Experience, Its Record in Early Printed Books Published in Facsimile, no. 174. Amsterdam: Theatrum Orbis Terrarum; New York: Da Capo Press, 1969.

Reinhard, Mariann. *On the Semantic Relevance of the Alliterative Collocations in "Beowulf."* Bern: A. Francke A. G. Verlag, 1976.

Richardson, Janette. "The *Summoner's Tale.*" In *Blameth Nat Me: A Study of Imagery in Chaucer's Fabliaux,* Studies in English Literature, vol. 58. The Hague: Mouton, 1970.

Rickard, P. "Semantic Implications of Old French Identical Rhyme." *Neuphilologische Mitteilungen* 66 (1965): 355–401.

Robertson, D. W. *A Preface to Chaucer: Studies in Medieval Perspectives.* Princeton: Princeton University Press, 1962.

Robinson, Edwin Arlington. "The Sheaves." In *Collected Poems of Edwin Arlington Robinson,* 870–71. New York: Macmillan, 1954.

Robinson, Fred C. *"Beowulf" and the Appositive Style.* Knoxville: University of Tennessee Press, 1985.

Sadowski, Piotr. *The Knight on His Quest: Symbolic Patterns of Transition in "Sir Gawain and the Green Knight."* Newark: University of Delaware Press, 1996.

Sanderlin, S. "Chaucer and Ricardian Politics." *Chaucer Review* 22 (1988): 171–84.

Saul, Nigel. *Richard II.* New Haven: Yale University Press, 1997.

Saussure, Ferdinand de. *Course in General Linguistics.* Translated by Roy Harris. Edited by Charles Bally, Charles Albert Sechehaye, and Albert Riedlinger. 3d ed. London: Duckworth, 1983.

Scattergood, V. J., ed. *The Works of Sir John Clanvowe.* Cambridge, England: D. S. Brewer; Totowa, N. J.: Rowman and Littlefield, 1975.

Schnyder, Hans. *"Sir Gawain and the Green Knight": An Essay in Interpretation.* The Cooper Monographs on English and American Language and Literature 6. Bern: Francke Verlag, 1961.

Shakespeare, William. *The Complete Works of Shakespeare.* Edited by George Lyman Kittredge. Boston: Ginn and Company, 1936.

——. *Hamlet.* Edited by Harold Jenkins. London: Methuen, 1982.

——. *Hamlet, Prince of Denmark.* Edited by Philip Edwards. Cambridge: Cambridge University Press, 1985.

Spearing, A. C. *The "Gawain"-Poet: A Critical Study.* Cambridge: Cambridge University Press, 1970.

——. *Medieval Dream-Poetry.* Cambridge: Cambridge University Press, 1976.

——. "Poetic Identity." In *A Companion to the "Gawain"-Poet,* edited by Derek Brewer and Jonathan Gibson, Arthurian Studies 38, 35–52. Cambridge; Rochester, N.Y.: D. S. Brewer, 1997.

——. *Readings in Medieval Poetry.* Cambridge: Cambridge University Press, 1987.

Speirs, John. *Medieval English Poetry: The Non-Chaucerian Tradition.* London: Faber and Faber, 1957.

Stanbury, Sarah. "*Pearl* and the Idea of Jerusalem." *Medievalia et Humanistica* n.s. 16 (1988): 117–31.

Stevens, Martin, and Kathleen Falvey. "Substance, Accident, and Transformations: A Reading of the *Pardoner's Tale.*" *Chaucer Review* 17 (1982): 142–58.

Stockton, Eric W. "The Deadliest Sin in the *Pardoner's Tale.*" *Tennessee Studies in Literature* 6 (1961): 47–59.

Strohm, Paul. "Chaucer's Lollard Joke: History and the Textual Unconscious." *Studies in the Age of Chaucer* 17 (1995): 23–42.

Szittya, Penn R. "Chaucer and Antifraternal Exegesis: The False Apostle of the *Summoner's Tale.*" In *The Antifraternal Tradition in Medieval Literature,* 231–46. Princeton: Princeton University Press, 1986.

Tatlock, J. S. P. "Chaucer and Wyclif." *Modern Philology* 14 (1916): 257–68.

——. "Notes on Chaucer: The *Canterbury Tales.*" *Modern Language Notes* 29 (1914): 140–44.

Thomas Aquinas, Saint. *Doctoris angelici divi Thomae Aquinatis sacri ordinis f.f. praedicatorum Opera omnia.* Edited by Stanisla Eduard Fretté and Paul Maré. 34 vols. Paris: Apud Ludovicum Vivès, 1871–80. Reprint, 1889–90.

Tolkien, J. R. R., and E. V. Gordon, eds. *Sir Gawain and the Green Knight.* 2d ed. Revised by Norman Davis. Oxford: Clarendon Press, 1967.

Tuck, J. Anthony. "Carthusian Monks and Lollard Knights: Religious Attitude at the Court of Richard II." *Studies in the Age of Chaucer: Proceedings* 1 (1984): 149–61.

Wallace, David. " 'Whan She Translated Was': A Chaucerian Critique of the Petrarchan Academy." In *Literary Practice and Social Change in Britain, 1380–1530,* edited by Lee Patterson, 156–215. Berkeley: University of California Press, 1990.

Walsh, Katherine. *Richard FitzRalph in Oxford, Avignon, and Armagh: A Fourteenth-Century Scholar and Primate.* Oxford: Clarendon Press, 1981.

Wentersdorf, Karl P. "The Motif of Exorcism in the *Summoner's Tale.*" *Studies in Short Fiction* 17 (1980): 249–54.

Wetherbee, Winthrop. *Geoffrey Chaucer: The "Canterbury Tales."* Landmarks of World Literature. Cambridge: Cambridge University Press, 1990.

Whiting, Bartlett J. "The Wife of Bath's Prologue." In *Sources and Analogues of Chaucer's "Canterbury Tales,"* edited by William Frank Bryan and Germaine Collette Dempster. Chicago: University of Chicago Press, 1941.

William of Saint Amour. "De periculis novissimorum temporum," printed under title "Scriptum Scholae Parisiensis, de periculis Ecclesiae." In *Fasciculus rerum expetendarum & fugiendarum . . . ,* edited by Ortuinus Gratius and Edward Brown, vol. 2, *Appendix . . . sive Tomus Secundus,* 18–41. London: impensis Richardi Chiswell, 1690. Reprint, Ann Arbor: University Microfilms, 1971, Early English Books, 1641–1700, 381:11.

——. *Opera omnia.* Constance [for Paris]: Alithophilos, 1632.

Williams, Arnold. "Chaucer and the Friars." *Speculum* 28 (1953): 499–513.

Wimsatt, William K. "One Relation of Rhyme to Reason." In *The Verbal Icon: Studies in the Meaning of Poetry,* 153–66. Lexington: University of Kentucky Press, 1954.

Wood, Chauncey. "Artistic Intention and Chaucer's Uses of Scriptural Allusion." In *Chaucer and Scriptural Tradition,* edited by David L. Jeffrey, 35–46. Ottawa: University of Ottawa Press, 1984.

Wordsworth, William. "Ode: Intimations of Immortality." In *The Poetical Works of William Wordsworth,* edited by Ernest De Selincourt and Helen Darbishire, 2d ed., 4:279–85. Oxford: Clarendon Press, 1952–72.

Workman, Herbert B. *John Wyclif, a Study of the English Medieval Church.* 2 vols. Oxford: Clarendon Press, 1926.

Wright, Thomas, and James Orchard Halliwell. *Reliquiae Antiquae: Scraps from Ancient Manuscripts Illustrating Chiefly Early English Literature and the English Language.* 2 vols. London: J. R. Smith, 1845.

Wrigley, Christopher. "*Sir Gawain and the Green Knight:* The Underlying Myth." In *Studies in Medieval English Romances: Some New Approaches,* edited by Derek Brewer, 113–28. Cambridge, England; Wolfeboro, N.H.: D. S. Brewer, 1988.

Wycliffe, John. "The Church and Her Members." In *Select English Works of John Wyclif,* edited by Thomas Arnold, 3:338–65. Oxford: Clarendon Press, 1869–71.

——. "De blasphemia contra fratres." In *Select English Works of John Wyclif,* edited by Thomas Arnold, 3:402–29. Oxford: Clarendon Press, 1869–71.

——. "De fundatione sectarum." In *John Wiclif's Polemical Works in Latin,* edited by Rudolf Buddensieg, Wyclif's Latin Works, 1:13–80. London: Published for the Wyclif Society by Trübner, 1883.

———. "De officio pastorali." In *The English Works of Wyclif, Hitherto Unprinted,* edited by F. D. Matthew, EETS 74, 405–57. London: Published for the Early English Text Society by Trübner, 1880.

———. "De ordinatione fratrum." In *John Wiclif's Polemical Works in Latin,* edited by Rudolf Buddensieg, Wyclif's Latin Works, 1:83–106. London: Published for the Wyclif Society by Trübner, 1883.

———. "De precationibus sacris." In *Select English Works of John Wyclif,* edited by Thomas Arnold, 3:224–25. Oxford: Clarendon Press, 1871.

———. "De quattuor sectis novellis." In *John Wiclif's Polemical Works in Latin,* edited by Rudolf Buddensieg, Wyclif's Latin Works, 1:233–90. London: Published for the Wyclif Society by Trübner, 1883.

———. "The Ecclesiastical Hierarchy." In *Selections from English Wycliffite Writings,* edited by Anne Hudson, 75–83. Cambridge: Cambridge University Press, 1978. Reprint, "Vae octuplex" in *Select English Works of John Wyclif,* ed. Thomas Arnold, 2:379–89.

———. "Exposicio textus Matthei XXIII." In *Opera minora,* edited by Johann Loserth and F. D. Matthew, Wyclif's Latin Works, 313–53. London: Published for the Wyclif Society by C. K. Paul, 1913.

———. "Fifty Heresies and Errors of Friars." In *Select English Works of John Wyclif,* edited by Thomas Arnold, 3:366–401. Oxford: Clarendon Press, 1869–71.

———. "Hou the Office of Curatis Is Ordeyned of God." In *The English Works of Wyclif, Hitherto Unprinted,* edited by F. D. Matthew, EETS 74, 143–63. London: Published for the Early English Text Society by Trübner, 1880.

———. "Purgatorium sectae Christi." In *John Wiclif's Polemical Works in Latin,* edited by Rudolf Buddensieg, Wyclif's Latin Works, 1:291–316. London: Published for the Wyclif Society by Trübner, 1883.

———. "Sermons on the Gospels for Sundays and Festivals." In *Select English Works of John Wyclif,* edited by Thomas Arnold, vol. 1. Oxford: Clarendon Press, 1869–71.

———. *Tractatus de apostasia.* Edited by Michael Henry Dziewicki. London: Published for the Wyclif Society by Trübner, 1889.

———. *Tractatus de blasphemia.* Edited by Michael Henry Dziewicki. London: Published for the Wyclif Society by Trübner, 1893.

Zietlow, Paul N. "In Defense of the Summoner." *Chaucer Review* 1 (1966): 4–19.

Index